Luci Yamamoto &
Gregg

KAUA'I

CONTENTS

Lonely Planet books provide independent advice. Lonely Planet does not accept advertising in guidebooks, nor do we accept payment in exchange for listing or endorsing any place or business. Lonely Planet writers do not accept discounts or payments in exchange for positive coverage of any sort.

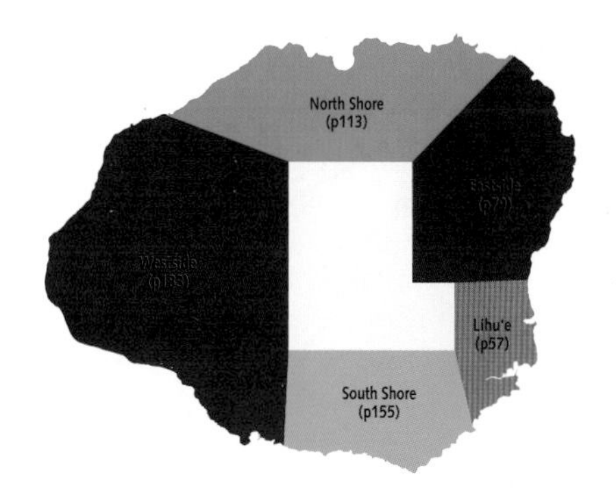

North Shore
(p113)
Westside
Lihu'e
(p57)
South Shore
(p155)

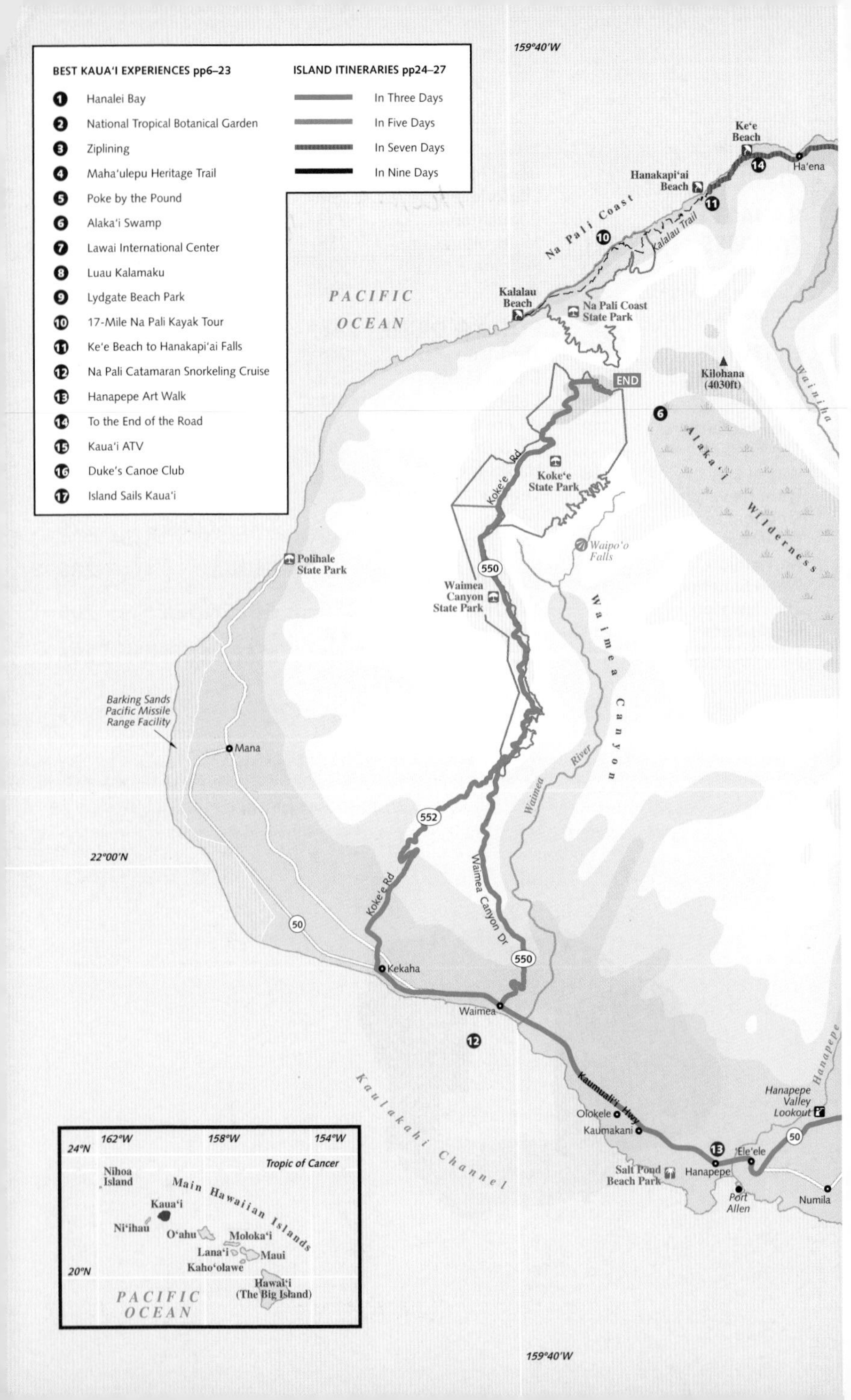

BEST KAUA'I EXPERIENCES pp6–23
1 Hanalei Bay
2 National Tropical Botanical Garden
3 Ziplining
4 Maha'ulepu Heritage Trail
5 Poke by the Pound
6 Alaka'i Swamp
7 Lawai International Center
8 Luau Kalamaku
9 Lydgate Beach Park
10 17-Mile Na Pali Kayak Tour
11 Ke'e Beach to Hanakapi'ai Falls
12 Na Pali Catamaran Snorkeling Cruise
13 Hanapepe Art Walk
14 To the End of the Road
15 Kaua'i ATV
16 Duke's Canoe Club
17 Island Sails Kaua'i
ISLAND ITINERARIES pp24–27
In Three Days
In Five Days
In Seven Days
In Nine Days
159°40'W
Ke'e Beach
Ha'ena
Hanakapi'ai Beach
Na Pali Coast
Kalalau Trail
PACIFIC OCEAN
Kalalau Beach
Na Pali Coast State Park
END
Kilohana (4030ft)
Wainiha
Alaka'i Wilderness
Koke'e Rd
Koke'e State Park
Waipo'o Falls
550
Waimea Canyon State Park
Polihale State Park
Waimea Canyon
Waimea River
Barking Sands Pacific Missile Range Facility
Mana
552
22°00'N
Koke'e Rd
Waimea Canyon Dr
50
550
Kekaha
Waimea
Kaulakahi Channel
Kaumuali'i Hwy
Hanapepe
Hanapepe Valley Lookout
Olokele
Kaumakani
50
Ele'ele
Salt Pond Beach Park
Hanapepe
Port Allen
Numila
162°W
158°W
154°W
24°N
Tropic of Cancer
Nihoa Island
Main Hawaiian Islands
Kaua'i
Ni'ihau
O'ahu
Moloka'i
Lana'i
Maui
Kaho'olawe
20°N
Hawai'i (The Big Island)
PACIFIC OCEAN
159°40'W

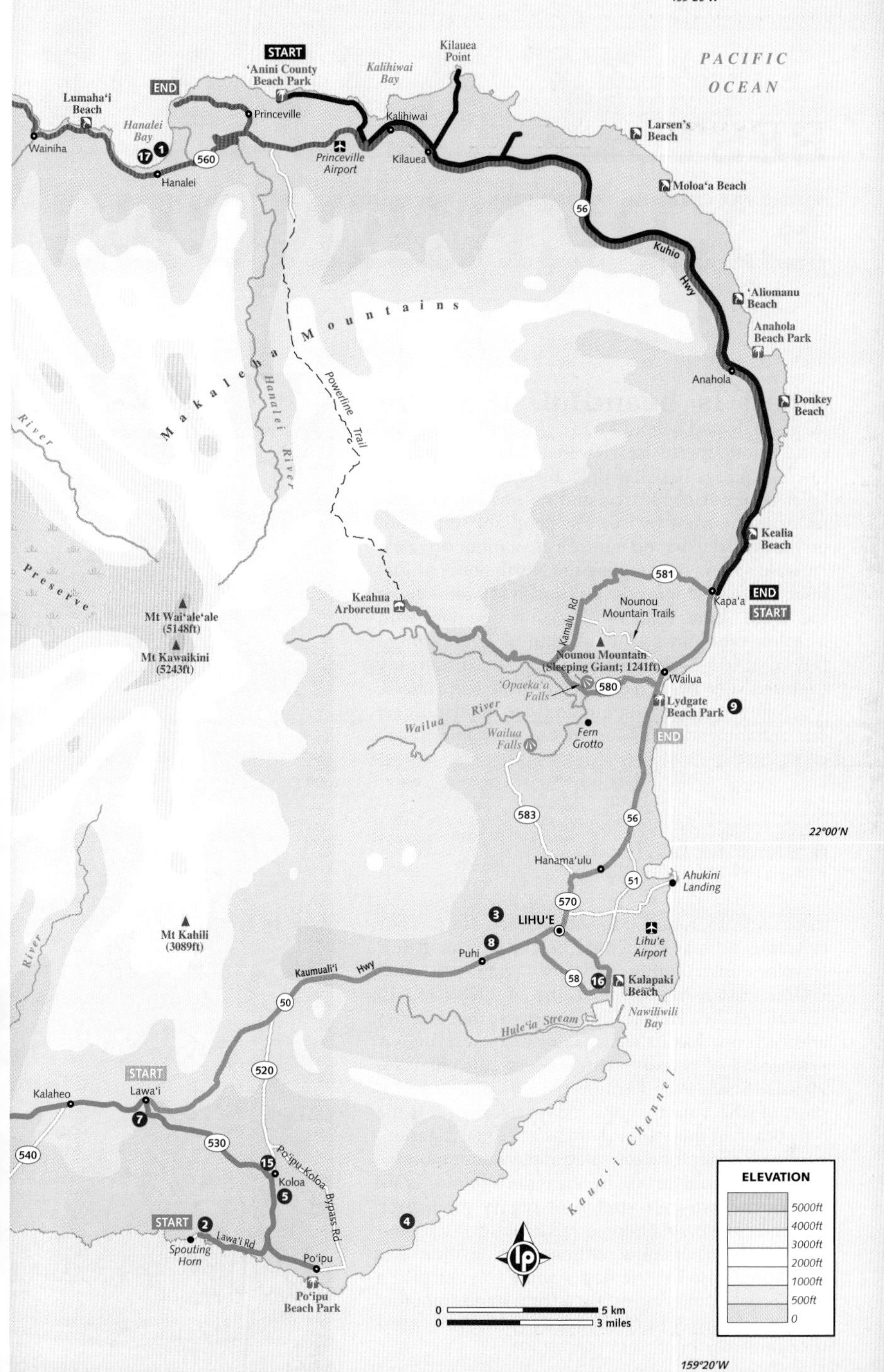
159°20'W
PACIFIC OCEAN
START
'Anini County Beach Park
END
Kilauea Point
Kalihiwai Bay
Lumaha'i Beach
Hanalei Bay
Princeville
Kalihiwai
Wainiha
Hanalei
560
Princeville Airport
Kilauea
Larsen's Beach
Moloa'a Beach
56
Kuhio Hwy
'Aliomanu Beach
Anahola Beach Park
Anahola
Donkey Beach
Makaleha Mountains
Hanalei River
Powerline Trail
River
Kealia Beach
581
Kapa'a
END
START
Kamalu Rd
Nounou Mountain Trails
Preserve
Keahua Arboretum
Mt Wai'ale'ale (5148ft)
Mt Kawaikini (5243ft)
Nounou Mountain (Sleeping Giant; 1241ft)
Wailua
'Opaeka'a Falls
580
Lydgate Beach Park
Wailua River
Wailua Falls
Fern Grotto
END
583
56
22°00'N
Hanama'ulu
Ahukini Landing
51
570
LIHU'E
Mt Kahili (3089ft)
Puhi
Lihu'e Airport
River
Kaumuali'i Hwy
58
Kalapaki Beach
50
Nawiliwili Bay
Hule'ia Stream
520
START
Kalaheo
Lawa'i
530
540
Po'ipu-Koloa Bypass Rd
Koloa
Kaua'i Channel
START
Lawa'i Rd
Spouting Horn
Po'ipu
Po'ipu Beach Park
ELEVATION
5000ft
4000ft
3000ft
2000ft
1000ft
500ft
0
0 5 km
0 3 miles
159°20'W

BEST KAUA'I EXPERIENCES

Small is beautiful. If you're skeptical, lo and behold Kaua'i, the diminutive doyenne among the major Hawaiian Islands. Here, no town surpasses 10,000 people. By law no building is taller than a coconut tree, and no one can circumnavigate the coast by car. The spotlight shines not on the artificial, but on nature's great outdoors. Be it emerald valleys overlooking the North Shore or turquoise waters lapping 50 miles of ivory sand along the South Shore, Kaua'i's epic landscape pops with a Technicolor punch that's all natural. Drive around this rural 555-sq-mile island once, and it's already captured your heart. To many, it is the real Hawaii. The following pages contain (in no particular order) our recommendations for an unforgettable Kaua'i experience.

❶ BEST BEACH: Hanalei Bay (p134)

You came to Kaua'i for some beach time. Your traveling companions could be children or fellow travelers entertaining their own views on what defines 'beach day.' Named one of 2008's top 10 Hawaii beaches, Hanalei Bay comprises four beaches and each one has its charms to satisfy everyone. A serene slice of paradise with modern conveniences, Hanalei Beach Park Pavilion (p135) is likely to hit most of what's on that beach day checklist. It is the only beach of those four that has a lifeguard station, making it easier for water-play in the winter months, when swells and strong rip currents abound. Walk or run the two-mile stretch of sugary sand, pack a picnic lunch or adopt a laissez-faire 'tude and practice the art of doing nothing. The 'pavilion' acts as a home base for the day if some in your group can't resist wandering off for a fruit-stand smoothie at Hanalei Taro & Juice Company (p141) or a stand up paddle surfing lesson (see p139).

LINDA CHING

LUCI YAMAMOTO

❷ BEST BOTANICAL WONDER: National Tropical Botanical Garden (p167)

It's clear why Kaua'i is nicknamed the 'Garden Isle.' Who could possibly imagine so many incarnations of green? If you've got a botanical bent (or if you simply enjoy pretty landscapes), don't miss the National Tropical Botanical Garden's three impressive gardens. In Po'ipu, Allerton Garden is the nature-made equivalent of a royal palace, featuring living 'rooms' with foliage borders accented with waterfalls, pools, fountains and statues. The adjacent McBryde Garden is vast and less manicured, holding the largest ex situ (off-site) collection of Native Hawaiian flora in existence. In Ha'ena, don't miss the most-Hawaiian garden of the three, Limahuli Garden (p148), the only non-irrigated location (no need, as the North Shore has rain to spare!), with excellent signs explaining which plants are native, Polynesian-introduced or Western-introduced. A nonprofit research institute, NTBG deserves kudos for its efforts to preserve native tropical plants (and for its LEED Gold Certified research building).

Who could possibly imagine so many incarnations of green?

❸ BEST EFFORTLESS THRILL: Ziplining (p43)

Surfing monster waves. Kayaking across open ocean. Trekking the precipitous Na Pali Coast. Most big thrills are reserved for diehards and daredevils. But there's one thing that anyone – young or old, fit or flab – can do. And live to brag about it. Ziplining is Kaua'i's latest and hottest adventure, almost unique in Hawaii (Maui is the other zip-happy island). Participants strap themselves in rock-climbing-style harnesses, which are attached to cables. To zip, just leap off the platform and – *whoosh!* – enjoy the fast-moving scenery while it lasts. Creative 'zippers' can try going backwards or in zany contortions (think Superman, lotus pose or upside down). And, if you find Kaua'i to be lacking in nightlife, try one outfit's unique 'after dark' tour.

LUCI YAMAMOTO

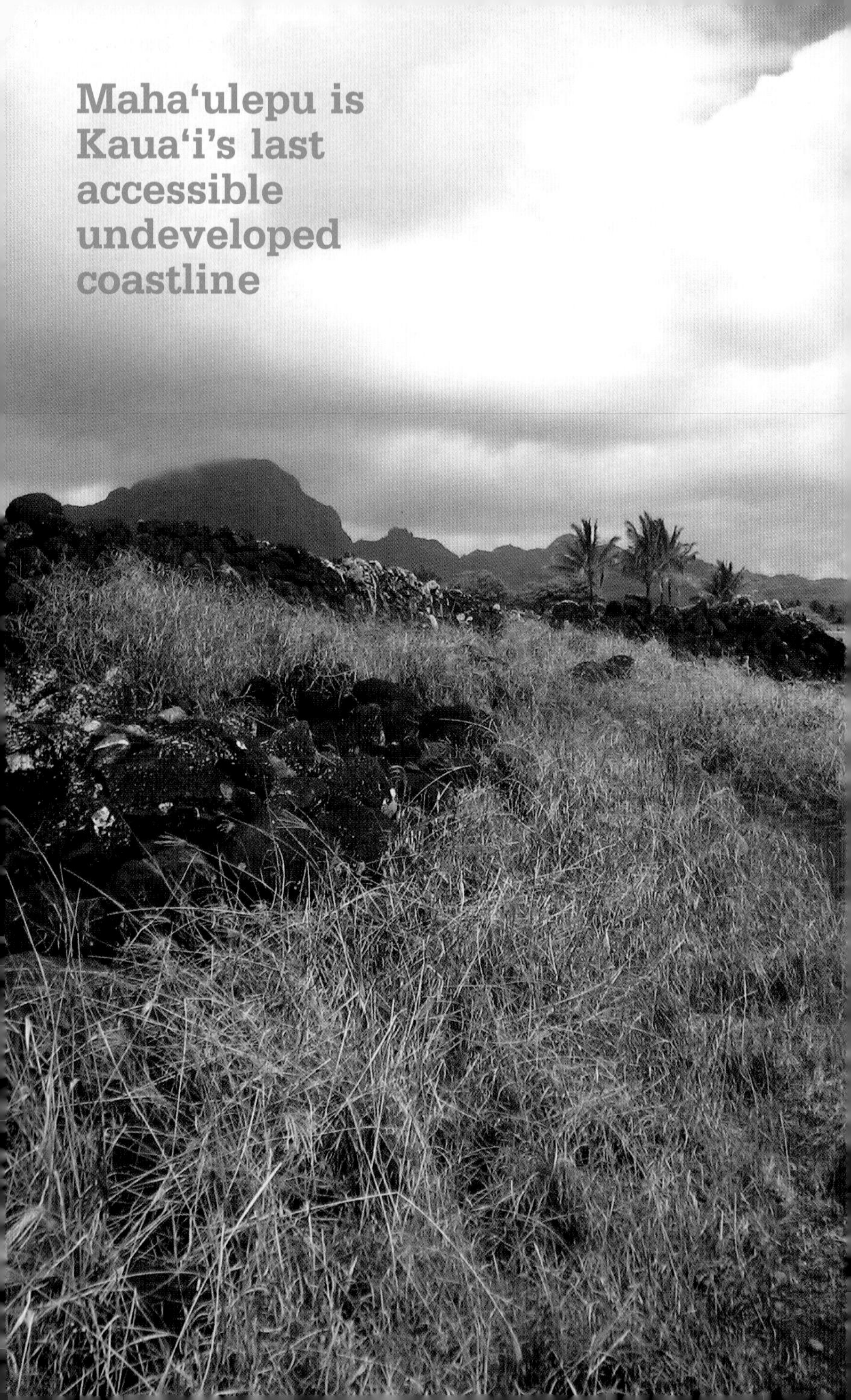
Maha'ulepu is
Kaua'i's last
accessible
undeveloped
coastline

LUCI YAMAMOTO

❹ BEST COASTAL HIKE: Maha'ulepu Heritage Trail (p168)

Ancient lithified sand dunes. If that sounds too academic (and even a tad boring), wait till you see them up close. The fascinating, steep, ridged cliffs of Maha'ulepu are visually stunning (and they'll make an eager armchair geologist out of you). Maha'ulepu is Kaua'i's last accessible undeveloped coastline, where the effects of five million years are obvious. Just compare these eroded limestone formations with the glassy black lava just formed on the Big Island! From your perch on the cliffs, peer down at the pounding surf and rock-strewn inlets, where monk seals occasionally haul themselves out to rest. Look to the left to find the stonewall remains of a Native Hawaiian heiau. Soon you'll reach Maha'ulepu Beach, where a pristine swath of velvety sand meets scattered rocks and relentless waves. Raw, rugged and remote, Maha'ulepu is utterly memorable. It's a wonderful place to escape the resort beaches and public parks, but tread lightly on this sacred sanctuary.

LUCI YAMAMOTO

❺ BEST BARGAIN MEAL: Poke by the Pound (p161)

A big-name chef in San Francisco is famous for his tuna *tartare*. But locals consider such fancy foods as overpriced renditions of Hawaiian-style *'ahi poke,* chunks of succulent raw tuna, seasoned typically with soy sauce, sesame oil, green onion, sea salt, *ogo* (seaweed) and *inamona* (ground-roasted) *kukui* (candlenut). Traditionally, Hawaiians used only the latter three ingredients, but as different immigrants arrived with their own staple seasonings, recipes evolved into today's tastebud-tangling varieties. *Poke* is an everyday dish, purchased by the pound at deli counters and places like the South Shore's Koloa Fish Market (for more great *poke* places, see the boxed text, p249). For the uninitiated palate, the popular sesame *'ahi* recipe is guaranteed to please, but adventurous eaters should try the gamut! Salted salmon with fresh onion and tomato. Chewy *tako* (octopus) in miso sauce. Minimalist Hawaiian style, which highlights the fish and its tang of the sea. Typically under $12 per pound, take-out *poke* makes a first-rate meal on the run.

This otherworldly rainforest is an unforgettable haven

❻ BEST NATIVE FOREST: Alaka'i Swamp (p217)

Soggy, muddy and misty, the Alaka'i Swamp might not sound appealing, but this otherworldly rainforest is an unforgettable haven for native plants and rare birds. At 4000ft to 4500ft in elevation, Alaka'i is not actually a swamp but rather a rainforest bog, filled with ferns, moss-covered tree trunks and vividly blooming *'ohia lehua*. Before the early 1990s, only scientists, intrepid hikers and pig hunters braved the thicket of brush and deep murk. Since then, a wooden boardwalk has made Alaka'i more accessible while it also protects the fragile terrain. Be prepared for sun, rain, hundreds of steps and, if the clouds refrain themselves, an awesome view.

LUCI YAMAMOTO

❼ BEST PLACE TO MEDITATE:
Lawai International Center (p161)

You can't help but whisper here, among the 88 miniature Buddhist shrines, sitting with unflappable dignity along a hillside path. Being among the shrines, you will grow quiet and composed, and become aware of the Lawa'i Valley's long history as a spiritual site. The ancient Hawaiians built a heiau (temple) here; during the early 1900s, Japanese plantation immigrants came here for Buddhist pilgrimages. After being abandoned once the sugar industry declined and settlers moved away, a group of dedicated residents struggled to purchase the site, and then strived to restore or replace all of the weathered, damaged shrines. Volunteers give public tours two Sundays per month.

LUCI YAMAMOTO

❽ BEST LUAU SHOW: Luau Kalamaku (p72)

Admit it. Ever since you watched the Brady Bunch enjoying a Hawaiian luau, you've wanted to try one yourself. Indeed, the 'commercial' luau has been a go-to attraction since the 1970s and 1980s. Today, luau shows are a well-oiled machine, serving hundreds of visitors nightly with the requisite buffet feast and Polynesian revue: it's catchy but not exactly novel. Kaua'i's Luau Kalamaku turns the same old show into mesmerizing dinner theater with a dash of Cirque du Soleil (think lithe dancers, flashy leotards and pyrotechnics) thrown in. The thrilling stageplay tells the story of one family's epic voyage to Hawaii, with heartfelt hula and Tahitian dancing – including the showstopping, nail-biting Samoan fire dance. Prepare to be impressed.

GREG ELMS

LUCI YAMAMOTO

9 BEST KID PLEASER: Lydgate Beach Park (p83)

You're vacationing with the kids. One wants to snorkel, another lives to Rollerblade, and the third wants simply to build sand castles all afternoon. Sounds daunting. But at Lydgate Beach Park in Wailua, it's a cinch to satisfy 'em all. The lifeguard-staffed beach is protected within a stone breakwater that forms two calm, shallow lagoons, ideal for munchkin snorkelers or learn-to-swimmers. Near the water, two giant playgrounds capture the imagination, with unique wooden mazes and bridges, kid-made ceramic mosaics, and classic swings and slides. Along the sand, there's a paved path, safe for pedestrians, cyclists, Rollerbladers and dogs on leashes – a simple feature but invaluable in a car-dominated place like Kaua'i. Scattered around are picnic tables, pavilions, restrooms and plentiful parking. Bring fixings for grilling, kick back and marvel that this wonderful place won't cost you a cent.

PETER HENDRIE

⑩ BEST FITNESS CHALLENGE: 17-Mile Na Pali Kayak Tour (p137)

A siren song of sorts, the Na Pali (the cliffs) Coast is inaccessible to vehicles and can be seen only by boat, helicopter or hike. That's why it draws some of the fittest and strongest from around the world, who've been lured by the notoriety of mastering this challenging stretch at ocean level. If you're fit enough to be mistaken for a superhero, a kayak tour around the Na Pali Coast could be your cup of tea (or energy drink). Not for the faint of heart, kayaking for eight hours along the stunning, sheared edges and turbulent waters has made even the guides turn queasy at times. The tour is offered only from May to September, so if you're here during that time frame – and if triathlons, marathons and the like are part of your more-than-once-a-year routine – then this might be for you. Added bonus? The two-hour beach lunch break.

⑪ BEST HIKE TO REMEMBER: Ke'e Beach to Hanakapi'ai Falls (p154)

A vertiginous tease, the hike from Ke'e Beach to Hanakapi'ai Falls can elicit awe, anticipation and impatience. But after you've climbed energetically around each rising, undulating curve, it delivers. You arrive at one of the most captivating sights the North Shore has to offer. At 2 miles in, Hanakapi'ai Beach is the first stop on the 11-mile Kalalau Trail. Just about 2 miles more and your parched, paradise-seeking self arrives at cold, pure pools of refreshment below the 100ft Hanakapi'ia Falls. You'll have to hike through a seemingly overgrown forest dense with everything from bamboo to wild orchids, so try to follow the stream and listen for the sound of rushing water when the trail seems to disappear. Upon arrival, plummeting, playful tropic birds brighten the roaring water above, with a flurry of tadpoles below. Those with hiking boots, agile feet and avid quadriceps will probably hike this roundtrip in four hours. Word to the wise: be generous with mosquito repellent and sunblock, and wear a swimsuit underneath. Pack a light snack, camera and water bottle.

MARK PARKES

CASEY MAHANEY

⓬ BEST UNDERWATER SIGHTSEEING: Na Pali Catamaran Snorkeling Cruise (p189)

It's somewhat luxe, to be sure. If you don't want to stroke, fly or hoof it around the Na Pali and you want to see the splendor of Kaua'i's marine life, then here's your chance. A half-day catamaran tour has guaranteed sightings of *honu* (sea turtles), spinner dolphins or whales, and also usually includes wine or beer and *pupu* (snacks). Snorkeling offers a chance to see vibrant tangs (think 'Dory' in *Finding Nemo)* and ever-regal *honu* up close. The canoe was the traditional method of voyage for the Polynesians, but indulging in a catamaran snorkeling cruise is less about tradition and more about the guilty pleasure of 'activity' without roughing it.

Hanapepe is better known as Kaua'i's 'art central'

⓭ BEST NIGHTLIFE: Hanapepe Art Walk (p193)

Local artists on the island anted up to dominate the main street real estate when the mom-and-pop businesses of the historic West Side town of Hanapepe were dropping like flies. Now every Friday is the Hanapepe Art Walk, when galleries are open late and the strip is awash in lookyloos with a hankering for art. Once dubbed the 'Biggest Little Town on Kaua'i,' Hanapepe's rep has evolved in recent years and it's now better known as an 'art central' of sorts. Peruse the galleries housing everything from kitsch Hawaiiana and Japanese-inspired watercolors to locally inspired interpretations of cubist, impressionist and expressionistic movements.

LINDA CHING

LUCI YAMAMOTO

⓮ BEST SCENIC DRIVE: To the End of the Road (p113)

Locals often refer to the main highway simply as 'the road.' Driving northwards from Kalihiwai, you'll emerge from a canopy of trees that rise from an undulating landscape, through a wild stretch slicing past a jungle-like mass over the river, beside the ocean. After the vine-laden Kalihiwai Bridge, you'll see patches of verdant fields where horses graze under tropical fruit-bearing trees, and teasing views here and there that let you just snatch glimpses of the Pacific. In Princeville, stop a moment at the Hanalei Valley Lookout to catch your first glimpses of *lo'i* (wet taro fields) and an assortment of native Hawaiian birds at the Hanalei National Wildlife Refuge (p132). Continue onward to Hanalei, passing first its famous historic bridge, then the six one-way bridges beyond (follow local courtesy and allow eight cars to pass first). Explore for a bit at the wet caves (p151) or the inspired Limahuli Garden (p148), winding up your afternoon at far-flung Ke'e Beach (p151) – the ultimate sunset perch.

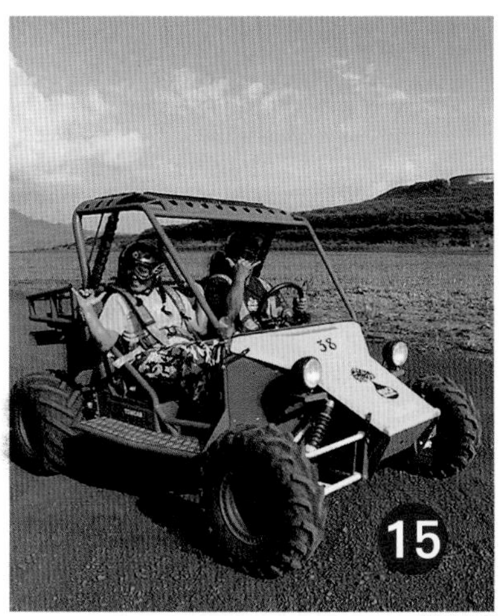

AMANDA GREGG

⓯ BEST ENVIRONMENTALLY SAVVY EFFORT: Kaua'i ATV (p161)

Of its 40 ATVs, 10 are environmentally friendly 'bio bugs' that rely on post-consumer recycled fuel from local restaurants. Sure, you'll smell like French fries at the end of the tour and yes, it costs an extra $20 for the upgrade, but 100% of that surplus goes toward Ho'opuka Learning Center, an after-school initiative to keep Hawaiian history alive for *keiki* (children). Added bonus? Supporting this kind of business helps keep Kaua'i the way most people love it: rife with open space, as it rewards landowners for leasing its acres for recreational use rather than becoming overdeveloped.

⓰ BEST POSTSUN PUPU & COCKTAILS: Duke's Canoe Club (p72)

Salt and sun have pounded you relentlessly and you loved every minute of it. But now you're too hungry to go all the way back to the hotel or B&B because chances are, once there, you won't have the energy to freshen up and head out. That's when you opt for Duke's Canoe Club at Kalapaki in Lihu'e. Whether you're covered in sand, wearing a stolen hotel towel, or still in a seafoam-green bridesmaid dress with a date you just met at a wedding, you're welcome. Named after the late renowned surfer, swimmer, waterman and Olympian Duke Kahanamoku, Duke's is one of those rare finds that attracts both locals and tourists because of its relaxed attitude, impressive ambience and good food. Not only does it serve food the latest on the island ('til 11pm) but its setting also means you can walk the scenic, coastal esplanade from its tiki torch entrance fronting the beach. And don't dismiss it as another chain. Though there's also a Duke's in Waikiki, this one's far better.

AMANDA GREGG

AMANDA GREGG

⓱ BEST SEAFARING EXPERIENCE: Island Sails Kaua'i (p140)

Spotted some outrigger canoe paddlers practicing in the water? Perhaps it's inspired you to learn more about the wayfinding arts that guided the deep-sea navigators of Oceania. Though there are four double-hulled voyaging canoes throughout the Hawaiian Islands and three more under construction, access isn't really possible for visitors. So for those who want to better understand traditional Polynesian navigational techniques, your best bet is a jaunt in a locally built outrigger sailing canoe. It took native Kauaian waterman Trevor Cabell of Island Sails more than 10 years to make his, guided by one simple idea: 'Leave the ocean as you found it.' You'll be on the water from 30 minutes to an hour, and all ages are welcome. While aboard, you're likely to spot some *honu,* and perhaps even catch some *'ahi* or barracuda. Though the canoe can't take more than six people, it's truly catered to your group, whether you're honeymooners, snorkel enthusiasts or just someone who wants to pick up a paddle and get a workout.

ISLAND ITINERARIES

See the itineraries at the beginning of each regional chapter for more detailed routes.

IN THREE DAYS *This leg: 58 Miles*

❶ **NATIONAL TROPICAL BOTANICAL GARDEN (p167)** Start day one immersed in glorious greenery, either touring the magnificent landscape art of **Allerton Garden** or exploring lush **McBryde Garden** at your own pace.

❷ **PO'IPU BEACH PARK (p164)** Next, stop at **Koloa Fish Market (p161)** for picnic fixings such as *poke* (chunks of marinated raw fish) and plate lunches, then join the family-friendly crowd at Po'ipu's version of a town square. Don't miss the sunset, sitting on the seawall or dining on the day's catch. For newbie snorkelers, this is a terrific walk-in spot.

❸ **NA PALI SNORKELING RAFT ADVENTURE (p199)** If you enjoyed shore snorkeling, ramp it up on day two: ride a zippy raft to open-ocean snorkeling along the Na Pali Coast, accessible only by sea or air.

❹ **HANAPEPE ART WALK (p193)** Backtrack to tiny Hanapepe to visit more than a dozen Kaua'i artists in their studios and see where Old West meets nouveau art. Go during the day or Friday's late-night openings.

❺ **WAIMEA CANYON (p206)** On day three, tie on your hiking shoes and journey upland to Kaua'i's colossal lava canyon, which the sure-footed can explore up close.

❻ **KOKE'E STATE PARK (p211)** First, stop at the **Koke'e Natural History Museum (p211)** for trail info. For a most unique nature setting, try the **Alaka'i Swamp Trail (p216)**, where a mountaintop rainforest takes you to a mystical muddy bog full of native plants and birds. Fit trekkers can try the **Nu'alolo loop hike (p215)** for breathtaking – if vertiginous – views.

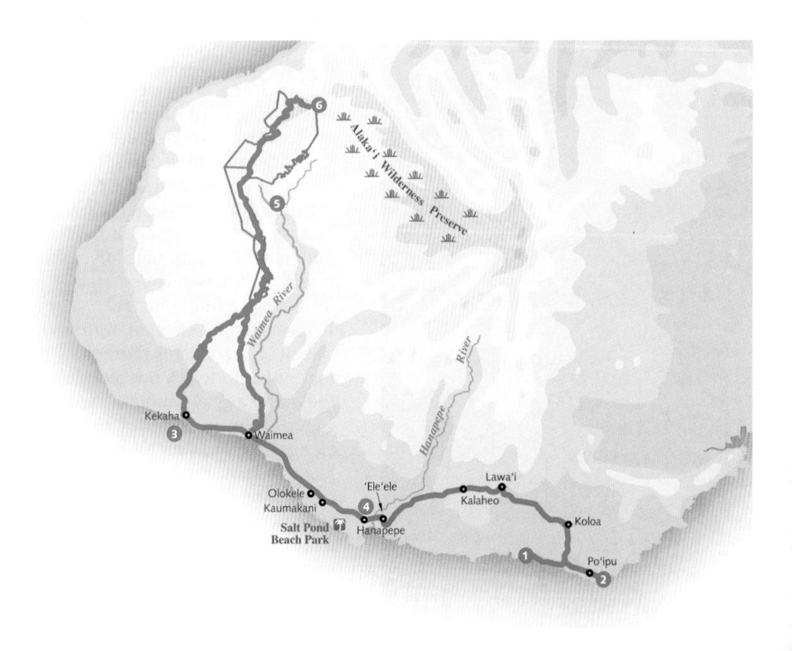

IN FIVE DAYS *This leg: 36 Miles*

8 ZIPLINING (p67) With five days on the island, plan your first three as above. On day four, entice yourself to rise (and hit the road to Lihu'e) with fresh malasadas (p70), and then go wild on treetop ziplines, where you can live that Tarzan fantasy.

9 KALAPAKI BEACH (p63) Sneak in an afternoon break at this easy-access beach, suited to most watersports, from bodyboarding to stand up paddle surfing. Don't be too miffed at the Marriott flanking the sand: its tropical bar (p70) is the island's liveliest.

10 LUAU KALAMAKU (p72) Sure, commercial luaus aren't exactly traditional, but you'll be wowed by this one. With pro-caliber performers who dance, sing and act their hearts out, this is a show you'll remember. Before dinner, hop on the historic Kaua'i Plantation Railway (p64), which winds past plots of native and introduced crops, plus a hungry herd of wild pigs.

11 WAILUA RIVER KAYAKING TOUR (p86) On day five, slather on sunscreen for a kayak paddle up the majestic Wailua River, sacred to Hawaiians. Bring your swimsuit for the highlight: a waterfall dip.

12 NOUNOU MOUNTAIN HIKE (p89) If kayaking is not your thing, work it out on the Sleeping Giant, atop which (or whom?) you'll see sweeping Eastside vistas. Notch up your experience with a guided tour (p41) by the island's most prominent geologist.

13 KEAHUA ARBORETUM (p85) Pack a lunch and drive up the scenic Kuamo'o Rd, which leads to 'Opaeka'a Falls (p85), a Hindu monastery (p84), and finally this serene picnic spot.

14 LYDGATE BEACH PARK (p83) If you're traveling with munchkins, now's the time for a kids' play date. With its Kamalani Playground and Kamalani Kai Bridge, bike path and gentle swimming lagoons, there's no time for fussiness at this easy-access park.

15 WAILUA MUNICIPAL GOLF COURSE (p90) *Sans* kids, you might prefer an affordable round of golf at this popular course, one of the top municipal courses in the state.

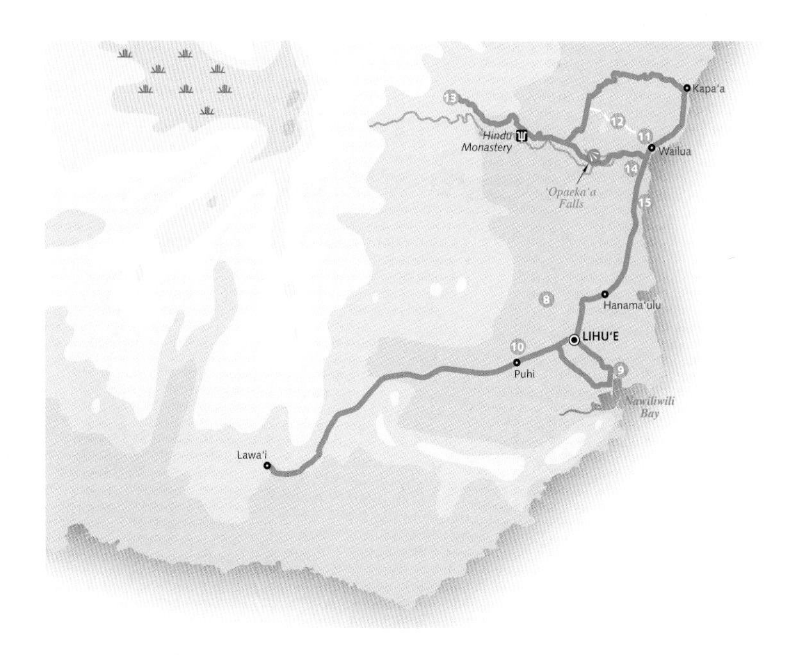

IN SEVEN DAYS *This leg: 52 Miles*

⑯ **LIMAHULI GARDEN (p148)** If you're staying for a week (the bare minimum, we say), follow the preceding five-day itinerary. On day six, head to the incomparably beautiful North Shore. First stop: Kaua'i's most natural, most Hawaiian garden, with flora bursting with health and greener than a Photoshopped glossy.

⑰ **HANALEI BAY (p134)** Perfectly circular, this sandy bay is arguably the island's finest. Fritter away the afternoon swimming, surfing or beach-walking, depending on the season. The manageable waves near the pier are ideal for beginner **surfing lessons (p139)**.

⑱ **HANALEI DINING (p141)** For dinner, try impeccable tapas at **Bar Acuda**, healthful pesci-vegetarian at **Postcards Café**, bargain gourmet plate lunches at **Polynesia Café** or fusion Middle Eastern at **Mediterranean Gourmet** in nearby Ha'ena. You won't go hungry in Hanalei.

⑲ **KALALAU TRAIL HIKE TO HANAKAPI'AI (p153)** On day seven, start early to hike the first leg of this rugged trail (though not if it's rainy). Turn around at Hanakapi'ai Beach or, for added sweat and adventure, hoof it to Hanakapi'ai Falls.

⑳ **KE'E BEACH (p151)** In summer, find a post-hike underwater panorama at this snorkeling hot spot. When Ke'e waters are too risky in winter (October to March), **'Anini Beach Park (p123)** is a worthy substitute.

㉑ **HANALEI TARO & JUICE COMPANY (p141)** No trip to Kaua'i is complete without experiencing the native staple, taro. This family-run farm offers **tours (p140)** and serves taro smoothies at this roadside kiosk.

㉒ **HANALEI RIVER PADDLE (p137)** Kaua'i's star river is the Wailua, but the Hanalei River is pleasantly small and secluded, meandering through the Hanalei National Wildlife Refuge and unbelievably green fields of taro.

㉓ **SUNSET OVER MAKANA MOUNTAIN (BALI HAI) (p126)** After winding your way through stunning emerald valleys and perfectly formed sandy beaches, savor another visual treat. Find a spot on the St Regis Princeville lawn and simply wait for sunset.

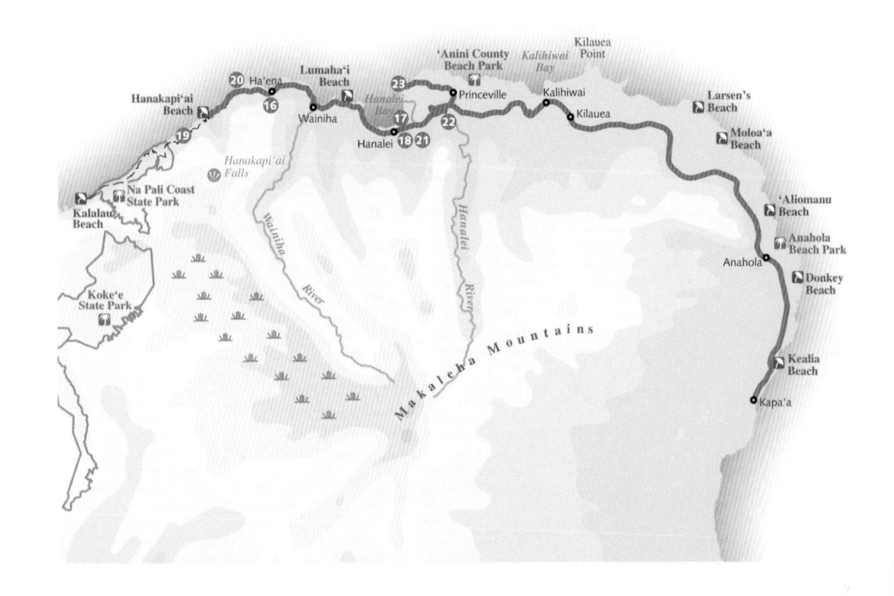

IN NINE DAYS *This leg: 26 Miles*

24 'ANINI BEACH PARK (p123) If you've planned nine days on Kaua'i, follow the first week as suggested. On your eighth day, unwind at this smooth-as-glass bay, protected by Kaua'i's largest coral reef. No waves for board sports, but snorkelers and windsurfers will be happy. A first-pick site for camping (or renting a dream beach house).

25 KILAUEA POINT NATIONAL WILDLIFE REFUGE (p117) Whether or not you're an Audubon fan, this nature area makes a scenic stop, with a historic lighthouse, rare native birds and whale watching in winter.

26 KILAUEA (p116) Formerly boondocks Kilauea is now home to multimillionaire transplants and stylish shops and eateries. Don't miss **Kong Lung Co (p121)** for Japanese tableware, kids' toys and other irresistibles. Or just cobble together a picnic at **Kilauea Town Market (p120)** and **Healthy Hut (p120)**.

27 NA 'AINA KAI BOTANICAL GARDENS (p118) On your last day, revisit your favorite place, kick back and let the island vibe sink in. Or, if you're up for another botanical extravaganza, visit this sprawling collection of meticulously manicured gardens, with an especially sweet children's area.

28 ANGELINE'S MU'OLAULANI (p111) Compared to Kaua'i's extravagant resort spas, this Hawaiian-owned bodywork center is distinctly rustic. Its signature treatment includes steam, *'alaea* salt scrub and double lomilomi massage, with two bodyworkers (four hands) working you over.

29 ANAHOLA BEACH PARK (p108) If you don't fancy a massage, check out this low-key beach, frequented mainly by local Hawaiian families. With swimmable waters and a backdrop of shady trees, you could easily while away the afternoon here.

30 KAPA'A (p98) End your trip in Kapa'a town, hanging out with a lively mix of old-time locals, bohemian seekers and grateful transplants. Cycle the **coastal path (p102)**, splash your baby at **Baby Beach (p100)**, talk story over a shave ice at **Hawaiian Blizzard (p104)** and munch down one last seared *'ahi* wrap at **Mermaids Café (p105)**.

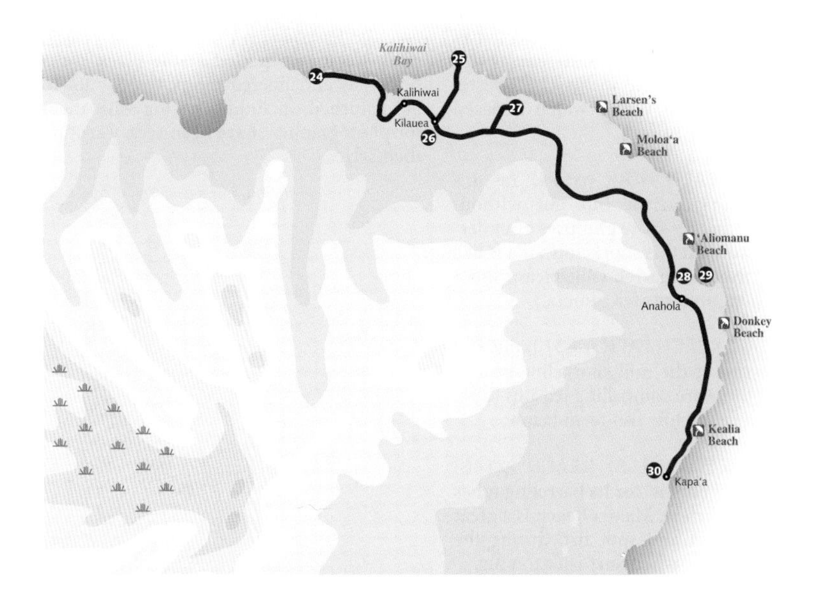

THE GOOD EARTH

❶ **CHOCOLATE ECO-TOUR AT STEELGRASS FARM IN WAILUA (p83)** Proud of your palate? Then try identifying one of the 500 notes said to be found in cacao (twice as many as in wine) by sampling local chocolate, some grown on-site. Learn about the upkeep of a hand-pollinated vanilla orchid and munch on organically farmed fruit or honey.

❷ **KAUA'I COFFEE COMPANY IN 'ELE'ELE (p186)** Honor your caffeine addiction on this self-guided tour of the state's largest coffee plantation. Roam through the environmentally responsible acres of this 100% renewable energy operation and rationalize your desire to inhale treats like malasadas, macadamia-nut ice cream or guava sherbet.

❸ **COCO'S KAUA'I B&B (p203)** Stay off the grid at this hydroelectric-powered B&B, located on a sugarcane ranch run by descendants of the Robinson family (owners of neighboring island Ni'ihau). If you feel like riding the waves, you're just a stone's throw from **Pakalas (p200)** surf spot.

❹ **HARAGUCHI RICE MILL IN HANALEI (p140)** This six-generation family farm in the Hanalei National Wildlife Refuge is rich with the Hawaiian tradition of taro farming and full of endangered native species.

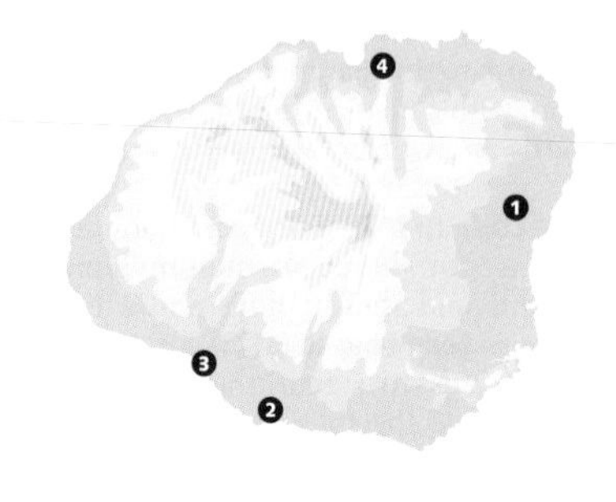

NATURE AT PLAY

❶ **KILAUEA POINT NATIONAL WILDLIFE REFUGE (p117)** Migratory sea and native Hawaiian birds plummet and soar at this intact lighthouse listed on the US Register of Historic Places. Whale watch between November and April.

❷ **PO'IPU BEACH PARK (p164)** Yes, it's chock-full of tourists, but not without reason. Getting up-close glimpses of underwater creatures at this snorkeling spot is like shooting fish in a barrel. (But please shoot only with an underwater camera.)

❸ **LYDGATE BEACH PARK (p83)** Tame, and not your run-of-the mill snorkeling experience, but those are compelling reasons to go. Sea turtles float while fish teem below.

❹ **MAKUA (TUNNELS) BEACH (p148)** Nicknamed 'Tunnels' for its barreling tubes that draw in surfers, Makua Beach is a great place to snorkel and spot fish during the summer months, when surf isn't too big.

❺ **KE ALA HELE MAKALAE (p102)** Navigate the Eastside on the new paved coastal path. Keep eyes peeled at the black rocks below, as endangered monk seals – not to be disturbed, including posing with them for photographs – have been seen warming themselves.

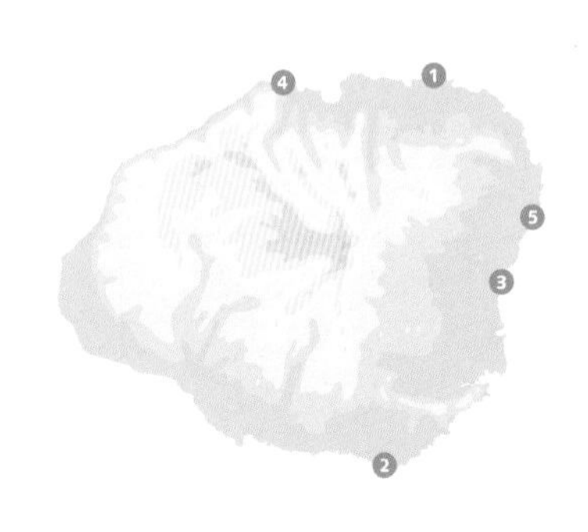

THE BEACH, INSPIRED

❶ **SUNSET AT POLIHALE (p206)** The island's westernmost point is known for its vibrant sunsets. Boasting the state's longest beach, it is Kaua'i's only *leina*, the Hawaiian culture's jumping-off point for spirits leaving this world and entering the next.

❷ **RELAX, 'ANINI-SIDE (p123)** Watch windsurfers, doze under a coconut tree or take a picnic for an early evening of roasted marshmallows and stargazing at this beach park with facilities and barbecue pavilions.

❸ **SUNRISE AT KEALIA BEACH (p108)** Surfers call it 'dawn patrol.' Regardless of whether you plan to jump in the water, sunrise can be spectacular at this eastern beach. You might find a few others here and there, some practicing yoga, some writing in journals. But chances are good you'll have it all to yourself.

❹ **SPECTATOR KITESURFING AT FUJII BEACH (p100)** It's a dangerous sport but somebody's got to do it. Live vicariously on any given windy day at this spot, where adventure-seeking wind junkies abound.

❺ **GLASS BEACH (p188)** While it's rare for many of us to meditate on what one grain of sand has experienced, walking this beach of discarded, softened junkyard treasures is like finding yourself inside a giant rock tumbler.

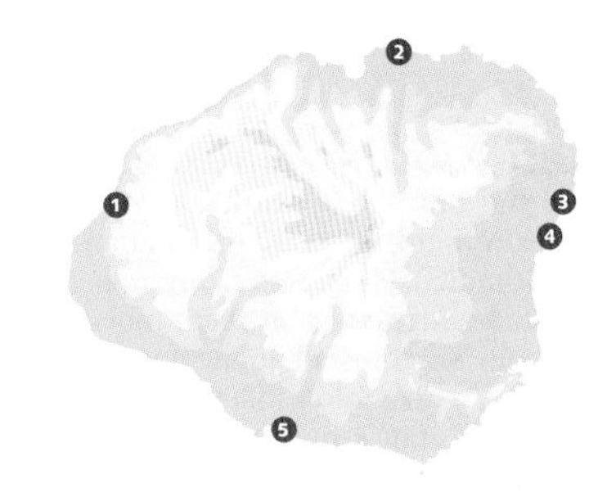

SURVIVAL OF THE FITTEST

❶ **BIKE THE POWERLINE TRAIL (p90)** Ride cautiously but with vigor over valley and into rainforest. The Wailua start is best for mountain bikers: steep, sometimes wide and usually muddy, it's not too technical but definitely requires endurance.

❷ **KAYAK THE NA PALI COAST (p137)** Plan at least two days for this seasonal opportunity to kayak the Mt Everest of the ocean. Camp kayaking requires swimming to shore, hiking extreme conditions, and smart planning.

❸ **HIKE TO KALALAU VALLEY (p152)** This 22-mile hike is sensory stimuli to the umpteenth: crashing waves below and eroding cliffs at your feet. Big surf can swallow up parts of this trail without apology. It can't be done in a day, but it's inarguably worth it.

❹ **HIKE THE BLUE HOLE (p90)** Strenuous, verdant and teeming with small obstacles you'd expect in a drainage path of Mt Wai'ale'ale, the second-wettest spot on earth.

❺ **BIKE (OR HIKE) THE MOALEPE TRAIL (p88)** While perhaps not the most physically challenging option for mountain biking aficionados, it still is among the most beautiful and lengthy, the latter of which depends upon your physical prowess. For an easier go, try it on foot.

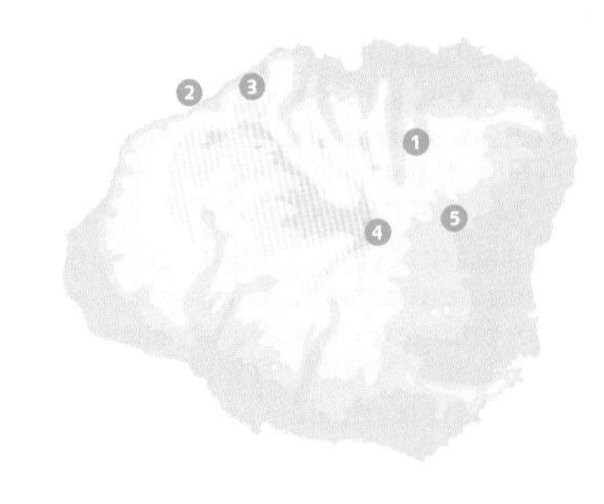

OUTDOOR ACTIVITIES & ADVENTURES

When Mother Nature designed Kaua'i, she must have worked overtime. Whether you venture *mauka* (toward the mountains) or *makai* (toward the sea), you'll find natural phenomena that far outshine anything that mere mortals can build. Simply put, Kaua'i is all about the Great Outdoors. Here, you can hike into a mammoth volcanic canyon or kayak the state's only navigable river. You can climb startlingly green valleys and steep, weathered cliffs, or whoosh from tree to tree on lofty forest ziplines. Offshore, you can snorkel amid the *honu* (Hawaiian sea turtles), go whale watching all winter, catch big-game fish or ride waves at forgivingly sandy-bottomed beaches. Whether you are a water baby or a landlubber, an athlete or a couch potato, you'll find fun activities for all abilities and levels of adventure. In this chapter we primarily recommend the best activities and locations, while destination chapters detail tour operators, rental shops, lessons and other specific information.

AT SEA

Of Kaua'i's 111 miles of coastline, sandy beaches constitute almost 50%. You need not drive far to find another — and yet another! — gorgeous beach. Water conditions are changeable, however. Note the seasonal changes in surf conditions: North Shore and Westside beaches are most hazardous around winter (November to March), when South Shore and Eastside beaches are quite calm. The pattern reverses in summer. Of course, conditions change daily and exceptions are the rule.

Before plunging in, click to **Kaua'i Explorer** (www.kauaiexplorer.com), a terrific, Hanalei-based resource on beaches, safety, marine life and much more. The best watersports map, available at bookstores and ocean-sports shops, is *Franko's Dive Map of Kaua'i* ($7), a waterproof fold-up that identifies all the top diving, snorkeling, surfing and kayaking sites.

MICAH WRIGHT

KAUA'I ACTIVITIES

A B 159°40'W C D

1 2 3 4 5 6

SIGHTS & ACTIVITIES

Acid Drop's....................(see 31)
Ahukini Landing....................1 F5
Alaka'i Swamp Trail....................(see 19)
Anahola Beach Park....................2 F3
'Anini Beach Park....................3 D2
Awa'awapuhi Trail....................(see 40)
BK's....................(see 31)
Brennecke's Beach....................4 E6
Cannons Beach....................5 C2
Center's....................(see 31)
General Store....................6 D6
Ha'ena Beach Park....................(see 5)
Hanalei Bay....................7 D2
Hanalei River....................8 D2
Hule'ia River....................9 E5
Kalalau Trail....................10 C2
Kalapaki Beach....................11 F5
Kalihiwai Stream....................12 E2
Kapa'a Beach Park....................13 F4
Kaua'i Lagoons Golf Course....................14 E5
Kawalkoi Stream Trail....................(see 19)
Ke Ala Hele Makalae....................15 F4
Kealia Beach....................16 F4
Ke'e Beach....................17 C2
Kikiaola Small Boat Harbor....................18 B5
Koai'e Canyon Trail....................(see 40)
Koke'e State Park....................19 B3
Koloa Landing....................20 D6
Kuilau Ridge Trail....................21 E4
Lydgate Beach Park....................22 F4
Maha'ulepu Beach....................23 E6
Maha'ulepu Heritage Trail....................(see 23)
Makua (Tunnels) Beach....................24 C2
Moalepe Trail....................25 E4
Na Pali Coast State Park....................26 B2
Nawiliwili Small Boat Harbor....................(see 11)
Nounou Mountain Trails....................27 E4
Nu'alolo Trail....................(see 19)
Nukumoi Point....................(see 31)
Pakalas (Infinities)....................28 B5
Pihea Trail....................(see 19)
Po'ipu Bay Golf Course....................29 E6
Po'ipu Beach....................30 D6
Po'ipu Beach Park....................31 D6
Port Allen....................32 C6
Powerline Trail....................33 D3

Bodyboarding & Bodysurfing
Cycling & Mountain Biking
Diving
Fishing
Golf
Hiking
Kayaking & Canoeing
Snorkeling
Surfing
Swimming
Water Skiing & Wakeboarding
Windsurfing & Kitesurfing

Na Pali Coast
Kalalau Trail
Kalalau Beach
Na Pali Coast State Park
Ha'ena
Wainiha
Kalihiwai Bay
Princeville
Hanalei
Princeville Airport
Powerline Trail
Kilohana (4030ft)
Alaka'i Wilderness Preserve
Wainiha River
Hanalei River
Makaleha
Mt Wai'ale'ale (5148ft)
Mt Kawaikini (5243ft)
Koke'e Rd
Waipo'o Falls
Polihale State Park
Barking Sands Pacific Missile Range Facility
Mana
Waimea River
Waimea Canyon
Waimea Canyon Dr
22°00'N
Pu'u Lua Reservoir
Kekaha
Waimea
Kaumuali'i Hwy
Hanapepe River
Mt Kahili (3089ft)
Hanapepe Valley Lookout
Kalaheo
Lawa'i
Olokele
Kaumakani
Hanapepe
'Ele'ele
Numila
Koloa
Spouting Horn
Lawa'i Rd
Po'ipu
Kaulakahi Channel
PACIFIC OCEAN
159°40'W

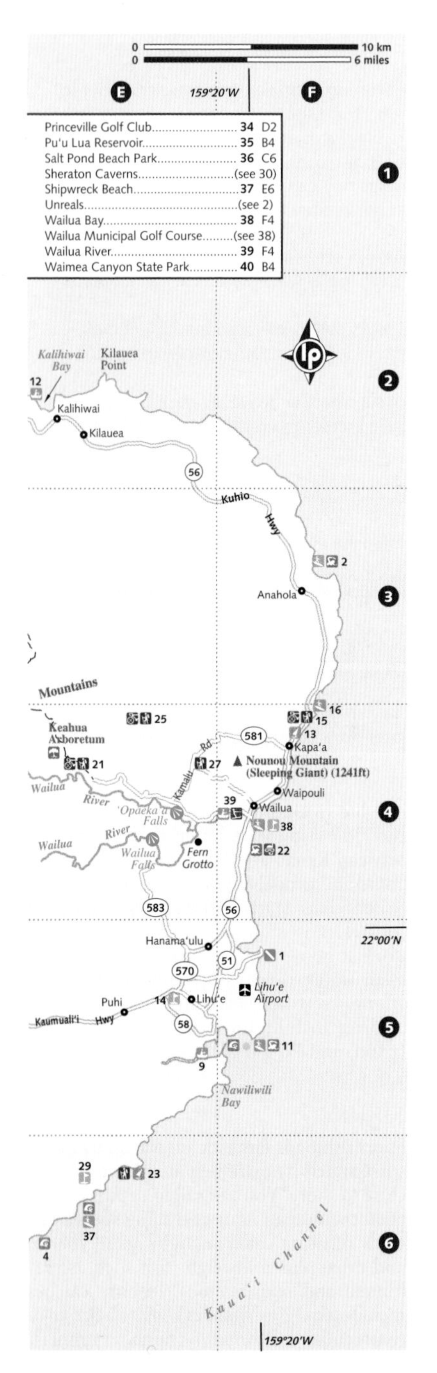

BODYBOARDING & BODYSURFING

While bodyboarding is less glamorous than surfing, it's more popular, more affordable and more doable (from day one). Bodysurfing appeals to minimalists who prefer to catch waves without a board, using only specialized fins. Unless you're a strong swimmer, stick to bodyboarding (and use a rashguard and fins). Good South Shore breaks include Po'ipu Beach (p166), Brennecke's Beach (p165) and, for the skilled, Shipwreck Beach (p166). On the Eastside, newbies should start at Kalapaki Beach (p63) near Lihu'e, while experts can test themselves at Kealia Beach (p108). Hanalei Bay (p134) near the pavilion is a top North Shore spot. Rentals cost around $5 per day and $20 per week at surf or snorkel shops.

DIVING

While Kaua'i waters cannot quite compare to the calm, clear waters off the Big Island's Kona Coast, diving is still excellent. South Shore waters see the most diving activity, but the North Shore reefs at Tunnels and Cannons are local favorites.

Note that the closest hyperbaric chambers for recompression therapy are located in Honolulu. If you encounter trouble, call ☎ 911 and the **Coast Guard Rescue Center** (on O'ahu ☎ 808-536-4336). **Divers Alert Network** (DAN; ☎ 919-684-8111, 800-446-2671; www.diversalertnetwork.org) gives advice on diving emergencies, insurance, decompression services, illness and injury.

Shore Dives

Top shore-diving site is Koloa Landing (p169), a great beginner spot that is conveniently located and allows easy entry. Others are Po'ipu Beach Park (p164), Ke'e Beach (p151) and Makua (Tunnels) Beach (p148) and Ahukini Landing (p64). Two-tank shore dives with equipment typically start at $85.

Boat Dives

Boat dives widen your options, with the best sites again along the South Shore: Sheraton

OCEAN SAFETY

Drowning fatalities have unfortunately become a recurring theme among travelers eager to plunge into the Pacific's beckoning blue. Ironically, it's the visitors who tend to underestimate the ocean's devastating power, while island surfers, lifeguards and canoe paddlers express profound awe and humility toward the waters they know so intimately.

Be aware of rip currents, fast-flowing ocean currents that can drag swimmers out into deeper water. Anyone caught in a rip should either go with the flow until it loses power or swim parallel to shore to slip out of it.

All waves are not made the same. They often come in sets, some bigger, some smaller, separated by as much as 20 minutes. Sometimes, a big rogue wave sweeps in and literally drags napping sunbathers into the ocean.

Waves breaking close to shore are called shorebreaks. When only a couple of feet high, they're generally fine for novices. Large shorebreaks, though, can slam down with enough force to knock you out.

Along steeply sloped beaches, undertows can occur where large waves wash back directly into incoming surf. If you get caught in one and pulled under the water, don't panic. Go with the current until you get beyond the wave.

Heed the basic warnings:

- Never turn your back on the ocean.
- Never swim alone. If you're an inexperienced swimmer, swim only at lifeguarded beaches. At beaches without lifeguards, swim only if (and where) the locals are doing so – they know better than you.
- Observe the surf for at least 20 minutes before entering. Look for sets, currents and other swimmers.
- Observe the wind. Windy conditions increase ocean chop.
- Don't walk on coastal rocks, where an unexpected wave can sweep you out. It's easy to misjudge the 'safe zone.'
- Don't assume that water conditions are consistent in all regions.
- Read the ocean tips and surf report at **Kaua'i Explorer** (www.kauaiexplorer.com).

Caverns, a series of partially collapsed lava tubes 10ft or more in height, with shafts of glowing sunlight illuminating their dim interior; Nukumoi Point, a shallow site and habitat for green sea turtles; and General Store, with sharks, octopuses, eels and the remains of an 1892 shipwreck. The hottest dive site for experienced divers, perhaps statewide, is Ni'ihau (p219), which features deep wall dives, lava formations, caves, plentiful marine life (including pelagics such as sharks) and clear waters. The often-choppy crossing between Kaua'i and Ni'ihau takes about 2½ hours and is doable only in summer.

Boat dives start at $120. For certification courses, most shops allow you to do coursework at home and then come to Kaua'i for open-water dives. Recommended outfits offering certification courses and all types of dives include those listed in the Koloa (p160) and Po'ipu (p170) sections.

Island Insights

Kaua'i's coastline features more extensive reef formations than the younger islands, but they're not really 'coral' reefs. Instead, various forms of stony coralline algae predominate. Regardless of their composition, the reefs provide an excellent habitat for colorful fish and invertebrates, enjoyed by snorkelers and divers around the island.

FISHING

Sport fishing is fantastic off Kaua'i, which is surrounded by extremely deep waters quite close to shore. You can sail to depths of over 6000ft within an hour at trolling speed. The day's offshore catch includes giant marlin and tuna, plus midweight fish such as mahimahi and *ono* (wahoo). Inshore catches include *uku* (gray snapper), *ulua* (jack), *kaku* (barracuda) and *kamanu* (rainbow runner).

Fishing charters depart mainly from Nawiliwili Small Boat Harbor (p68) in Lihu'e and Port Allen (p188). Among the dozens, if not hundreds, of charters advertised, we especially recommend those listed in the Lihu'e chapter (p68).

Ask about sharing the catch if you want to keep what you hook. Seasickness is common, so take medication before you depart; try to plan a charter when seas are calm (of course, who can predict the weather?).

Freshwater bass fishing is possible in artificial reservoirs; also rainbow-trout fishing is an annual summer event at the **Pu'u Lua Reservoir** (Map p212). To cast independently you'll need a freshwater license from the **Division of Aquatic Resources** (☎ 274-3344; www.hawaii.gov/dlnr/dar; 7-day tourist license adult/child $10/4), or consider going out with expert bass fisherman Tom Christy of **Cast & Catch** (☎ 332-9707; half-day charter for 1 or 2 people $265).

KAYAKING

River Kayaking

With seven rivers, including the only navigable one statewide, river kayaking is the rage here. The Wailua River tour, which includes a dip at a 130ft waterfall, is the classic. Due to the river's popularity, the county strictly regulates its use (eg no tours on Sundays). Most outfitters are located in Wailua (p86), Hanalei (p137) and Lihu'e (p68). Kayaks rent from single/double $25/50 per day and guided Wailua River tours range from $40 to $98.

If you're seeking a solitary nature experience, you should visit Kaua'i's other rivers, smaller but perhaps more charming and leisurely. Hanalei River (p137) and Kalihiwai Stream (p122) are highly recommended. A handful of tours (p68) navigate the Hule'ia River, which passes through the off-limits Hule'ia National Wildlife Refuge.

Sea Kayaking

Officially all sea kayaking off Kaua'i must be done on tour because of rough surf. Beginners can learn in Po'ipu (p170) and Hanalei (p137), while the fit and ambitious can challenge themselves on the grueling 17-mile Na Pali journey (p137), possible only in summer.

RESPONSIBLE DIVING & SNORKELING

The popularity of underwater sports is causing serious damage to many sites. Help preserve Kaua'i's reef and marine ecosystems with these tips:

- Respect Native Hawaiian cultural practices and sacred places, including fishing grounds.
- Avoid touching living marine organisms or dragging equipment across reefs. Even the gentlest contact can damage polyps. Never stand on coral. If you can't move without kicking coral, you don't belong there.
- Practice and maintain proper buoyancy control to avoid colliding with the reef. Make sure you're correctly weighted and that your weight belt is positioned so that you stay horizontal.
- Be fin conscious. Even without contact, heavy fin strokes near the reef can damage delicate organisms. When treading water in shallow reef areas, take care not to kick up clouds of sand, which can smother fragile reef life.
- Do not use reef anchors or ground boats on coral (anchoring in sand is better). Encourage dive operators to establish permanent moorings at popular sites.
- Collecting live coral or rock is illegal. Also resist the temptation to buy coral or shells. Removing such natural objects is ecologically damaging and mars the beauty of a site.
- Remove all trash, including found litter or abandoned fishing gear (hooks, lines, nets). Plastics are especially harmful to marine life. Turtles can mistake plastic for jellyfish and eat it.
- Do not disturb marine animals. It's illegal to come within 30ft of turtles and 150ft of whales, dolphins and the Hawaiian monk seal. Limit your observation of an animal to 30 minutes.
- Never feed marine animals and fish. You will disturb their normal eating habits. Boycott dive and snorkel shops that sell fish food (and voice a complaint).
- Spend as little time as possible within underwater caves; your air bubbles may be trapped within the roof, leaving previously submerged organisms high and dry.
- Sunscreen protects human skin but kills coral polyps. Use rash guards instead.

KITESURFING

Kitesurfing, also known as kiteboarding, is an emerging sport that combines surfing maneuvers, windsurfing speed and the aerial thrills of paragliding. If you're already a surfer or windsurfer, try it! But the experience requires a lesson; no one in the island rents such specialized gear. Lessons wildly vary in price, so shop around.

Most lessons are given in Hanalei (p138). Spectators, watch the action at Kapa'a Beach Park, Hanalei Bay and along the Maha'ulepu Coast (boxed text, p168).

SNORKELING

Snorkeling is the least snobby of ocean activities. Almost anyone can do it, simply by choosing a beach suited to one's experience level and swimming skills. If you choose shore snorkeling (ie entering the water from the beach, instead of motoring out in a boat), you'll also save money and the environment. Top spots include Po'ipu Beach Park (p164), with dense fish populations and frequent turtle spotting, on the South Shore; Salt Pond Beach Park (p191), with its shallow waters, on the Westside; Lydgate Beach Park (p83), for a protected lagoon perfect for kids, on the Eastside; and 'Anini Beach Park (p123), Ke'e Beach (p151) and Makua (Tunnels) Beach (p148), for the most spectacular setting (both above and below water), on the North Shore.

Snorkeling Cruises

To reach the spectacular waters along the Na Pali Coast, your only options are to go by boat or raft. Tours leave from Port Allen (p189), Kikiaola Small Boat Harbor (p199) and Hanalei Bay (p139). Departures from Hanalei on the North Shore are recommended because they navigate past the whole scenic Na Pali Coast. Morning trips generally have calmer seas, and dolphins. Book as early in your trip as possible, as high surf or foul weather can cancel tours (or at least the snorkeling part). Seasickness is common: if you're prone, take remedies 24 hours before departure.

The major difference in tours is the type of boat used: either catamarans (sailing or motorized) or rafts. Certainly, rafts are the most exhilarating, bouncing along the water and entering caves (in mellower weather), but most lack any shade, restroom or comfy seating, so they're not for everyone (folks with bad backs should beware). The best rafts are rigid-hull inflatables, with hard bottoms that allow smoother rides, and note that large rafts might include a restroom and canopy. Sit in back for less jostling.

Catamarans are cushier, with smooth rides, ample shade, restrooms and crowd-pleasing amenities, like trampolines for sunning and water slides. Some catamarans sport sails (and actually use them), while others are entirely motorized.

ANCIENT VOYAGERS, MODERN PADDLERS

The first Polynesians arrived here by paddling outrigger canoes across 2000 miles of open ocean. Today, modern islanders certainly don't use outrigger canoes for everyday transportation, but paddling remains a popular activity. On Kaua'i alone, there are dozens of canoe clubs, which train regularly and compete in such events as the annual **Na Pali Challenge** (www.napalichallenge.com) in August.

While paddlers might train in single or double canoes, they often race in six-person vessels that literally glide (as if above the water) when paddlers are working in optimum synchronicity. This ancient sport spurs much camaraderie among paddlers, who span all ages.

Many visitors (with visions of the *Hawaii Five-O* opener dancing in their heads) want to give paddling a go. But most canoe tours are passenger rides, eg on the Wailua River (p84) and in Hanalei Bay (p140). One option for actual paddling: a trip up the Hanalei River with Hawaiian Surfing Adventures (p139).

Watching canoe paddlers practice or race is always exciting. Most clubs practice in the Wailua River, Hanalei Bay or Kalapaki Beach. Check the **Garden Island Canoe Racing Association** (www.gicra.org) website for race dates. To learn more about outrigger canoe paddling, see Steve West's comprehensive books at www.kanuculture.com.

Stand up paddle surfing in Hanalei Bay AMANDA C GREGG

STAND UP PADDLE SURFING

In the 1960s, Waikiki watermen developed stand up paddle surfing (SUP) when teaching groups of learner surfers. Standing on their boards, using a paddle to propel themselves, they could easily view their surroundings. In the early 2000s, SUP emerged as a global sport when big-name pros started doing it as a substitute when waves were flat.

On Kaua'i, you might see stand up paddlers at the beach and be tempted to try it. But note that it's much harder than it looks. Novices will struggle to control both their boards (which are bigger than surfboards) and their paddles, creating hazards for anyone around them. In fact, there's much animosity between traditional surfers and stand up paddlers, who tend to claim all the waves, can cause collisions and injuries, and are said to ruin the 'vibe' of the line-up. The two sports are actually quite incompatible, and some are pushing to get SUP surfing banned at most surf breaks.

If you're still keen, lessons are offered at various spots islandwide, particularly Hanalei Bay (p139) and Kalapaki Beach. Lessons and rentals tend to be unadvertised and unofficial so just look for surf-instructor trucks (with lots of boards) and ask around.

SURFING

Ever since the 1970s when surf bums flocked to the North Shore, Kaua'i has been known as a surf mecca. Today Hanalei remains a surf town, and many islanders start or end their day catching waves. The best time of year for surfing depends on your skill level. For experienced surfers, the North Shore is terrific in winter, especially at Hanalei Bay (p134) and Tunnels Beach (p148), where winter waves average 6ft to 8ft (with 20ft or

LIFEGUARD-PROTECTED BEACHES

- **Hanalei Bay** (p134) At the Hanalei Beach Park Pavilion and at Wai'oli (Pine Trees) Beach Park.
- **Lydgate Beach Park** (p83)
- **Po'ipu Beach Park** (p164)
- **Salt Pond Beach Park** (p191)
- **Kekaha Beach Park** (p204)
- **Kealia Beach** (p108)
- **Ha'ena Beach Park** (p148)

Lifeguard staffing is subject to change, so call the **Ocean Safety Bureau** (☎ 241-6506) to confirm this information.

KAUA'I SURF BEACHES & BREAKS *Jake Howard*

As a tourist in Hawaii, there are some places you go and there are some places you don't go. For many local families the beach parks are meeting places where generations gather to celebrate life under the sun. They're tied to these places by a sense of community and culture, and they aren't eager for outsiders to push them out. As a conscious traveler, it's important to understand this. Most folks who live in Hawaii are happy to share the spots that have become gentrified over the past 100 years, and usually will greet you with open arms – but they do reserve the right to protect some of their sacred surf grounds.

In the water, basic surf etiquette is vital. The person 'deepest,' or furthest outside, has the right of way. When somebody is already up and riding, don't take off on the wave in front of them. Also, remember you're a visitor out in the line-up, so don't expect to get every wave that comes your way. There's a definite pecking order and, frankly, as a tourist you're at the bottom. That said, usually if you give a wave, you'll get a wave in return. In general, be generous in the water, understand your place and surf with a smile, and you should be fine.

The Garden Isle is one of Hawaii's most challenging islands for surfers. On the North Shore, a heavy local vibe is pervasive; though **Hanalei Bay** (p134) offers some of the best waves among the islands, it is also one of the most localized. With Princeville Resort overlooking the break, residents may be a bit more understanding of out-of-towners in the water at Hanalei than at other North Shore spots, but surfing with respect is a must. Between localism and the inaccessibility of the Na Pali Coast, not to mention a sizable tiger shark population, you may want to pass on surfing the North Shore.

As a general rule, surf tourism is relegated to the South Shore around Po'ipu (p164). Chances are good that you'll be staying in this popular area anyway, which is perfect because there are some fun waves to be had here. Breaking best in the summer on south swells, spots like **BK's**, **Acid Drop's** and **Center's** challenge even the most advanced surfers. First-timers can get their feet wet at nearby **Brennecke's** (p165). Only bodyboarding and bodysurfing are permitted here – no stand-up surfing – and it's a great place to take the family.

On the Northeast Coast, **Unreals** breaks at Anahola Bay. It's a consistent right point that can work well on easterly wind swell, when *kona* (leeward) winds are offshore.

Surfing lessons and board hire are available mainly in Hanalei (p139) and in Po'ipu (p170). To find the swells, call the **surf hotline** (☎ 335-3720).

Jake Howard is a senior writer at Surfer *magazine and lives in San Clemente, CA.*

higher surf possible at any time). Nowadays, the North Shore breaks are crowded year-round, especially when the surf is under 6ft and attracts the masses (bigger surf means smaller crowds). The vibe in the line-ups can be aggressive, with everyone trying to claim a piece of the action.

The South Shore is best in summer, where hugely popular Po'ipu Beach Park (p164) crowds up, while Shipwreck Beach (p166) and Maha'ulepu Beach (p168) draw only the experts. Pakalas (p200), also known as Infinities, near Waimea, is the Westside's hottest break, but the unprotected western waters mean winter breaks are treacherous. Transitional swells happen on the Eastside, when surfers hit Kealia Beach (p108), Wailua Bay (p86) and Kalapaki Beach (p63). Eastside swells often break on distant reefs and hence get blown out except during early-morning hours and *kona* (leeward) wind conditions. Check on current swells at www.kauaiworld.com/surfreport or call the **surf hotline** (☎ 335-3720).

Surfing lessons and board rentals are available primarily in Hanalei (p139) and Po'ipu (p170).

SWIMMING

You can find protected swimming lagoons year-round at Lydgate Beach Park (p83), Salt Pond Beach Park (p191) and 'Anini Beach Park (p123). Elsewhere, swimming is a seasonal sport. On the North Shore, swimming is lovely in summer, when waters are glassy at Ke'e Beach (p151) and Hanalei Bay (p134). In winter, when giant swells pound the North Shore, head to the South Shore, especially Po'ipu Beach Park (p164). For a

list of beaches with lifeguards on duty, see the boxed text, p37.

Lap swimmers who need lanes and walls will enjoy the new Olympic-sized YMCA pool in Lihu'e (p69).

WATER SKIING & WAKEBOARDING

Water skiing is not a major sport on Kaua'i, and only one company is permitted to tow skiers on the Wailua River: Water Ski, Surf & Kayak Company (p90), in Wailua. But the calm, freshwater river is a nice place to learn. You can also try wakeboarding, the water equivalent of snowboarding, in which you're towed behind a boat on a single board.

WHALE WATCHING

Plan a trip a winter trip and lock in a wildlife-watching bonus: the annual humpback whale migration. Coming 6000 miles from Alaska, the *kohola* are seen from late November to late March. It's possible to whale watch from land, but seeing the massive creatures close-up from a boat will give you the shivers. Many of the snorkeling cruise companies also offer whale-watching tours, which depart either from Hanalei (p139), Port Allen (p189) or Kikiaola Small Boat Harbor (p199).

Top Picks

WHALE WATCHING FROM LAND

- **Kilauea Point National Wildlife Refuge** (p117)
- **Lookout between Kapa'a and Kealia Beach** (Map p101) Reached by taking the paved turnout into the small parking lot.
- **Po'ipu Beach Park** (p164)

WINDSURFING

While Kaua'i lacks Maui's world-class windsurfing beaches, it does have some decent sites: 'Anini Beach Park (p123), with calm, shallow, reef-protected waters, is ideal for beginners. Instructors use specialized jumbo boards that offer stability and small, lightweight sails. More experienced folks can likely handle Makua (Tunnels) Beach (p148) and Maha'ulepu Beach (p168).

ON LAND

Landlubbers, prepare to be impressed! Kaua'i boasts the greenest, steepest mountains and valleys found across the Hawaiian Islands,

THAR SHE BLOWS!

You're not the only species that chooses to winter in balmy Hawaii. From November to March, as many as 10,000 humpback whales migrate from the Gulf of Alaska to Hawaiian waters. The shallow, warm waters constitute a key habitat for the endangered whales, and nearly two-thirds of the entire North Pacific population migrates the 3000-mile distance.

The whales feed all summer in the cool, nutrient-rich Alaskan waters, while they mate, birth and nurse their young all winter (during which they rarely eat). Males compete for female attention, slamming each other with their powerful tail flukes, emitting mysterious sounds and breaching (propelling their bodies into the air). The chance to witness these colossal creatures, which measure up to 50ft long and weigh 45 to 50 tons, is reason enough to schedule a winter visit. Of all whale species, humpbacks have the longest pectoral flipper, about a third of their body length. The undersides of their tail flukes are as distinctive as our fingerprints.

The 11½-month gestation period means that females impregnated in a given winter will return to the same waters to give birth the next winter. Then, after feeding all summer in the Gulf of Alaska, a newly weaned calf may follow its mother back to the breeding grounds the following winter. Humpbacks reach young adulthood at four to six years.

In 1970, the US Fish and Wildlife Service designated the humpback whale as an endangered species. To learn more, check the website of the **Hawaiian Islands Humpback Whale National Marine Sanctuary** (☎ 246-2860; www.hawaiihumpbackwhale.noaa.gov).

Mountain biking near Po'ipu ANN CECIL

making for phenomenal hiking, especially around Waimea Canyon and along the Na Pali Coast. Golfers can play at world-class courses, while kids will forget about Disney rides when they can go ziplining atop real-live trees.

ATV

For environmental reasons, we generally recommend crossing the countryside by horse rather than by ATV. But there's one company, Kaua'i ATV (p161), that commendably offers biodiesel vehicles. Renting one is optional and entails a $20 extra fee. So if you decide to go, do the right thing and choose a BioBug!

CYCLING

It's *possible* to ride along the belt highway in the Westside, South Shore and most of the Eastside. But is it *recommended*? On one hand, Kaua'i has no bike lanes along the highway, and road shoulders can be narrow or nonexistent. On the other, distances are short and you might welcome a substitute for the maddening Eastside crawl. Overall, only experienced cyclists should consider cycling as transportation on Kaua'i.

Once the Eastside coastal path, Ke Ala Hele Makalae (boxed text, p102), is completed, however, cycling from Lihu'e all the way to Anahola will be doable for the masses. For now, the path is used only recreationally in short stretches near Lydgate Beach Park (p83) and from Kapa'a Beach Park (p100) to Donkey Beach (boxed text, p110). Bear in mind, because it's a shared-use path rather than a bike throughway, your speed must accommodate pedestrians and others around you.

Cycling the North Shore, past Princeville, is impossible along the narrow, cliffside highway.

GOLF

Kaua'i has only nine golf courses, but there's something for every taste and budget. Pros and experts can try the world-class St Regis Princeville Golf Club (p127), Kaua'i Lagoons Golf Club (p68) and Poi'pu Bay Resort Course (p171). Budget or novice players can try the Wailua Municipal Golf Course (p90), considered among the nation's finest municipal courses, and Kukuiolono Golf Course (p180), where nine holes cost only $8.

To save on resort fees, golf in the afternoon for the 'twilight' rate or book through **Tee Times Hawaii** (www.teetimeshawaii.com), which offers savings of 10% to 40%.

HELICOPTER TOURS

The helicopter dilemma: you're loath to add to noise and air pollution. But your heart is set on a bird's-eye view of Kaua'i's inaccessible mountains and valleys, especially the mysterious, cloud-cloaked Mt Wai'ale'ale.

Ultimately you'll go with your gut (and budget). But here are a few tips: check the **Stop Disrespectful Air Tourism** (www.stopdat.org) website for recommended helicopter companies; schedule a chopper tour early in your trip in case it's cancelled due to bad weather; plan a morning flight, for the best lighting and least cloud cover; and choose a company that is an FAA-certified 135 air carrier and a pilot who is 135-certified, which basically means that they're better trained and maintained under the Federal Aviation Administration.

Most companies fly Eurocopter AStar helicopters, which fit four passengers in back and two with the pilot in front. But at least

RECOMMENDED HELICOPTER COMPANIES

Operator	Tour	Price	Extras
Island Helicopters (www.islandhelicopters.com)	50- to 55-minute circle island	$178	
Jack Harter Helicopters (www.helicopters-kauai.com)	60- to 65-minute circle island	$229-259	Doors-off, four-passenger Hughes 500 choppers available; can do custom charters
Mauna Loa Helicopters (www.maunaloahelicopters.com)	60-minute circle island	$199-239	Private tours for two or three passengers; doors-off aircraft optional
Ni'ihau Helicopters (www.niihau.us)	Half-day tour	$365	Only tour to Ni'ihau; beach landing
Safari Helicopters (www.safarihelicopters.com)	55-minute circle island/ 90-minute 'eco-tour'	from $160/250	Exclusive Westside landing; talk with Keith Robinson about his conservation efforts

three outfits fly the four-passenger, doors-off Hughes 500, which puts you closer to the windy, misty elements.

An alternative to helicopters are fixed-wing airplanes, but they cause more noise pollution and, according to the Kaua'i Sierra Club, they tend to disturb neighborhoods more blatantly. To respect island residents, we recommend choosing a chopper, if you must fly.

Except as noted, all tours depart from Lihu'e Airport. Princeville departures typically cost more.

HIKING

If you don't explore the island on foot, you're missing out on Kaua'i's finest (and free) terrestrial offerings. Hiking takes you up mountaintop rain forests, along steep coastal cliffs and down a colossal lava canyon – places you can't get to by car. Trails range from easy walks to precarious treks, so there's something for all skill levels. For the most variety, head to Waimea Canyon State Park (p208) and Koke'e State Park (p213). Don't miss the Pihea Trail (p215), which connects to the Alaka'i Swamp Trail, for a look at pristine native forestland. Hardier trekkers can combine the Nu'alolo Trail with the Awa'awapuhi Trail (p215) for breathtaking views of the Na Pali Coast.

Along the Na Pali Coast, the once-remote Kalalau Trail (p152) now attracts anyone with two legs – but only for the doable first section to Hanakapi'ai Beach. Eastside hikes head inland and upward, such as the Nounou Mountain Trails (p89), which afford sweeping mountain-to-ocean views. In addition to official trails, Kaua'i's vast coastline allows mesmerizing ocean walks, particularly along the cliffs of the Maha'ulepu Coast on the Maha'ulepu Coast (boxed text, p168) and the endless carpet of sand along Kekaha Beach Park (p204).

Guided Hikes

The Kaua'i chapter of the **Sierra Club** (☎ 651-0682; www.hi.sierraclub.org/kauai/kauai.html) leads guided hikes (suggested donation $3) ranging from beach clean-up walks to rigorous overnighters. Advance registration might be required; check the website in advance.

Top Picks

HIKING TRAILS

- **Canyon Trail to Waipo'o Falls** (p214)
- **Awa'awapuhi & Nu'alolo Trails loop hike** (p215)
- **Kalalau Trail to Hanakapi'ai Beach** (p153)
- **Nounou Mountain Trails** (p89)
- **Maha'ulepu Heritage Trail** (p168)

Island Insights

Thirty-four of Kaua'i's trails are managed by **Na Ala Hele** (☎ 274-3442; www.hawaiitrails.org), a commendable state program under the Department of Land and Natural Resources. The user-friendly website provides key facts about each trail, which might help you decide which ones match your fitness level. The staff welcomes inquiries and will send you a detailed topographic map by mail for $6; see website for details.

Koke'e Natural History Museum (p211) also offers guided hikes, dubbed 'Wonder Walks,' for a nominal donation during summer months.

For the ultimate learning experience, hike with geologist Chuck Blay's company, **Kaua'i Nature Tours** (☎ 742-8305; 888-233-8365; www.kauainaturetours.com; tours adult $100-130, child 7-12yr $75-85). Tours run from six to 10 hours and include lunch and transportation (you get your money's worth).

Hiking Safety

Among the major Hawaiian Islands, Kaua'i is the eldest and it shows. Weathered by waves, winds and rains, the lava terrain is eroded and can be unstable, especially along cliffs. Never go beyond fenced lookouts.

Rain is always a factor, especially on the North Shore and up at Koke'e and Waimea Canyon. Trails that are doable in dry weather can become precariously slippery with mud. Worse, flash floods are real threats wherever there are stream or river crossings. Never cross a waterway during heavy rains.

Wear appropriate footwear: while Chacos or Tevas are fine for easy coastal walks, definitely wear hiking or running shoes for major trails. Bring more water than you expect to need, plus first-aid supplies and snacks. Cell phones can be handy, but will probably lack access in remote areas.

Most accidents occur not due to a trail's inherent slipperiness or steepness, but because hikers take unnecessary risks. Don't hike alone. Don't go off-trail or bushwhack new trails. Don't dare yourself to perch on the cliff edge. Locals, especially parks and forestry officials, have little patience for tourists who take risks, only to require expensive rescue missions that jeopardize others' safety.

HORSEBACK RIDING

Vast pastureland stretches from open coastal cliffs to jungly rain forests – providing ample terrain for horseback riding. A handful of stables offer tours, mainly for beginners. On the South Shore, CJM Country Stables (p171) rides along the Maha'ulepu Coast, while on the North Shore, Princeville Ranch Stables (p127) and Silver Falls Ranch (p123) traverse green pastures, streams and waterfalls. In Kapa'a, Esprit De Corps Rid-

RESPONSIBLE HIKING

- Remove all trash, including any left by others. 'Trash' includes not only plastics, cigarette butts and food waste, but also used toilet paper and feminine-hygiene products. Do not burn or bury it.
- Use established toilets if available. Doing your business elsewhere increases the risk of water-source contamination. If no toilet is available, dig a hole 6in deep and 320ft from the nearest water source, and bury your waste.
- Don't use detergent or toothpaste in or near waterways, even if they are biodegradable. Instead, for personal washing, use biodegradeable soap and a container of water at least 160ft away from the nearest waterway.
- Stay on existing trails. Creating new ones only increases ground erosion and damage, especially on cliffs.
- Walk across a mud patch if a trail crosses one. Trying to skirt around it will only expand the patch.
- Do not remove any plants. Minimal picking of wild fruit is OK.
- Observe 'kapu' signs, which mean 'prohibited' or 'no trespassing.'

ing Academy (p102) offers the most varied selection of rides, making it the best option for advanced riders.

MOUNTAIN BIKING

If you aren't afraid of mud and puddles, go wild on countless dirt roads and trails islandwide. Running roughly north to south, the Powerline Trail is a decent, if muddy, option – and you can start from either Wailua (p90) or from Princeville (p128). Near the coast, the cane-haul road between Anahola and Donkey Beach will one day be paved with concrete as part of Ke Ala Hele Makalae (boxed text, p102), but it remains mountain-biking turf till then. The dirt roads near Po'ipu, above Maha'ulepu Beach, are flat but nice and dry, and you're less likely to encounter showers here. For a solitary ride, your best bets are the hunter roads at Waimea Canyon State Park (p206). For more information contact **Na Ala Hele** (www.hawaiitrails.org) and Kauai Cycle (p96), a retail/rental shop with a knowledgeable crew.

For the ultimate non-workout workout, Outfitters Kaua'i leads an all-downhill tour (p210) on Waimea Canyon Dr between the 12-mile marker and Kekaha.

SPAS

Forget the stereotype of wives going to the day spa when their husbands are golfing: we know that nowadays the spa 'lifestyle' is also attracting males. By far the biggest and most luxurious resort spa is Anara Spa (p171), a 20,000-sq-ft tropical garden fantasyland at the Grand Hyatt Kaua'i in Po'ipu, but consider Kaua'i Marriott's Alexander Day Spa and Salon (p68) in Lihu'e for its eco-consciousness. Hanalei Day Spa (p149) is known for its ayurvedic treatments and gorgeous North Shore location. On the Eastside, the Aveda Spa (p96) features soothing, Asian decor and its iconic botanical potions, but a better deal is Spa by the Sea (p102), where there are fewer frills but outstanding professionals. For an only-on-Kaua'i experience, book a signature steam, scrub and lomilomi massage treatment at Angeline's Mu'olaulani (see the boxed text, p111), run by a Hawaiian family in rural Anahola. If you're used to plush robes and marble floors, you might find the setting a tad rustic, especially for the $150 cost – but what price local flavor?

YOGA

Considering Kaua'i's plethora of ayurvedic practitioners and longtime hippie culture, it's surprising that the yoga scene is so limited. If you are a serious student and hail from a 'yoga town,' you might be disappointed by the lack of good studios here. But there are two excellent teachers on the North Shore: for Ashtanga yoga, try Bhavani Maki's longtime studio, Yoga Hanalei (p139), where this devoted disciple of Patthabi Jois offers both Mysore-style and led classes. Open-minded types who want to explore body alignment should try a class with the innovative Michaelle Edwards of Mana Yoga (p128) between Princeville and Kilauea.

ZIPLINING

Ziplines, which first appeared in Costa Rica canopy parks, are now proliferating across the US mainland. But location matters – and Kaua'i's magnificent forests can't be beat. This outdoor adventure requires neither skill nor training, but participants must meet age and weight restrictions. Half-day tours typically cost from $125 to $145.

In Lihu'e, Just Live (p67) is recommended because they feature canopy-based ziplines: once you're in the trees, you don't touch ground till the end. In addition to their general zipline tour, you can zip by full moon or challenge yourself to a ropes-course-inspired tour that includes rappelling, climbing and more.

The three other outfits offer fun combination tours that also include swimming holes and picnic lunches. Kaua'i Backcountry Adventures (p67) in Lihu'e and Princeville Ranch Adventures (p128) offer similar combination zip-swim tours. Outfitters Kaua'i (p67) offers multi-activity tours and an especially thrilling set of ziplines that are strung with more slack or have vertical drops, both which give a bungee effect.

GREEN KAUA'I

To ancient Hawaiians, being 'green' and 'sustainable' weren't fads. While they planted, harvested, fished, hunted and ate to their satisfaction (or perhaps their chief's), little was wasted. The native population took seriously their *kuleana* (responsibility) to use the *'aina* (land) wisely, perhaps because they regarded nature as sacred. Today the island is threatened by overdevelopment, traffic, exorbitant real estate and dependence on imported fuel and food. Such problems are not unique, but they're exacerbated on a small isolated island. Now that tourism is the number-one industry in Hawaii, tourists must join residents in honoring the *kuleana* to act sustainably by leaving a negligible footprint.

ENVIRONMENTAL ISSUES

Kauaians have a love-hate attitude toward tourism, which drives the economy but also catapults the cost of living. Overdevelopment and land speculation are the biggest woes, but traffic, helicopter noise and disrespect for Native Hawaiian culture also irk residents. In the mid-2000s, resort and luxury-end development went gangbusters, with over 5000 residential units and 6100 resort units set for development. The largest project, Po'ipu's massive Kukui'ula community, is guaranteed to be another enclave of wealthy second-home buyers. Such exclusive communities can't help but shift island demographics away from people who are really connected to the local area.

Simply put, real estate remains out of reach for many *kama'aina* (those born and raised here), despite the economic downturn and market drop in 2008. Mainlanders might come bargain hunting, but many locals can't afford a modest home. Kilauea used to be an affordable town for Princeville workers, but now it's a desirable spot for monied new arrivals, while Ha'ena's former Hawaiian community is now displaced by vacation mansions.

Ironically, locals can seem a tad lackadaisical about environmental awareness. Driving is a way of life

AIMÉE GOGGINS

Island Insights

In 2007 **Hawaii 2050** (www.hawaii2050.org), a 25-member statewide task force, created a sustainability plan for the 21st century. Developed mainly by elected and government officials, the ambitious (and unwieldy) plan strove to reflect the people's concerns about the economy, natural resources, community and Native Hawaiian culture. Now the taskforce has disbanded, it's up to policymakers to sift through the reams of documentation and actually implement the recommendations.

here, and the status vehicle is the biggest, baddest monster truck you can afford. Hybrid (eg Prius) sightings are rare. Bus transit is limited mainly to highways, although ridership markedly increases with gas prices. Perhaps because towns originated along the highway, county planners seem oblivious to pedestrian-oriented neighborhoods or high-density town centers (or any town centers at all!).

Energy costs are higher on Kaua'i than on the other Hawaiian Islands (and anywhere in the US). Despite abundant sunlight, however, few households or businesses have installed photovoltaic panels. Commendably, Kaua'i Coffee Company (p186) produces all of its own electricity, and the National Tropical Botanical Garden's (p167) new research building received Kaua'i's first LEED Gold Certification (Leadership in Energy and Environmental Design).

Sustainable Agriculture

A hot issue on Kaua'i is food security. About 90% of the island's food is imported, despite its natural biodiversity. A growing contingent of small-scale organic farmers argues that island agriculture is no longer viable by the old model: corporate-scale, industrialized monocropping (eg pineapples and sugarcane) enabled by chemical fertilizers, pesticides and herbicides. Instead, family farms growing diverse crops — for the table or for sale locally, not only globally — would always be sustainable.

Nobody goes into farming to make money, especially on Kaua'i, where limited resources mean that land, water and labor costs are comparatively high. Huge parcels of agricultural land are occupied by major multinational corporations, such as Monsanto, Syngenta Seeds and Pioneer Hi-Bred International, for growing genetically modified (GMO) crops, mainly corn. Minds differ on the risks of genetic modification, but it's clear that island crops should benefit island residents and not multinational corporations.

Exotic orchids at the South Shore's McBryde Garden (p168)

LINDA CHING

Unfortunately, established businesses (and locals themselves) tend to resist change. Safeway and even island-based supermarket chains prefer the blemish-free consistency of mainland-imported apples and oranges. And locals tend to buy whatever's cheapest.

Consumer demand drives the market. Take a stand and buy local!

KAUA'I GOES GREEN

Proud of its independent image, Kaua'i has long attracted progressive types, including '70s hippies, midlife career-changers, youthful wanderers, nature lovers and environmental activists. Also, *kama'aina* loathe to see their island altered. Activism

ISLAND VOICES

NAME: LOUISA WOOTEN
OCCUPATION: LIFELONG FARMER, BOB AND LOUISA WOOTEN'S KAUAI KUNANA DAIRY (p118)
RESIDENCE: KILAUEA

When did you start farming on Kaua'i? In the 1970s, my husband and I were general organic farmers, growing mango, avocado, citrus, starfruit. We were among the 10 farmers who started the first Kaua'i County Sunshine Market in 1978. Today there are 12 farmers markets islandwide.

What's it like to raise goats? We've raised goats and free-range chickens since 1979. At any given time, we're milking 25 out of our herd of 40. Goats are as smart as dogs. They're easy to care for and produce excellent-tasting milk. We hand-raise them from the time they're born, so they bond to us.

Are your dairy products organic? Our produce is certified organic, but our cheese and eggs are not. That's because it's very difficult to bring organic feed into the state of Hawaii. If we ship it over and the inspectors find a single bug, they fumigate the whole batch and it's ruined.

How is Kaua'i faring in agriculture today? We have no [dairies that can process cow's milk], and limited beef and pork. Coffee and taro are major crops, but the biggest is unfortunately GMO-seed corn, planted by big corporations like Monsanto. You can see the cornfields from Lihu'e all the way to Kekaha. I am strongly opposed to GMO crops in general because they promote chemical use and discount the need for natural biodiversity. Why not plant crops to feed ourselves? Why not grow organic seed corn and organic feed for my goats?

Why aren't we seeing more local farming? The cost of land is prohibitive. The Big Island is fortunate to have so much relatively cheap land. The other limiting factor is labor. Currently, a farm owner cannot rent on-site housing to workers. That's to prevent vacation rentals on ag land [land zoned for agricultural purposes].

How does a small farmer make it in the modern agricultural system? Ours is a family-owned farm, run by my husband and me, plus our two sons and a daughter-in-law. Everyone plays a key role. The place would fall down around our ears if not for Bob, a mechanical genius and general contractor, who built our buildings and maintains the machinery, plumbing and electricity. To be a farmer means wearing many different hats.

SUSTAINABLE ICON

Throughout this book, our Sustainable icon indicates listings that demonstrate an active sustainable-tourism policy. Some are dedicated to environmental conservation and/or education, others preserve Hawaiian identity and culture, and many are owned and operated by residents with deep roots to the *'aina* (land). For quick reference, these listings are compiled in the GreenDex (p295).

remains more fringe than mainstream, but the dedicated few have spurred a green movement (which currently hovers around chartreuse).

The challenges are many and unrelenting: overfishing, landfill capacity, US military presence, invasive species, affordable housing, watershed management, chain stores, suburbanization, ancient Hawaiian burial sites and *iwi* (bones) (see p240), and more.

Recycling has come and gone over the years, but the county currently accepts the usual suspects (see Recycling Tips at www.kauai.gov/recycling). Curbside pickup remains elusive, but the statewide HI-5 Bottle Bill (which charges a refundable 5¢ deposit for glass, aluminum and plastic bottles labeled 'HI 5¢') has encouraged recycling.

Preservation of native species is a constant effort both by the State Department of Land and Natural Resources and by private groups such as the National Tropical Botanical Garden (p167) and Keith Robinson (see p189), who for three decades has tried to propagate hundreds of endangered native plants on his land.

Kaua'i depends on petroleum for energy production, but some companies are exploring alternatives. Green Energy Hawaii (www.greenenergyhawaii.com) has plans for hydroelectric power by 2009 and for carbon-neutral biomass-to-energy (BTE) power by 2010. In September 2008, Kaua'i's last sugar plantation, Gay & Robinson, announced plans to cease sugar operations and start ethanol production.

Green organizations abound, from enviro watchdog Malama Kaua'i (www.malamakauai.org) to Hui o Laka (www.kokee.org/about-hui-o-laka), an effective community-based group that presents guided hikes, operates the Koke'e Natural History Museum, helps eradicate invasive species and offers great volunteering opportunities. The organization Malama Maha'ulepu (www.malama-mahaulepu.org) is an excellent model of grassroots activism. It has spurred widespread community interest through educational outreach about the privately owned Maha'ulepu Coast (see p168), considered the last undeveloped accessible coastline on the island.

SUSTAINABLE KAUA'I

Tourism might be Kaua'i's Trojan Horse: sure, islanders are grateful for the economic boost. But what is the real price of hotels and condos, helicopter tours and snorkeling cruises? It's impossible to offset all environmental costs of travel, but visitors can minimize their effects.

The Malama Kaua'i Green Map (www.malamakauai.org/aboutGreenMap.php) is a decent starting point to find sustainable businesses, but it's far from complete and based on self-identification as 'green.'

Transportation

There's no getting around it. You need a car on Kaua'i. Period. But choose as small a rental car as feasible. Drive efficiently, without unnecessary backtracking. Pick three home-base accommodations around the island. Then, at each place, keep your

Island Insights

Should tourists be restricted to staying in resort areas or free to lodge in residential neighborhoods? Kaua'i, along with Maui and O'ahu, is pushing toward the former, in response to residents opposed to vacation rentals being too close to their homes. Here, the county in 2008 restricted residential vacation rentals (eg cottages) to Visitor Destination Areas (VDAs) located mostly in Princeville, Po'ipu and coastal Wailua-Kapa'a and Lihu'e (with exceptions for pre-existing units). The upshot? In the longterm, you'll find fewer vacation-rental houses outside the touristy hotspots.

A white egret rests on a hedge of hibiscus HOLGER LEUE

sightseeing within that region. When traveling between major points along the highway, take the bus. (It's a swell way to meet locals.)

Food

Why come here to eat Kellogg's cornflakes and Sunkist oranges from Safeway? You're on Kaua'i. Buy locally grown produce, locally caught fish and locally made cheese, preserves, breads and baked goods instead of the familiar imported national brands. See p248 for locavore recommendations. On the road, eating takeout is a given. But try to avoid takeout containers (bring your own mug or reusable utensils) or choose establishments that use biodegradable containers (see www.alohawedeliver.com for a list). If you find a restaurant serving imported feta or a grocer carrying only California fruit, use your tourist clout and request the homegrown stuff!

Accommodations

Turn off air-conditioning when you're out, or don't use it at all. Fans and tradewinds are usually enough to keep rooms cool after dark, no kidding. Also reuse towels; turn off lights and TV when unnecessary. Make a case for going green and ask the management to set out recycling bins, use eco-conscious cleaning products and energy-efficient light bulbs, and turn off AC and lights in vacant rooms. Tell them to get off the grid with solar or hydro power. When guests speak, proprietors listen.

GREEN SHOPPING TIPS

- Buy locally made souvenirs and gifts. Beware of fakes, such as 'Hawaiian' quilts and shell lei made in the Philippines.
- Bring your own shopping bags or reuse the bags given to you.
- Recycle bottles, cans, cardboard, newspaper, mixed paper, glass, aluminum, #1 and #2 plastics. Return HI-5 (Hawaii 5¢) bottles for redemption or give them to locals.
- Avoid buying bottled water. The drinkability of Kaua'i water might surprise you.
- Don't buy junk souvenirs (often plastic and made in China) that you'll discard the minute you return home.
- Give away bodyboards, coolers and other items you don't plan to take home with you.
- Do not buy shells or coral. Their sale encourages the demand everywhere.
- Refuse the shell lei given at luau and tell the management that they're unnecessary.

Top Picks

KAUA'I-MADE GIFTS

- **Nature CD recordings of Kaua'i birdsong and other enchanting soundscapes** (www.soundshawaiian.com)
- **Malie Organics botanical bath and body products** (p188)
- **Koa handcrafts and furniture** (p74 and p106)
- **Recycled-fabric bags by Denise Tjarks** (www.denisetjarks.com)
- **Fresh homemade chips from Taro Ko Chips Factory** (p194)
- **Silver and sea glass jewelry by Caitlin Ross Odom** (www.caitlinrossodom.com)
- **Award-winning liliko'i-wasabi mustard from Aunty Lilikoi Passion Fruit Products** (p203)
- **Kaua'i-themed T-shirts from Pohaku T's** (p162) **and Puahina Moku o Kaua'i Warrior Designs Hawaii** (p195)
- **Genuine Ni'ihau shell jewelry** (www.niihau.us)
- **'Alaea salt and other seasonings from Aloha Spice Company** (www.alohaspice.com)

ON THE GROUND

While nothing can fully offset the carbon that was released from your flight here, you can reduce further harm to the *'aina* without forgoing any of its charms. When possible, choose the lower-impact option: go shore diving instead of motoring out by boat. Or go outrigger-canoe sailing with Island Sails (p140) for a uniquely Hawaiian experience powered by human, not petroleum, energy.

Hiking is suited to all fitness levels and requires only a pair of sturdy shoes. For the price of an ATV or helicopter tour, you can see the same terrain up close and personal on an expert-led hiking tour with Kaua'i Nature Tours (p41). That said, if you do choose a gas-guzzling option, choose the right outfit: Kaua'i ATV (p161) offers biodiesel vehicles and donates some of their profits to local children's causes.

Supporting Kaua'i's environment also means supporting the native and local people. Choose businesses run by residents who contribute to the community. For starters, stay at inns and B&Bs and interact with real island folks. (The best choices are both locally owned and off-the-grid green, such as hydro-powered Coco's B&B (p203) near Waimea and solar-powered Aikane Kaua'i (p176), a beach house in Po'ipu.

When possible, buy local. Why buy generic souvenirs when you can find handmade edibles, beauty products, clothing, jewelry and much more? By supporting local businesses, you keep profits here.

Finally, if you don't learn about Native Hawaiian history and culture during your visit, you have overlooked the soul of Hawaii. Visit attractions that teach about Hawaiian culture, such as Limahuli Garden (p143), Kaua'i Museum (p64) and Angeline's Mu'olaulani (p111).

Check the Kaua'i Green Map at www.malamakauai.org for a list of green businesses across Kauai'i. For more tips, read *50 Simple Things You Can Do to Save Hawai'i* (2007) by Gail Grabowsky.

HELPFUL ORGANIZATIONS

Aloha We Deliver (☎ 631-9138; www.alohawedeliver.com) A handy list of restaurants that use biodegradable take-out tableware, made of bagasse or corn, not Styrofoam.

Island Breath (www.islandbreath.org) Dig deep into local issues with these links to newspaper and independent articles on Kaua'i's hot-button sustainability topics.

Kaua'i Explorer (www.kauaiexplorer.com) While known mainly for its outstanding ocean-safety tips, this refreshingly concise site also contains preservation tips and a handy 'Where to Recycle' guide.

Malama Kaua'i (☎ 828-0685; www.malamakauai.org) This Kilauea-based grassroots organization is the island's watchdog, dedicated to protecting the 'aina's ecosystems and culture with a biweekly KKCR public-radio show, volunteering opportunities and more.

Save Kaua'i (www.savekauai.org) Community-run website with links to background information on key issues such as agriculture, food security, water resources and Native Hawaiian rights.

Sierra Club (www.hi.sierraclub.org/kauai) A pioneer in the environmental movement, the Kaua'i chapter offers guided outings, such as strenuous hikes and full-moon walks.

Zero Waste Kaua'i (www.zerowastekauai.org) This small group is currently pushing for curbside recycling collection, a ban on Styrofoam and other plastics and ways to reuse trash; click on the 'Recycle Guide' link for recycling info.

A Hawaiian monk seal snoozes on the beach LINDA CHING

THE ENVIRONMENT

Kaua'i is the oldest (and fourth-largest) of the major inhabited Hawaiian Islands, with volcanic rocks dating back over five million years. Unlike the shiny black terrain seen on the lava-spewing island of Hawai'i the Big Island (a baby at 450,000 years old), Kaua'i displays the effects of time and erosion, with weathered summits, mountaintop bogs and rainforests, deeply cut valleys, extensive sandy beaches, coral and algal reefs, and rust-colored soil indelible to both memory and your white sneakers. Because its volcanic origins lie hidden under a carpet of forests, ferns and shrubland, its landscape, particularly along the North Shore, is overwhelmingly lush and strikes many as the ultimate tropical beauty.

THE LAND

The state of Hawaii's eight major islands grab the world's attention, but the Hawaiian archipelago actually comprises more than 100 distinct volcanoes. The oldest, Meiji Seamount, is 80 million years old. The chain is inching northwestward (imagine a geo-conveyor belt) at about 3.5in per year, moving with the Pacific tectonic plate. All of the islands, including Kaua'i, will shrink and sink until they become atolls and seamounts.

Perhaps duped by its round shape, scientists for decades believed that a single volcano formed Kaua'i. But on the basis of evidence collected since the 1980s, scientists now think that Kaua'i's entire eastern side 'slumped' along an ancient fault line, leaving a steep *pali* (cliff) along Waimea Canyon's western edge. Then, lava from another shield volcano, four-million-year-old Lihu'e, flowed westward to the *pali* and ponded against the cliffs. The black and red horizontal striations along the canyon walls represent successive volcanic eruptions; the red color shows where water seeped through the rocks, creating rust from the iron inside.

Now shrunken by age, Kaua'i is also slowly subsiding into the ocean floor. Don't worry, the rate is less than an inch per century. Still, those inches have cost the island 3000ft in elevation, making today's high point the 5243ft Kawaikini. Among the most visually spectacular valleys is Kalalau, with curtain-like folds, knife-edge ridges, and a drop of 4000ft at the two lookouts where the road ends in Koke'e State Park (p211). Views of Na Pali are spectacular but seen only from the deck of a boat,

THE REST OF THE HAWAIIAN ARCHIPELAGO

The familiar eight Hawaiian Islands that constitute the US State of Hawaii are just a small part of the entire Hawaiian archipelago. Beyond Kaua'i and Ni'ihau lies the grand chain of the **Northwestern Hawaiian Islands**, which comprise 33 tiny islands and atolls spread over 1400 miles. Their total land area is less than 5 square miles.

On June 15, 2006, then US President George W Bush declared the Northwestern Hawaiian Islands the USA's first Marine National Monument. Encompassing around 140,000 sq miles, **Papahanaumokuakea Marine National Monument** is now the largest protected marine area in the world, and seven times larger than all other US marine sanctuaries combined.

The Northwestern Hawaiian Islands contain the largest and healthiest coral-reef system in the US – it's home to 7000 marine species, a quarter of which are endemic to Hawaii. The islands also support around 14 million seabirds, including 19 native species. Furthermore, the island beaches are primary breeding grounds for the endangered Hawaiian monk seal and green sea turtle.

Closest to Kaua'i (and visible on clear days), at a distance of 130 miles, is 900ft **Nihoa**, which encompasses an area of just 160 acres. Next in line is 10-million-year-old **Mokumanamana (Necker)**, hardly even an island as it comprises less than 64 acres of land. Continuing northwest, and barely above sea level, are the bumps of **French Frigate Shoals**, **Gardner Pinnacles**, **Maro Reef**, **Laysan Island**, **Lisianski Island**, **Pearl and Hermes Atoll**, and **Midway Atoll**, followed at last by the 30-million-year old **Kure Atoll**. Beyond this outpost, another 2000-mile-long chain of sunken islands known as guyots, or seamounts, dot the ocean floor all the way past the Aleutian Islands to the Kamchatka Peninsula (Russia). Here, ancient islands are sunken below the Eurasian continental plate, with deep oceanic trenches marking the boundary.

Human history on these islands extends back to the first Polynesian voyagers to arrive in Hawaii. In modern times, the most famous of these is Midway Atoll, an unorganized and unincorporated territory of the US, which was a convenient refueling stop for military aircraft enroute to Japan during World War II (hence the name). On June 4, 1942, six months after the infamous Japanese attack on Pearl Harbor, the US Navy devastated the Japanese naval forces in the Battle of Midway – now considered the turning point of the war in Japan's control of the Pacific Ocean. Today, it's the only island of the chain that is open to visitors (for more information see www.fws.gov/midway).

the windows of a helicopter – or, for the fit and eco-conscious, from the Nu'alolo-Awa'awapuhi Trail (p215) in Koke'e or the grueling 11-mile Kalalau Trail (p152).

WILDLIFE

The Hawaiian Islands are the most isolated landmasses on earth. Only the hardiest species of plants and animals could survive the long journey over 2400 miles of open ocean. Scientists estimate that new species arrived once every 70,000 years. They included no amphibians, no browsing animals, no pines, no mosquitoes and only two mammals, which were a bat and a seal.

The flora and fauna that did arrive found a rich, ecologically diverse land to colonize. As they developed in isolation for at least 70 million years, many of these indigenous (native) species became endemic to the islands, meaning that they're found nowhere else in the world. Through natural selection, the original colonizers then evolved into thousands of new species through 'adaptive radiation.' Lacking predators or much competition, these species dropped defensive protections: thorns, poisons and strong odors disappeared.

When the first humans arrived, they brought about 25 foreign animals and plants today classified as Polynesian introductions, including pigs, chickens, rats, *niu* (coconuts), *mai'a* (bananas), called western introductions (or alien). They include relatively benign crops and ornamental plants, as well as notoriously invasive and devastating pests, such as cattle, fountaingrass, miconia and ivy gourd. The extinction rate in Hawaii is unsurpassed in the US. As for remaining species, Hawaii is home to over 300 endangered and rare species (see www.fws.gov/pacificislands for details).

Land Animals & Marine Life

With no native amphibians or reptiles, and only two native mammals, the endangered hoary bat and monk seal, the islands' main attractions for wildlife enthusiasts are birds or ocean creatures. Up to 10,000 migrating North Pacific humpback whales come to Hawaiian waters for calving each winter (November through April), and whale watching (p39) is excellent off Kaua'i's South Shore, with most boats departing from Port Allen Harbor (p189). Pods of spinner dolphins, with their acrobatic spiraling leaps, regularly approach boats cruising in Kaua'i waters, and can also be seen from the shoreline off Kalihiwai Bay (p122) and Kilauea Point (p117) on the North Shore.

Threatened *honu* (green sea turtles) are traditionally revered by Native Hawaiians as an *'aumakua* (family deity). Snorkelers often see *honu* feeding on seaweed along rocky coastlines or in shallow lagoons. Endangered Hawaiian monk seals (see p166) occasionally haul up onshore, a thrill for beachgoers, who by law must observe the seals from a distance. Federal and state laws protect all four of these species from harassment.

Top Picks

VIEWING NATIVE SPECIES

- **Whale watching in winter from land or from sea** (p39)
- **Hiking the Alaka'i Swamp Trail among native trees and rare birds** (p215)
- **Identifying native versus introduced plants at Limahuli Garden** (p143)
- **Bird watching at Kilauea Point National Wildlife Refuge** (p117)
- **Spotting a monk seal (from a generous distance) at Po'ipu Beach Park** (p166) **or along the Maha'ulepu Coast** (p168)
- **Snorkeling among *honu* (green sea turtles)** (p36)

Birds

On Kaua'i, the bird population is lucky to avoid the mongoose, a predator common to the other islands but nonexistent here. To learn more about Kaua'i's birds, **Birds of Kaua'i** (www.kauaibirds.com) is a good starting point, while **SoundsHawaiian** (www.soundshawaiian.com) is a real treat for the ears, with crisply recorded examples of native birdsong.

WHY FLY?

When did you last hear a helicopter overhead? Chances are, you can't remember. Island residents unfortunately have a different answer: chopper noise is a daily nightmare. This might seem piddly next to greenhouse gases and global warming, but if you're constantly barraged by droning helicopters (or, worse, loud biplanes), your quality of life surely suffers. Further, crashes have occured near towns, including Ha'ena and Wainiha, causing those on the ground to worry about their own safety.

The Sierra Club and other island advocacy groups have long pushed for limits on commercial aircraft's freedom to fly over residential neighborhoods and FAA-designated noise-abatement areas. But for now it's a voluntary system. Thus the Sierra Club recommends that passengers ask pilots to avoid sensitive areas, such as the Kalalau Trail and popular beaches.

To stop 'disrespectful air tourism,' a group called **StopDAT** (www.stopdat.org) is seeking to pinpoint the best and worst tour companies. Advocates emphasize common courtesy: would you want tourists constantly flying over your hometown? They decry those who come for Kaua'i's rural serenity yet contribute to the opposite qualities by taking noisy tours.

And in case you're wondering just how much carbon you'll need to offset for that 60-minute tour: most helicopter companies fly Eurocopter AStars, which consume 38 to 40 gallons of fuel per hour's flight, when carrying seven passengers. Smaller choppers, such as the Robinson R44s flown by Mauna Loa Helicopters, seat up to four and use less than 25 gallons for a similar tour.

WATER BIRDS

Lowland wetlands feature four endangered waterbirds that are cousins of mainland species: the Hawaiian duck, coot, moorhen and stilt. The best place to view these is the Hanalei National Wildlife Refuge (p132) on the North Shore; an overlook near Princeville Shopping Center provides a great view of their habitat, shallow ponds and cultivated taro fields.

The endangered nene, Hawaii's state bird, is a long-lost cousin of the Canada goose. Nene once numbered as many as 25,000 on all the islands, but by the 1950s only 50 were left. Intensive breeding programs have raised their numbers to over a thousand on three islands: Maui, Kaua'i and Hawai'i. You might see them in Hanalei wetlands, around golf courses and open fields, and at the Kilauea Point National Wildlife Refuge (p117).

FOREST BIRDS

Native forest birds are more challenging to observe, but the keen-eyed will find eight native species remaining at Koke'e State Park (p211), especially in the Alaka'i Wilderness Preserve (p218). *'Apapane,* a type of honeycreeper, is the most abundant: a bright-red bird the same color as the lehua flowers from which it takes nectar. Honeycreepers are a uniquely Hawaiian subfamily (Drepanidinae) with more than 50 species that evolved over millions of years from a finch-like ancestor, a spectacular example of adaptive radiation.

Today, over half of those bright-colored species, along with two-thirds of all native Hawaiian birds, are extinct, the victims of aggressive, introduced birds or infectious diseases. Hurricane 'Iniki (1992) also contributed to this catastrophic decline: it was the last time three species were seen on Kaua'i.

Plants

Ancient Hawaiians would scarcely recognize Kaua'i, having never encountered the tropical flowers, fruit and lush landscape that today epitomizes the island. Mango came

SUPERFERRY NON GRATA

In August 2007, when the **Hawaii Superferry** (p275) sailed toward Nawiliwili Harbor for its first arrival, some 300 Kaua'i protestors blocked its entry. Three dozen people even swam in the gargantuan ferry's path, shouting, 'Go home, go home!' Ultimately, service from O'ahu to Maui (but not to Kaua'i) launched in December 2007, but the whole enterprise was terminated indefinitely in March 2009, when the Hawaii Supreme Court deemed the Superferry's Environmental Impact Statement (EIS) invalid.

Why was opposition to the ferry so furious? Many protesters were suspicious of the politcal process that ushered the Superferry to Hawaii – or, as they claim, Governor Linda Lingle's disregard of state environmental laws, as she gave the Superferry a green light without an EIS. When the State Supreme Court eventually mandated an EIS, Lingle got a bill passed that changed the environmental requirements, which allowed the ferry to continue operating while the statement was being prepared.

Actually, the opponents themselves were not 'anti-ferry' but, rather, anti-Superferry. They wanted smaller, passenger-only, publicly owned and slower-moving boats. Their main concerns were nighttime collisions with whales, worsened traffic on Neighbor Islands, spread of environmental pests and plundering of natural resources by non-residents. Indeed, during the Superferry's brief run between O'ahu and Maui, O'ahu residents were frequently caught taking home *'opihi* (a prized edible limpet), crustaceans, algae, rocks, coral and massive quantities of reef fish.

That said, not all locals were opposed. In fact, many locals (especially O'ahu residents) viewed the Superferry as a convenient way to visit friends and family on Neighbor Islands. They also cited the need for an alternate, fuel-efficient mode of transportation between the islands (though the enormous vessels are actually gas guzzlers). They also pointed to the existing Matson barges already carrying potential pests between the islands.

For a compelling, if overwhelmingly detailed, account, read *The Superferry Chronicles* by Koohan Palk and Jerry Mander, which also analyzes the ferry's questionable ties to US military and commercial interests.

THE WILD BUNCH

Before you get too annoyed at the thousands of wild chickens on Kaua'i, understand their backstory: the first chickens to populate Hawaii were jungle fowl *(moa)*, introduced by the first Polynesians. These vividly colored birds later crossbred with domestic chickens brought by westerners. During plantation days, Kaua'i's wild-chicken population was kept in check by field fires (a regular event before harvest, to allow more efficient reaping). But when the sugar industry went bust in the 1980s, the chicken population boomed.

When Hurricane 'Iwa and Hurricane 'Iniki struck in 1982 and 1992 respectively, they obliterated the cages of Kaua'i's fighting cocks, adding even more chickens to the wild. With no mongoose or snake population to act as predators, wild chickens proliferated.

You'll see them perched in trees, running across fields, roaming parking lots and otherwise strutting their stuff across the island. Most locals have accepted the chickens, but warn of their *lolo* (crazy) schedules: instead of crowing only at dawn, they cock-a-doodle-doo at random times and seem confused by a full moon or any late-night light. Before you book accommodations, ask if there are chickens living within earshot. Or just wear earplugs.

from Asia. Macadamia nuts from Australia. Coffee from Africa. Today, many botanists and farmers advocate biodiversity, so alien species aren't necessarily bad. But, of Hawaii's 1300 endemic native plant species, over 100 are extinct and 273 are endangered. It's worth noting which are native species that developed here before human contact.

NATIVE PLANTS

Native flora abounds: over 90% of Hawaii's 1000-plus plant species are endemic to the islands, meaning that they naturally occur nowhere else on earth. To see native forests, try Koke'e State Park (p211) and the 10,000-acre Alaka'i Swamp Wilderness Preserve (p217). Along the Pihea and Alaka'i Swamp Trails (p215), you'll see the most abundant rainforest tree, ohia lehua, a hardwood with bright red or orange pompomlike flowers that provide nectar for forest birds. Another dominant is *lapalapa*, with long-stemmed leaves that flutter in the slightest breeze.

Among the best-known species is koa, an endemic hardwood that is Hawaii's most commercially valuable tree, with its fine woodworking qualities, rich color and swirling grain. Look for koa trees and their distinctive crescent-shaped leaves at lower elevations (under 4000ft) along the rim of Waimea Canyon; some of the tallest ones, planted in the 1930, are along the dirt roads below the Koke'e Natural History Museum.

Despite the rampant development along it, the coastal shoreline is also a good place to find native plants. The harsh environment – windblown, salt-sprayed, often arid land with nutrient-poor, sandy soil – requires plants to have special survival adaptations, such as growing flat along the ground, becoming succulent or developing waxy leaf coatings to retain moisture. One common example is the *naupaka*, with its iconic white half-flower (see the boxed text, p175). You can also see native coastal plants at Kilauea Point National Wildlife Refuge (p117).

INTRODUCED PLANTS

About two dozen species are Polynesian introductions (called canoe plants), which arrived some 1500 years ago in the voyagers' great double-hulled sailing canoes. Taro, bananas and sugar cane became key agricultural crops and remain so today. Taro cultivation remains much the same as it was centuries ago. See www.canoeplants.com for details on the canoe plants.

Island Insights

Around Waimea Canyon, look for koki'o ke'oke'o (white hibiscus). This species is not only endemic to the Hawaiian Islands, it's also found only on Kaua'i. (The Hawaii state flower is the yellow hibiscus.) Flowers bloom white in the morning and turn pink by the afternoon. Like most species of hibiscus, flowers last a single day. But while most hibiscus have no scent, *koki'o ke'oke'o* has a strong, sweet fragrance.

NATIONAL, STATE & COUNTY PARKS

About 30% of Kaua'i is protected as state parks and nature reserves. For hiking, don't miss Waimea Canyon State Park (p206) and Koke'e State Park (p211), with their spectacular elevated views and numerous trails and campsites. On the Eastside, Nounou Mountain (p89), with three steep but scenic hikes, is well-maintained forest-reserve land.

Ha'ena State Park (p150) is another favorite, as it has Ke'e Beach, a fantastic snorkeling spot, and the start of the Kalalau Trail (p152). The miles of sandy beach at Polihale State Park (p206) offer escape from crowds, but beware two potential threats: hazardous ocean conditions and the bone-rattlingly rough 5-mile gravel road to get there.

Most of Kaua'i's best and easiest-access beaches are designated as county parks, such as sunny Po'ipu Beach Park (South Shore; p164); serene 'Anini Beach Park (North Shore; p123); and family-friendly Lydgate Beach Park (Eastside; p83).

RUSTIC VS RENOVATED

Since the mid-2000s some Kaua'i residents have slammed the State Department of Land and Natural Resources for its Koke'e State Park improvement plans. The idea of an entry gate, additional lookouts and signs, expanded parking lots and a 'park identity' rankle those who want to keep Koke'e a rustic, minimally touristy sanctuary (see www.savekokee.org). But state officials argue that such measures allow entry by buses (replacing individual cars) and enhance both security and the visitor experience. This type of dichotomy is the status quo on Kaua'i.

There are no national parks on the island, but there are three federal refuges, including the accessible Kilauea Point National Wildlife Refuge (p117), which has spectacular wildlife watching (seasonal whales and the only diverse seabird colony on the main Hawaiian Islands).

KAUA'I'S TOP PROTECTED AREAS

Nature Area	Features	Activities	Page
Alaka'i Wilderness Preserve	rainforest, bogs, forest birds, boardwalk	hiking, bird watching	p217
'Anini Beach Park	sandy beach, calm waters	swimming, windsurfing, picnicking	p123
Ha'ena State Park	sandy beach, historic Hawaiian sites, marine life	swimming, snorkeling	p150
Hanalei Bay	scenic circular bay, sandy beaches, winter waves	surfing, swimming	p134
Hanalei National Wildlife Refuge	scenic views, taro fields, endangered waterbirds	bird watching (limited access)	p132
Hule'ia National Wildlife Refuge	river, endangered waterbirds	bird watching (limited access)	p68
Kilauea Point National Wildlife Refuge	seabirds, coastal plants, nene, historic lighthouse	bird watching, whale watching	p117
Koke'e State Park	trails, waterfalls, forest birds and plants, interpretive center	hiking, camping, bird watching	p211
Maha'ulepu Coast*	lithified sand-dune cliffs, sandy beaches, heiau	walking, windsurfing, surfing	p168
Na Pali Coast State Park	challenging trails, coastal flora, seabirds, archaeological sites	hiking, camping	p151
Polihale State Park	coastal dunes, state's longest beach (dangerous currents) p206	walking, sunset watching, camping	p206
Waimea Canyon State Park	colossal gorge, forestland	hiking, camping	p206

*Private property not under governmental protection

LIHU'E

Simply put, Lihu'e is a reality check. Sure, this modest island capital might lack beachy charm or a lively town square. But Lihu'e's ordinariness is an asset. You'll find good-value shops and restaurants, plus a critical mass of actual locals, rather than tourists. You might not welcome seeing Wal-Mart and Costco, but they're reminders that residents here are not on permanent vacation. Its saving grace is natural beauty, from sandy, sport-friendly Kalapaki Beach to the stately green slopes of the Haupu Mountains. While Lihu'e can't compete with the tourist cachet of Po'ipu and Princeville, that reputation might be changing, with a luxury Four Seasons on the way.

LIHU'E ITINERARIES

IN TWO DAYS *7 miles*

❶ **KALAPAKI BEACH (p63)** Beat the jet-lag blahs at Lihu'e's best beach. With a location fronting the **Kaua'i Marriott Resort (p77)**, Kalapaki has a touristy vibe, but it's also consistently good for swimming, bodyboarding and surfing.

❷ **HAMURA SAIMIN (p70)** Steaming bowls of noodle soup might seem incongruous in tropical heat, but saimin is an island tradition – and this hole-in-the-wall is famous for superlative homemade noodles.

❸ **LUAU KALAMAKU (p72)** Cross a Hawaiian luau with polished dinner theater and you get Lihu'e's best nighttime entertainment, the 'theatrical' luau at **Kilohana Plantation (p64)**. Expect a compelling adventure-romance, with mesmerizing hula, Tahitian and Samoan dancing.

❹ **ZIPLINING (p67)** On day two, wake up to high-speed thrills on a forest zipline tour that requires no skills, just an adventurous spirit (and trust in equipment maintenance!).

❺ **FISH EXPRESS (p71)** There's no place like Kaua'i for affordable fresh fish. Try a variety of different kinds of *poke* (chunks of marinated raw fish) at this well-stocked fish market.

❻ **DUKE'S CANOE CLUB (p72)** Always jammed, this beachfront favorite is tops for lively, people-watching fun. Budget watchers can opt for drinks and *pupu* (appetizers) at the downstairs **Duke's Barefoot Bar (p70)**.

❼ **SOUVENIR SHOPPING (p74)** You're on Kaua'i, so why buy fake souvenirs? The Koa Store offers affordable genuine koa crafts, while Kapaia Stitchery is a mecca for quilters and crafters. A great one-stop shop for books and assorted island-made crafts is Kaua'i Museum's gift shop.

Big bowls o' noodles at Hamura Saimin

LINDA CHING

FOR HISTORY & CULTURE

❶ KAUA'I MUSEUM (p64) If you find most museums imposing, try this tiny but captivating collection of historical artifacts and contemporary art. Special events include the annual **May Day Lei Contest & Fair (p69)**, celebrating Kaua'i's floral masterpieces.

❷ MENEHUNE FISHPOND (p66) There's something magical about this emerald pool along the Hule'ia River. It must be the *menehune*, Hawaii's legendary (though apocryphal) 'little people.'

❸ GROVE FARM HOMESTEAD (p67) This sleepy homestead belies a rich history from the plantation era that forever changed the old Hawaiian way of life.

❹ KILOHANA PLANTATION (p64) Amid manicured grounds and a handsome manor you'll find a historic railroad ride, gourmet restaurant, upmarket shops and a luau show featuring impressive Kaua'i talent.

❺ 'KAUA'I STYLE' HAWAIIAN SLACK KEY GUITAR FESTIVAL (p70) Don't miss this fantastic (and free) chance to hear slack key masters from across the Hawaiian Islands.

❻ TIP TOP CAFÉ (p70) Chances are you'll be among only locals at this long-running diner, where specialties range from oxtail soup and meaty plate lunches to hearty pancakes and fresh sashimi.

❼ KAUA'I COMMUNITY RADIO (p62) Turn your dial to KKCR and listen to non-commercial programming done completely by Kauaians. Local hosts riff on Hawaiian issues, jazz, sustainability and more.

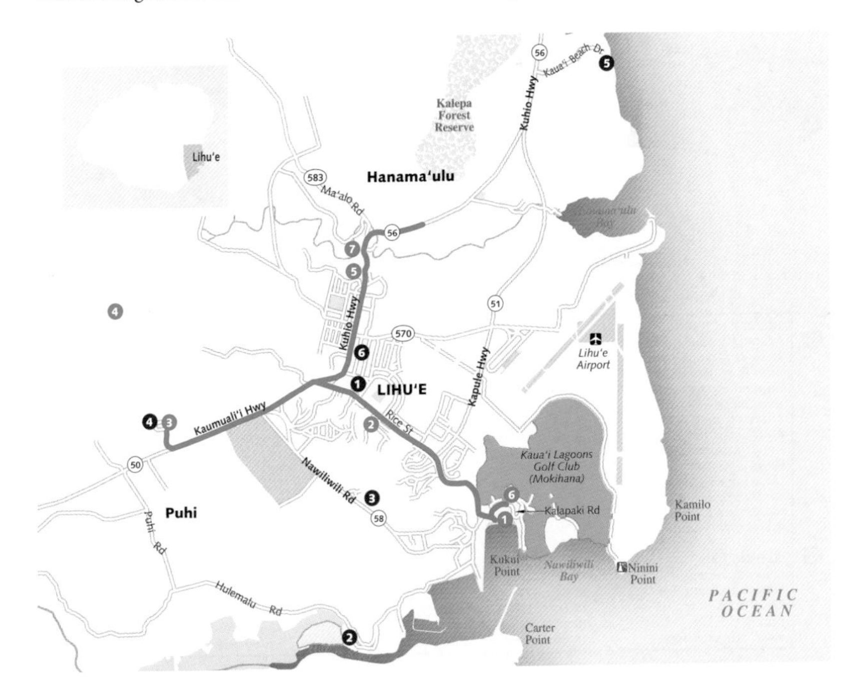

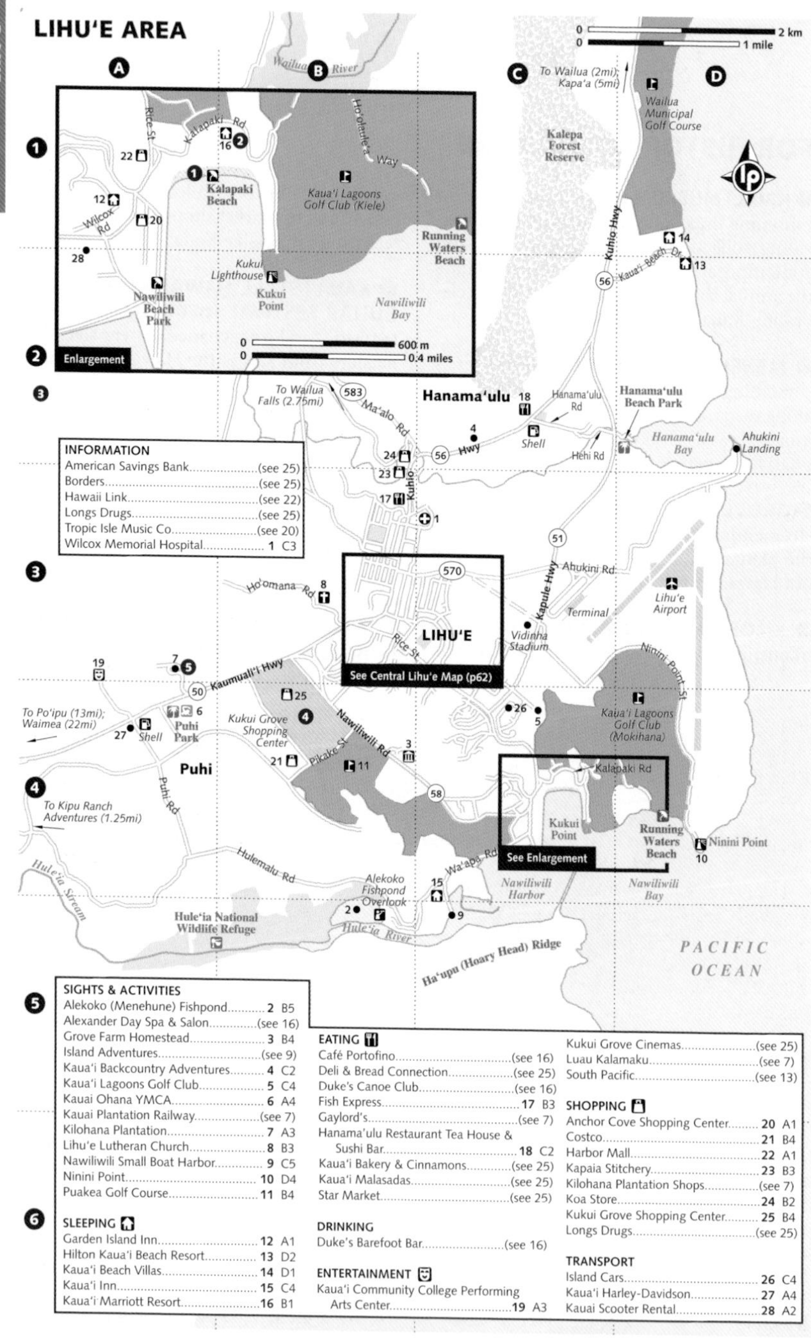
LIHU'E AREA
Enlargement
See Enlargement
See Central Lihu'e Map (p62)
0 600 m
0 0.4 miles
0 2 km
0 1 mile
Wailua River
To Wailua (2mi); Kapa'a (5mi)
Wailua Municipal Golf Course
Kalepa Forest Reserve
Rice St
Kalapaki Rd
Ho'olaule'a Way
Kalapaki Beach
Kaua'i Lagoons Golf Club (Kiele)
Wilcox Rd
Running Waters Beach
Kukui Lighthouse
Kukui Point
Nawiliwili Beach Park
Nawiliwili Bay
Kuhio Hwy
Kaua'i Beach Dr
To Wailua Falls (2.75mi)
Ma'alo Rd
Hanama'ulu
Hanama'ulu Rd
Hanama'ulu Beach Park
Hanama'ulu Bay
Ahukini Landing
Shell
Hehi Rd
Ahukini Rd
Kapule Hwy
Terminal
Lihu'e Airport
Ho'omana Rd
LIHU'E
Vidinha Stadium
Ninini Point St
Kaumuali'i Hwy
To Po'ipu (13mi); Waimea (22mi)
Puhi Park
Kukui Grove Shopping Center
Nawiliwili Rd
Pikake St
Kaua'i Lagoons Golf Club (Mokihana)
Puhi
Puhi Rd
To Kipu Ranch Adventures (1.25mi)
Kukui Point
Running Waters Beach
Ninini Point
Hulemalu Rd
Wa'apa Rd
Alekoko Fishpond Overlook
Nawiliwili Harbor
Nawiliwili Bay
Hule'ia Stream
Hule'ia National Wildlife Refuge
Hule'ia River
Ha'upu (Hoary Head) Ridge
PACIFIC OCEAN
INFORMATION
American Savings Bank (see 25)
Borders (see 25)
Hawaii Link (see 22)
Longs Drugs (see 25)
Tropic Isle Music Co (see 20)
Wilcox Memorial Hospital 1 C3
SIGHTS & ACTIVITIES
Alekoko (Menehune) Fishpond 2 B5
Alexander Day Spa & Salon (see 16)
Grove Farm Homestead 3 B4
Island Adventures (see 9)
Kaua'i Backcountry Adventures 4 C2
Kaua'i Lagoons Golf Club 5 C4
Kauai Ohana YMCA 6 A4
Kauai Plantation Railway (see 7)
Kilohana Plantation 7 A3
Lihu'e Lutheran Church 8 B3
Nawiliwili Small Boat Harbor 9 C5
Ninini Point 10 D4
Puakea Golf Course 11 B4
SLEEPING
Garden Island Inn 12 A1
Hilton Kaua'i Beach Resort 13 D2
Kaua'i Beach Villas 14 D1
Kaua'i Inn 15 C4
Kaua'i Marriott Resort 16 B1
EATING
Café Portofino (see 16)
Deli & Bread Connection (see 25)
Duke's Canoe Club (see 16)
Fish Express 17 B3
Gaylord's (see 7)
Hanama'ulu Restaurant Tea House & Sushi Bar 18 C2
Kaua'i Bakery & Cinnamons (see 25)
Kaua'i Malasadas (see 25)
Star Market (see 25)
DRINKING
Duke's Barefoot Bar (see 16)
ENTERTAINMENT
Kaua'i Community College Performing Arts Center 19 A3
Kukui Grove Cinemas (see 25)
Luau Kalamaku (see 7)
South Pacific (see 13)
SHOPPING
Anchor Cove Shopping Center 20 A1
Costco 21 B4
Harbor Mall 22 A1
Kapaia Stitchery 23 B3
Kilohana Plantation Shops (see 7)
Koa Store 24 B2
Kukui Grove Shopping Center 25 B4
Longs Drugs (see 25)
TRANSPORT
Island Cars 26 C4
Kaua'i Harley-Davidson 27 A4
Kauai Scooter Rental 28 A2

HIGHLIGHTS

❶ **BEST BEACH:** Kalapaki Beach (p63)
❷ **BEST VIEW:** Beachside table at Duke's Barefoot Bar (p70)
❸ **BEST ACTIVITY:** Ziplining from tree to tree (p67)
❹ **BEST JUNK FOOD:** Malasadas (p70)
❺ **BEST FAMILY TOUR:** Kilohana Plantation Railroad (p64)

Highlights are numbered on the map on p60.

HISTORY

pop 5674

Born as a sugar town, Lihu'e's sugar mill (still standing south of town along Kaumuali'i Hwy) was Kaua'i's largest. The plantation relied solely on rainwater during its early years, but then William Harrison Rice, who bought the company in the early 1860s, became the first planter in Hawaii to irrigate sugarcane fields. The plantation closed in 2001, ending more than a century of operation.

Now Lihu'e's economy relies not only on tourism but also on retail, which is obvious from all the big-box stores at Kukui Grove Shopping Center (p74). You might not think an island of 62,000 needs a Costco but, in October 2006, it got one.

Lihu'e's ethnic mix reflects the plantation era, with Japanese representing just under 30% of the population, followed by Caucasian and mixed-race individuals, each about 20% of the population. The virtually contiguous communities of Puhi (population 1186) and Hanama'ulu (population 3272) both comprise majority Filipino populations.

ORIENTATION

The main business district of Lihu'e is surrounded by highways: Kuhio Hwy (Hwy 56) along the west, Kapule Hwy (Hwy 51) along the east, Ahukini Rd (Hwy 570) along the north, and Nawiliwili Rd (Hwy 58) along the south. The town's main drag, Rice St, runs east–west past the government buildings and post office.

INFORMATION

Bookstores

Borders (Map p60; ☎ 246-0862; Kukui Grove Shopping Center, 3-2600 Kaumuali'i Hwy; 🕑 9am-10pm Mon-Thu, to 11pm Fri & Sat, to 8pm Sun) Large chain with wide range of books, CDs and DVDs; stocks lots of local selections unavailable on the mainland. In-store Starbucks café.

Tropic Isle Music Co (Map p60; ☎ 245-8700; www.tropicislemusic.com; Anchor Cove Shopping Center, 3416 Rice St; 🕑 9am-9pm) Huge selection of Hawaii-specific books, CDs, stationery, food, toiletries, fabrics – you name it. See website for complete online store.

Emergency

Police, Fire & Ambulance (☎ 911)

Police Station (Map p62; ☎ 241-1771; 3060 Umi St) For nonemergencies, incident reporting and information.

Sexual Assault Crisis Line (☎ 245-4144)

Internet Access

Unless you have your own computer, free internet access is rare in Lihu'e. One option is **Kukui Grove Shopping Center** (Map p60; 3-2600 Kaumuali'i Hwy; 🕑 9:30am-7pm Mon-Thu & Sat, 9:30am-9pm Fri, 9:30am-6pm Sun; wi-fi), where the mall's free wi-fi zone runs from Sears through the food court and central walkway. If you can't do without table and espresso, pay for access at the mall's two Starbucks locations.

For dinosaur-age dial-up service, **Hawaii Link** (Map p60; ☎ 246-9300; www.hawaiilink.net; 2950 Kress St; 🕑 10am-6pm Mon-Fri, 9am-noon Sat) offers a $10 deal for two weeks.

Laundry

Lihu'e Laundromat (Map p62; ☎ 332-8356; Rice Shopping Center, 4303 Rice St; 🕑 24hr)

Media

NEWSPAPERS

Garden Island (www.kauaiworld.com) Kaua'i's daily newspaper is very lean and locally focused, but it's a good source for current island events and issues.

RADIO

KITH 98.9FM Contemporary island music, including Hawaiian and reggae, plus local-favorite covers of American pop classics. Upbeat choice for island cruising.

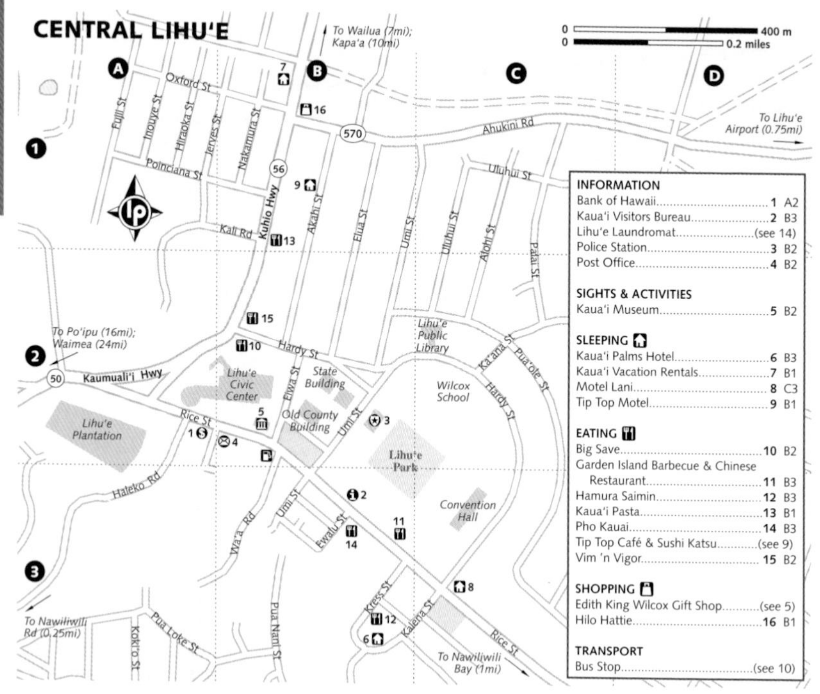

our pick **KKCR 90.9FM** (www.kkcr.org) Kaua'i Community Radio is 100% volunteer-run, listener-supported and non-commercial. Excellent spectrum of music programming, plus call-in talk shows, interviews and live in-studio performances. No NPR or PRI national programs. Based in Hanalei, you can listen islandwide at 91.9FM.

KQNG 93.5FM (www.kongradio.com) Known as KONG radio, this popular station plays mainstream US pop and contemporary island music. DJs Ron Wiley (mornings) and Marc Valentine (afternoons) are island institutions.

KQNG 570AM News, sports and talk, including syndicated shows by Rush Limbaugh, Dr Dean Edell, Mitch Albom and Al Franken.

KTOH 99.9FM Oldies, classic hits from the 1960s to 1990s.

KUAI 720AM The best station for news, every hour on the hour, plus extended coverage at 7am, noon and 5pm on weekdays.

Island Insights

In September 2008, *National Geographic Adventure* magazine ranked Lihu'e third in the West Coast category of its '50 Best Places to Live' list.

TELEVISION

KVIC A televised loop of Kaua'i tourist information on channel 3.

Medical Services

Longs Drugs (Map p60; ☎ 245-7771; Kukui Grove Shopping Center, 3-2600 Kaumuali'i Hwy; store 7am-10pm Mon-Sat, 8am-8pm Sun, pharmacy 8am-9pm Mon-Sat, 9am-6pm Sun)

Wilcox Memorial Hospital (Map p60; ☎ 245-1010, TTY 245-1133; 3420 Kuhio Hwy) Kaua'i's only major hospital. Emergency services 24 hours.

Money

Banks with 24-hour ATMs:

American Savings Bank (Map p60; ☎ 246-8844; Kukui Grove Shopping Center, 3-2600 Kaumuali'i Hwy)

Bank of Hawaii (Map p62; ☎ 245-6761; 4455 Rice St)

Post

Longs Drugs (above) has an in-store postal center offering photocopying, FedEx and

UPS, and US Postal services (rates are slightly lower at a post office).

The main **Post office** (Map p62; ☎ 800-275-8777; 4441 Rice St, Lihu'e, HI 96766; 🕑 8am-4:30pm Mon-Fri, 9am-1pm Sat) holds poste restante (general delivery) mail for a maximum of 30 days.

Tourist Information

Kaua'i Visitors Bureau (Map p62; ☎ 245-3971, 800-262-1400; www.kauaidiscovery.com; Suite 101, 4334 Rice St) offers a monthly calendar of events, bus schedules and list of county-managed Sunshine Markets (farmers markets) for the sale of Kaua'i produce. Order a free 'vacation planning kit' online.

Island Insights

Established as Kaua'i's principal port in 1930, **Nawiliwili Harbor** (Map p60) is actually an artificial harbor. No natural deepwater harbors exist along Kaua'i's entire coast, so part of Nawiliwili Bay was dredged and protected with a breakwater to create one. Today, cargo carriers Matson and Young Brothers dock here twice weekly with all necessary imported goods. In Hawaii, 80% of all consumer goods are imported, and on Kaua'i virtually everything arrives at this harbor. During dockworker strikes, locals immediately stock up on toilet paper, batteries and canned goods (including Spam).

BEACHES

The only beach worth noting is Kalapaki Beach, which attracts a mixed crowd of locals and tourists (mostly guests of the Marriott). Due to the proximity of Nawiliwili Harbor, however, it might disappoint those seeking a rural, not-a-building-in-sight setting.

KALAPAKI BEACH

Kalapaki Bay (Map p60) is small, square-shaped and well protected within the larger Nawiliwili Bay, so its sandy **beach** is remarkably versatile. The calmer waters toward the east are good for swimming, while the swells toward the west draw bodyboarders and surfers. Due to its sandy (rather than reef) bottom, the waters are poor for snorkeling. But overall, it's a gem, not only for ocean sports but also for picnicking, watching the surf action, grabbing a drink at Duke's Barefoot Bar (p70) and just hanging out. It's easily overlooked because it's hidden behind a row of touristy shops and the large Kaua'i Marriott Resort (p77).

Due to the proximity of Nawiliwili Harbor, you'll see ship traffic, barge containers and other industrial objects in the distance. Hence the beach is less exotic than those on the North and South Shores, but the forgiving wave action here is a real plus. Parking is available close to the water at the hotel's north end (signs direct you to public/beach parking).

NAWILIWILI BEACH PARK

With Kalapaki Beach a minute away, there's no good reason to come here. But, in case you're curious about Nawiliwili Harbor, the

Enjoying the sun at Kalapaki Beach

MICAH WRIGHT

island's major port, take a look around **Nawiliwili Beach Park** (Map p60). It ain't a show-stopper, with a seawall running its length. Gargantuan cruise ships dock at Nawiliwili Harbor, while smaller boats, including deep-sea fishing charters (p68) and kayak tours (p68), leave from nearby Nawiliwili Small Boat Harbor.

HANAMA'ULU BEACH PARK

This small neighborhood beach is like a small neighborhood pub – it won't knock your socks off, but it's fine for low-key hanging out. With sandy banks, grassy fields and welcome shade from ironwood trees, it's nice for picnicking. As for swimming, the bay is protected, but the waters are silty (and therefore rather murky) due to runoff from Hanama'ulu Stream. You'll find mostly locals here, pole-fishing or gathering with friends and family. Nearby **Ahukini Landing** is known as a shore-dive site.

SIGHTS

Lihu'e's museum and historical attractions can give a decent grounding in the island's background. Kilohana Plantation is the most polished of the lot. But while modest, the others are bargains and never overly taxing or time-consuming.

KILOHANA PLANTATION

our pick Map p60; www.kilohanakauai.com; Kaumuali'i Hwy; admission free; 9:30am-9:30pm Mon-Sat, to 5pm Sun

Island Insights

Kaua'i's Wilcox family was the model for James Michener's famous epic, *Hawaii.*

If you're curious about how Kaua'i's powerful sugar barons lived, visit this handsome **plantation estate**, which today contains a variety of classy attractions: **Gaylord's** (p72) restaurant, a train tour (see the boxed text, below) and carriage rides, a luau show and upscale shopping. The meticulously kept property feels welcoming, and guests are invited to wander around.

Plantation owner Gaylord Parke Wilcox, once the head honcho of **Grove Farm Homestead** (p67), built the house in 1936. The 15,000-sq-ft Tudor-style mansion has been painstakingly restored, and its legacy as one of Kaua'i's distinguished historic houses is unquestioned. Antique-filled rooms and Oriental carpets laid over hardwood floors lead you past cases of poi pounders, koa bowls and other Hawaiiana to a row of gallery shops.

In an island take on hansom cabs, Clydesdale horses take visitors on **carriage rides** (☎ 246-9529; 20min ride adult/child $12/6; 11am-5pm) across the 35-acre grounds, including gardens and livestock barns.

KAUA'I MUSEUM

Map p62; ☎ 245-6931; www.kauaimuseum.org; 4428 Rice St; adult/child 6-12/student 13-17/senior

ALL ABOARD!

It's not obvious, but Kaua'i relied on railroads between the late 1880s and early 1900s, the sugar era. Workers would catch the morning train out to the fields and spend the day moving cars loaded with cut cane to the mills, or moving bags of processed sugar to the nearest ship landing. None of the trains were meant for passenger use. A handful of still-working train engines are preserved at the Grove Farm Homestead Museum (p67).

Although Kaua'i's railroads are long gone, you can ride the **Kauai Plantation Railway** (☎ 245-7245; www.kauaiplantationrailway.com; 40min ride adult/child 3-12 $18/14; departures on the hour, 10am-2pm), a restored historic train that passes fields of staple island crops (such as sugarcane, banana, coffee and taro), groves of tropical fruits and livestock including cattle and horses. The open-air replica cars are beautiful and allow a clear view of the fields. The Plantation Railway takes seriously its role as historian and preserver: it has acquired two genuine steam engines that ran in early-20th-century O'ahu and is working to restore them.

The highlight for city slickers (especially the underage ones) is stopping to feed bread to the herd of wild pigs here. The humorous, young, local guides give the tour a stamp of authenticity. To enjoy more of Kilohana Plantation's attractions, ask about the longer train–hike–lunch tour.

ISLAND VOICES

NAME: SYLVIA AKANA
OCCUPATION: SALES AND MARKETING ASSOCIATE, KAUA'I MUSEUM (oPPOSITE)
RESIDENCE: WAILUA

Where are you from? I grew up in Kekaha, in the plantation camps. It was a hunter-gatherer lifestyle – you had to be resourceful. For a kid, it was fun and very multicultural: I'd watch Japanese movies and eat Japanese food with my friends.

How would you define 'Native Hawaiian'? I am one-quarter Hawaiian. When I taught as a *kupuna* (Hawaiian elder) in the public schools, I would tell the kids, 'If you were born here, you're Hawaiian, too. Do you dance hula? Do you surf? If yes, you're Hawaiian.' Sure, there is 'Hawaiian' and there is '*koko* (blood) Hawaiian.' But what really matters is your *pu'uwai,* your heart. When you can look at a people and embrace them, you're one of them.

How do you view tourism? It's wonderful, a way for locals who don't or can't travel to meet other people. But there are too many timeshares and condos, which create a sense of loss. Loss of places to fish, hunt and gather. Loss of the simple life.

Do tourists understand the value of Hawaiian artifacts? No. When I tell them the price of a *lauhala* (pandanus leaf) hat or Ni'ihau shell jewelry, they say, 'It's not worth that much,' or even, 'That's totally ridiculous!' They don't understand the labor involved.

What about heiau (Hawaiian temples)? Visitors must learn the protocols of visiting heiau and other sacred places. Go with an attitude of respect and understanding. Don't step over boundary lines. Don't leave any gifts, especially non-Hawaiian objects like crystals. Just show gratitude.

Our heiau are not enclosed. They're out in the open to allow gods to see and hear us when we pray. But, in their meaning, our temples are like your temples. Treat them with similar respect.

Anything else you'd tell visitors? Visitors should understand the *huna* (invisible essence) of words: 'aloha' is not just hello and goodbye. Aloha is breathing deeply and inviting the breath of God between people. They should understand the traditional Hawaiian values that existed well before Christianity: *lokahi* (to work together), *malama* (to take care) and *pono* (to make right). Hawaiians converted to Christianity because it matched their traditional values.

$10/1/3/8, 1st Sat of month free; 9am-4pm Mon-Fri, 10am-4pm Sat

For a grounding in Kaua'i's history, check out this modest but interesting **museum**. If you're new to the islands, it's worth taking a **guided tour** (free with admission; 10:30am Tue-Fri). Free **Hawaiian quilting demonstrations** (9am-noon Wed & Thu) and **lauhala (pandanus leaf) weaving demonstrations** (1pm Mon & Wed) are given year-round. Check the website for special exhibits, including the annual lei competition (p262) and biennial Hawaiian and contemporary quilt exhibit.

Straightforward, well-written displays explain the Hawaiian Islands' volcanic genesis and Kaua'i's unique ecosystems. Collections include early Hawaiian artifacts such as *kapa* (bark cloth), wooden bowls and ceremonial lei. Upstairs the collection covers the sugar and pineapple plantation era. One telling display juxtaposes replicas of a plantation worker's spartan shack and an early missionary's spacious bedroom, furnished with an extravagant four-post koa (prized Hawaiian hardwood) bed.

WAILUA FALLS

Wind your way 4 miles north of Lihu'e to the falls made famous in the opening credits of the *Fantasy Island* TV series. While officially listed as 80ft, the falls (off Map p60) have been repeatedly measured at between 125ft to 175ft. Indeed, this gushing double waterfall (Wailua means 'two waters') misting the surrounding tropical foliage is a fantastic photo op, especially when the falls merge into one wide cascade after downpours.

At the lookout spot, a sign warns: 'Slippery rocks at top of falls. People have been killed.' Heed it. Many have slipped while trying to scramble down the steep, untamed path.

Wailua Falls PHOTO CREDIT

To get here from Lihu'e, follow Kuhio Hwy north and turn left onto Ma'alo Rd (Hwy 583), which ends at the falls after 4 miles.

ALEKOKO (MENEHUNE) FISHPOND

Although the lookout is far from the pond, you won't regret a quick stop to admire this tranquil, 39-acre *loko wai* (freshwater fishpond; Map p60), surrounded by a vast area of forest. According to legend, Kaua'i's *menehune* (little people) formed the fishpond overnight when they built the 900ft stone dam across a bend in the Hule'ia River. Holes in the structure allowed young fish to enter the pond but not to escape once grown. The dam is now covered by a thick green line of mangrove trees.

The pond was productive with mullet until 1824, when Kaua'i's leader Kaumuali'i died and *ali'i* (chiefs) from O'ahu and Maui ruled the island as absentee landlords. With no *ali'i* to feed and maintain the pond, it sorely declined. Later the surrounding area was planted with taro and rice. Today it is privately owned and not in use.

The US Fish & Wildlife Service owns the lands surrounding the fishpond (about 240 acres of river basin and steep forested slopes along the north side of Hule'ia River). In 1973 the area was designated the **Hule'ia National Wildlife Refuge** (http://pacificislands.fws.gov/wnwr/khuleianwr.html) and now provides breeding and feeding grounds for endemic water birds. The refuge is closed to the public, but kayak tours (p68) along Hule'ia River drift through it.

To get to the overlook, drive up Hulemalu Rd for 0.5 miles.

NININI POINT

You'll enjoy solitude from other tourists here (Map p60), where 360-degree vistas show jets swooping in the sky above and waves crashing against the rocks below. Looking east, soaring cliffs cut off rainbows and, closer in, golfers tee off near a beckoning scoop of beach. These terrific views from Ninini Point are made more so by its 100ft **lighthouse** marking the northern entrance to Nawiliwili Bay. Here, Hawaiians still fish, pick *'opihi* (edible limpet) and gather *limu* (edible seaweed).

The road to the lighthouse begins off Kapule Hwy, just over 880yd south of the intersection with Ahukini Rd and marked with two concrete slabs. You'll walk for just over 2 miles, past a guard gate (usually empty) and through Hole 12 of the Mokihana Golf Course, most of it rutted dirt road, before you reach the short spur to the lighthouse.

Running Waters Beach (the little slice of sand visible from Ninini Point) is not swimmable but makes a nice picnic spot. To find it, return to Hole 12 and park in the lot just before it, then follow the signs for 'Shore Access.' Turn right at Whaler's Brew Pub and descend to its parking lot, where you'll see another 'Shore Access' sign to your left. It's a steep, quick walk to the beach below.

GROVE FARM HOMESTEAD

Map p60; ☎ 245-3202; Nawiliwili Rd; 2hr tour adult/child under 12 $5/2; tours 10am & 1pm Mon, Wed & Thu

History buffs might enjoy this plantation museum, open only for prearranged tours, but kids might grow restless. Grove Farm was among the most productive sugar companies on Kaua'i, and George Wilcox, the son of missionaries Abner and Lucy Wilcox, built this well-preserved farmhouse in 1864. It feels suspended in time, with rocking chairs sitting dormant on a covered porch and untouched books lining the shelves of the musty library.

LIHU'E LUTHERAN CHURCH

Map p60; ☎ 245-2145; 4602 Ho'omana Rd; services 8am & 10:30am Sun

Atop a curvy country lane just off Kaumuali'i Hwy (Hwy 50) is Hawaii's oldest Lutheran church, a quaint clapboard house of worship, with an incongruously slanted floor that resembles a ship's deck and a balcony akin to a captain's bridge. German immigrants built this church, styling it after their own late-19th-century boat. The building is actually a faithful 1983 reconstruction of the 1885 original, which was leveled in Hurricane 'Iwa in 1982.

ACTIVITIES

Ziplining & Multi-Activity Tours

The 'sport' of ziplining arose in Costa Rican jungles, but it's similarly suited to Kaua'i's tree-filled rainforests. No special athleticism needed (only courage), but you must pass weight and age restrictions, which vary widely.

Don't Miss

- **Liliko'i (passion fruit) chiffon pie at Hamura Saimin** (p70)
- **May Day lei contest and display at Kaua'i Museum** (p64)
- **Tooling around town and the backroads on a moped** (p78)
- **Morning photo op at Alekoko (Menehune) Fishpond** (opposite)
- **Local-watching at the Borders bookstore Starbucks – the only cafe in town and an unexpected gem** (p61)
- **Ziplining at night with community-minded company Just Live** (below)
- **Local grinds (eats) at Tip Top Café & Sushi Katsu** (p70)

our pick **Just Live** (☎ 482-1295; www.justlive.org; Kuhio Hwy; tours $79-125) The difference between this outfit and the rest: it offers the only canopy-based zipping, meaning you never touch ground after your first zip. The 3½-hour zip tour includes seven ziplines and five bridge crossings, 60ft to 80ft off the ground in 200ft Norfolk pines. Test your mettle on the Eco-Adventure tour, which ups the ante with the rappelling and freefalling Monster Swing. Profits from commercial tours allow the company to offer community youth programs at low/no cost. Minimum age is nine.

Kaua'i Backcountry Adventures (Map p60; ☎ 245-2506, 888-270-0555; www.kauaibackcountry.com; Kuhio Hwy; tour incl lunch $125) Offers a 3½-hour zipline tour with seven lines, elevated as high as 200ft above the ground and running as far as 900ft (three football fields). Afterward, refuel on a picnic lunch at a swimming pond. Groups run as large as 11. Minimum age is 12.

Outfitters Kaua'i (Map pp164–5; ☎ 742-9667, 888-742-9887; www.outfitterskauai.com; Po'ipu Plaza, 2827-A Po'ipu Rd; 4hr tour adult/child 7-14 $125/99, 8hr tour incl lunch adult/child under 15 $175/135). Offers two multi-activity tours near Lihu'e that combine zipping, hiking, waterfall swimming and that idealized 'rope-swinging' (blame it on those old Mountain Dew commercials). The half-day tour includes four zips (which are especially thrilling and fast, due to the way they're strung) while the full-day tour includes only one. Minimum zipping age is seven, but the all-day Safari tour (which adds kayaking to the mix) is open to any age because zipping is optional.

Top Picks

LIHU'E FOR KIDS

- **Inner-tube ride in backcountry waterways** (below)
- **Old-fashioned plantation train** (p64)
- **Multi-activity jungle adventure** (p67)
- **Kalapaki Beach day** (p63)
- **Kids' aloha wear at Kapaia Stitchery** (p74)
- **Kauai Ohana YMCA kiddie pool** (opposite)

Kayaking & Canoeing

The only way to navigate the Hule'ia River and see the Hule'ia National Wildlife Refuge is on a commercial tour. The best are offered by **Outfitters Kaua'i** (p67), which combines kayaking and hiking (tours adult/child 3-14 including lunch $108/84, without lunch $104/7). It's a cinch, downwind for only 2 miles, with a return trip not by kayak but by motorized canoe.

Island Adventures (☎ 246-6333; www.kauaifun.com; Nawiliwili Small Boat Harbor; tour incl lunch adult/child 6-12 $89/69) offers a 4½-hour tour in the Hule'ia National Wildlife Refuge, where you'll paddle 2.5 miles into the refuge, hike to two private waterfalls, swim and picnic. If you can't hike eight to 10 flights of uneven steps, take a pass.

Tubing

Part historical site, part lazy-man cruise, 'tubing' means floating down former sugar-plantation irrigation ditches in old-fashioned inner tubes. **Kaua'i Backcountry Adventures** (Map p60; ☎ 245-2506, 888-270-0555; www.kauaibackcountry.com; Kuhio Hwy; 3hr tour incl lunch $100; 🕑 departures 9am, 10:30am, 1pm & 2:30pm Mon-Sat, 9am & 1pm Sun) offers the island's only tubing tour, which ends with lunch at a swimming hole. Great for the whole family (including kids as young as five).

ATV

Can driving an ATV across pristine ranchland really constitute an 'ecotour'? A **Kipu Ranch Adventures** (off Map p60; ☎ 246-9288; www.kiputours.com; tours from driver/child/senior & passenger $125/72/100) tour does let you see a gorgeous, otherwise inaccessible landscape – including the Ha'upu mountain range, Kipu Kai coast and Hule'ia River, plus cattle, wild pigs, pheasants, peacocks and turkeys – but gas-powered vehicles are hard to endorse. For a green option, try Kaua'i ATV Tours (p161).

Golf

The original two Jack Nicklaus–designed 18-hole par-72 courses at **Kaua'i Lagoons Golf Club** (Map p60; ☎ 241-6000, 800-634-6400; www.kauailagoonsgolf.com; Kaua'i Marriott, 3351 Ho'olaule'a Way; club rental $55, green fees morning $125-175, afternoon $105-125) were called Kiele and Mokihana. In 2008, both courses began undergoing a major renovation that will last through 2010. During this period, only one combined 18-hole experience is available. Guests of the Kaua'i Marriott receive discounted rates (morning/afternoon $115/95).

The lush cliffs of Mt Ha'upu serve as a backdrop to the Robin Nelson–designed **Puakea Golf Course** (Map p60; ☎ 245-8756, 866-773-5554; www.puakeagolf.com; 4315 Kalepa Rd; green fees incl cart before 11am $135, 11am-2pm $79, after 2pm $59, club rental $40), which first opened in 1997 (with an odd 10 holes) and became an 18-hole course in 2003. Located near Kukui Grove Shopping Center.

Fishing

Many charters depart from Nawiliwili Small Boat Harbor (Map p60), but see p34 for other sport fishing locations. The following outfits are top-notch:

our pick **Lahela Ocean Adventures** (☎ 635-4020; www.sport-fishing-kauai.com; 4hr per person $219, 4hr private charter per 6 passengers $625) Captain Scott Akana is named by other fisherman as the island's best and a real pro. Spectators ride at half price. Detailed website answers all your questions and more.

Happy Hunter Sport Fishing (☎ 639-4351, 634-2633; www.happyhuntersportfishing.com; 4hr private charter per 6 passengers $625) Captain Harry Shigekane has 30 years of experience and sails a fantastic 41ft Pacifica. Private charters only.

Spas

Alexander Day Spa & Salon (Map p60; ☎ 246-4918; www.alexanderspa.com; Kaua'i Marriottt Resort; 50min massage $115; 🕑 8am-7pm) strives to pamper guests in the most ecofriendly way, using biodegradable water cups, recycled paper products and CFL (compact fluorescent light) bulbs.

Swimming

Lap swimmers, get your fix at the open-air, Olympic-sized pool at the new **our pick** **Kauai Ohana YMCA** (Map p60; ☎ 246-9090; Kaumuali'i Hwy across Kilohana Plantation; day pass $10; 🕐 5:30am-9am & 11am-7pm Mon-Fri, 7am-7pm Sat, 10am-6pm Sun). Teach tots to swim in a nifty learning pool with 1ft to 4ft steps. Weight room is also available. YMCA members from any state, show your card to pay only $5.

TOURS

We don't recommend most general bus tours, but the half-day, 4WD backroads tour by **Aloha Kaua'i Tours** (☎ 800-452-8113; www.alohakauaitours.com; adult/child under 13 $80/50) takes you across private land from Kilohana Crater to the Maha'ulepu Coast (p168). This scenic road trip is ideal for history or geography buffs, or those who prefer driving to hiking.

Helicopter Tours

Most helicopter tours fly from Lihu'e Airport (Map p60). The going rate for a 50- to 60-minute flight is around $200. Book online for major discounts. See p40 for more on helicopter tours.

A good choice for couples or trios is **Mauna Loa Helicopters** (☎ 245-4006; www.maunaloahelicopters.com; 60min tour $199-239), which also runs a flight school. Highly qualified pilots don't skimp on full 60-minute private tours for up to three passengers. Small groups allow for more-personalized interaction between pilot and passengers. You can choose a doors-off tour for $10 to $20 more per person. Singles should choose a non-private tour, as the cost would be prohibitive.

The following tours allow six passengers, which can seem crowded (if you get stuck in the middle), but they give 60-minute (or close) rides and have well-qualified pilots:

Island Helicopters (☎ 245-8588, 800-829-8588; www.islandhelicopters.com; 50-55min tour $178) Longtime, small company.

Jack Harter Helicopters (☎ 245-3774, 888-245-2001; www.helicopters-kauai.com; 60-65min tour $229-259) You get your money's worth of air time here. Choose from standard enclosed, six-passenger AStars ($229) or doors-off, four-passenger Hughes 500s ($259). Longer 90- to 95-minute tours offered.

our pick **Safari Helicopters** (☎ 246-0136, 800-326-3356; www.safarihelicopters.com; 55/90min tours from $160/250) Besides fair prices, this outfit offers a fascinating tour that lands on a cliff overlooking Olokele Valley in Waimea. The landowner, Keith Robinson (whose family owns Ni'ihau and 42,000 Kaua'i acres), chats with passengers about his conservation work with endangered species.

Top Picks

LIHU'E SPLURGES

- **Wine-and-food pairings by top chefs at the Spring Gourmet Gala** (right)
- **Oceanfront suite at Kaua'i Marriott Resort** (p77)
- **Helicopter tour with a wildlife refuge landing** (right)
- **18 holes at Kaua'i Lagoons Golf Club** (opposite)
- **Alexander Day Spa** (opposite)
- **Luau Kalamaku** (p72)

FESTIVALS & EVENTS

E Pili Kakou i Ho'okahi Lahui (www.epilikakou-kauai.org) Annual two-day hula retreat in late February features top kumu hula from across the islands. Current venue is the Hilton Kaua'i Beach Resort.

Spring Gourmet Gala (☎ 245-8359; Kaua'i Community College; admission $100; 🕐 6pm) Save your appetite for the island's highest-end gourmet event in early April, featuring food-and-wine pairings by famous Hawaii chefs. Funds support the Kaua'i Community College's culinary arts program. The 300 tickets sell out fast.

our pick **May Day Lei Contest & Fair** (☎ 245-6931; www.kauaimuseum.org; admission free) Established in the early 1980s, the annual Kaua'i Museum lei contest on May 1 spawns legendary floral art.

Kaua'i Polynesian Festival (☎ 335-6466; www.kauaipolynesianfestival.org) This four-day event in late May features rockin' competitions in expert Tahitian, Maori, Samoan and hula dancing, plus food booths and cultural workshops, held at various locations.

Fourth of July Concert in the Sky (☎ 246-2440; admission $7-10; 🕐 3-9pm) Enjoy island foods, live entertainment and the grand finale fireworks show set to music; held at Vidinha Stadium (Map p60). Proceeds benefit Kauai Hospice.

Kaua'i County Farm Bureau Fair (☎ 332-8189; Vidinha Stadium; admission adult/child $4/2) Old-fashioned family fun at Vidinha Stadium (Map p60) in late August, with carnival rides and games, livestock shows, petting zoo, hula performances and lots of local-food booths.

Aloha Festivals Ho'olaule'a & Parade (☎ 245-8508; www.alohafestivals.com; admission free) This statewide event in early September starts on Kaua'i with a parade from Vidinha Stadium (Map p60) to the historic county building lawn. The *ho'olaule'a* includes an appearance by Kaua'i's royal court.

our pick **Kaua'i Composers Contest & Concert** (☎ 822-2166; www.mokihana.kauai.net; admission $10-15; 7pm) The signature event of the Kaua'i Mokihana Festival, this contest in mid- to late September showcases homegrown musical talent; held at Kaua'i Community College (Map p60).

'Kaua'i Style' Hawaiian Slack Key Guitar Festival (☎ 239-4336; www.slackkeyfestival.com; Kaua'i Beach Resort; admission free; noon-6pm) This opportunity to see master slack key guitarists for free is not to be missed. Held in mid-November.

Lights on Rice Parade (☎ 246-1004; Rice St; admission free; 6:30pm) Disney had its Main Street Electrical Parade. Kaua'i has this charming parade of illuminated floats in early December.

EATING & DRINKING

DUKE'S BAREFOOT BAR

Bar $

Map p60; ☎ 246-9599; Kaua'i Marriott Resort, Kalapaki Beach; tropical drinks $7.25, wine per glass $6-16; 11am-11pm

For a convivial, Waikiki-style tropical bar, hurry and grab a beachside table here (before the nonstop evening queue). It's a thrifty substitute for **Duke's Canoe Club** (p72), with similar full-fledged menu items including fresh fish tacos ($11), crab wontons ($8) and Hula Pie ($6.50), a mound of macadamia ice cream atop chocolate-cookie crust that is now legend.

HAMURA SAIMIN

Diner $

Map p62; ☎ 245-3271; 2956 Kress St; noodles $3.75-4.50; 10am-10pm Mon-Thu, to midnight Fri & Sat, to 9pm Sun

An island institution, Hamura's is a hole-in-the-wall specializing in homemade saimin (noodle soup). Service can be abrupt (think Soup Nazi) so don't hem and haw. Expect crowds at lunchtime, slurping noodles elbow-to-elbow at orange U-shaped counters. It's stifling inside with noodles boiling and no air-con. Save room for their other specialty, *liliko'i* (passion fruit) chiffon pie.

TIP TOP CAFÉ & SUSHI KATSU

Diner/Sushi $

our pick **Map p62; ☎ 245-2333; 3173 Akahi St; breakfast mains $4.50-10, lunch mains $5.50-11; café 6:30am-2pm, Sushi Katsu 11am-2pm & 5:30-9pm Tue-Sun**

The stark white building might give you pause, but inside you'll find a pleasantly retro diner teeming with locals filling up on good, ol' fashioned eats. The main draws are its famous pancakes and oxtail soup. Meat eaters, go local with *loco moco* (two fried eggs, hamburger patty, rice and gravy), saimin and beef stew. Sushi Katsu offers value-priced sushi and Japanese dishes.

MMM... DOUGHNUTS

If you, like Homer Simpson, rank the all-American classic doughnut (with a hole) among your favorite foods, you'll gobble up the Portuguese *malasada* (without a hole). Sugar-coated but not too sweet, the best of these palm-sized beauties combine lightness with satisfying heft. Try the island's two best *malasada* makers.

Malasadas taste best when hot, so a stop at our pick **Kaua'i Malasadas** (Map p60; Kukui Grove Shopping Center, 3-2600 Kaumuali'i Hwy; 3 pieces $1.25; from 9am Mon-Sat) is a must. Look for Marlena Bunao in her one-woman stand in front of Kmart. She keeps her *malasadas* (rolled in either sugar or cinnamon-sugar) toasty under a heat lamp and stays open from morning until *pau* (finished), sold out.

With additional filled varieties, some might prefer **Kaua'i Bakery & Cinnamons** (Map p60; ☎ 246-4765; www.kauaibakery.com; Kukui Grove Shopping Center, 3-2600 Kaumuali'i Hwy; pastries 49¢-$1.75, cakes & pies $8-16; 7am-7pm Mon-Thu & Sat, to 9pm Fri, to 6pm Sun), full-service bakery in the mall. In addition to cream- or chocolate-filled *malasadas*, you can indulge in old-fashioned cinnamon rolls, apple turnovers, bread pudding and much more.

A local treat: sweet, creamy Portuguese *malasadas*

LUCI YAMAMOTO

DELI & BREAD CONNECTION
Sandwiches $

Map p60; ☎ 245-7115; Kukui Grove Shopping Center, 3-2600 Kaumuali'i Hwy; sandwiches $5-7; 9:30am-7pm Mon-Thu & Sat, to 9pm Fri, 10am-6pm Sun

If you're hankering for an all-American, meal-sized sandwich, this local favorite eatery will satisfy. Find classics like hot tuna melts and classic clubs. Vegetarians won't starve with a non-meat burger layered with mushrooms, pesto and melted mozzarella. Fringe benefit: it's at the mall but it's not a chain.

FISH EXPRESS
Fish Market $

our pick Map p60; ☎ 245-9918; 3343 Kuhio Hwy; lunch $6-7.50; 10am-6pm Mon-Sat, to 5pm Sun

Fish lovers, this is a no-brainer. One day, order chilled deli items, from fresh *'ahi poke* (cubed, marinated raw fish) to green seaweed salad, by the pound. The next day, try a healthful plate lunch of blackened *'ahi* with guava-basil sauce, plus rice and salad ($8.50) or a gourmet *bentō* (Japanese box lunch). You might end up here every day (lunch is served to 3pm daily).

GARDEN ISLAND BARBECUE & CHINESE RESTAURANT
Chinese/Local $

Map p62; ☎ 245-8868; 4252 Rice St; plate lunches $5-6.25, entrées $7-9; 10am-9pm

Tasty, filling, cheap Chinese food. No surprise, it's a hit. For a true local (if lowbrow) experience, try this bustling family-style eatery. The lengthy menu includes Chinese, Japanese and Hawaiian dishes, which is a red flag on the mainland but rather common in Hawaii. Try the simpler veg dishes, like black mushrooms with Chinese broccoli.

PHO KAUAI
Vietnamese $

Map p62; ☎ 245-9858; Rice Shopping Center, 4303 Rice St; noodle soups from $8; 10am-9pm Mon-Sat

Hidden in a strip mall, this no-frills eatery serves steaming bowls of well-made *pho* (Vietnamese noodle soup). Choose meat or veg toppings, such as curry chicken, grilled shrimp, snow peas or eggplant. No credit cards.

KAUA'I PASTA
Italian $$

Map p62; ☎ 245-2227; 4-939B Kuhio Hwy; mains $9-15; 11am-2pm & 5-9pm

For a sit-down restaurant that's neither a fast-food joint nor a resort splurge, this centrally located Italian bistro is your ticket. Colorful salads meld diverse flavors, such as peppery arugula, creamy goat cheese and sweet tomatoes. Hot focaccia sandwiches, classic pasta mains and luscious tiramisu would pass muster with mainland foodies.

HANAMA'ULU RESTAURANT TEA HOUSE & SUSHI BAR Japanese $$

Map p60; ☎ 245-2511, 245-3225; 3-4291 Kuhio Hwy; mains $7-10, special platters $17-20; 11:30am-9:30pm Tue-Sun

This fixture on the outskirts of Lihu'e stands out mainly for its historic tea house setting. The food is good but not great, and the menu suspiciously includes Chinese dishes, but that's the island way. They're known for crispy fried dishes, from Chinese ginger chicken to Japanese tempura and *tonkatsu* (breaded cutlets). Avoid the dismal front dining room; request seating in the quaint tea house in back.

GAYLORD'S Hawaii Regional Cuisine $$$

Map p60; ☎ 245-9593; www.kilohanakauai.com/gaylords.htm; Kilohana Plantation, Kaumuali'i Hwy; lunch $8-14, dinner $20-35; 11am-2pm & 5:30-9pm Mon-Sat, 9-2pm & 5:30-9pm Sun

Discerning minds generally agree that **Kilohana Plantation** (p64) makes a handsome setting. Amid the manicured lawns, white tablecloths and formal dining room, you can daydream about the life of a plantation lord. But picky palates do differ on the quality of dishes like filet mignon bathed in *liliko'i* sauce, and shiitake–prime rib salad with Maui onions and Kamuela tomatoes. We want to love this place, but it needs more consistency.

CAFÉ PORTOFINO Italian $$$

Map p60; ☎ 245-2121; www.cafeportofino.com; Kaua'i Marriott Resort, Kalapaki Beach; appetizers $8-12, mains $16-29; 5-9:30pm

A textbook example of 'romantic,' this oceanfront *ristorante* appeals to particular tastes. Some appreciate the white tablecloths, low lighting and solo harpist, but others find chef Maximillian Avocadi's food overpriced and the formal atmosphere too staid. The traditional Italian menu features fine pastas and lots of veal, such as house specialty *osso buco* (veal shank).

DUKE'S CANOE CLUB Hawaii Regional Cuisine $$$

Map p60; ☎ 246-9599; Kaua'i Marriott Resort; appetizers $8-11, mains $18-30; 5-10pm

Princeville and Po'ipu resort restaurants might be more elegant and refined. But you won't find an evening spot more fun and lively than Duke's, holding court on Kalapaki Beach. The steak-and-seafood menu is not very innovative, but dishes are well executed. The fresh catch baked 'Duke's style' with garlic, lemon and basil glaze is a winner. Expect a touristy crowd (matching alohawear is not uncommon). To cut costs, go to the downstairs bar (p70) instead.

For groceries, Lihu'e's branch of the **Big Save** (Map p62; ☎ 245-6571; 4444 Rice St; 7am-11pm) island chain is decent but lacks a deli. (Note that the Big Save parking lot and entrance is actually off Hardy St, which is just north of Rice St.) **Star Market** (Map p60; ☎ 245-7777; Kukui Grove Shopping Center, 3-2600 Kaumuali'i Hwy; 6am-11pm) carries much the same stock. **Vim 'n Vigor** (☎ 245-9053; 3-3122 Kuhio Hwy; 9am-7pm Mon-Fri, to 5pm Sat) carries vitamins and supplements, health foods, organic produce and bulk staples. Finally, the food department of Costco (p75) might surprise you with fresh *poke* and gourmet cakes by Icing on the Cake (p91).

ENTERTAINMENT

Shows

LUAU KALAMAKU

our pick Map p60; ☎ 877-622-1780; www.luaukalamaku.com; Kilohana Plantation; adult/child 3-11/student 12-18 $95/45/65; 5pm Tue & Fri

A cut above the standard commercial show you'll find elsewhere in Hawaii, this luau is smooth dinner theater. Unlike the usual Polynesian-dance revue, the presentation centers on a compelling stageplay about seafaring and romance. Featuring hula, Tahitian and awesome Samoan fire dancing, the choreography is sophisticated and without too much cringe-worthy 'embarrass the tourist' forced dancing. The buffet dinner is above average, with 360-degree seating around a circular stage. The setting at Kilohana Plantation (p64) is ideal for before-dinner meandering.

SOUTH PACIFIC

Map p60; ☎ 246-0111; Hilton Kaua'i Beach Resort, 4331 Kaua'i Beach Dr; adult/child incl tax $71/63; 5:30pm Wed

If you've never seen Rodgers and Hammerstein's *South Pacific,* it's worth your while to catch this ongoing dinner-theater pro-

ISLAND VOICES

NAME: ANSON LARDIZABAL
OCCUPATION: MUSICIAN, SINGER AND ACTOR, LUAU KALAMAKU (Opposite)
RESIDENCE: HANAMA'ULU

Where did you grow up? I'm a third-generation native of Hanama'ulu. I bought my childhood home from my parents 15 years ago. Most of the same families are still here and look out for each other.

What's your musical background? After high school, I moved to northern California: Gilroy and Hollister, where I learned to ride Harleys, went to junior college and transferred to UC Santa Cruz. But I left after a year to play the keyboards professionally: heavy metal stuff, opening for acts like Journey and Bon Jovi. I had long hair and I was 50lb lighter.

Eventually I left the industry and moved back. There was family pressure. There were too many negatives, the drugs and corruption. My Catholic upbringing made me see, 'I'm not like this.'

What was it like to move back? When I returned, I knew that I was different inside. But, to my old friends and family, I was not a different person. So I had to behave according to context. That's what you learn from living away from Hawaii. You become street smart. No one can teach that to you.

How did you land your major role in the luau? I was hired as a keyboard player, but I knew I could do the stage role. In high school and college, I studied drama and theater, including musicals. Broadway *kine!* Like *West Side Story* and *Oklahoma!* I was always stereotyped by my look: played the thug, bouncer, rough guy. I had vocal training in California, but the *mana* (spirit) comes from church singing.

In the luau, you play a Hawaiian man although you're Filipino. Is that acceptable? I look Hawaiian. Big bones. But I went to the *kupuna* (Hawaiian elders) for their blessing. I had to make it *pono* (right), to feel good about [taking] the role. Actually, a lot of real Hawaiians are not interested in this type of thing. They've been hurt enough already.

Do you enjoy interacting with the audience after the show? We all enjoy meeting the tourists. You give aloha and it comes back. You just hope people want to learn about Hawaii for the right reasons, not only to exploit it, make money, treat it like a *National Geographic* display.

Where do you like to ride your Harley? Koke'e (p211) makes a good ride. The North Shore is too congested. Kaua'i is small so you need a different attitude. You [don't] need [to] put in so many miles. Pack a picnic and go beach. Just enjoy nature and the open air.

duction directed by Brenda Turville and produced by Alain Dussaud and the Hawaii Association of Performing Arts. Line up early; seating is first come, first served.

Cinemas

For mainstream first-run movies, **Kukui Grove Cinemas** (Map p60; ☎ 245-5055; Kukui Grove Shopping Center, 3-2600 Kaumuali'i Hwy; adult/child $6/4,

before 5pm $4) is your standard shopping-mall fourplex. It's also a venue for the **Hawaii International Film Festival** (www.hiff.org).

Concerts

The **Kaua'i Community College Performing Arts Center** (Map p60) is home to the **Kaua'i Concert Association** (☎ 245-7464; www.kauai-concert.org), offering classical, jazz and dance concerts (tickets $30 to $45) at 7pm. Past performers include singer Angelique Kidjo, the Rubberbanddance Group and Alison Brown.

SHOPPING

Lihu'e's only major mall is **Kukui Grove Shopping Center** (Map p60; ☎ 245-7784; 3-2600 Kaumuali'i Hwy), which contains mostly chain stores, such as Macy's, Sears, Longs Drugs, Borders, Kmart, Radio Shack and banks. Near Nawiliwili Harbor, **Anchor Cove Shopping Center** (Map p60; ☎ 246-0634; 3416 Rice St) and **Harbor Mall** (Map p60; ☎ 245-6255; 3501 Rice St) draw mainly tourists from cruise ships and the nearby Marriott. Take a pass.

KOA STORE

our pick Map p60; ☎ 245-4871, 800-838-9264; www.thekoastore.com; 3-3601 Kuhio Hwy; 9am-6pm Mon-Sat, 10am-5pm Sun

Don't bother with 'Made in China' fakes sold cheap at touristy gift shops. Come to this welcoming shop for genuine koa handicrafts. Other stores carry higher-end masterpieces, but this place has affordable souvenirs, such as sleek chopsticks and desk accessories. Many items come in three grades, from the basic straight-grain koa to the rare, almost three-dimensional premium 'curly' koa.

KAPAIA STITCHERY

Map p60; ☎ 245-2281; 3-3551 Kuhio Hwy; 9am-5pm Mon-Sat

A quilter's heaven, this longtime shop features countless cotton fabrics, plus island-made patterns and kits. Stop here also for handmade gifts, such as children's clothing, Japanese kimono, potholders and an assortment of bags.

EDITH KING WILCOX GIFT SHOP

Map p62; www.kauaimuseum.org/store; Kaua'i Museum, 4428 Rice St; 9am-4pm Mon-Fri, 10am-4pm Sat

This gem of a gift shop at **Kaua'i Museum** (p64) features a variety of genuine Hawaiian crafts, such as Ni'ihau shell jewelry, koa woodwork and *lauhala* (pandanus leaf) hats, plus books on Hawaii and collectible ceramics. Enter the shop, free of charge, through the museum lobby.

GET DIRTY

Today, dyeing T-shirts with ecofriendly dirt isn't a novelty anymore. But the idea originated on Kaua'i back in the 1990s, after Hurricane 'Iniki slammed the island and blanketed everything (including blank white T-shirts) with the island's famous rust-red soil. The rich color is essentially rusted volcanic rock, with the redness coming from iron oxide. Among the Hawaiian Islands, only Kaua'i features such plentiful red dirt, thanks to 5 million years of erosion.

Locals might warn you to keep the dirt off towels and anything you'd prefer to keep clean and white. Once stained with island dirt, nothing can remove the telltale color. So while a red-dirt shirt is itself dirt-proof, it's liable to stain everything else in your laundry until it's been washed a few times.

Minds differ on who first invented the red-dirt shirt, but we recommend the **Real Dirt Shirt Hawaii** (☎ 888-918-5658; www.realdirthawaii.com) and **Red Earth Hawaii** (☎ 245-5123, 800-799-5834; www.redearthhawaii.com), both of which use all-natural dyeing processes and feature screen-printed, Kaua'i-themed designs. Red Earth Hawaii also offers kids' tees and women's tank tops and halters. Check websites for island retailers. The **Original Red Dirt Shirt** (☎ 335-5670, 800-717-3478; www.dirtshirt.com; 4350 Waialo Rd, 'Ele'ele; 8am-5pm Mon-Fri, 9am-5pm Sat & Sun) is a large company that's hard to miss, but they charge more and seem rather corporate, also producing Arizona-dirt shirts that closely resemble the Kaua'i ones.

The red-dirt T-shirt craze peaked in the 1990s, and by now the shirts are passé to locals. But it's still a cute way to take home an actual piece of Kaua'i. Note: when it's new, be sure to wash your T-shirt separately – and don't wear it in the rain!

Kaua'i Museum (p64)

JOHN ELK III

KILOHANA PLANTATION SHOPS

Map p60; www.kilohanakauai.com/shopping.htm; Kaumuali'i Hwy; most shops 10am-9pm Mon-Sat, to 4pm Sun

Nestled in an elegant historic manor, these classy shops will please the discriminating shopper. Find high-end jewelry, original art, woodwork, Raku pottery and aloha shirts. The picturesque historic setting is reason enough to stop here.

Two statewide chain stores are worth mentioning: on the positive side, **Longs Drugs** (Map p60; ☎ 245-7771; Kukui Grove Shopping Center, 3-2600 Kaumuali'i Hwy; 7am-10pm Mon-Sat, 8am-8pm Sun) is much more than a drugstore. Go here for an impressive selection of locally made products, from children's books to macadamia nuts to snacks galore.

As for **Hilo Hattie** (Map p62; ☎ 245-3404; www.hilohattie.com; 3-3252 Kuhio Hwy; 8:30am-6:30pm), that tourist beacon along Kuhio Hwy, all we can say is caveat emptor. While it's a convenient one-stop shop for generic souvenirs (eg macadamias), beware of exorbitant prices and a plethora of mediocre items made in China and the Philippines. Decades ago, Hilo Hattie hired local seamstresses to sew aloha attire but today, all clothing is foreign-made and, ironically, not good value. If you're seeking cheap shirts and trinkets, **Costco** (Map p60; ☎ 241-4000; www.costco.com; 4300 Nuhou St; 11am-8:30pm Mon-Fri, 9:30am-6pm Sat, 10am-6pm Sun) is far superior and carries some quality, locally made merchandise.

SLEEPING

Lihu'e's sleeping options are limited mostly to a few hotels, from the high-end Marriott to no-frills motels in the nondescript town center. Unlike on the Eastside, few B&Bs and inns operate in residential neighborhoods. For vacation-rental homes, contact **Kauai Vacation Rentals** (Map p62; ☎ 245-8841, 800-367-5025; www.kauaivacationrentals.com; 3-3311 Kuhio Hwy), where owner Lucy Kawaihalau is one of the island's most experienced and dedicated rental agents.

KAUA'I PALMS HOTEL
Motel $

Map p62; ☎ 246-0908; www.kauaipalmshotel.com; 2931 Kalena St; r from $75-85; office 7am-8pm;

The best budget option in town, Kaua'i Palms is a two-story, open-air motel with 28 tidy rooms. All include refrigerator, cable TV and windows on opposite walls to allow cooling cross-breezes. Pay more for rooms with kitchenettes and air-con. Wi-fi guaranteed only in lobby.

KAUA'I INN
Hotel $$

Map p60; ☎ 245-9000, 800-808-2330; www.kauai-inn.com; 2430 Hulemalu Rd; r with kitchenette incl breakfast $129-149;

In an ordinary residential area near **Alekoko Fishpond** (p66), this quiet inn offers a simple home base away from traffic and crowds. While not fancy, the 48 rooms include refrigerator and microwave; air-con costs $10 per day. Ground-floor rooms have back porches, while 2nd-floor rooms are larger but sans lanai. Rooms vary in decor and bed count; ask for tile floors over carpet. Three rooms for guests with disabilities are available.

GARDEN ISLAND INN
Hotel $$

our pick Map p60; ☎ 800-648-0154; www.gardenislandinn.com; 3445 Wilcox Rd; r $99-150, suite $145-180;

You won't find the Marriott's beachfront cachet and mega pool here. But this two-story inn across the street holds its own for value and friendliness. Rooms are modest but cheerful, with tropical decor, overhead

The Kaua'i Marriott Resort's pool overlooks Kalapaki Bay

ANN CECIL

fans, quality double beds and kitchenettes. The real gems are the suites on the 2nd and 3rd floors, with large, ocean-view lanai. **Kalapaki Beach** (p63) is just a minute away.

KAUA'I BEACH VILLAS
Condo $$

Map p60; ☎ reservations 800-367-5025; www.kauaivacationrentals.com; 1br unit per week $810-1250, 2br unit per week $1050-1750;

Just north of the Hilton, these condos are like Starbucks coffee: not fantastic, but definitely better than average. Units include full kitchen, washer/dryer, and lots of space (the 2-bedroom/2-bathroom units give two couples ample privacy). Buildings F, G and H are closest to the ocean and afford the best views – but the lagoon (artificial fountain) ain't bad at all! The pool is rather pathetic, but for $15 per day, guests can use the Hilton's amenities. Kauai Vacation Rentals, which manages 30 of the 60 condos, can steer you to an appropriate unit.

HILTON KAUA'I BEACH RESORT
Hotel $$$

Map p60; ☎ 245-1955, 888-805-3843, www.hilton.com; 4331 Kaua'i Beach Dr; r $189-229;

Located just north of Lihu'e, the 350-room Hilton will strike you as either conveniently central or in the middle of nowhere. It lacks the Marriott's prime location on Kalapaki Beach, but it does offer a quieter setting and lower rates. Rooms are business-class level, and there are restaurants and a spa on-site. Complimentary shuttle service to Coconut Marketplace (p93; from 10am to 4pm Saturday to Monday) in Wailua is also offered.

KAUA'I MARRIOTT RESORT
Hotel $$$

our pick Map p60; ☎ 245-5050, 800-220-2925; www.marriotthotels.com; 3610 Rice St; r $219-429;

Among Kaua'i's big-name hotels, the Marriott shines in every category. Fantastic, user-friendly beach. Two top golf courses. The island's liveliest oceanfront restaurant. Stunning 26,000-sq-ft, four-part pool fronting the beach. Hawaiian touches such as nene (Hawaiian geese) and a koa canoe in the grand atrium. Quick drive to varied eateries. You get the picture. On the downside, it is a gargantuan complex with 366 hotel rooms and 464 timeshare rooms: finding your door can be a major hike. Room decor and amenities are standard and rather staid. And it seems niggardly to charge $13 per day for in-room internet access.

Lihu'e's two cheapest motels are bleak (and cannot compare to similarly priced digs on the Eastside) but if necessary, here they are:

Motel Lani (Map p62; ☎ 245-2965; 4240 Rice St; r $55) You'd suffer consequences if you lodged your boss or mother here. But if the bottom line is your bottom line, consider this six-room flat. Located off a main street, the bare-bones rooms are shabby but clean and include a small refrigerator (no TV or phone). If you're seeking a substitute for the island's sketchy hostels, this is it.

Tip Top Motel (Map p62; ☎ 245-2333; tiptop@aloha.net; 3173 Akahi St; r $65;) Consider this budget motel only in a pinch. The price is simply too high for the drab institutional decor (picture white cinder-block walls, linoleum floors, iron-gated windows and fluorescent lighting). Rooms include cable TV and either a king or two twin beds. There is one saving grace: yummy pancakes at the motel's highly recommended restaurant (p70).

GETTING THERE & AWAY

Air

All commercial flights arrive at **Lihu'e Airport** (LIH; ☎ 246-1448; www.hawaii.gov/dot/air ports/kauai/lih; visitor hotline 6:30am-9pm), located 1.5 miles east of Lihu'e.

The small airport is simple to negotiate, and the only problem you might encounter is rush-hour traffic as you exit Lihu'e. Try to avoid arriving in the late afternoon, as traffic will be crawling in either direction.

Boat

The only seafaring options are cruises, such as the seven-day, four-island tour offered by **Norwegian Cruise Line** (see p275). On Kaua'i, the *Pride of America* docks at Nawiliwili Harbor on Thursdays, for one night.

Bus

As the hub for the **Kaua'i Bus** (p275), Lihu'e has service to all major island regions, including Hanalei, the Eastside and the Westside. Check website for current schedules.

Car & Motorcycle

Kaua'i remains very rural, with only one coastal highway connecting all major destinations. If you miss a turn, chill out. You cannot get lost here.

For car rentals, see p276.

At a cost of almost $200 per day, plus a $1000 security deposit, the price might deter some, but **Kaua'i Harley-Davidson** (Map p60; ☎ 241-7020, 877-212-9253; www.kauaih-d.com; 3-1866 Kaumuali'i Hwy; per day $167-188) does brisk business renting its 26-bike fleet. More affordable are mopeds, available at **Kauai Scooter Rental** (☎ 245-7177; www.kauaimopedrentals.com; 3371 Wilcox Rd; 8am-5pm) for $59 per day (from 8am to 5pm) and $75 for 24 hours. Staffers train new moped users until they're confident enough to hit the road – and there's no obligation if you change your mind. See p278.

GETTING AROUND

To/From the Airport

To pick up rental cars, customers generally check in at the booths outside the baggage-claim area and then catch vans to the actual lots. Here's a tip: go straight to the rental-car lot, where you can also check in (with less of a queue).

Taxicabs are rarely used because most visitors rent cars, but you can find them (as well as phones to call one) at curbside of the baggage-claim area. Average fares from Lihu'e airport include Kapa'a ($20), Lihu'e ($10) and Po'ipu ($35 to $40).

Bus

Kaua'i Bus (p275) serves Lihu'e with a shuttle that runs hourly from 6am to about 7pm, with stops at obvious destinations such as Kukui Grove Shopping Center, Lihu'e Airport, Vidinha Stadium, Wal-Mart, Wilcox Memorial Hospital and Big Save. There's also a lunch shuttle that runs at 15-minute intervals within central Lihu'e.

Car & Motorcycle

Kaua'i is a driving town, so most businesses have parking lots and street parking is relatively easy to find. Metered parking in Lihu'e costs 25¢ for 30 minutes. For information about car and motorcycle rentals, see left or p276.

Horses grazing by the road to Wailua Falls (p66)

MERTEN SNIJDERS

EASTSIDE

Since ancient times, people have revered the majestic Wailua River, surrounded by mountaintop forests, grassy pastures and pounding surf; to appreciate the real Eastside, venture *mauka* (mountainward) or *makai* (seaward), beyond the strip malls and highway traffic. Kaua'i's population is concentrated here, creating enough critical mass for variety in restaurants, shops and people – more 'real life' than 'resort living.' Along the highway, Wailua, Waipouli and Kapa'a blend into the 'Coconut Coast,' a commercial stretch that's either eyesore or efficient, take your pick. To the north is Anahola, a rustic land where Native Hawaiians constitute 70% of all residents.

EASTSIDE ITINERARIES

IN TWO DAYS *This leg: 10 miles*

❶ **SMALL TOWN CAFÉ (p104)** Enjoy your first sunrise at this Kapa'a coffeehouse, painted an unmistakable turquoise blue. Kick back with gourmet coffee and pastries, the local daily or free wi-fi.

❷ **KE ALA HELE MAKAMAE (p102)** Before the noon heat, cruise the coastal path on a bike (or walk, jog or rollerblade) from **Kapa'a Beach Park (p100)** to past **Donkey Beach (p110)**.

❸ **KEALIA BEACH (p108)** In the afternoon, surfers and sunbathers should head to this beach for formidable waves and a fierce tan. For toddlers, the best choice is **Fujii Beach (p100)**, known for its shallow, calm waters.

❹ **SHAKA TACOS (p104)** On Friday nights, catch jazz musicians Denny Morouse and David Braun at this open-air Kapa'a eatery. Go early: Kaua'i's midnight is 9pm.

❺ **WAILUA RIVER KAYAK TOUR (p86)** Start day two with an invigorating kayak paddle up the largest river across Hawaii. Your sweat will be rewarded by a waterfall swim.

❻ **KEAHUA ARBORETUM (p85)** Pack some picnic foods and head to Wailua's refreshingly lush upcountry, where tall trees and a babbling brook couldn't be more picturesque.

❼ **TIN CAN MAILMAN (p93)** Whether or not you're a Hawaiiana collector, this overflowing shop of rare books and quality memorabilia makes for compelling browsing. Continue your shopping spree up the coast: modern fashionistas can find unique temptations at **Bambulei (p93)** and **Marta's Boat (p98)**, or for aloha shirts and dresses, try **Hula Girl (p106)**.

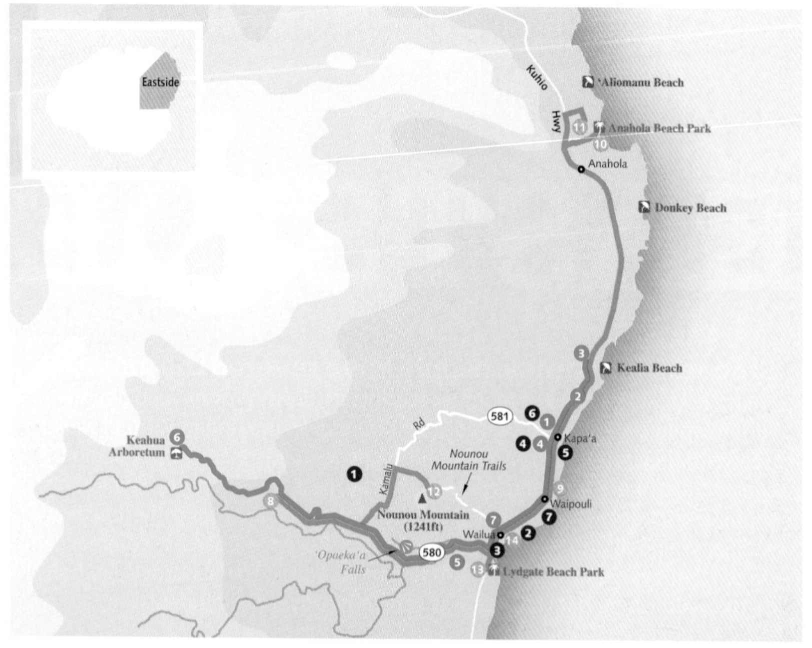

IN FOUR DAYS *This leg: 26 miles*

❽ KAUA'I HINDU MONASTERY (p84) On your third day, visit the grounds of a magnificent Hindu monastery, where the tropical foliage surpasses most parks and a massive stone temple is under construction.

❾ PAPAYA'S NATURAL FOODS (p97) Stop at the island's longtime go-to health-food store for takeout lunch fixings. Then choose a beach spot and spread a *goza* (straw mat) for an impromptu picnic.

❿ ANAHOLA BEACH PARK (p108) Most visitors miss this rural beach, frequented by neighborhood residents, many Native Hawaiian. Much of Anahola is designated as Hawaiian Home Lands, which are reserved for homesteading by the native people. It's a sweet spot for swimming (and surfing at the south end) but tread lightly: respect the locals.

⓫ ANGELINE'S MU'OLAULANI (p111) For an only-on-Kaua'i experience, get a genuine Hawaiian *lomilomi* massage at this longtime family-run center. If you want more variety of facial and body treatments, including an oceanfront massage, try Spa by the Sea (p102) in Kapa'a.

⓬ NOUNOU MOUNTAIN HIKE (p89) Welcome the morning of day four by climbing the 'Sleeping Giant' – Nounou Mountain – from any one of its three approaches. You can expect a steep, sweaty hike, with a reward of panoramic views from mountain to ocean.

⓭ LYDGATE BEACH PARK (p83) Finish up your stay with a leisurely afternoon at this kid-pleasing beach park. The little ones will find hours of amusement in its gigantic, community-made playgrounds.

⓮ KINTARO (p92) If you want to dine among the locals, head out early to this phenomenally popular Japanese restaurant, which specializes in expertly done *teppanyaki* (table cooking on a gas grill).

FOR FOODIES

❶ CHOCOLATE FARM TOUR (p83) Learn about Kaua'i-grown cacao at a thriving family farm, where you'll also see groves of bamboo, tropical flowers, vanilla and fruit trees. The clincher is the 11-course dark-chocolate tasting, featuring fine chocolate from around the world.

❷ HUKILAU LANAI (p92) Fine dining need not be froufrou, as shown by the casually elegant dining room and simply delicious Hawaii regional cuisine found here.

❸ ICING ON THE CAKE (p91) For elegant cakes made to order, this patisserie never fails to impress. If the coconut macaroons are available, don't think twice: buy them all.

❹ HAWAIIAN BLIZZARD (p104) No trip to Kaua'i is complete without a heaping cup of shave ice, specifically the superior creations made by the island's low-key guru of this uniquely Hawaiian treat.

❺ PONO MARKET (p104) Curious about the local plate lunch, *poke* (marinated raw fish) and Spam *musubi* (Japanese rice ball)? Go for it, but only at the tried-and-true local favorites like this family-run shop.

❻ KAPA'A FARMERS MARKET (p253) To find locally grown produce, you can cozy up to the locals – or simply bring a bag and wad of bills to the farmers market.

❼ SWEET MARIE'S HAWAII (p97) Gluten-free goes decadently gourmet, with lusciously moist cakes and hearty fruit-and-nut-filled muffins that would please any palate.

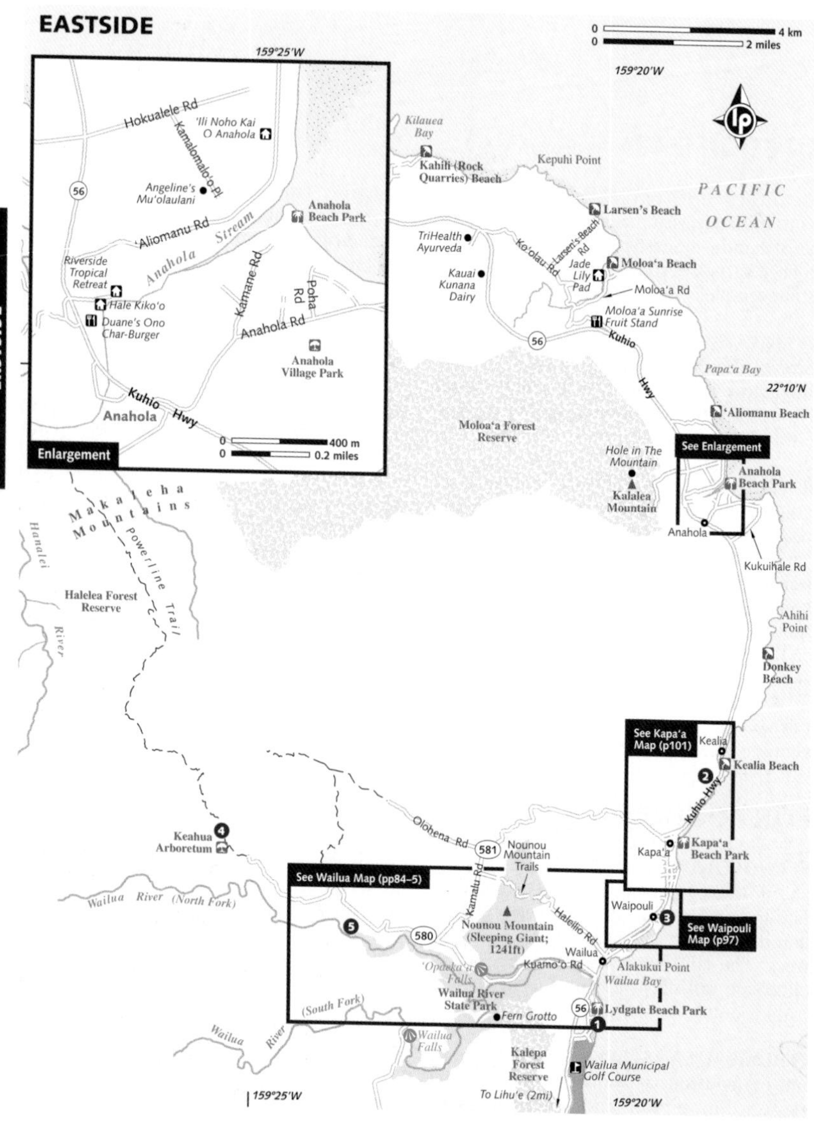

WAILUA

pop (incl Wailua Homesteads) 6650

If you're looking for an Eastside home base, it's hard to top Wailua. Unlike the touristy meccas you'll find up north and down south, it's a low-key vacation spot – and that's a compliment. Choose an oceanfront condo for a 24/7 soundtrack of waves or else head to lush, upcountry Wailua Homesteads (pop 4567) for B&Bs and vacation rentals. Wailua's other attractions include a whimsical kiddie playground, a gigantic Hindu monastery, and the only navigable river in the entire state.

HIGHLIGHTS

❶ **BEST BEACH:** Lydgate Beach Park (below)
❷ **BEST VIEW:** Sunrise along the coastal path (p102)
❸ **BEST ACTIVITY:** Surfing with Ambrose Curry (p96)
❹ **BEST LITTLE-KNOWN PICNIC SPOT:** Keahua Arboretum (p85)
❺ **BEST UNEXPECTED SIGHT:** Kaua'i Hindu Monastery (p84)

Highlights are numbered on the map on p82.

Orientation

Don't look for a town center. Most attractions are scattered along Kuhio Hwy (Hwy 56) or along Kuamoʻo Rd (Hwy 580), which leads *mauka* (inland). To get to Kapaʻa or beyond, take the Kapaʻa Bypass Rd, which runs from Coconut Plantation to north Kapaʻa.

Beaches

LYDGATE BEACH PARK

our pick You name it, Lydgate's got it. Safe swimming, convenient shore snorkeling, two children's playgrounds, game-sized soccer fields, a 2.5-mile bicycle/pedestrian path, pavilions, picnic tables and ample parking. A volunteer group (www.kamalani.org) built and continues to maintain the park's unique features, especially the multi-featured **Kamalani Playground** (found at the north end) and the simpler, two-level **Kamalani Kai Bridge** (at the south end). If you're seeking a secluded, pristine beach, Lydgate might seem too built-up. But most families will appreciate having multiple diversions for multiple (or easily bored) kids. Remember, the shallow seawater pool is calm thanks to the protective stone breakwater, but beware of the open ocean beyond the pool. Other amenities here include changing rooms, rest rooms, showers, drinking water and a lifeguard. To get here, turn *makai* (seaward) on Kuhio Hwy between the 5- and 6-mile markers.

Sights

See the **Kaua'i Heritage Trail** (wailuaheritagetrail.org) website and map for an overview of major sights.

SMITH'S TROPICAL PARADISE

☎ 821-6895; www.smithskauai.com/tropical_garden.html; Wailua River Marina; adult/child 3-12 $6/3; 🕓 8:30am-4pm

CACAO: THE NEXT BIG BEAN

The world's chocolate comes mainly from West Africa, Brazil, Equador, Malaysia and Indonesia. But Kaua'i's humid tropical climate and regular rain allows the prized cacao bean to grow here, too. It's among the specialty crops that local-agriculture proponents are touting for Hawaii's next generation of farmers. Learn more about diversified agriculture and cacao growing at **our pick** **Steelgrass Farm** (☎ 821-1857; www.steelgrass.org; adult/child 12 & under $60/free; 🕓 9am-noon Mon, Wed & Fri), which offers a unique chocolate farm tour that includes an 11-course chocolate tasting of single-estate dark chocolate bars produced around the world, including the Big Island's 'Original Hawaiian Chocolate Factory, ' American Dagoba and French Valrhona.

Their other crops are timber bamboo and vanilla, but the 8-acre farm features hundreds of thriving tropical species, which you'll also see on the tour. It's a fantastic introduction if you're curious to see what thrives on Kaua'i, from avocados and citrus to soursop and jaboticaba.

The owners, Will and Emily Lydgate, are the great-grandchildren of Kaua'i minister and community leader John Mortimer Lydgate, namesake of Lydgate Beach Park (above). The property was not an inheritance, as 'JM' had no desire to acquire land or profit from the sugar industry. With this thriving example of a 'teaching farm' – meant to experiment with workable crops – the Lydgates are trying to encourage a shift away from the monocrops and sheer capital outlays of industrial agriculture toward small-scale farming and diversified crops instead.

Read more about the family's intriguing history on the website; specific location info is given out when booking a tour.

Other gardens might have fancier landscaping or loftier goals, but you can't beat Smith's for value. For six dollars, you can leisurely stroll a loop trail past a serene pond, grassy lawns and island-themed gardens. The setting can seem Disney-esque, with an Easter Island replica and tour trams, but it's appealingly unpretentious and large enough to accommodate all. The Smith's family-run luau (p92) is held on the garden grounds.

KAUA'I'S HINDU MONASTERY

☎ 822-3012; www.himalayanacademy.com; 107 Kaholalele Rd; 9am-noon

Serious pilgrims and curious sightseers alike are welcome at the island's splendid Hindu monastery, set on 458 acres of buoyantly thriving rainforest above the Wailua River. The astoundingly green setting (enhanced by the monks' back-breaking gardening) equals that of a commercial garden. The temples, Ganesh statues and other structures are devoted to the god Shiva. While visitors can access a limited area (self-guided tour) from 9am to noon daily, we highly recommend taking a free guided tour offered once a week; call ☎ 888-735-1619 for tour dates and parking reservations.

Currently the temple in use is **Kadavul Temple**, where guests can see the world's largest single-pointed quartz crystal, a 50-million-year-old, six-sided wonder that weighs 700lb and stands over 3ft tall. In the temple, meditating monks have been rotating in three-hour vigils round the clock since the temple was established in 1973.

Under construction is the ambitious **Iraivan Temple**, a monumental and almost incongruously imposing structure that's being entirely hand-carved from white granite by a village of artisans in Bangalore, India.

KAMOKILA HAWAIIAN VILLAGE

☎ 823-0559; Kuamo'o Rd; self-guided tour adult/child 5-12 $5/3; 9am-5pm

While not a must-see, this replica village is a pleasant diversion, especially for kids. It's located along the Wailua River and includes traditional structures, from Canoe House to Chief's Assembly House, amid thriving gardens of guava, mango and banana trees.

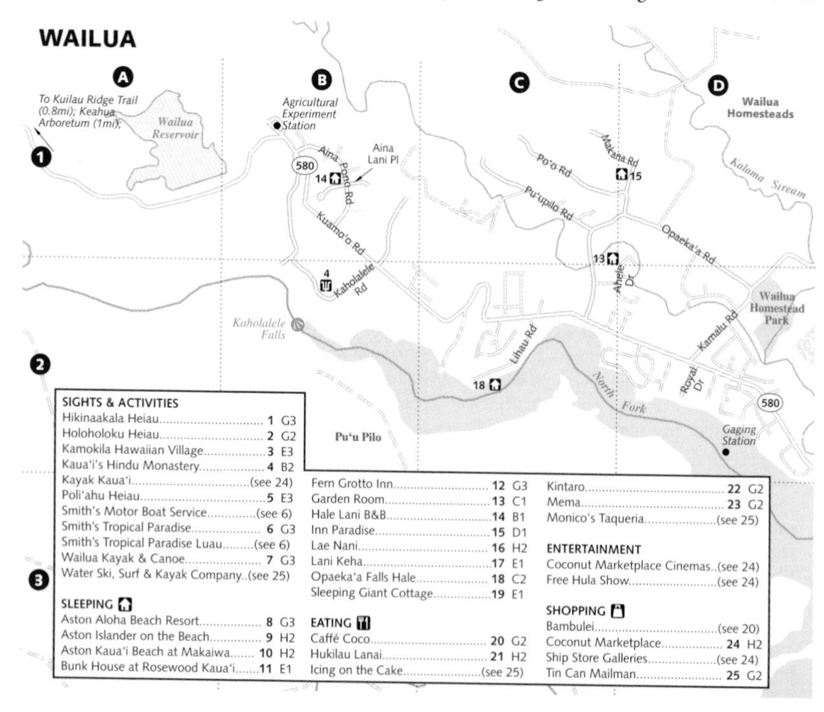

Use your imagination! You're on your own here, but the site is modest and the simple map given is sufficient.

Kamokila also offers **outrigger canoe tours** (adult/child $30/20; departures hourly 9:30am-2:30pm), which include a paddle, hike and waterfall swim. Because you start farther upriver from the mouth, the trip is shorter than going by kayak (see p86) and a Hawaiian guide is guaranteed.

To get here, turn south from Kuamo'o Rd, opposite 'Opaeka'a Falls. The half-mile road leading to the village is very steep and narrow.

'OPAEKA'A FALLS

Kuamo'o Rd, btwn 1-mile & 2-mile markers

While not a showstopper, this 40ft waterfall makes an easy roadside stop. For the best photo conditions, go in the morning. Don't be tempted to try trailblazing to the base of the falls. The steep cliffs are perilous, as shown in 2006 when two tourists died after falling almost 300ft while hiking. Instead, after viewing the falls, cross the road for a fantastic photo op of the Wailua River.

Island Insights

Take a look at **Nounou Mountain**. What do you see?

Islanders see the Sleeping Giant. According to legend, an amicable giant fell asleep on the hillside after gorging at a luau. His *menehune* ('little people') friends tried to rouse him by throwing stones. But the stones bounced from his full belly into his open mouth and lodged in his throat. He died in his sleep and turned into rock.

Now he rests, stretched with his head in Wailua and his feet in Kapa'a. At an elevation of almost 1250ft, the giant's forehead is the highest point on the ridge.

KEAHUA ARBORETUM

Kuamo'o Rd

A local favorite picnic spot at the end of Kuamo'o Rd, this arboretum resembles storybook countryside, with grassy fields, gurgling stream and groves of teak, eucalyptus, shower and other tall trees. Locals

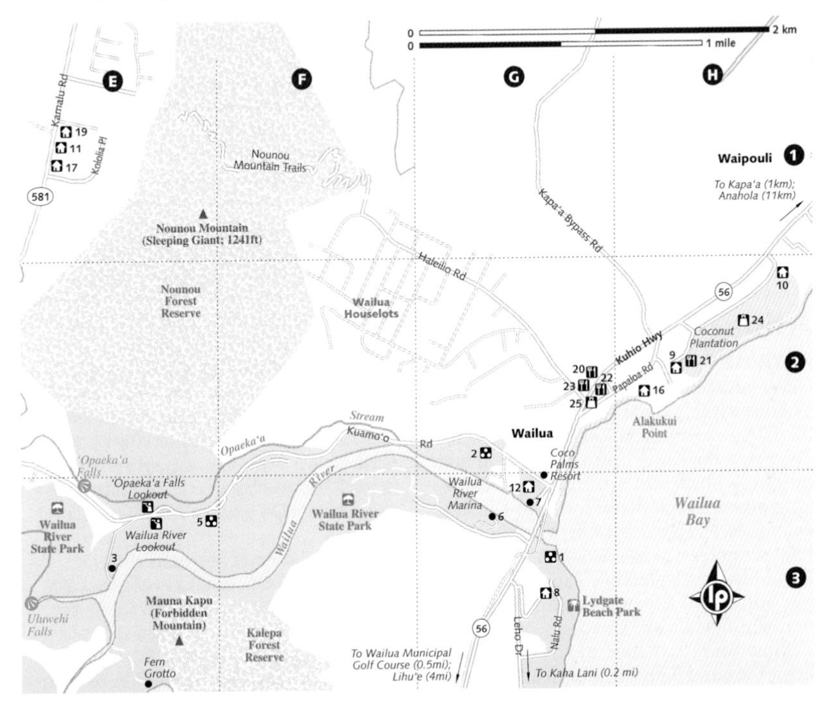

The Wailua River is the only navigable river in Hawaii

LUCI YAMAMOTO

enjoy swimming or splashing in the freshwater stream and pools, but remember that the water can contain the leptospirosis bacterium. The road continues past the arboretum parking lot, but you must cross water – not recommended if you're driving a standard car, especially if rainy.

WAILUA BAY

Despite its natural beauty, this sandy bay is generally a 'drive-by' attraction. The water is typically too rough for swimming, although a summer surf break toward the south draws locals and surf students. The sweeping stretch of sand is nice for walking but its location at the heavily trafficked Wailua Bridge makes the beach annoyingly visible and noisy.

Activities

KAYAKING

Never kayaked? No problem. The legendary Wailua River paddle is a doable 5 miles for all ages and fitness levels. Tours usually don't pass the Fern Grotto and instead take the river's north fork, which leads to a mile-long hike through dense forest to Uluwehi Falls (Secret Falls), a 130ft waterfall. The hike scrambles over rocks and roots, and if muddy it will probably cause some slippin' and slidin'. Tip: wear sturdy, washable, non-slip sandals like Chacos.

Most tours last four to five hours and depart around 7am or noon (call for exact check-in times). The maximum group size is 12, with paddlers going out in double kayaks. The pricier tours include lunch, but on budget tours, you can store your own food in coolers and waterproof bags. Bring a hat, sunscreen and mosquito repellent.

Experienced paddlers might want to rent individual kayaks and go out on their own. Prices wildly vary. Note that not all tour companies are licensed to rent individual kayaks. Kayakers must stay on the north side of the river, while the Smith's boats (see opposite) cruise in the center. No kayak tours or rentals are allowed on Sundays. Of course, non-commercial kayaks are always allowed on the river, seven days a week.

Of the following companies, Kayak Kaua'i and Outfitters Kaua'i are big and established, with many other tour offerings. But the two recommended little guys offer better value for this basic tour.

our pick **Kayak Wailua** (☎ 822-3388; www.kayakwailua.com; Kuhio Hwy, Wailua; tour per person $40) This small, family-owned outfit specializes in Wailua River tours. They keep boats and equipment in tip-top shape and provide dry bags for your belongings and a nylon cooler for your BYO snacks. If you prefer to speed ahead of the group, they're flexible enough to accommodate different preferences.

our pick **Wailua Kayak Adventures** (Map p97; ☎ 822-5795, 639-6332; www.kauaiwailuakayak.com; Kuhio Hwy, Waipouli; s/d kayaks per day $25/50, tour per couple $85; check-in 7am & 1pm) Go here for the cheapest individual kayak rentals. They offer three, budget-friendly Wailua River tours (which include generous snacks at the waterfall). Call for times, as they vary slightly for each tour. Located behind Lemongrass restaurant in Waipouli.

Wailua Kayak & Canoe (Map pp84-5; ☎ 821-1188; Wailua River State Park; s/d kayak per 5hr $45/75, tour per person $55-90) Located at the boat ramp on the north bank, this outfit is very convenient for individual rentals (no need to transport the kayak). Tour quality is fine but their prices have skyrocketed since 2006.

Kayak Kaua'i (Map pp84-5; ☎ 826-9844, 800-437-3507; www.kayakkauai.com; Coconut Marketplace, 4-484 Kuhio Hwy, Wailua; d kayak per person per day $27, tour per adult/child under 12 $85/60; check-in 7:45am & 12:15pm) This longstanding and reputable outfit, with shop locations in Wailua and Hanalei (p133), offers river and sea kayaking tours, including the Na Pali challenge. Rates run high, but lunch is included. A good choice if you need a Japanese- or Spanish-fluent guide.

Outfitters Kaua'i (Map pp164-5; ☎ 742-9667, 888-742-9887; www.outfitterskauai.com; Po'ipu Plaza, 2827-A Poipu Rd, Po'ipu; kayak per person per day $40, tour adult/child 5-14 $98/78; check-in 7:45am) Known for their multi-adventure tours, this established outfit is good except for their steep prices.

BOAT RIDES

If you're curious to see the legendary **Fern Grotto**, there's only one way to get up close – or at least as close as you can get. **Smith's Motor Boat Service** (☎ 821-6892; www.smithskauai.com; adult/child 2-12 $20/10; departures every 30min 9-11:30am & 12:30-3:30pm) has had exclusive rights since 1946 to ply the river in covered riverboats (they're the size of a bus) to the grotto. Bear in mind that since the heavy rains and rockslides of 2006, visitors cannot enter the grotto itself but must stay on the wooden platform quite a distance from the shallow cave.

Island Insights

The 12-mile-long Wailua River is the state's only navigable river. It's formed by the convergence of two large streams, known as its north and south forks, which are both fed by Mt Wai'ale'ale.

THE SACRED WAILUA RIVER

To ancient Hawaiians, the Wailua River was among the most sacred places across the islands. The river basin, near its mouth, was one of the island's two royal centers (the other was Waimea) and home to the high chiefs. Here, you can find the remains of many important heiau (religious sites) including:

Hikinaakala Heiau (rising of the sun) sits south of the Wailua River mouth, which is today the north end of Lydgate Beach Park (p83). In its heyday, the long, narrow temple (c AD 1200) was aligned directly north to south, but only a few remaining boulders outline its original massive shape. The neighboring **Hauola Pu'uhonua** (dew of life; place of refuge) is marked by a bronze plaque. Ancient Hawaiian *kapu* (taboo) breakers were assured safety from persecution if they made it inside.

Believed to be the oldest *luakini* (temple of human sacrifice) on the island, **Holoholoku Heiau** is located a quarter mile up Kuamo'o Rd on the left. The whole area was royal property: toward the west, against the flat-backed birthstone (marked by a plaque reading 'Pohaku Ho'ohanau' (royal birthstone), queens gave birth to future kings. Only a male child born here could become king of Kaua'i. Another stone a few yards away, marked 'Pohaku Piko,' was where the *piko* (umbilical cords) of the babies were left.

Perched high on a hill overlooking the meandering Wailua River, the well-preserved **Poli'ahu Heiau**, another *luakini,* is named after the snow goddess Poli'ahu, one of the volcano goddess Pele's sisters. Poli'ahu Heiau is located immediately before the 'Opaeka'a Falls lookout, on the opposite side of the road.

Bear in mind, unmarked Hawaiian heiau might not catch your eye. Although they were originally imposing stone structures, most now lie in ruins, covered with scrub. It takes a leap of imagination for non-Hawaiians to appreciate heiau, but they are still powerful, set in places of great mana (spiritual energy).

Find an excellent brochure on the Wailua complex of heiau at www.hawaiistateparks.org/pdf/brochures/Hikinaakala.pdf. For a compelling history on the Wailua River's meaning to ancient Hawaiians, see Edward Joesting's *Kauai: The Separate Kingdom*.

The famous Fern Grotto LINDA CHING

The Fern Grotto, formed below an overhanging cliff at the base of **Mauna Kapu** (Forbidden Mountain), looks rather tired nowadays, having suffered from a localized drought since the 1990s, when the sugar plantations above the cliff went out of production and weren't irrigated anymore. The elongated sword ferns and delicate maidenhair seem to be struggling. If you're expecting an eye-popping emerald cascade, you might as well find old pictures.

Still, the 1½-hour round-trip ride has its charms. Think hokey but homespun. Along the leisurely ride out, a guide (or two, if Japanese-speakers are aboard) narrate facts and anecdotes about the river. At the wooden platform, musicians serenade all couples with 'Ke Kali Nei Au,' known as the 'Hawaiian Wedding Song' after Elvis Presley sang it in English in *Blue Hawaii*. The return trip features Hawaiian music and hula. Most passengers come from tour groups and tend toward the older and less adventurous.

HIKING

Eastside hikes ascend into Kaua'i's tropical-jungle interior. Expect humid air, red dirt (or mud) and slippery patches after rains. All mileage distances given here are one way. See the Eastside Trails map (p89).

KUILAU RIDGE & MOALEPE TRAILS

The **Kuilau Ridge Trail** (2.1 miles) is recommended for its sheer beauty: emerald valleys, colorful birds, dewy bushes, thick ferns and glimpses of misty Mt Wai'ale'ale in the distance. After 1 mile, you'll see a grassy clearing with a picnic table; continue east in descending switchbacks until you reach the **Moalepe Trail** (2.25 miles). From here on, you'll see Nounou Mountain and the Makaleha Mountains.

While they are independent trails, the two are often mentioned together because they connect to each other and can be hiked in sequence. Both are moderate hikes and among the most visually rewarding on Kaua'i. Remember, the trails don't complete a circuit so you will have to retrace your steps on a 9-mile out-and-back trek. Mountain bikers would also enjoy these forestland trails, although they're used mostly by hikers and hunters.

If you plan on doing only one trail, choose the Kuilau Ridge Trail because it takes you immediately into the forest wilderness, while the first mile of the Moalepe Trail crosses the simple, treeless pastureland of the Wailua Game Management Area. Both trails are well maintained and signposted.

The Kuilau Ridge Trail starts at a marked trailhead on the right, found just before Kuamo'o Rd crosses the stream at the Keahua Arboretum, 4 miles above the junction of Kuamo'o Rd and Kamalu Rd. The Moalepe Trail trailhead is at the end of Olohena Rd where it bends into Waipouli Rd.

Island Insights

Charles E King, who wrote 'Ke Kali Nei Au' (now known as the 'Hawaiian Wedding Song') in 1926, is among Hawaii's revered composers. He was one-quarter Native Hawaiian and raised among royalty: Queen Emma was his godmother. Queen Lili'iuokalani was his music teacher. Fluent in the Hawaiian language, King strove to keep Hawaiian music true to its roots, with Hawaiian lyrics, Hawaiian themes and the melodic quality *nahenahe* (sweet) rather than 'jazzed up.'

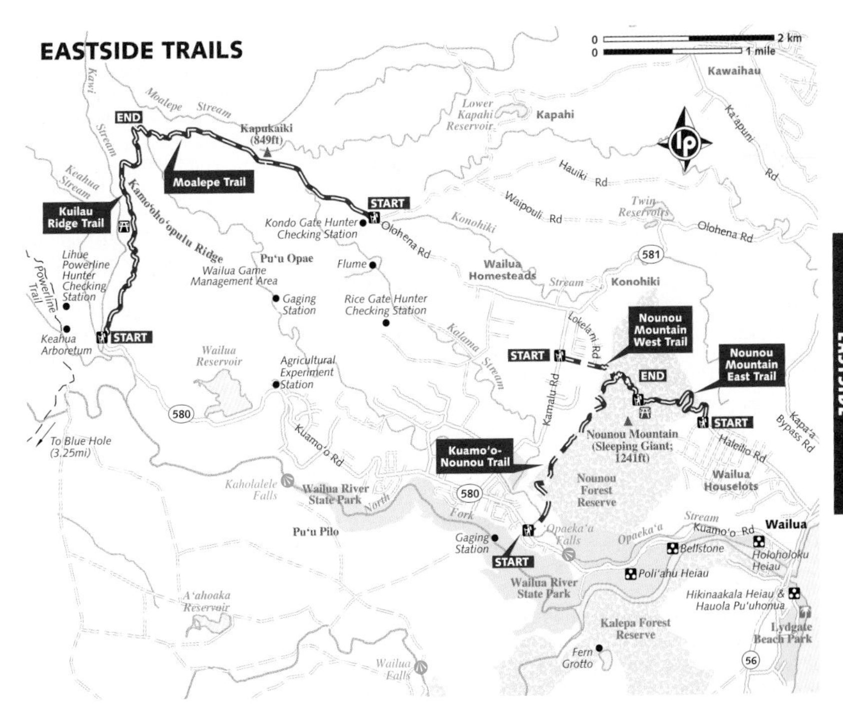

NOUNOU MOUNTAIN TRAILS

Climbing Nounou Mountain (Sleeping Giant), you'll ascent over 1000ft, but the views of Kaua'i's Eastside panorama are a worthy reward. You can approach the mountain from the east on the **Nounou Mountain East Trail** (1.75 miles), from the west on the **Nounou Mountain West Trail** (1.5 miles) and from the south on the **Kuamo'o-Nounou Trail** (2 miles). The trails meet near the center.

Visitors tend to prefer the exposed East Trail because it offers sweeping views of the ocean and distant mountains. The well-maintained trail is moderately strenuous, climbing through wild thickets of guava, *liliko'i* (passion fruit) and ironwood. The trail is steep, with switchbacks almost to the ridge. At the three-way junction near the top, take the left fork, which will lead to the summit, marked by a picnic shelter. Now atop the giant's chest, only his head prevents you from a 360-degree view. Climbing farther is extremely risky and not recommended.

It's best to do this hike early in the morning, when it's relatively cool and you can witness daylight spreading across the valley. The hard-packed dirt trail is exceedingly slippery when wet; look for a walking stick (hikers will sometimes leave some near the trailhead).

The East Trail starts at a parking lot a mile up Haleilio Rd in the Wailua Houselots neighborhood. When the road curves left, look for telephone pole #38 with the trailhead sign.

The West Trail ascends faster, but it's better to take if you prefer a cooler forest trail. Much of the hike is shaded by towering Norfolk pines and other trees. There are two ways to access the trailhead: from

Island Insights

Mt Wai'ale'ale (5148ft), almost smack in the middle of the island, is considered the second-wettest place on earth, averaging 460in of rain annually. Mawsynram, India, averages about 7 inches more per year, but its rainfall is seasonal.

Kamalu Rd, near telephone pole 11, or from the end of Lokelani Rd, off Kamalu Rd. Walk through a metal gate marked as a forestry right-of-way.

The Kuamo'o-Nounou Trail runs through groves of trees planted in the 1930s by the Civilian Conservation Corps; it connects with the West Trail. The trailhead is right on Kuamo'o Rd, near a grassy field between the 2- and 3-mile markers.

For guided hikes, the gold standard is geologist Chuck Blay's company, **Kaua'i Nature Tours** (☎ 742-8305, 888-233-8365; www.kauainaturetours.com; adult/child 7-12 $115/85), which offers an all-day tour that includes lunch and transportation.

GOLF

Ranked among the finest municipal golf courses nationally, the **Wailua Municipal Golf Course** (☎ 241-6666; green fees weekday/weekend & holidays $32/44, optional cart rental $18, club rental from $29) is an 18-hole, par-72 course off Kuhio Hwy immediately south of Wailua. Plan ahead because morning tee times are reserved perhaps a week in advance at this popular course, designed by former head pro Toyo Shirai. After 2pm, green fees drop by half and no reservations are taken.

Just before press time, the county announced a possible major increase in fees during the next seven years. If adopted, the weekday rate would jump 47% to $60 in the first year and then $5 more every other year. Call to check before you head over.

WATER SKIING AND WAKEBOARDING

The only non-ocean waterskiing in the state is found here on the Wailua, only from the Wailua Bridge to the first big bend in the river.

Try waterskiing or wakeboarding with a tow by **Water Ski, Surf & Kayak Company** (☎ 822-3574; Kinipopo Shopping Village, 4-356 Kuhio Hwy; per 30/60min $75/140; 9am-5pm Mon-Fri, 9am-noon Sat). The company also rents water equipment, including surfboards (per day/week $10/50, $200 deposit), bodyboards (per day/week $5/20, $75 deposit) and snorkel gear (per day/week $5/15, $75 deposit).

MOUNTAIN BIKING

While the **Powerline Trail** (which covers 13 miles, between Wailua and Princeville) is used mainly by hunters, it's a decent option for diehard mountain bikers. Hikers might find the trek rather too long, too

THE MYSTERIOUS BLUE HOLE

How close can you get to Mt Wai'ale'ale by foot? If you can find **Blue Hole** (off Map p89) you're there. It's not a 'hole' per se but a pool fed by a pretty stream and waterfall.

To get here, take Kuamo'o Rd up to Keahua Arboretum. Unless you're driving a 4WD, you should park in the lot and hike in. The unpaved road is head-jarringly rough, and the mud can engulf ordinary cars. Either way, head left onto Wailua Forest Management Rd. After less than 1.5 miles, you'll reach a junction; turn right (a gate blocks the left direction). Go straight for about 2 miles. Along the way, you'll pass an otherworldly forest of false staghorn, guava, eucalyptus and native *mamane* and *ohia*. The dense foliage introduces you to a rainbow of greens, from deep evergreen to eye-popping chartreuse.

This setting substituted for Costa Rica in *Dragonfly* and for the prehistoric era in *Jurassic Park*. As you drive in, look to your left at a wide clearing, which served as the trailer camp during filming. When Kevin Costner drove down this dirt road while filming *Dragonfly*, the weather was dry, so sprinklers were installed alongside to simulate rain.

You will then reach a locked yellow gate; it is meant to keep out cars, but the state allows foot traffic (the mud actually deters most people from willingly hiking here). This gate is where the entrance gate to *Jurassic Park* stood. From here you must slosh 1320yd till you reach the dammed stream, which is the north fork of Wailua River. The stream rises and falls depending on the season and rainfall. Occasionally it is deep enough for kids to swim.

Blue Hole is a quiet, secluded spot, not a tourist destination by a long shot. To avoid getting stuck or lost, join **Aloha Kaua'i Tours** (☎ 800-452-8113; www.alohakauaitours.com; adult/child 5-12 $80/50) for a half-day tour that includes rain gear, walking sticks and snacks.

exposed and, especially toward the north, too monotonous (although that might be just the challenge you relish!). The trail is never crowded and it traverses an otherwise inaccessible north–south region. Beware of hidden, steep drop-offs hidden in the dense foliage. Expect to slog through mud and puddly ruts.

The south end of the trail begins across the stream at the Keahua Arboretum (p85), at the end of Kuamo'o Rd. Consider starting from the Princeville end, where it's less messy. Just south of Princeville, look for the Princeville Ranch Stables (p127) turnoff. This is Po'oku Rd. The trail starts about 2 miles down this road, near an obvious water tank.

The Powerline Trail is actually a former maintenance road for the electric powerlines running along the mountains between Wailua and the North Shore. When the powerlines were established back in the 1930s, county officials used land vehicles to access them. Today helicopters are the mode of choice, so the road has fallen into disuse.

Top Picks

EASTSIDE FOR KIDS

- **Lydgate Beach Park and giant playgrounds** (p83)
- **Pono Market ice-cream concoctions** (p104)
- **Riding coaster bikes along the coast** (p102)
- **Fun Factory arcade** (☎ 822-3660; Waipouli Town Center; games 50¢-$1; 10am-10pm, to midnight Fri & Sat)
- **Baby Beach for tots** (p100)
- **Shave ice** (p104)
- **Wailua River kayaking** (p86)
- **Keahua Arboretum picnic** (p85)
- **Marta's Boat (for girls)** (p98)
- **Esprit De Corps Riding Academy** (p102)

Festivals & Events

Taste of Hawaii (www.tasteofhawaii.com; Smith's Tropical Paradise; admission $85-95; 11:30am-4pm) On the first Sunday in June, the Rotary Club of Kapa'a hosts the 'Ultimate Sunday Brunch,' a casual outdoor event featuring samples by 50 of Hawaii's distinguished chefs. With additional booths offering wines, microbrews, ice cream and desserts, you're liable to stuff yourself silly here.

Aloha Festivals Royal Court Investiture (☎ 332-7888; www.alohafestivals.com; admission incl lunch $18) The statewide Aloha Festivals in late August are launched on each island with the presentation of a royal court. Held at Kamokila Hawaiian Village, the event includes special ceremonies of traditional chanting and hula.

Eating

ICING ON THE CAKE — Bakery $

our pick **☎ 823-1210; www.icingonthecakekauai.com; Kinipopo Shopping Village, 4-356 Kuhio Hwy; cookies $1.25-1.75, 6in/9in cakes from $25/40**

Trained in northern California, pastry chef Andrea Quinn has a knack for elegant designs and sophisticated flavors. Nothing is too cute or too sweet. While she specializes in made-to-order cakes, she also produces gourmet treats such as cocoa-nib shortbread, pecan brownies and exquisite coconut macaroons. Check the website for other retail locations islandwide.

MONICO'S TAQUERIA — Mexican $

our pick **☎ 822-4300; Kinipopo Shopping Village, 4-356 Kuhio Hwy; mains $8-14; 11am-3pm & 5-9pm**

As a general rule, you can't find 'real' Mexican food on Kaua'i. But Monico's won't disappoint. Everything tastes fresh and rings true, from the generous plates of burritos and tacos to the freshly made chips, salsa and sauces. Run by a local girl and her Mexican husband, it's also your ticket for affordable island fish entrées.

MEMA — Thai $$

☎ 823-0899; 4-369 Kuhio Hwy; mains $9-18; 11am-2pm Mon-Fri, 5-9pm nightly

While not stark-raving awesome, Mema serves decent dishes that can be tailored to your meat-philic or meat-phobic preference: you choose either tofu, chicken, pork, beef, fish or shrimp. The cozy dining room is modest but a cut above the standard local-diner setting.

CAFFÉ COCO — Eclectic $$$

☎ 822-7990; www.restauranteur.com/caffecoco; 4-369 Kuhio Hwy; salads & sandwiches $5-14.50, meals $16-21; 11am-9pm Tue-Fri, 5-9pm Sat & Sun

At this rustic little hideaway, chefs fuse Asian, Middle Eastern and other 'exotic' flavors into healthful dishes that would

…d. The *'ahi* is
…roccan spices
…or seared and
…vasabi cream.
…serts include
…ious mosqui-

Japanese $$$

☎ 822-3341; 4-370 Kuhio Hwy; appetizers $3.50-6, meals $14-20; 5:30-9:30pm Mon-Sat

Night after night, this local favorite packs 'em in. No wonder: from thick-cut slices of sashimi to a shrimp/fish/veg tempura combination, the main dishes shine in both quality and quantity. The owner is Korean, but the cuisine is authentic Japanese. A specialty is the sizzling, crowd-wowing *teppanyaki,* for which chefs show off their stuff tableside on steel grills.

HUKILAU LANAI Hawaii Regional Cuisine $$$

our pick ☎ 822-0600; www.hukilaukauai.com; 520 Aleka Loop; dinner $16-27; 5-9pm Tue-Sun

Wailua's eateries tend toward T-shirt–casual, but if you want to ramp up the setting, your best bet is Hukilau Lanai. The open-air dining room is casually elegant, while the menu features top local ingredients, from Kilauea goat cheese to Lawa'i Valley *warabi* (fiddlehead fern). Standouts include the fish entrees, feta-and-sweet-potato ravioli and *'ahi poke* nachos. For an affordable splurge, arrive from 5pm to 6pm for the early-bird tasting menu, which pairs six courses with five wines ($40) or food only ($28). It's in Kaua'i Coast Resort at the Beachboy.

Entertainment

The best night life in Wailua is curling up in bed before the roosters wake you. Or, if the price isn't a deterrent, a commercial luau might be a decent diversion. **Smith's Tropical Paradise** (☎ 821-6895; www.smithskauai.com; Wailua River Marina; luau adult/child 3-6/child 7-13 $75/19/30; 5pm Mon, Wed & Fri) launched their luau in 1985, and today it's a Kaua'i institution, attracting droves of tourists. It's a lively affair, run with lots of aloha spirit by four generations at the lovely 30-acre garden. The multicultural show features Hawaiian, Tahitian, Samoan, Filipino, Chinese, Japanese and New Zealand dances.

While touristy, the **free hula show** at the Coconut Marketplace (☎ 822-3641; 4-484 Kuhio

Get some fresh, local *'ono grinds* (good food) at Pono Market (p104)

ANN CECIL

Don't Miss

- **Hukilau Lanai's locavore menu offerings** (opposite)
- **Fish tacos at Monico's** (p91)
- **Hollywood-site spotting with Hawaii Movie Tours** (p103)
- **Hawaiiana collectibles at Tin Can Mailman** (right)
- **Organic breads at Country Moon Rising bakery** (p104)
- **Splurge-worthy fashions at Marta's Boat** (p98)
- **Blue Hole tour with Aloha Kaua'i Tours** (p90)
- **Taste of Hawaii gourmet smorgasbord** (p91)
- **Homemade *manju* (Japanese pastry) from Pono Market** (p104)
- **Using the Kapa'a Bypass Rd during traffic jams** (see Map p101)

Hwy; 5pm Wed) are fun and lively, featuring **Leilani Rivera Bond** (www.leilanirivera.com) and her *halau* (troupe). She's the daughter of famous Coco Palms entertainer Larry Rivera, who joins the show on the first Wednesday monthly.

Another anytown option is a movie at a mall. **Coconut Marketplace Cinemas** (821-2324; 4-484 Kuhio Hwy; adult/child/senior $7.25/4.25/5.50, shows before 6pm $4.25) screens first-run flicks.

Shopping

The touristy **Coconut Marketplace** (www.coconutmarketplace.com; 4-484 Kuhio Hwy; 9am-9pm Mon-Sat, 10am-6pm Sun) feels like a throwback, a once-popular venue now deserted, with too many vacant spaces. Amid midrange island attire, jewelry, T-shirts and gifts is one worthy stop: Ship Store Galleries.

BAMBULEI

823-8641; www.bambulei.com; 4-369D Kuhio Hwy; 10am-6pm Mon-Fri, 10am-5pm Sat

Find the antithesis of 'generic' and 'chain store' at this irresistible women's boutique. The fashions are feminine and made for women who've outgrown the teenage surfer-chick look. The drapey sweaters, platform sandals and kimono-fabric accessories aren't haute couture, but they're affordable and unique. Also find vintage clothing and retro home decor.

TIN CAN MAILMAN

our pick 822-3009; www.tincanmailman.net; Kinipopo Shopping Village, 4-356 Kuhio Hwy; 11am-7pm Mon-Fri, noon-4pm Sat

Brimming with rare books and antiques, this little shop will delight Hawaiiana collectors. The wide selection of new and used books (including many on the Hawaiian Islands) is reason enough to come, but the collection of vintage LPs, aloha shirts, maps, photos, postcards, jewelry and other artifacts is downright fascinating.

SHIP STORE GALLERIES

822-4999, 800-877-1948; www.shipstoregalleries.com; Coconut Marketplace, 4-484 Kuhio Hwy; 9am-5pm Tue-Sat

Art galleries can be intimidating, but this spacious showroom is refreshingly welcoming. Longtime staff is friendly, whether you're browsing or buying. Featured maritime artist Raymond Massey lives in New York, but he's created an extensive, fascinating series on seafaring to the Hawaiian Islands. Notable Kaua'i painters include Leslie Tribolet, who does mesmerizing portraits, and Dolores 'Dee' Kirby, whose unostentatious landscapes are keepers. Also see Marco Cannella's riffs on the Old Masters' still lifes: hidden *menehune* give them a local twist.

Sleeping

Note that many condos, B&Bs and inns require a three-night minimum and charge a one-time cleaning fee of $50 to $250 or more, depending on unit size. For condos, we list contact info for the agency managing the majority of units, but also check www.vrbo.com and smaller agencies. **Rosewood Kaua'i** (822-5216; www.rosewoodkauai.com) represents not only condos but also many outstanding vacation rental homes in Wailua and Kapa'a (p106).

BUNK HOUSE AT ROSEWOOD KAUA'I — Inn $

822-5216; www.rosewoodkauai.com; 872 Kamalu Rd; r with shared bathroom $50-60;

If you like the *idea* of bunk-bed hostels but you can't live without privacy and cleanliness, you're in luck. The three small studios

EASTSIDE

WHAT EVER HAPPENED TO COCO PALMS?

Old-timers might recall **Coco Palms Resort** (Map pp84-5, cnr of Kuhio Hwy & Kuamo'o Rd) as Hollywood's go-to wedding site during the 1950s and 1960s. Built in 1953, it was Kaua'i's first resort, and its romantic lagoons, gardens, thatched cottages, torch-lit paths and coconut groves epitomized tropical paradise. The highest-profile onscreen wedding here was when Elvis Presley wed Joan Blackman in the 1961 film *Blue Hawaii*.

At its height, the Coco Palms was a playground for Hollywood's leading males and their lithe ingenues, and the trendiest mainland couples came here to get hitched. But it was also an old-Hawaii place where guests knew hotel staff on a first-name basis and returned year after year.

In 1992, Hurricane 'Iniki demolished the then-396-room hotel, which sat in benign neglect for years. In spring 2006, a new owner announced a $220 million plan to resurrect Coco Palms as a condo-hotel, but plans fell through. By fall 2007, the 19-acre property was back on the market. The county has toyed with the idea of acquiring the property (which is historically significant as the ancient Hawaiian royal seat) and turning it into a public park.

The site remains abandoned except for weddings performed by **Larry Rivera** (☎ 822-3868; larryrivera@hawaiian.net) of Blue Hawaii Weddings. Rivera, a local musician and celebrity who made his career at Coco Palms, recreates elaborate *Blue Hawaii* fantasy weddings on the grounds, which he and a tiny team of lifetime Coco Palms employees maintain with TLC.

To read more about this historic resort, see www.coco-palms.com, an unofficial website created by its fans.

here are cheerful and tidy, and they have private entrances and kitchenettes. Just outside are a shared bathroom, outdoor shower and gas grill. For a step up, inquire about the picturesque Victorian Cottage ($145), and Thatched Cottage ($135), which are also on the storybook-pretty property, complete with white picket fence. The cleaning fee is $25.

LANI KEHA Inn $

☎ 822-1605; www.lanikeha.com; 848 Kamalu Rd; s/d from $65/75;

Solo travelers and sociable types will appreciate the low-key, communal atmosphere in this longtime guesthouse. Nothing fancy, the three rooms feature *lauhala* (pandanus leaf) mat flooring, king beds and well-worn but clean furnishings. Gather round the kitchen and living room.

GARDEN ROOM Inn $

our pick ☎ 822-5216, 822-3817; www.rosewoodkauai.com; 6430 Ahele Dr; r $75;

Find serenity in an immaculate studio overlooking a gorgeous pond with waterlilies and *koi* (Japanese carp). The aptly named room is compact (hotel-room size) but delightful, with a private entrance, kitchenette and generous welcome basket. Expect to be charmed by the host couple, longtime Kaua'i residents who make their guests feel welcome.

SLEEPING GIANT COTTAGE Cottage $$

☎ 505-401-4403; www.wanek.com/sleepinggiant; 5979 Heamoi Pl; 1br cottage $95;

Surrounded by tropical foliage and three open-air lanai, this plantation-style bungalow makes a private, spacious and quiet retreat. The amiable owner lives on the island but off-site, so staying here gives the impression of living here (dream on). The interior features hardwood floor, full kitchen, comfortably sized bedroom and living/dining room, plus a huge screened patio facing a backyard garden. Rates drop for weekly or longer stays; cleaning fee $50.

INN PARADISE B&B $$

our pick ☎ 822-2542; www.innparadisekauai.com; 6381 Makana Rd; studio/1br/2br units incl breakfast $85/100/120

Consistently rated highly by travelers, this longtime B&B sets the standard. Classy units. Spectacular garden view. Charming innkeepers. Pick from three different-sized units, all with private entrance and kitchen or kitchenette. Reasonable rates, scrumptious breakfast fixings and shared washer/dryer clinch the deal.

OPAEKA'A FALLS HALE B&B $$

our pick ☎ 888-822-9956; www.opaekaafallskauai.ws; 120 Lihau St; 1br units incl breakfast $110-130;

You'll have no problem stretching your legs in these two immaculate units, which at a whopping 1000+ sq ft each are bigger than the average city apartment. Each includes full kitchen and private lanai, phone and washer/dryer, plus a lovely swimming pool and breakfast fixings; cleaning fee $50. If you can afford it, choose the larger upstairs suite for DSL internet access and panoramic views of Wailua's emerald valleys.

FERN GROTTO INN Cottages $$

☎ 821-9836; www.ferngrottoinn.com; 4561 Kuamo'o Rd; cottages $99-150, house $275;

There's a charmingly retro feel to these remodeled, 1940s plantation-style cottages near the Wailua River dock. The cottages and house vary in size, but all feature hardwood floors, tasteful furnishings, TV/DVD, shared laundry, and kitchen or kitchenette. Rates are slightly high, but the location near the highway reduces driving. The friendly on-site owner couple go the extra mile to ensure guests' comfort.

HALE LANI B&B B&B $$

☎ 823-6434, 877-423-6434; www.halelani.com; 283 Aina Lani Pl; studios $125-135, 2br unit $165, 1br cottage $185, all incl breakfast;

Located at the top of Kuamo'o Rd, this sparkling clean B&B comprises four cheerful units, all of which make efficient use of space and include kitchenette and private outdoor hot tub. If you dislike forced morning chitchat, you'll appreciate the minimal socializing here, as home-cooked breakfasts arrive at your door in a cooler. One quibble: rates are on the high side.

ASTON ALOHA BEACH RESORT Hotel $$

☎ 823-6000, 888-823-5111; www.alohabeachresortkauai.com; 3-5920 Kuhio Hwy; r $99-219, 1br cottages from $189;

The hotel is three-star average. But the location is appealing. You're within walking distance to the kid-friendly Lydgate Beach Park. Don't expect much more from this 216-room hotel than the standard amenities and B-level restaurants and grounds. In fact, maintenance can be slack, and you might find broken elevators. Bottom line: the basic rooms are a decent deal, but don't bother with the overpriced cottages.

ASTON ISLANDER ON THE BEACH Hotel $$

☎ 822-7417, 877-997-6667; www.astonhawaii.com; 440 Aleka Pl; r $140-230;

Among midrange hotels, you can't top the Islander. It's not a resort, so don't expect frills, but all 186 rooms were renovated in fall 2005 and, with granite countertops, flat-panel TVs and stainless-steel and teak furnishings, they feel modern and upscale. For internet access, room connections cost $10 per 24 hour period; free wi-fi in lobby. Web specials can snag you an oceanfront room for $135.

ASTON KAUA'I BEACH AT MAKAIWA Hotel $$$

☎ 822-3455, 800-760-8555; www.astonhawaii.com; 650 Aleka Loop; r $150-380;

For a presentable business-class hotel, look no further. The 300-plus-room Kaua'i Beach has a classy, efficient feel, from the

Wailua Bay (p86) ANN CECIL

EASTSIDE

soaring lobby full of plush seating to the sedately pleasant pool. Rooms pamper the business traveler with dark woods, black-marble counters and work desk with rolling chair. A $12 hotel fee buys you parking, local calls, internet access and daily paper. Book early and online for amazing deals.

KAHA LANI Condo $$$
☎ 822-9331; www.castleresorts.com; 4460 Nene Rd; 1br units $150-250, 2br units $180-300;
If exterior location matters more to you than interior design, this older condo is ideal. The prime location just south of Lydgate Beach Park means easy-access sandy strolls and morning dips. Units vary in quality, some with sadly worn furnishings, but overall they include all the usual amenities and are decent value. Expect to rise with the roosters – a great number live on the grounds.

LAE NANI Condo $$$
☎ 822-4938, 800-688-7444; www.outrigger.com; 410 Papaloa Rd; 1br/2br units from $215/235;
All of the condos along Papaloa Rd are good, but this five-building property is particularly appealing. Rates aren't the cheapest, but it's set along a pleasant stretch of beach, far enough from the highway for nighttime quiet. Outrigger manages almost 60 of the 84 units and provides on-site support, but also check with other agents. Buildings 3 and 5 include the most oceanfront units; building 1 is far from the highway and parking lot.

WAIPOULI

Sandwiched between Wailua and Kapa'a, Waipouli is less a town than a cluster of restaurants and grocers, plus a drugstore and other basic businesses. But don't let the strip-mall setting fool you. Here you'll find the island's best health-food store, artisan bakeries, an Aveda spa and other gems. It's a convenient place to stock up and grab a bite.

Information

There are ATMs inside Foodland supermarket in Waipouli Town Center and, just a minute north, inside Safeway in Kaua'i Village. Both are located on the *mauka* side of Kuhio Hwy.

Longs Drugs (☎ 822-4915; Kaua'i Village; store 7am-10pm Mon-Sat, 8am-8pm Sun, pharmacy 8am-9pm Mon-Sat, 9am-6pm Sun) Pharmacy and over-the-counter drugs, plus excellent prices on household products, beach supplies, grocery items and souvenirs.

Activities

Bear in mind that rentals are here but the actual activities are elsewhere.

SURFING

Don't miss a chance to meet surf guru Ambrose Curry of **Ambrose's Kapuna** (☎ 822-3926; www.ambrosecurry.com; 770 Kuhio Hwy; per hr $35), who offers to 'take people surfing' (not to 'give surf lessons'). If you're baffled, then you have much to learn from this longtime surfer/philosopher once aptly dubbed a tribal elder. Originally from California, Curry has lived on Kaua'i since 1968 and is also an artist and board maker.

SNORKELING

The cool thing about **Snorkel Bob's** (☎ 823-9433; www.snorkelbob.com; 4-734 Kuhio Hwy; basic snorkel sets per day/week $2.50/9, better sets $8/32, bodyboards $6.50/26; 8am-5pm Mon-Sat) is if you're island-hopping, you can rent gear on Kaua'i and return it on the Big Island, O'ahu or Maui.

CYCLING

Kauai Cycle (☎ 821-2115; www.kauaicycle.com; 4-934 Kuhio Hwy; per day/week cruiser $20/110, mountain or road bike $30/165; 9am-6pm Mon-Fri, to 4pm Sat) sells, services and rents bikes maintained by experienced cyclists. Prices include helmet and lock.

SPAS

Enter a world of Japanese *shōji* screens, soft lighting, earth tones and botanical aromatherapy at **Aveda Spa** (☎ 823-1488; www.kauaispasalon.com; Outrigger Waipouli Beach Resort & Spa, 4-820 Kuhio Hwy; 60min massage or facial $135, haircuts $45-65; 9am-6pm Mon-Sat, 10am-6pm Sun) – and the Eastside's traffic will drift far, far away. Treatments include relaxing extras: imagine lounging in a cushy massage chair while

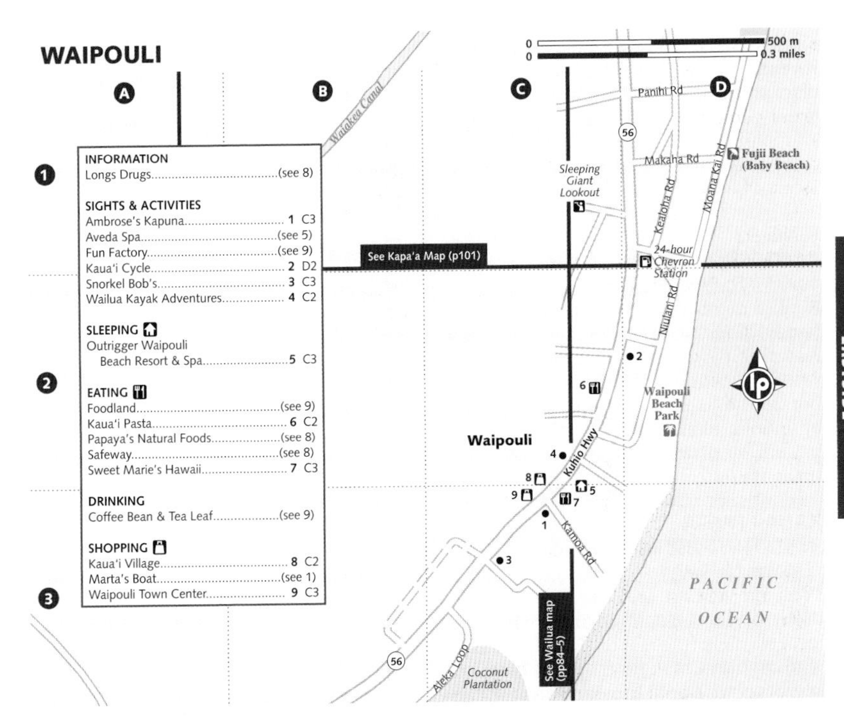

getting a pedicure ($70 to $115). Take advantage of numerous monthly specials.

Courses

Kaua'i Heritage Center (☎ 346-7574; www.kaieie.org) offers lectures and workshops by Kehaulani Kekua, a respected and very articulate *kumu* hula (teacher of hula). The Friday lectures are free, while the hands-on Saturday workshop cost $30. Nowhere else can you find such genuine teachings on the ancient Hawaiian lunar calendar or the significance of Kaua'i's hula heiau.

Eating & Drinking

SWEET MARIE'S HAWAII — Bakery $

our pick ☎ 823-0227; www.sweetmarieskauai.com; 4-788 Kuhio Hwy; baked goods $2.25-10, 6in/8in cakes from $50/75; 7am-5pm Tue-Sat

Chef Marie Cassel's 100% gluten-free desserts are proof positive that wheat is overrated. Just taste her melt-in-the-mouth white-chocolate *liliko'i* cake or gooey coconut–vanilla bean tapioca (non-dairy, believe it or not). Cassel is a phenomenal one-woman show, baking away from 4am. She also offers specialty cakes (soy- or dairy-free, too), cooking lessons and private chef services. Look for the bakery sign across from Foodland.

COFFEE BEAN & TEA LEAF — Cafe $

☎ 822-4754; www.coffeebeanhawaii.com; Waipouli Town Center, 4-771 Kuhio Hwy; drinks from $4; 6am-9pm Sun-Thu, to 9:30pm Fri & Sat;

At this clean-cut franchise, you'll find the gamut of Americanized coffee and tea concoctions. Starbucks fans will fit right in.

PAPAYA'S NATURAL FOODS — Deli/Grocer $

☎ 823-0190; Kaua'i Village, 4-831 Kuhio Hwy; dishes $5-8, salad per lb $7; store 9am-8pm Mon-Sat, deli to 7pm Mon-Sat

At Kaua'i's biggest health-food store, you'll find a nouveau-hippie contingent, locavore-leaning mainland transplants and vegetarian/vegan types. National brands might seem expensive, so look for weekly or monthly sales. Produce is not cheap because it's either organic or local. It's the convenient place to stock up on bulk items (including grind-your-own peanut butter), vitamins and supplements, bottled water, healthful deli fixings and island specialties such as Kilauea honey and goat cheese.

KING & I — Thai $

☎ 822-1642; Waipouli Plaza, 4-901 Kuhio Hwy; mains $7-11; 4:30-9:30pm

Ranked number one by locals, this friendly, family-run restaurant offers a lengthy menu featuring flavors such as curries popping with kaffir lime and lemongrass, fiery or not, as you like. Vegetarians will find loads of options, like flavorful eggplant and tofu in chili oil or a mound of traditional pad thai with tofu.

KAUA'I PASTA — Italian $$

☎ 822-7447; 4-939B Kuhio Hwy; mains $9-15; 5-9pm Tue-Sun

With no view to speak of, the food had better be good. And, judging from steady local clientele (the real test), it is. The chef, who cut his teeth at Roy's (p173) in Po'ipu, serves savory *panini* (hot sandwiches), classic pasta dishes and a perfectly simple (or simply perfect) Caprese salad with local basil and tomatoes and fresh mozzarella.

For groceries, chain giant **Safeway** (☎ 822-2464; Kaua'i Village, 4-831 Kuhio Hwy; 24hr) caters to mainland tourists with its familiar brands, plus American-style deli and bakery. A slightly better option is local chain **Foodland** (Waipouli Town Center; 6am-11pm), with a decent selection of gourmet and health brands, eg Kashi and Scharffen Berger. But neither stocks much local produce at all.

Foodies will prefer Papaya's Natural Foods (p97). Another recommendation for local produce and national health brands is Cost U Less (p105) in nearby Kapa'a.

Shopping

Waipouli's two main shopping malls are **Waipouli Town Center** (4-771 Kuhio Hwy) and **Kaua'i Village** (☎ 822-4904; 4-831 Kuhio Hwy). One notable boutique is the irresistible **Marta's Boat** (☎ 822-3926; 770 Kuhio Hwy; 10am-6pm Mon-Sat), which will delight 'princesses of all ages' with feminine and sexy threads from Paris, LA and New York. Distinctive lingerie and frocks shine, but locally made jewelry and excruciatingly cute little girls' outfits also enchant. Expect big-city price tags. 'Surf for World Peace' T-shirts (hand-painted by owner Marta Curry's husband, surfer and artist Ambrose Curry; p96) make cool souvenirs.

Sleeping

Waipouli is sandwiched between Wailua and Kapa'a, both with plentiful options; see p93 and p106 respectively.

OUTRIGGER WAIPOULI BEACH RESORT & SPA — Condo $$$$

☎ 822-6000, 800-688-7444; www.outrigger-waipouli.com; 4-820 Kuhio Highway; 1br/2br units from $295/425;

The Eastside's fanciest condo is new (c 2006), law-firm handsome and consistently well furnished with 37" flat-screen TVs, washer/dryer and extra bathroom per unit. The property lacks a swimmable beach, but compensates with a saltwater 'river pool,' sand-bottom hot tubs and an Aveda spa. Outrigger represents 100 of the 196 total units, but also check www.vrbo.com. One caveat: only the svelte can lounge on the stick-thin balconies in one-bedroom units.

KAPA'A

pop 9472

The only walkable town on the Eastside, Kapa'a is a charmer. The eclectic population of old timers, new transplants, nouveau hippies and tourists coexist smoothly. Retro diners and domestic shops mingle with live jazz, Bikram yoga and your choice of espresso drinks. A new bike/pedestrian path runs along the part-sandy, part-rocky coast, the island's best vantage for sunrises. Kapa'a's downfall: it sits right along the highway. Try crossing the road during rush hours!

To avoid the paralyzing Kapa'a-to-Wailua crawl, take the Kapa'a Bypass Rd. Note that except in the heart of Kapa'a, you will definitely need a car.

Information

INTERNET ACCESS

Business Support Services (☎ 822-5504; fax 822-2148; 4-1191 Kuhio Hwy; computer per 15 min $2.50;

ISLAND VOICES

NAME: KENNETH KUBOTA
OCCUPATION: ESPRESSO BAR PROPRIETOR, PONO MARKET (p104); MARRIAGE LICENSE AGENT
RESIDENCE: KAPA'A

Tell me the history of Pono Market. In 1968, my parents acquired Pono Market, which was a meat market (pork) back then. Times change and by 1980 we converted it into a convenience store, like today's 7-Eleven. In the 1990s, we faced big competition when the **ABC Store** (p106) chain arrived. And then Foodland and Safeway came. So we decided to focus on food: plate lunches, *poke*, local favorites.

Who are your typical customers? We open early, so construction workers and schoolkids can come. It's a neighborhood place. People walk in and we greet them by name. If they ask for 'the usual,' we know what they want, like on Cheers. Everything is fresh. The *poke* is made in batches throughout the day. Fast service, good food. People come back.

Why did you open an espresso bar? In the late 1990s, after running a dry-cleaning business for a decade, I sold it and took a break. I read, exercised and worked at **Borders** (p61), which had an espresso café [now Starbucks]. That initiated my interest in coffee. I tell kids, 'Don't look only at your paycheck.' You're also getting paid to learn.

Are locals into the cafe scene? When the Borders café opened, people *loved* it. Finally, a place to sit and read or talk. Until then, there was no place to hang out. And they were willing to pay for expensive coffee.

In addition to customers, you see lots of tourist couples come in for marriage licenses. What's a marriage-license agent anyway? To make it easier for tourists (or locals) to get a marriage license, Kaua'i has four agents islandwide, plus the main office in Lihu'e. I've been issuing marriage licenses since 2000, and I do almost 1000 per year. The busiest months are May and June, but Valentine's Day is also popular. August 8, 2008, was busy because eight is good luck to Asians, and July 7, 2007, was huge.

I take a picture of each couple. Some are clearly having fun. Some look nervous. Some, you think, 'Are you sure you want to get married?' The oldest couple I met were ages 93 and 85.

How has Kapa'a changed since you grew up here? [It's] grown way beyond what the land and infrastructure can bear. The older generation didn't expect it. In 1962, the mayor said that we need four-lane roads. People laughed. But look at today's traffic. He had foresight.

8am-6pm) No atmosphere but cheap internet access, plus faxing, copies and stamps.

Java Kai (823-6887; 4-1384 Kuhio Hwy; 6am-7pm;) With its tiny interior and queues at the counter, this cafe can feel cramped for lengthy websurfing, but it's fine in a pinch.

our pick **Small Town Café** (821-1604; 4-1495 Kuhio Hwy; computer per 10 min $1, wi-fi free; 5:30am-1pm;) Rustic, island-style coffee bar with lots of seating, indoor and outdoor.

LAUNDRY

Kapa'a Laundry Center (822-3113; Kapa'a Shopping Center, 4-1105 Kuhio Hwy; 7:30am-9:30pm, last wash 8pm)

MEDICAL SERVICES

Samuel Mahelona Memorial Hospital (☎ 822-4961; fax 823-4100; 4800 Kawaihau Rd) Primarily a long-term care facility, this longstanding hospital expanded services to include basic emergency care in late 2005. Serious cases are transferred to Lihu'e's Wilcox Memorial Hospital (p62).

MONEY

First Hawaiian Bank (☎ 822-4966; 4-1366 Kuhio Hwy) 24-hour ATM.

Island Insights

Ask locals born before 1950 about their first job, and chances are they worked for Kapa'a's pineapple cannery, which was located where the Pono Kai Resort now sits. The pineapple industry left in the early 1960s, and today tourism has by and large replaced agriculture as the area's economic backbone.

POST

Post office (☎ 800-275-8777; Kapa'a Shopping Center, 4-1101 Kuhio Hwy; 8am-4pm Mon-Fri, 9am-2pm Sat)

Beaches

KAPA'A BEACH PARK

From the highway, you'd think that Kapa'a was beach-less. But there's a mile-long ribbon of beach that's very low-key and local. While the whole area is officially a county park called Kapa'a Beach Park, that name is commonly used only for the north end, where there's a grassy field, picnic tables and a public pool.

The best sandy area is at the south end, informally called **Lihi Beach**, where you'll find locals hanging out and talking story. A good starting point for the paved coastal path is the footbridge just north of the beach – just turn *makai* on Panihi from the highway.

Further to the south is **Fujii Beach**, nicknamed **Baby Beach**, because an offshore reef creates a shallow, placid pool of water that's perfect for toddlers. Located in a modest

Palm trees silhouetted at sunrise, Kapa'a Beach Park

LINDA CHING

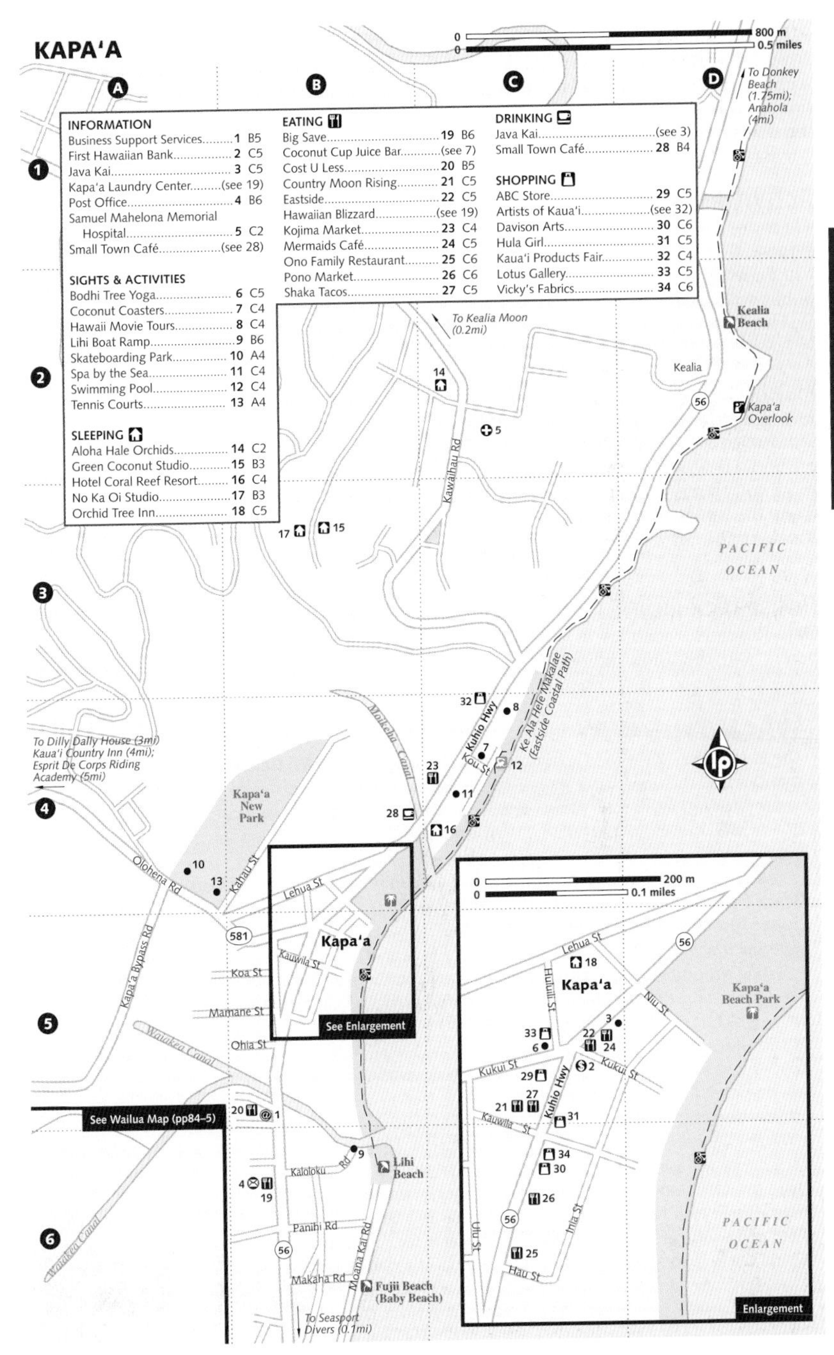
KAPA'A
0 800 m
0 0.5 miles
INFORMATION
Business Support Services 1 B5
First Hawaiian Bank 2 C5
Java Kai 3 C5
Kapa'a Laundry Center (see 19)
Post Office 4 B6
Samuel Mahelona Memorial Hospital 5 C2
Small Town Café (see 28)
SIGHTS & ACTIVITIES
Bodhi Tree Yoga 6 C5
Coconut Coasters 7 C4
Hawaii Movie Tours 8 C4
Lihi Boat Ramp 9 B6
Skateboarding Park 10 A4
Spa by the Sea 11 C4
Swimming Pool 12 C4
Tennis Courts 13 A4
SLEEPING
Aloha Hale Orchids 14 C2
Green Coconut Studio 15 B3
Hotel Coral Reef Resort 16 C4
No Ka Oi Studio 17 B3
Orchid Tree Inn 18 C5
EATING
Big Save 19 B6
Coconut Cup Juice Bar (see 7)
Cost U Less 20 B5
Country Moon Rising 21 C5
Eastside 22 C5
Hawaiian Blizzard (see 19)
Kojima Market 23 C4
Mermaids Café 24 C5
Ono Family Restaurant 25 C6
Pono Market 26 C6
Shaka Tacos 27 C5
DRINKING
Java Kai (see 3)
Small Town Café 28 B4
SHOPPING
ABC Store 29 C5
Artists of Kaua'i (see 32)
Davison Arts 30 C6
Hula Girl 31 C5
Kaua'i Products Fair 32 C4
Lotus Gallery 33 C5
Vicky's Fabrics 34 C6
To Donkey Beach (1.75mi); Anahola (4mi)
To Kealia Moon (0.2mi)
Kealia Beach
Kealia
Kapa'a Overlook
Kawaihau Rd
PACIFIC OCEAN
Ke Ala Hele Makalae (Eastside Coastal Path)
Kuhio Hwy
Kou St
Moikeha Canal
To Dilly Dally House (3mi) Kaua'i Country Inn (4mi); Esprit De Corps Riding Academy (5mi)
Kapa'a New Park
Olohena Rd
Kahau St
Lehua St
Kapa'a
Kauwila St
Koa St
Mamane St
Ohia St
Kapa'a Bypass Rd
Waikaea Canal
See Enlargement
See Wailua Map (pp84–5)
Kaloloku Rd
Lihi Beach
Panihi Rd
Moana Kai Rd
Makaha Rd
Fujii Beach (Baby Beach)
To Seasport Divers (0.1mi)
0 200 m
0 0.1 miles
Hulili St
Niu St
Kapa'a Beach Park
Kukui St
Uhu St
Inia St
Hau St
Enlargement
EASTSIDE

neighborhood that attracts few tourists, this is a real locals' beach, so don't make a loud scene here. In addition to the toddler action, you might catch a few kitesurfers in the deeper waters offshore.

Activities

There are free **tennis courts** and a **skateboarding park**, along with a field for baseball, football and soccer in Kapa'a New Park, and a public **swimming pool** (☎ 822-3842; admission free; 10am-4:30pm Thu-Mon) at Kapa'a Beach Park.

FISHING

Join gregarious Captain Terry of **Hawaiian Style Fishing** (☎ 635-7335; 4hr charter per person $100) on his 25ft boat. He takes four anglers at most and shares the catch. Charters depart from the small boat ramp at the end of Kaloloku Rd, off Kuhio Hwy.

HORSEBACK RIDING

Dale Rosenfeld qualifies as a 'horse whisperer,' and the tours offered by her **Esprit De Corps Riding Academy** (☎ 822-4688; www.kauaihorses.com; Kualapa Pl; tours $130-390, lessons per hr $55) are small (five max), personalized and varied (longer tours for more-skilled riders). Groups never exceed five riders, ages 10 and above. She also offers honeymoon rides and weddings on horseback. The ranch is located about 5.5 miles above Kapa'a town; see website for directions.

SPAS

For a satisfying alternative to pricey resort spas, try **Spa by the Sea** (☎ 822-2171; www.spabytheseakauai.com; 4-1558 Kuho Hwy; 50min massage or facial $110), which shares a building near the ocean with a chiropractor and physical therapist. Massage therapists are all hand-picked and highly qualified. If you're torn between massage or facial, the Menehune Meditation ($115) includes 30 minutes of each.

YOGA

Bikram types craving a hot room might like **Bodhi Tree Yoga** (☎ 822-5053; www.bodhitree

WALK THIS WAY

The Eastside's newest road is not meant for cars; **our pick** **Ke Ala Hele Makalae** ('the Path that Goes by the Coast') is a shared-use path reserved for pedestrians, bicyclists and other non-motorized modes. At 10ft wide and paved in concrete, it's jumpstarted locals into daily fitness: walking, jogging, cycling, rollerblading and, perhaps, forgoing the local habit of driving everywhere.

In Kapa'a, the path currently starts at the **Lihi Boat Ramp** at the south end of Kapa'a Beach Park (p100) and ends just past Donkey Beach (p110) at **Ahihi Point** (Map p82), a 4-mile stretch. But this constitutes only a small piece of the ambitious facility, which will run over 16 miles all the way from Lihu'e to Anahola Beach Park (p108).

While a loud minority has complained about pouring concrete along the coast, especially near the Wailua River, which is sacred to Native Hawaiians, most appreciate the easy-access path, which is now like a town square in motion. Proponents point out that an official path is critical to preserving public shoreline access (a legal right in Hawaii). Often, such access is blocked when private landowners post no-trespassing signs or set up gates, or when trails are deemed unsafe by authorities.

Sunrise walks are brilliant but, for an added kick, rent a coaster bike! **Coconut Coasters** (☎ 822-7368; www.coconutcoasters.com; 4-1586 Kuhio Hwy; bike rentals per 1hr/4hr from $8.50/18; 7am-6pm Tue-Sat, 9am-4pm Sun) specializes in hourly rentals for the path. Classic single-speed coasters are just right for the gentle slope north, but you can upgrade to a three-speed model ($9.75 per hour) for an extra-cushy ride. Owners Melissa and Spark Costales meticulously maintain their fleet and exude aloha spirit. For daily or weekly rentals of coaster, mountain or road bikes, try **Kauai Cycle** (p96), located at the south end of the path.

A nonprofit community group called **Kaua'i Path** (www.kauaipath.org) is promoting and maintaining the path; see the website for more info. Note: the path is wheelchair accessible.

KAUA'I ON THE SET!

Hollywood has tapped Kaua'i more than 75 times to stand in for tropical locales around the world. Keep your eyes peeled for these famous settings:

- *South Pacific* (1957): the North Shore's Lumaha'i Beach, with Makana mountain in the background, became an icon.
- *Blue Hawaii* (1961): Elvis remains omnipresent at Wailua's Coco Palms Resort.
- *Donovan's Reef* (1963): the Nawiliwili Harbor area, including the original Kaua'i Inn, were backdrops for Lee Marvin and John Wayne.
- *Gilligan's Island* pilot (1963): Moloa'a Bay was the pilot site for the shipwrecked SS *Minnow*.
- *King Kong* (1976): remote Honopu Valley on the Na Pali Coast was the giant gorilla's island home.
- *Fantasy Island* (1978–84): the waterfall shown during this TV series' opening credits is Kaua'i's own Wailua Falls.
- *Raiders of the Lost Ark* (1981): rugged landscapes near Hule'ia Stream (outside Lihu'e) and Kalaleo Mountain (north of Anahola) stood in for South American jungles.
- *The Thorn Birds* (1983): old Hanapepe town became an Australian Outback town in the Richard Chamberlain TV mini-saga.
- *Honeymoon in Vegas* (1992): Lihu'e sites including the airport, police station and hospital make an appearance along with Nicholas Cage; the manager of Hanalei Inn has a bit part as an airline pilot.
- *Jurassic Park* (1993): Hanapepe and Lawa'i Valleys became the valley of the dinosaurs for Steven Spielberg's *Jurassic Park*; all three films in the series were partly filmed on the Garden Isle.

Film buffs can indulge their big-screen fascination with *The Kaua'i Movie Book* by Chris Cook. See p242 for more on movies shot on Kaua'i.

yogakauai.com; Dragon Bldg, Suite 10, 4504 Kukui St; drop-in class $16). Otherwise head to the North Shore for the island's best teachers.

DIVING & SNORKELING

Eastside waters are less protected by reefs and more choppy due to easterly onshore winds. Diving and snorkeling are therefore very limited here. Still, there's a small branch of Po'ipu-based **Seasport Divers** (☎ 823-9222, 800-685-5889; www.seasportdivers.com; 4-976 Kuhio Hwy), where you can rent diving, snorkeling and other ocean gear.

Tours

In air-conditioned 'theaters on wheels,' movie buffs can cruise the island with **Hawaii Movie Tours** (☎ 822-1192, 800-628-8432; www.hawaiimovietour.com; 4-885 Kuhio Hwy; adult/child under 12 from $89/79; office 7:30am-6pm), stopping at film sites while viewing movie clips on a video monitor. The standard land tour is fine, but it's worth paying extra for the 4WD option (adult/child 5-11 $95/85), an adventurous ride that takes you off-road to the base of Mt Wai'ale'ale (*Jurassic Park* territory) and includes lunch at Lydgate Beach Park (p83).

On the **Kapa'a Town Walking Tour** (☎ 245-3373; www.kauaihistoricalsociety.org; adult/child $15/5; 10am & 4pm Tue, Thu & Sat), knowledgeable local guides point out landmarks, describe Kapa'a's sugar and pineapple boom days and, best of all, 'talk story' and answer questions. Advance reservations are required.

Festivals & Events

Heiva I Kaua'i Ia Orana Tahiti (☎ 822-9447; Kapa'a Beach Park; admission $5) In early August, dance troupes from as far away as Tahiti, Japan and Canada join groups from Hawaii in this Tahitian dancing and drumming competition. Free admission for kids age six and under.

our pick **Coconut Festival** (☎ 651-3273; www.kbakauai.org; admission free) Celebrate all things coconut! Events during the two-day festival in early October include coconut-pie–eating contests, coconut cook-off, cooking demonstrations, music, hula, crafts and food.

Eating & Drinking

Roadside restaurants abound, none terrible, some terribly touristy. Here are several local-favorite picks. Note that Kapa'a's famous vegan eatery, Blossoming Lotus, closed in December 2008 after a successful five-year run.

HAWAIIAN BLIZZARD

Shave Ice $

www.hawaiianblizzard.com; Kapa'a Shopping Center, 4-1101 Kuhio Hwy; small cup $3; noon-5pm Mon-Fri

Keep your eyes peeled for shave-ice virtuoso Aaron Furugen's plain white van outside Big Save. He's been perfecting the art of shave ice since the 1980s – and you can taste his expert touch. Sit on 'da bench,' savor your colorful treat and 'talk story' with the neighborhood regulars. Really thirsty? Pay $7 for 'all you can eat'!

COUNTRY MOON RISING

Bakery $

822-2533; 4-1345 Kuhio Hwy; loaf $5; 7am-5pm Mon-Thu, 7am-3pm Fri & Sat, 9am-3pm Sun

Using organic flour and sea salt, dedicated bakers hand-form generous 24oz loaves of bread and giant cookies. The sprouted wheat sourdough has a pleasantly chewy bite (which somewhat compensates for its imperceptible sourness) and the tropical sweet breads, featuring taro, mac nuts or pineapple. Other draws include locally grown papayas, takeout sandwiches and chilled coconuts with straws. Hours are changeable, and the bakery's often open into the early evening.

JAVA KAI

Cafe $

823-6887; www.javakai.com; 4-1384 Kuhio Hwy; coffee drinks $1.50-4.50; 6am-5pm Mon-Sat, 7am-1pm Sun

Always busy, this Kaua'i-based micro-roastery is best for grabbing a cup to go. The muffins, scones and cookies are baked fresh here, but it can feel like an oven inside. Sidewalk seating is limited.

SMALL TOWN CAFÉ

Cafe $

our pick 821-1604; 4-1495 Kuhio Hwy; coffee drinks $3-5; 5:30am-1pm & 6:30-9pm Tue-Thu;

This indie coffeehouse's electric-blue paint job would be *inexcusable* on lesser establishments. Here, the zingy color modernizes the airy retro building, where plentiful indoor/outdoor seating invites leisurely chats or websurfing. The organic, free-trade coffee suits the hippie/boho crowd. The only downside? It's closed just when you're getting comfy.

COCONUT CUP

Juice Bar $

823-8630; 4-1586 Kuhio Hwy; fruit smoothies $6-7, sandwiches $8; 9am-5pm

The non-chain alternative to Jamba Juice, this roadside stand is a thirst-quenching oasis. Stop here for generously endowed sandwiches from albacore tuna to avocado veggie and fresh-squeezed organic orange or carrot juice ($6 for 16oz).

PONO MARKET

Deli $

our pick 822-4581; 4-1300 Kuhio Hwy; plate lunch $6.50; 6am-6pm Mon-Fri, 6am-4pm Sat

Go local! Fill up on local *grinds* at this longtime hole-in-the-wall, now with a full-fledged espresso bar. At lunch, line up for generous plate lunches, homemade sushi rolls, fresh *'ahi poke* and savory delicacies such as dried *opelu* (mackerel scad) and smoked marlin. Don't miss the barista's sweet specialty, the Roselani Espress: vanilla bean ice cream topped with a shot of espresso.

SHAKA TACOS

Mexican $

823-0012; 4-1345 Kuhio Hwy; burritos $8-10; 7:30am-9pm Mon-Sat, 7:30am-3pm Sun;

In a casual patio setting, this taqueria might not serve virtuoso Mexican food. But the live music on Friday evenings (6:30pm to 9pm) showcases two awesome musicians – jazz saxophonist Denny Morouse, a longtime pro from New York, and talented trumpeter David Braun from Chicago. The charged sounds might seem incongruous with the laidback island vibe, but appreciate talent when you encounter it. A rare example of small-town 'night' life.

ONO FAMILY RESTAURANT

Diner $

822-1710; 4-1292 Kuhio Hwy; breakfast mains $8.50-11, lunch mains $4.50-8.25; 7am-2pm daily & 5:30-9pm Wed-Sat

Nothing fancy, yet something special: that's the appeal of Kaua'i's longtime diners. If you're a hearty-breakfast lover, don't miss the *'ahi* specials (benedict, omelet or burrito, $11) or veg omelets ($10). Locals love the banana pancakes, served with warmed syrup. Lunch items, from saimin to meat-and-rice plates, tasty but not exactly calorie conscious. For years serving only breakfast and lunch, the restaurant added dinner

Hawaii's iconic shave ice, made fresh at Hawaiian Blizzard LUCI YAMAMOTO

hours in late 2008, with a simple menu of saimin (hot noodle soup) and local-style *pupu* (appetizers).

MERMAIDS CAFÉ Cafe $

☎ **821-2026; 4-1384 Kuhio Hwy; wraps & plates $9.50-11; 11am-8:45pm**

If real local food makes you feel your arteries clogging, try the healthful wraps and plates at this walk-up counter. Southeast Asian satay or coconut-curry flavors liven up tofu or chicken 'plate lunches,' while the bestselling seared *'ahi* and *nori* (dried seaweed) wrap would be flawless with a more restrained dollop of sauce. Limited outdoor seating; buy takeout and walk to Kapa'a Beach.

EASTSIDE Hawaii Regional Cuisine $$$

☎ **823-9500; www.theeastsidekauai.com; 4-1380 Kuhio Hwy; lunch mains $9-13, dinner mains $19-32; 11:30am-2:30pm & 5:30-9pm**

Opened in late 2008, this newcomer boasts a breezy open-air dining room, gracious staff and a brief menu of fish, chicken and meat. Think dressed-up versions of down-home eats. No concept is novel, but the nimble execution of entrees, from *misoyaki* (miso-marinated) mahimahi ($23) to *hulihuli* (rotisserie) chicken ($17), makes up for it.

For groceries, stock up at **our pick Cost U Less** (☎ 823-6803; www.costuless.com; 4525 Akia Rd; 9am-8pm Mon-Fri, 9am-7pm Sat, 9am-6pm Sun), which carries not just mainstream brands but also local produce and meat, plus 'natural' brands, such as Kashi and Tom's of Maine. Most items are sold in large, family sizes. No membership is needed.

Local chain **Big Save** (☎ 822-4971; Kapa'a Shopping Center, 4-1101 Kuhio Hwy; 7am-11pm) has a deli, while the smaller **Kojima Market** (☎ 822-5221; 4-1543 Kuhio Hwy; 8am-7pm Mon-Fri, to 6pm Sat, to 1pm Sun) is rather limited but does carry local meat and produce.

Shopping

VICKY'S FABRICS

☎ **822-1746; www.vickysfabrics.com; 4-1326 Kuhio Hwy; 9am-5pm Mon-Sat**

Established in the early 1980s, Vicky's is a gem for quilters and homemakers. Find a wide selection of Hawaiian, Japanese and batik print fabrics. Longtime owner and seamstress Vicky also offers some handmade quilts, pincushions and bags.

ARTISTS OF KAUA'I

☎ 652-7430; www.artistsofkauai.ifp3.com; Kaua'i Products Fair grounds, Kuhio Hwy; 9am-5pm Wed-Sun

Seven Kaua'i artists share a gallery to display their outstanding works in oils, pencil, watercolor and photography. Four are Kaua'i born and raised, including William Keala Kai, who does classic pencil sketches of ancient Hawaiian artifacts and canoes, and photographer Kerry Oda, whose diverse collection includes mesmerizing wildlife shots of monk seals, whales and *honu* (Hawaiian sea turtles).

LOTUS GALLERY

☎ 822-9300; www.jewelofthelotus.com; Dragon Bldg, 4504 Kukui St; 10am-6pm Tue-Sat

A 19th-century bronze Ganesha sculpture. Hand-carved lingam stones. Asian dynasty replica gold jewelry. This fascinating gallery features authentic art and collectibles from such countries as India, Tibet and Thailand. If you're drawn to non-Western spirituality, you'll love the exotic treasures here.

HULA GIRL

☎ 822-1950; www.welovehulagirl.com; 4-1340 Kuhio Hwy; 9am-6pm Mon-Sat, 10am-5pm Sun

Aloha-shirt aficionados will find a wide selection of quality, name-brand shirts ($40 to $125) at this shop – take a moment to feel the silky-soft Tori Richard line in cotton lawn ($70 to $75). This family-run shop is a standout for quality Hawaii souvenirs (eg clothing, jewelry, island-made ceramics, art prints, books), and beyond that simply a fun place to browse.

DAVISON ARTS

our pick ☎ 821-8022; www.davisonarts.com; 4-1322 Kuhio Hwy; 9am-noon Mon, 9am-5pm Tue-Fri, 10am-2pm Sat

For the ultimate splurge, find worthy temptation in Hayley Davison's magnificent koa furniture and John Davison's striking paintings inspired by Kaua'i's landscapes. If you're unclear about why koa, a prized native Hawaiian hardwood, is so exalted, the lustrous pieces here will make the point. The generously sized rocker, a classic, starts at $3500.

It's just a chain convenience store, but **ABC Store** (☎ 823-0081; 4-1359 Kuhio Hwy; 6am-11pm) is locally owned and carries a mesmerizing array of macadamia nuts, sundries, snacks, beer and souvenirs at competitive prices.

Don't bother with the outdoor market, **Kaua'i Products Fair**, at the north end of town. Too many stalls are hawking cheap imitations marked as Kaua'i-made.

Sleeping

If you're seeking accommodations right in town, pickings are slim. Kapa'a has only one hotel, and almost all B&Bs and inns are situated way beyond walking distance. In case you're wondering about the ideally located Pono Kai Resort, we're sorry to say that it's primarily a midrange timeshare, with a limited number of exorbitantly priced vacation rentals.

That said, driving *mauka* to residential neighborhoods leads through picturesque pastures, sweeping views and excellent B&Bs and inns. Remember to ask about minimum-night requirements.

ALOHA HALE ORCHIDS Inn/Cottage $

☎ 822-4148; www.yamadanursery.com; 5087-A Kawaihau Rd; r $55, 1br cottage $85

SHOPPING FOR ALOHA SHIRTS

Whet your appetite for Hawaii's modern-day uniform with two in-depth reads: *The Hawaiian Shirt* (1984), by H Thomas Steele, and *The Art of the Aloha Shirt* (2002), by DeSoto Brown and Linda Arthur. Check out the following and find your match:

- **Hula Girl** (Kapa'a, above) for an upscale, vintage selection.
- **Kapaia Stitchery** (Lihu'e, p74) for custom-made shirts.
- **Pohaku T's** (Koloa, p162) for shirts handmade by a well-known Kaua'i seamstress.

Top Picks

EASTSIDE COST CUTTERS

- **Tour by donation at Kaua'i Hindu Monastery** (p84)
- **Stocking up on groceries at Cost U Less** (p105)
- **Wailua Municipal Golf Course's affordable green fees** (p90)
- **$6 garden admission at Smith's Tropical Paradise** (p83)
- **Vacation rental units at Aloha Hale Orchids** (opposite)
- **Massages and other treatments at Spa by the Sea** (p102)
- **Walking the coastal path** (p102)
- **Hiking the Kuilau Ridge, Moalepe or Nounou Mountain Trails** (p88)
- **Rent a kayak and paddle the Wailua River on your own** (p86)
- **Free hula show at Coconut Marketplace** (p92)

Budget travelers, you're in luck. Choose from two clean, quiet, value-priced units located at a residential orchid nursery. The studio is ideal for singles and contains queen bed, mini refrigerator and TV, while the airy one-bedroom cottage has a full kitchen, TV, windows on all walls, washer and clothesline. One drawback: no wi-fi.

ORCHID TREE INN
Inn $

☎ 822-5359; www.vrbo.com/118213; Lehua St; 2br units s/d $85/90;

Sick of driving? This inn is among the few located smack in Kapa'a and within walking distance of shops and eateries. Two compact but tidy units include two bedrooms, full kitchen, washer/dryer and a sofa sleeper. The chatty owner carefully landscapes the grounds with Taoist and feng shui influences, hence the red motif in bougainvillea and hibiscus. Ideal for sociable types who appreciate Asian philosophies. Long-term stays encouraged.

GREEN COCONUT STUDIO
Inn $$

our pick ☎ 647-0553; www.greencoconutstudio.com; 4698 Pelehu Rd; studio $98-105;

Modest on the outside, this upstairs studio will wow you when you step inside. It's fantastically airy, literally lined with windows (and a wraparound veranda) that allow spectacular coastal views and cooling cross-breezes. The layout makes great use of space, allowing a comfy satellite-TV setup and a kitchenette with full-sized fridge and the gamut of appliances. There's a $75 cleaning fee for brief stays, and additional guests cost $20 per night.

NO KA OI STUDIO
Inn $$

☎ 651-1055; www.vrbo.com/125884; 4691 Pelehu Rd; studio $95;

Wake up to sunshine in this comfy studio with full kitchen, shared washer/dryer and wraparound lanai (veranda) overlooking Kapa'a and the distant coast. While nearby Green Coconut Studio is airier with more windows, this lanai affords more privacy from street traffic. Avid surfers themselves, the host family is an excellent resource on Kealia Beach and surfing. There's a $75 cleaning fee for brief stays; deep discounts for weekly and monthly stays.

KEALIA MOON
Cottage $$

☎ 822-5216; www.rosewoodkauai.com; 5111 Hassard Rd; 2br cottage $135;

Ideal for two couples or a family of four, this immaculate cottage affords much privacy on a quiet residential street. There are two bedrooms, two bathrooms, full kitchen, washer/dryer, multiple flat-screen TVs and a simple, local-style garage patio (the island version of the front stoop). The owners, who live next door, give enormous welcome baskets.

DILLY DALLY HOUSE
B&B $$

☎ 821-0192; www.dillydallyhouse.com; 6395 Waipouli Rd; r $125-155, suite $165, cottage $185;

If you've never tried a B&B, let this standout give you a fantastic first impression. Units vary in size, but all feature chic furnishings, Tempurpedic mattresses on bed-frames fit for royalty, washer/dryer, private entrance and lanai. The 3.5-mile upcountry drive to the house might seem long and confusing at first, but the reward is panoramic mountain and ocean views. The host couple serves scrumptious multi-course breakfasts, such as taro pancakes with scrambled eggs and sausage quiche with fried paprika potatoes. Additional guests, add $20 per night.

KAUA'I COUNTRY INN Inn $$

☎ 821-0207; www.kauaicountryinn.com; 6440 Olohena Rd; 1- & 2-br units $130-180, 3br cottage from $249;

Located four miles above Kapa'a, this inn deftly blends modern creature comforts and country hospitality. In the main house, four units gleam with rich hardwoods and include flat-screen cable TVs, iMac computers with DSL, wi-fi, kitchen facilities and either one or two bedrooms. Kids under 12 are not allowed in suites but are welcome in the three-bedroom cottage out back. Fringe benefit: guests can view the owner's astounding collection of Beatles memorabilia.

HOTEL CORAL REEF RESORT Hotel $$

☎ 822-4481, 800-843-4659; www.hotelcoralreefresort.com; 4-1516 Kuhio Hwy; r $110-289;

Kapa'a's sole hotel has one major advantage: oceanfront location. Otherwise, it's a basic hotel, with smallish rooms and the expected amenities such as air-con and flat-screen TV. Budget rooms ($110 to $125) face the parking lot and Kuhio Hwy. Oceanfront rates wildly vary: if you snag a $149 room, grab it. During busy periods, the same room goes for $289.

KEALIA BEACH

Visible from the highway at the 10-mile marker, this wide, long sandy beach is prime turf for local surfers and bodyboarders. The sandy bottom slopes offshore very gradually, making it possible to walk out far to catch long rides back. But the pounding barrels are treacherous and definitely not recommended for novices. A breakwater protects the north end, so swimming and snorkeling are occasionally possible there.

Parking is plentiful in a paved lot, but the beach is also accessible by bike or foot along the coastal path (p102), which runs along the beach. There are restrooms, picnic tables and pavilions, but no trees or natural shade. Sunscreen is a must.

ANAHOLA

Blink and you'll miss the predominantly Native Hawaiian village of Anahola, where there are subdivisions of Hawaiian Homestead lots at the southern and northern ends. Pineapple and sugar plantations once thrived here, but today the area is mainly residential. The few who lodge here will find themselves in rural seclusion among true locals.

Grouped together at the side of Kuhio Hwy, just south of the 14-mile marker, Anahola's modest commercial center includes a **post office** (8am-4pm Mon-Fri, 9:30-11:30am Sat), burger stand and convenience store.

See the Eastside map (p82) for all places in Anahola and beyond.

Beaches

ANAHOLA BEACH PARK

Hidden from the highway, this locals' beach makes an easy getaway – more secluded yet still drive-up accessible. Because this county park sits on Hawaiian Home Lands,

A wind-blown tree stands guard at Kealia Beach

LINDA CHING

ISLAND VOICES

NAME: LUKE HITCHCOCK
OCCUPATION: KAPA'A HIGH SCHOOL FRESHMAN AND COMPETITIVE SURFER
RESIDENCE: KAPA'A

Are you a local? I was born in New Mexico and lived in California, but I moved here nine years ago, when I was five. Now, with all the people I know and warm water to surf, I feel that I belong here. I feel local.

When did you learn to surf? When I was nine, my older brother took me out. At first I was really scared. But then I would ride the whitewash all the way in and get so excited and want to do it [again]. Now I surf almost every day at **Kealia Beach** (opposite).

How have you done in competitions? I won the Hawaii State Championship for 2006–07. I've also done pretty well nationally, and in 2007 I placed second in the open boys category and second in the national middle school division. I'm currently first in the Kaua'i juniors division.

Do you enjoy competing? It feels great to win. And I am happy to make any finals. Surfing opens a lot of opportunity for me. I travel to California and other places; my sponsor, Hurley, pays my contest fees and travel expenses. I get to meet a lot of people who support me in achieving my goals.

Name your favorite meal. Pono Market (p104) plate lunch or *bentō* is the best. I'll also eat Spam *musubi* or something from Burger King.

What do you enjoy doing on Kaua'i? My favorite place is **Anahola** (opposite). All my friends go there, and we surf and just hang out around the beach. I love to surf and go camping all over the island: **Polihale** (p206), **Hanalei** (p133), Kealia, and especially Anahola because it's beautiful country living and just fun.

What do you do on rainy days? Watch TV or surf movies. I'm not into playing video games (eg Wii or PlayStation). I'd rather be outdoors.

What do you want to be when you grow up? A professional surfer.

Where would you take visiting tourist kids? I would take them to Kealia Beach because it's close to my house, and I would tell them, 'Don't be edgy, just lay back, slow down and enjoy the island lifestyle.'

you'll probably share the beach with Hawaiian families, especially on weekends. Remember, it's their beach: respect the locals. The wide bay, fringed with a decent swath of lovely sandy beach, is a surfers' hot spot at the choppier south end. But toward the north, waters are calm enough for swimming. There are two ways to get here: for the south end, turn off Kuhio Hwy onto Kukuihale Rd at the 13-mile marker, drive a mile down and then turn onto the dirt beach road. For the north end, take 'Aliomanu Rd at the 14-mile marker and park in the sandy lot.

'ALIOMANU BEACH

Secluded 'Aliomanu Beach is another spot frequented primarily by locals, who pole- and throw-net fish and gather *limu* (seaweed). It's a mile-long stretch of beach; you can get to the prettier north end by turning onto 'Aliomanu Rd Second), just past the 15-mile marker on Kuhio Hwy. Don't take 'Aliomanu Rd (First), a mile south, by mistake! Then turn left onto Kalalea View Dr, go 880yd and turn right at the beach access sign.

Activities

If you're an open-minded traveler looking for an only-on-Kaua'i experience, book in a session for some authentic *lomilomi* massage at **Angeline's Mu'olaulani** (see the boxed text, opposite).

To sample traditional Ayurvedic therapies, try **TriHealth Ayurveda** (☎ 828-2104, 800-455-0770; http://trihealthayurvedaspa.com; Kuhio Hwy; treatments $130-275; by appointment) in a simple bungalow just off the highway. Therapists are trained both locally and in Kerala, India. A popular treatment includes a sensual hot-oil massage, synchronized by two therapists, followed by heady relaxation in a rather intimidating horizontal steamer. Located between the 20- and 21-mile markers.

Eating & Sleeping

For information about camping in Anahola Beach Park, see p259.

DUANE'S ONO CHAR-BURGER Drive-in $

☎ 822-9181; 4-4350 Kuhio Hwy; burgers $5-7; 10am-6pm Mon-Sat, 11am-6pm Sun

Amid a world of phonies, here's the real deal. Try the Old-Fashioned (cheddar, onions and sprouts) or the Local Girl (Swiss cheese, pineapple and teriyaki sauce). Add crispy thin fries and some melt-in-your-mouth onion rings. And you're not alone: check out the autographed photos of famous fans, from Chuck Norris to Steve Tyler.

HALE KIKO'O Inn $

our pick ☎ 822-3922; www.halekikoo.com; 4-4382-B Kuhio Hwy; studio units s $70-80, d $75-90 (cleaning fee $75);

Who would guess that such chic digs exist along this unnamed, unpaved lane? Choose from two charming, modern studios, each with full kitchen. The downstairs unit is large enough for living room and features stylish slate floors, lava-rock pillars, garden patio and artsy outdoor shower. The upstairs unit is more ordinary but brighter, with windows aplenty and a deck.

'ILI NOHO KAI O ANAHOLA B&B $$

☎ 821-0179, 639-6317; www.kauai.net/anahola; Aliomanu Rd; r with shared bathroom incl breakfast $100-120

This simple guesthouse fronting Anahola Beach ain't cheap, but if you dream of rolling out of bed and onto a sandy beach in under a minute, it might be worth the price. The four compact but tidy rooms (which share two bathrooms) surround a central

DONKEY BEACH

Unofficially known as a nude site, this beach is secluded and scenic but rarely swimmable. It's a rugged place to escape the highway and cars, with rocks scattered at the water's edge, windswept ironwood trees, and native flowers *naupaka* and *'ilima* adding dashes of color.

Summer swells might be manageable, but stay ashore if you're an inexperienced ocean swimmer. From October to May dangerous rip currents and a powerful shorebreak take over.

The beach is accessible in two ways: you can cycle or walk the coastal path (p102) and turn *makai* (toward the ocean). Or you can drive along Kuhio Hwy to the parking lot about halfway between the 11- and 12-mile markers; look for the small 'Public Shoreline Access' sign. Restrooms are open at the parking lot.

This access path cuts through a 300-acre, 29-lot planned community called **Kealia Kai** (www.kealiakai.com). Note that public nudity is illegal in Hawaii, and the Kealia Kai developer has cracked down on folks baring all.

While Donkey Beach is not Kaua'i's finest, it's a proud example of public shoreline access. Sure, you're surrounded by exclusive private properties, but you have an equal right to enjoy that light sweet sand.

HAWAIIAN HEALING HANDS

In the late 1970s, Angeline Kaihalanaopuna Hopkins Locey moved back to Hawaii after years of living in California. Back in her native land, Angeline, who is three-quarters Native Hawaiian and grew up on O'ahu, experienced a cultural homecoming as well as a geographical one. She embraced Hawaiian healing, studied with *lomilomi kumu* (traditional Hawaiian massage teacher) Margret Machado on the Big Island, and in the mid-1980s established a homestead in Anahola, where she began to share her gift of therapeutic touch with the community. Over the years 'Auntie Angeline,' now in her late seventies, became a local icon, and today her son Michael and granddaughter Malia carry on her legacy.

Angeline's Mu'olaulani (☎ 822-3235; www.angelinelomikauai.com; Kamalomalo'o Pl; massage treatment $150; 9am-3pm Mon-Fri by appointment only) is an authentic introduction to Hawaiian healing practices and remains untouristy and frequented mainly by locals. Don't expect plush towels, glossy marble floors or an endless menu of face and nail pamperings. A trip to Angeline's is more like visiting a friend's bungalow, with an outdoor shower, wooden-plank deck, massage tables separated by curtains, and simple sarongs for covering up.

The signature treatment costs as much as a resort-spa massage, but the three-step process does include time in a steam room, a vigorous salt scrub and a special four-hands, two-person *lomilomi* massage (traditional Hawaiian healing massage). The four-hands method prevents you from fixating on a particular tender area – the mind cannot focus on all four hands, so it must disengage and let the body relax and receive the treatment. But if you'd prefer a single massage therapist (or other treatments like hot stones), just ask. During the treatment, therapists might spontaneously break into *oli* (Hawaiian chant), which adds a unique and powerful element. If you chat with Michael or Malia, their reverence for the ancient healing arts is clear, and their desire to share their culture would make any visitor feel welcome.

As an expression of *ho'okipa* (hospitality), the Loceys invite guests to stay and sip a drink on the patio after the treatment. The facilities (including showers and sauna) are unisex, but the staff is glad to provide same-sex facilities upon request.

lanai, where guests can 'talk story' and fill up on home-cooked breakfasts. The hosts are Native Hawaiian activists who now run a B&B on Hawaiian Home Lands for which they fought long and hard. The cleaning fee is $80.

RIVERSIDE TROPICAL RETREAT Inn $$

☎ 823-0705; www.vrbo.com/9186; 4-4382 Kuhio Hwy; ste $125;

Spiritual seekers would appreciate this rustic bungalow, surrounded by green forest, river, mountains and pasture. The one-bedroom suite is well worn rather than spanking new, but includes kitchenette and lots of louvers for ventilation. One of the host couple, Tatiana, is an Ayurvedic practitioner and offers specially prepared meals, bodywork, counseling and other spiritual guidance for additional fees.

KO'OLAU ROAD

The peaceful, scenic loop drive along Ko'olau Rd takes you through rich green pastures dotted with soaring white egrets and bright wild flowers. It makes a nice diversion and is the way to reach untouristed Moloa'a Beach or Larsen's Beach (no facilities at either). Ko'olau Rd connects with Kuhio Hwy 880yd north of the 16-mile marker and again 180yd south of the 20-mile marker.

For a quick bite, the **Moloa'a Sunrise Fruit Stand** (☎ 822-1441; Kuhio Hwy & Ko'olau Rd; juices & smoothies $3-6.25, sandwiches $5.50-7; 7:30am-6pm Mon-Sat, 10am-5pm Sun) offers healthful sandwiches on multigrain bread, taro burgers and brown-rice vegetarian sushi. Located between the 16- and 17-mile markers.

Moloa'a Beach

Off the tourist path, this classically curved bay appeared in the pilot for *Gilligan's Island*. To the north, there's a shallow protected swimming area good for families; to the south, the waters are rougher but there's more sand. When the surf's up, stay dry and safe – go beach walking instead. Toward the

Island Insights

Only longtime locals bore witness to an Anahola landmark, **Hole in the Mountain**. The *puka* (hole) in **Pu'u Konanae** is now more like a sliver, since a landslide transformed the once-obvious landmark. Legend says the original hole was created when a giant threw his spear through the mountain, causing the water stored within to gush forth as waterfalls. From slightly north of the 15-mile marker along Hwy 56, look back at the mountain, down to the right of the tallest pinnacle: on sunny days you'll see a smile of light shining through a slit in the rock face.

back of the beach, which is fed by Moloa'a Stream, there's plenty of shade, making for an ideal picnic or daydreaming spot.

To get here, follow Ko'olau Rd and turn onto Moloa'a Rd, which ends 1320yd down at a few beach houses and a little parking area.

Cross jaw-jarringly unpaved roads to find **Jade Lily Pad** (☎ 822-5216; www.rosewoodkauai.com; near Moloa'a Rd; 2br house $295), a beach house on stilts beside a tranquil stream. With two bedrooms, two bathrooms, full kitchen, lanai with Jacuzzi and airy cathedral ceilings, it's a spacious retreat for adventurous couples or families.

Larsen's Beach

This long, golden-sand beach, named after L David Larsen (former manager of C Brewer's Kilauea Sugar Company), is good for solitary strolls and beachcombing. Although the water is shallow, snorkeling can be good when the waters are very calm, usually only in the summer. Beware of a vicious current that runs westward along the beach and out through a channel in the reef.

When the tide is low, you might share Larsen's with Hawaiian families collecting an edible seaweed called *limu kohu*. The seaweed found here is considered to be some of the finest in all of Hawaii. Otherwise, it will be you, the sand and the waves.

To get here, turn onto Ko'olau Rd from whichever end (ie where it intersects either Kuhio Hwy or Moloa'a Rd), go just over a mile then turn toward the ocean on a dirt road (easy to miss from the south: look for it just before the cemetery) and take the immediate left. It's 1 mile to the parking area and then a five-minute walk downhill to the beach.

Anahola Beach Park (p108) is a local family favorite

ANN CECIL

NORTH SHORE

Simply put, the North Shore is a way of life. Agelessness, defying the odds and inspired idealism are common themes among its residents. Chock-full of natural playgrounds, the North Shore is the story behind why many visitors turned their trip to Kaua'i into a lifetime stay – it was just too heartbreaking to leave. With fewer plantation-era locals, the transplant-heavy North Shore marks a sharp demographic shift that's easy to sense the further north you drive. One could almost say the number of organic markets, highbrow restaurants and '60s-like attitude increases in direct proportion to the number of miles driven away from Lihu'e.

NORTH SHORE ITINERARIES

IN TWO DAYS *This leg: 17 miles*

❶ **KILAUEA POINT AND LIGHTHOUSE (p117)** Ease into your surroundings with sweeping views at the northernmost point of the island; it doubles as a National Wildlife Refuge and sanctuary for Hawaii seabirds.

❷ **KONG LUNG CENTER (p120)** Stroll among the shops and grab a quick bite to go at **Pau Hana Pizza (p120)** or do the 'sit down' thing at the **Lighthouse Bistro (p120)**.

❸ **MAKUA (TUNNELS) BEACH (p148)** Take a pleasant drive north through Hanalei past several one-way bridges. Past the 8-mile marker is Makua (Tunnels) Beach, where reef-snorkeling and swimming opportunities abound.

❹ **MANINIHOLO DRY CAVE (p149)** Get a peek at the inside of this cave, across the street from **Haena Beach Park (p148)**, which lost half its width to sand from a 1957 tsunami.

❺ **LIMAHULI GARDEN (p148)** Start your morning at Limahuli (meaning 'upturned hand') Garden, honoring the Hawaiians who built agricultural terraces out of lava rock and planted taro, on a self-guided tour of this National Tropical Botanical Garden.

❻ **KAULU PAOA HEI'AU (p151)** Head to **Ke'e Beach (p151)** and while there take a moment to visit one of the most cherished heiau *(*Hawaiian temples).

❼ **MEDITERRANEAN GOURMET (p149)** Cap off your day with a meal of fish and scallop ceviche, banana leaf baked *'ahi* or free-range rosemary rack of lamb at Ha'ena's version of a high-end restaurant.

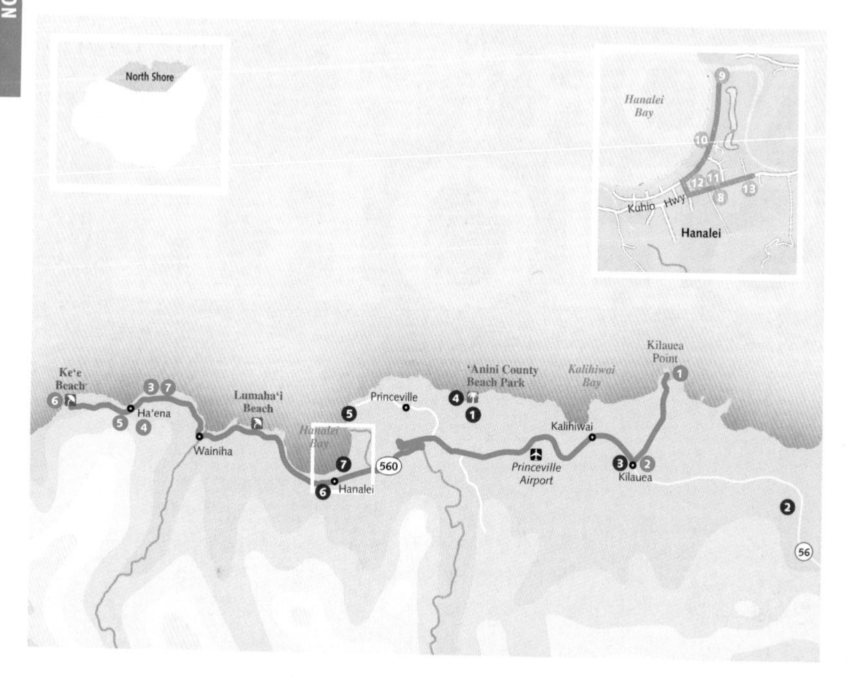

IN FOUR DAYS *This leg: 3 miles*

8 **JAVA KAI (p141)** After following the two-day itinerary, rise and shine with a cold, black-tea-and-milk Chai Anu, a Shark Bite (a sundae-like blend with espresso) or a spicy Point Break smoothie with ginger, papayas and coconut milk at this morning hot-spot.

9 **HANALEI RIVER (p139)** Take a kayak tour or stand up paddle lesson for almost-guaranteed athletic success in an idyllic setting.

10 **HANALEI BEACH PARK PAVILION (p135)** Turquoise, alluring water, pristine sailboats and waterfall-laden mountain views are all part of what makes this a scenic don't-miss spot for a lazy beach day.

11 **POLYNESIA CAFÉ (p141)** Take a stroll through the Ching Young Village shopping center and grab a scrumptious paper-plate breakfast or early to-go lunch.

12 **EVOLVE LOVE GALLERY (p143)** Peruse the work of fishermen-artists and intricately small, rare shell lei – woven like tiny ropes. Sunrise shell and Kahelalani shell, made in the tradition of the Ni'ihau-style lei, are also found here, as are paintings and other forms of local art.

13 **POSTCARDS CAFÉ (p142)** Enjoy a healthy, well-prepared dinner at this pescetarian restaurant a short stroll across the street.

FOR LOVERS

1 **ORCHID COTTAGE (p124)** Stay at a secluded B&B such as this one where you can pluck fruit for breakfast like Adam and Eve.

2 **KAUAI KUNANA DAIRY (p118)** Start gathering for an evening sunset beach picnic with a tour of this dairy and sampling of goat cheeses.

3 **BANANA JOE'S FRUITSTAND (p119)** Choose from a smattering of local honeys, chocolate and, of course, exotic fruit – and pick up a lei for your better half.

4 **'ANINI BEACH (p123)** Stroll hand in hand, fall asleep under a tree, frolic in the sun and bathe in the sea in this mellow setting.

5 **BLACK POT BEACH PARK (HANALEI PIER) (p135)** Head north for a sunset *pupu* tryst – try to get there before 6pm for ample picnicking time.

6 **BAR ACUDA TAPAS & WINE (p142)** If high-end is the name of the game for you, splurge on a $20 glass of wine or enjoy sliced honeycomb, apples and artisan cheese at this candlelit tapas and wine spot.

7 **TAHITI NUI (p142)** Now you're primed for some late-night drinks and flirting at this 'happening' dive bar classic.

KARL LEHMANN

Kilauea Point Lighthouse

HIGHLIGHTS

❶ **BEST BEACH:** 'Anini Beach Park (p123)
❷ **BEST VIEW:** Kilauea Point (opposite)
❸ **BEST ACTIVITY:** Hike to Hanakapia'i Falls (p154)
❹ **BEST SUNSET SWIM:** Black Pot Beach Park (Hanalei Pier) (p135)
❺ **BEST DIVE BAR:** Tahiti Nui (p142)

KILAUEA

pop 2075

The northernmost point of the island is a different kind of beautiful. Kilauea doesn't offer much in the way of oceanfront property but most of its residents enjoy a lush atmosphere where vegetation abounds and people sightings are more sparse. This old plantation town has become somewhat of a farm country for the entitled, teeming with organic grocers, moss-laden buildings and a historic lighthouse that serves as a wildlife refuge, whale watching spot and vantage point for dramatic, scenic bluffs. Sleepy, unassuming and vibrant, this town is known for its 'ag' lands and 'North Shore' idealism.

Most eating and shopping options can be found at the two shopping centers off the main street, Kilauea Rd (also known locally as Lighthouse Rd).

Beaches

KAHILI (ROCK QUARRIES) BEACH & POOLS OF MOKOLEA

Rugged and great for serious surfers when the winds behave, but there's a rip current from Kilauea Stream's outflow, so beware. Voyeurism for the vicarious is easy here, as fisherman and surfers are at work and play. If the waves are suitable for surfing, it's likely not safe for swimming.

Public access is via Wailapa Rd, which begins midway between the 21- and 22-mile markers on Kuhio Hwy. Follow Wailapa Rd north for less than 880yd beyond Kuhio Hwy and then turn left on the unmarked dirt road (4WD recommended) that begins at a bright-yellow water valve.

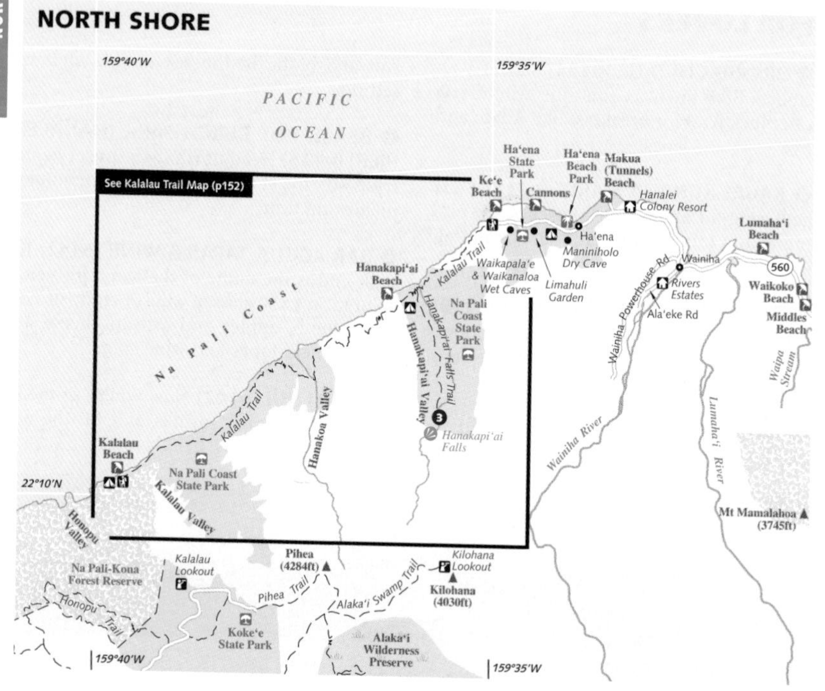

KAUAPEA (SECRET) BEACH

It's often been argued how 'secret' it really is, but this deflowered location is still renowned for its reclusive qualities. But take note: even though it's illegal, people have been known to drop trou at this locale. So if that offends, perhaps this spot isn't for you. Off in the distance is an island known as Moku'ae'ae, a bird sanctuary. Accessing the beach requires a trek of about 15 minutes that is dangerous during inclement weather.

The trail starts off Kalihiwai Rd. Turn *makai* (seaward) down an unmarked dirt road and follow it to its end to the parking area; the trailhead begins in the plum trees. Follow the trail to the bottom to the western end of the beach. The expanse of beach will be to the right and a rocky coast to your left. If the swells are down, you can consider strolling left instead of right where the trail meets the beach. Continue left *only* if the water is calm (ie no crashing waves – or you risk getting sucked out to sea). The lava rocks are about a quarter of a mile down.

Sights

KILAUEA POINT NATIONAL WILDLIFE REFUGE

☎ 828-1413; www.fws.gov/kilaueapoint; Lighthouse Rd; adult/child under 16 $5/free; 10am-4pm, closed federal holidays

It's not just about soaring tropic birds, but sweeping views that include the possibility of an occasional whale breaching in the distance. The drive to the lighthouse passes horses grazing and bright fields. Even just overlooking the bluffs from the cul-de-sac fronting the lighthouse is worth it. Red-footed boobies, wedge-tailed shearwaters, red-tailed and white-tailed tropic birds and Laysan albatross are among the birds you could see, or Kaua'i's nene, the endangered Hawaiian goose. Look for sea turtles and spinner dolphins in spring and summer, and for humpback whales in winter. You'll also see Moku'ae'ae Island, which is teeming with protected wildlife. To get there, turn *makai* (toward the ocean) onto Kolo Rd, then take a left onto Kilauea Rd. Drive 2 miles to the refuge entrance where the road ends.

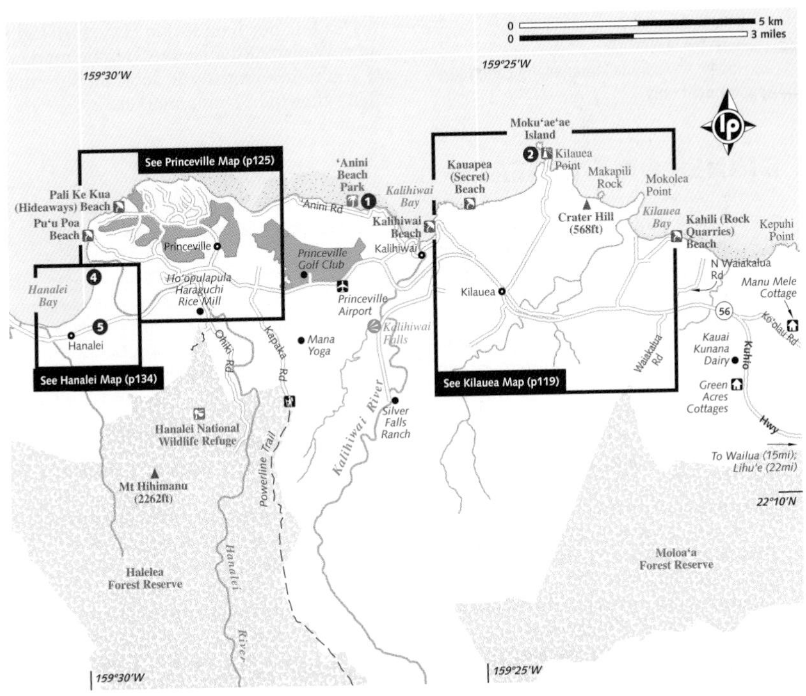

Top Picks

NORTH SHORE FOR KIDS

- **Magic Dragon Toy & Art Supply Co** (p130)
- **Surf lessons** (p139)
- **Island Sails** (p140)
- **Hanalei Beach Park Pavilion** (p135)
- **Hanalei Dolphin Fish Market** (p142)
- **Ki Ho'alu – slack key guitar concerts** (p143)
- **Lappert's ice cream** (p128)
- **Kokonut Kids** (p143)
- **Pat's Taqueria** (p141)

CHRIST MEMORIAL EPISCOPAL CHURCH

☎ 826-4501; 2518 Kolo Rd

After turning onto Kolo Rd from Kuhio Hwy, just past the 23-mile marker if you're heading north, look immediately for this short and small-but-striking church. Built in 1941 of lava rock, the headstones in the churchyard, also of lava rock, date back to a Hawaiian Congregational church.

KAUAI KUNANA DAIRY

☎ 651-5046; www.kauaikunanadairy.com; tours by appointment only

The only micro-dairy on the island, with 20 does, they have a knack for goat cheese and even ecofriendly beauty products made with goats' milk. This family farm is also certified organic for its fruits and vegetables and specializes in such homemade treats as pesto, dressing and bread.

NA 'AINA KAI BOTANICAL GARDENS

☎ 828-0525; www.naainakai.com; 4101 Wailapa Rd; tours $25-70; by reservation, Tue-Fri

The newest project within this husband-and-wife operation pays tribute to Hawaiian culture with the Na'aina Kai *ahupua'a* (traditional Hawaiian land division), paying homage to the traditional island way of island life. A small mountain waterfall travels past replica huts and through *lo'i* (taro wet fields) and sweet potato fields into an 'ocean.' This artistic and cultural feat, when complete, will house 15 bronze inhabitants canoe-building, mat weaving and kapa-making. If the *ahupua'a* isn't enough for you, there's also 240-acres of botanical gardens. Also on the grounds: a beach, a bird-watching marsh and forest with 60,000 South and East Asian hardwood trees.

Heading north on Kuhio Hwy, turn right onto Wailapa Rd after the 21-mile marker. If you're heading south, look for the turn (left) after the 22-mile marker.

DINNER ON THE BEACH

If terms like 'pita,' 'raw,' 'gluten-free' or 'organic' are among those oft' coined in your preferred eating requisites, then perhaps a personal gourmet chef beachside is a dream come true. Here's a smattering of at-your-service pros:

- our pick **Foraging Fork** (☎ 635-5865; www.foragingfork.com; dinner per couple $300) Following the mantra 'from the soil to the soul,' North Shore chef AJ Deraspe is an inventive, hard-core foodie and a well-educated gourmet with a penchant for local, organic and sustainable farming to boot. Whether it's a meal drop-off, romantic dinner or larger beach party, Deraspe can cater (pun intended) to almost every known diet. (He got his Ayurvedic training in India and Nepal.) Vegan, raw, gluten-free, religious restrictions – you name it, chances are he can whip it up.
- **Dining in Nature** (☎ 808-345-6931; www.dininginnature.com; completely customized dinner per couple $295) Alkaline, vegetarian or not and, depending on your preference, local and organic. From the allergy-challenged to the high-maintenance but small-carbon-footprint–seeking, sustainable chefs Chris Hamby and Valerie Adair specialize in gluten-free gourmet for those with even the most rigid of diets. They'll bring the linens and silver, and leave you with a photo memento and beach bonfire. Limousine package available.
- **Heavenly Creations** (☎ 821-9300; www.heavenlycreations.org; dinner per couple $285) Combinations can include blackened shrimp with *liliko'i* (passion fruit) glaze, local goat cheese, olive or artichoke tapenade, local fresh fish with macadamia and grilled pineapple with coconut ice cream for dessert.

NORTH SHORE

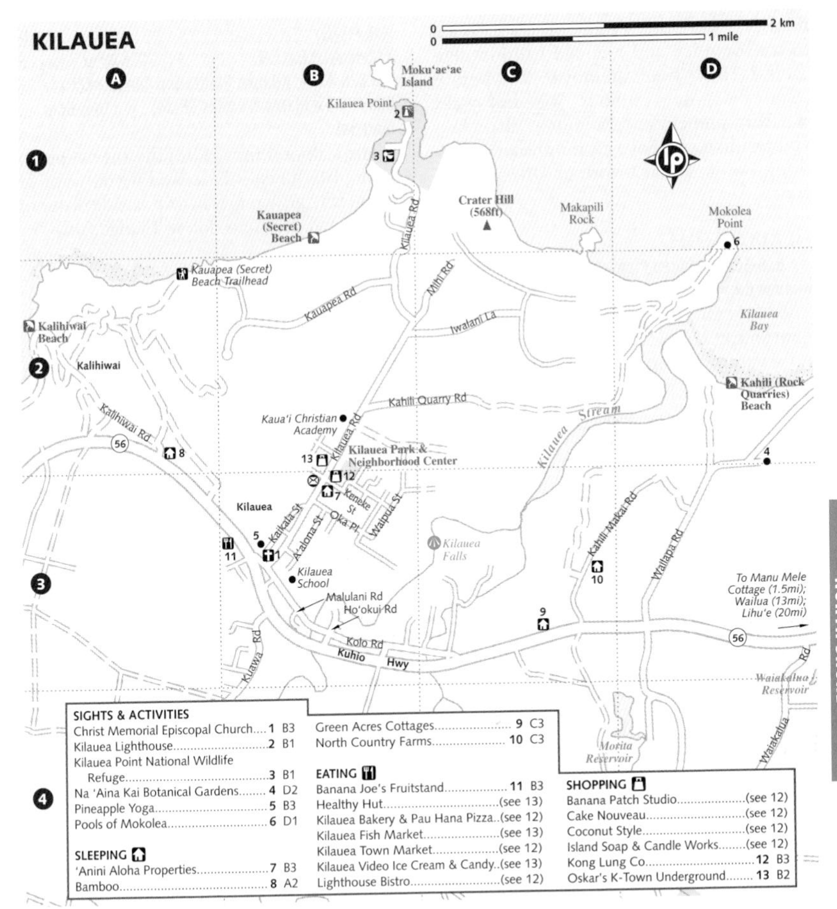

Activities

Check out **Pineapple Yoga** (☎ 652-9009; www.pineappleyoga.com; drop-in classes $15; 7:30-9:30am, Mon-Sat) for Ashtanga yoga classes. There are no classes on Sundays, when there's a full moon and on new moon days. It's located in the parish house of the Christ Memorial Church, across the street from the Menehune Mart gas station.

Eating

KILAUEA VIDEO ICE CREAM & CANDY
Ice Cream/Gelato $

our pick ☎ 828-1822; Kilauea Plantation Center, 4270 Kilauea Rd; noon-9:30pm

The owner of this buzzing little shop has a lot of obvious pride in his family, his business and his products. If you want a perfect pick-me-up on a warm day, whether it be gelato, creamy tropical ice cream or a live-culture, low-calorie Carpigiani, everything here is served up in a low-key, happy-go-lucky style. Mango lychee and banana ice creams or the Carpigiani twist offer unique refreshment.

BANANA JOE'S FRUITSTAND
Fruit Stand $

☎ 828-1092; www.bananajoekauai.com; 5-2719 Kuhio Hwy; 9am-6pm Mon-Sat

This low-rent–looking shack just past the 24-mile marker on the *mauka* side of the road is a smoothie-producing gem. Want to try some icy and blended fruition delicacies? How 'bout atemoya? Rambutan? Mamey sapote? Liliko'i? Soft not waxy starfruit, pomelo and kumquats also make you feel like you have accomplished something exotic. Great before or after any sun sports.

HEALTHY HUT
Snacks $$

☎ 828-6626; Kilauea Plantation Center, 4270 Kilauea Rd; 8:30am-9pm

This organic grocer offers some antioxidant snacks coupled with some guilty pleasures: cacao nibs and kefir, buttery Anahola granola, and an array of local, organic fruits and veggies.

KILAUEA BAKERY & PAU HANA PIZZA
Pizza $$

☎ 828-2020; Kong Lung Center, 2484 Keneke St; pastries $4, pizza $15-33; 6:30am-9pm

It's hard to wait in line while smelling whatever it is that's cooking. Tropical Danishes, cookies – they are all resoundingly odiferous. The pizza (served from 10:30am) has a thick crust, but if you're OK with that, it's usually drenched in a generous heaping of toppings. Opt for pineapple as one of them; just remember it's not really 'authentic' Hawaiian.

Don't Miss

- A crash course in exotic fruit names at Banana Joe's Fruitstand (p119)
- Sushi and martinis just before sunset at the lobby bar at the St Regis Princeville (p130)
- Sunset at Ke'e Beach (p151)
- Local ingredients only pupu (appetizers) like honeycomb, goat cheese and apple at Bar Acuda Tapas & Wine (p142)
- A glimpse of the Waikapala'e and Waikanaloa wet caves, said to have been dug by fire goddess Pele (p151)
- Early-morning surf at Black Pot Beach Park (Hanalei Pier) (p135)
- Testing your native flora savvy at Limahuli Garden (p148)
- Camping at 'Anini Beach Park (p123)
- Kayaking up Kalihiwai Stream (p122)

KILAUEA FISH MARKET
Sandwiches/Wraps $$

☎ 828-6244; Kilauea Plantation Center, 4270 Kilauea Rd; plates & wraps $8-14; 11am-8pm Mon-Sat

There's a good mix of healthy-meets-local–style plate lunches here, and if you want to get locally grown greens with a side order of marinated meat, no one will judge you.

LIGHTHOUSE BISTRO
Eclectic $$$

☎ 828-0480; Kong Lung Center, 2484 Keneke St; lunch mains $12-20, dinner mains $18-36; noon-2pm & 5:30-9pm Mon-Sat, 5:30-9pm Sun

The ambience is great at this expensive but romantic spot, though the pastas are overpriced. Live music, usually solo artists, makes it great for a date, as does their wine list.

KILAUEA TOWN MARKET
Vegetarian $$$

☎ 828-1512; Kong Lung Center, 2484 Keneke St; 8am-8pm Sun-Thu, to 8:30pm Fri & Sat

Great for organic wines, stinky (in a good way) cheeses, local produce from farmers and much more for the high-end discerning palate. If you're heading to the beach for your own picnic or back to your room for some yummy in-house dining, this is a great place to check out.

Shopping

BANANA PATCH STUDIO

☎ 828-6522; Kong Lung Center, 2484 Keneke St; 10am-6pm

Custom ceramic tile work and designs, and Hawaiiana art. Though it's not a one-of-a-kind stop, it's worthy of window shopping or sneaking a peek at the murals, local art and Hawaiiana.

CAKE NOUVEAU

☎ 828-6412; Kong Lung Center, 2484 Keneke St; 11am-6pm

If you need a boutique-y dress for your upcoming date night or just a shopping fix, this store offers pricey (albeit cute) dresses, slacks, tops and skirts with the accessories to match.

COCONUT STYLE

☎ 828-6899; Kong Lung Center, 2484 Keneke St; 11am-6pm

Bali-inspired furniture, art and hand-painted silk batiks pepper this modest, earthy and tropical showcase next door to the Kong Lung Island Soap & Candle Works.

ISLAND SOAP & CANDLE WORKS

828-1955; www.islandsoap.com; Kong Lung Center, 2484 Keneke St; 9am-9pm

While not exclusive to Kaua'i or Kilauea (other shops are in Kapa'a and Princeville, to name a few), this store is where you can watch them make and cure soaps that are so pretty that they look good enough to eat. Vibrant, fragrant and unique, there are boatloads of Kilauea-only made soap 'flavors' like mango cream coconut, vanilla lavender cream and chocolate and espresso, along with 'grime' bars, perfect for those toting *keiki* (child). The shop also gives its leftover makings to elementary schools on-island to use for crafts.

KONG LUNG CO

828-1822; Kong Lung Center, 2484 Keneke St; 11am-6pm

This shop has several contrived 'themes' that make for an interesting hodgepodge in-house catalog to complement its uppity staff. If you are a true Asian art aficionado, this stop might annoy you. Along with overly marked-up imports and plenty of 'Far East' tchotchkes to peruse, they do, however, sell pricey reclaimed silk kimonos and boutique-style *keiki* clothes.

Top Picks

NORTH SHORE SUNSET SPOTS

- **Ke'e Beach** (p151)
- **Hanalei Beach Park Pavilion** (p135)
- **'Anini Beach Park** (p123)

OSKAR'S K-TOWN UNDERGROUND

our pick 828-6858; www.oskarskauai.com; Kilauea Plantation Center, 4270 Kilauea Rd; 10am-7pm Mon-Sat, 11am-6pm Sun

This shop stocks baby shoes, gently used and recycled baby clothes and organic toddler outfits along with a selection of unique and island-inspired beach wear for adults; there's a smattering of gift souvenirs to choose from.

Sleeping

No hotels or condos exist in Kilauea – and a new B&B limitation has made it 'interesting' challenge-wise for owners to advertise.

Ke'e Beach (p151) as seen from the Kalalau Trail MICAH WRIGHT

That said, many vacation rentals are keeping a low profile. Search **Vacation Rentals by Owner** (VRBO; www.vrbo.com).

GREEN ACRES COTTAGES Cottage $

☎ 828-0478, 866-484-6347; www.greenacrescottages.com; 5-0421-C Kuhio Hwy; cottages $75;

They're not actually cottages, but these small studios are a good bargain and close to plenty of local-growing fruit. Each has its own private entrance and kitchenette.

MANU MELE COTTAGE Cottage $$

our pick Map pp116-17; ☎ 828-6797, 652-2585; www.kauaibirdsongcottage.com; cottage $150

Meaning 'bird song' in Hawaiian, the cute Manu Mele Cottage boasts a canopy bed, exotic hardwood furniture, high-end tub, full kitchen and washer/dryer. There's a one-time cleaning fee of $100. The cottage is very secluded, located southeast of Kilauea town, in an area technically called Waipake. Heading north toward Kilauea, take a right on Ko'olau Rd.

NORTH COUNTRY FARMS Cottage $$

☎ 828-1513; www.northcountryfarms.com; cottage $150

You've got to call for an appointment, but if they have openings, it's a good deal if you want the ability to stroll around in the morning and pick fruit from their farm. Though they claim to be minutes from the beach, keep in mind they're inland, and it is 'just minutes' if you're *driving*. Choose from one of two cottages similar to each other, but each unique in their own charming way.

'Anini Beach Park

LINDA CHING

PLUMERIA MOON Cottage $$$$

Map pp116-17; ☎ 828-0228; www.kauaivacationhideaway.com/plumeria; 4180 N Waiakalua St; cottages $295;

Though Kilauea is inland, what this pricey getaway lacks in affordability, it makes up for in seclusion. Just one bedroom, it is ideal for honeymooners, with its private hot tub and off-the-beaten-track feel. It also has a gas grill for dining in.

KALIHIWAI

pop 717

Sandwiched between Kilauea and 'Anini, Kalihiwai ('water's edge' in Hawaiian) is a hidden treasure that's easy to pass by. The main indication that it's on the *makai* side is Kalihiwai Bridge, which curves dramatically after an abundance of towering albesia trees. Most venture here to discover the remote beach. Kalihiwai Rd was at one point a road that passed Kalihiwai Beach, connecting with the highway at two points. A tidal wave in 1957 washed out the Kalihiwai Bridge. The bridge was never rebuilt, and now there are two Kalihiwai Rds, one on each side of the river.

Beaches

KALIHIWAI BEACH

Remote, small and surrounded by lush grounds, it's an ideal frolicking spot for sunbathing, sandcastle building and, swells permitting, swimming, bodyboarding and surfing along the cliff on the east side.

Kalihiwai Stream offers an ideal spot for a short kayak jaunt if you've rented one (see opposite) and don't feel like trying the more-crowded rivers of Wailua or Hanalei. Launch at the beach and into Kalihiwai Valley, where you should keep eyes peeled for Kalihiwai Falls. Note: the falls are on land leased by Princeville Ranch Stables and you might be shooed away. The beach has no facilities.

To get here, take the first Kalihiwai Rd if you're heading north on Kuhio Hwy, roughly 880yd from Kilauea.

NORTH SHORE

Activities

KAYAKING

The closest outfit that will rent you a kayak is **Kayak Kauai** (Map p134; ☎ 826-9844; www.kayakkauai.com; single/double $29/54; ⏰ 8am-5:30pm, to 8pm in summer). Though they'll allow you an unsupervised rental on Kalihiwai, they do not allow renting kayaks for the Wailua River, Na Pali coast or any open ocean.

PILATES

Up your fitness at **Pilates Kaua'i** (☎ 639-3074; www.pilateskauai.com; 2540 Halocline Rd; per hr one person $75, couple $45; groups of 3 or more $30; ⏰ by appointment only). Owner Laurie Antonellis is a positive, well-experienced instructor with years of bodywork behind her. Ask about mat classes and group sessions.

HORSEBACK RIDING

Saddle up with **Silver Falls Ranch** (☎ 828-6718; www.silverfallsranch.com; Kamo'okoa Rd; 90min trail ride $95, 2-/3-hr trail ride $115/135) for an inland, lush ride amid the North Shore landscape at the end of Kamo'okoa Rd. Daily rides include a shorter trek or a ride to the falls, which includes a waterfall swim and picnic lunch.

Sleeping

BAMBOO

our pick Map p119; ☎ 828-0811; www.surfsideprop.com; 3281 Kalihiwai Rd; 1br house per week $1100;
Overlooking the Kalihiwai Valley and a 10-minute walk to either 'Anini or Kalihiwai Beaches, this is a charming getaway attached to a larger house inhabited by the owners. A private entrance takes you up steep stairs to this cozy but well-appointed spot that works well for two people. A small deck offers views of lush vegetation. Guests have exclusive rights to a hot tub, and the full bathroom overlooks an impressively landscaped garden where couples have gotten married. There's also citrus, avocados, bananas, and flowers for guests to pluck at their leisure. Other features include a full kitchen, a gas BBQ on the lanai and free long-distance Canada and mainland US calls. Kayak, snorkel gear and beach chairs are included. There's a $250 security deposit and a $100 cleaning fee. If you the owners also offer accom **Orchid Cottage** (p124) and **Plumeria** (p125) in 'Anini.

'ANINI

Don't dismiss 'Anini, home of the quintessential 'vacation rental,' as some on-the-beaten-path strip. Secluded, serene and rented by such names as Tom Petty, the drive along the road fronting 'Anini Beach is as scenic as it is perfect for house – ahem, excuse us – mansion window-shopping. But this secluded area remains somewhat secret and is still lauded by local families with summer homes here. The beach park is spacious, with calmer water in the summer months that can be safe for kids, though keep in mind it's not lifeguarded. Also ideal for stand up paddle surfing or snorkeling in its huge reef. Above all, it's also home to some of the best windsurfing conditions to be found.

From Lihu'e, head north on Kuhio Hwy, cross Kalihiwai Bridge, turn onto the second Kalihiwai Rd (there are two) and bear left onto 'Anini Rd.

Beaches

'ANINI BEACH PARK

our pick Perfect for camping or barbecuing, 'Anini's beach park has some of the most reliable conditions for water sports, as it bubbles over a lagoon and is protected by one of the longest and widest fringing reefs in the Hawaiian Islands. At its widest point, the reef extends over 1600ft offshore. The park is unofficially divided into day-use, camping and windsurfing areas. While weekends might draw crowds, weekdays are low key. Facilities include rest rooms, showers, changing rooms, drinking water, picnic pavilions and BBQ grills.

Activities

SWIMMING & SNORKELING

With practically no shorebreak and average water depth of 4ft to 5ft, lap swimming is easier here than elsewhere, though there aren't lifeguards.

Swimming and snorkeling are good in the day-use area and in front of the camping area; conditions are best when the tide is high. The water is shallow, but the long barrier reef means lots of juvenile fish.

WINDSURFING

Windsurfing teacher extraordinaire Celeste Harvel from **our pick** **Windsurf Kaua'i** (☎ 828-6838; windsurfkauai@aol.com; 3hr lesson $100, board rental per hr $25; rentals 10 am-4pm, lessons 9am & 1pm Mon-Fri) has been teaching windsurfing for 31 years and is all about getting you out there and having some fun. Harvel can take up to six people per class, which consists of an hour on land and two on the water. 'Plenty time,' she says. She'll outfit you with gear, including booties and rashguards ('rashies'). Call in advance for a reservation.

Sleeping

'Anini rentals are pricey, ranging from $1100 to $10,500 weekly, not including cleaning fees and security deposits. Keep in mind that most will also add an 11.416% excise and accommodation tax on top of weekly rates. Our initial list got smaller as several B&Bs that were operating without proper licensing have since closed under a recent county bill known as 2204, which allows vacation rentals only in specific zones on the island (or grandfathers in those that were already permitted outside those zones). You can still find some deals here, however. Search **Vacation Rentals By Owner** (VRBO; www.vrbo.com) if our listings don't suit your needs.

Camping is another option, and it's primo at 'Anini Beach Park (p123), with facilities and frolicking room aplenty. Right on the water, it has its shaded areas, too, and can be chilly in the winter at night. The beach park is relatively spacious, although it crowds up on weekends, when local families arrive. (See p259 for county park permit information.) No camping is allowed on Tuesdays.

ORCHID COTTAGE — Guesthouse $$$$

our pick ☎ **828-0811; www.surfsideprop.com; 3585 'Anini Rd; 1br house per week $1199;**

The guesthouse of **Plumeria Cottage** (opposite), this tucked-away, cozy paradise getaway is perfect for a writer seeking an inspiring work-away-from-home spot, honeymooners or a couple with a young child. Just a short stroll up the street to 'Anini Beach, its size is small but it makes up for it with quaint and charming accoutrements. Outside is a private shaded reading or relaxing area with garden and teak furniture. Inside embellishments include mahogany floors, adorable kitchen and office nook overlooking a tropical fruit-bearing garden and partial ocean view. Includes free long-distance calls to Canada and mainland US and use of kayaks, bicycles, snorkel gear and beach chairs. There is a three-night minimum stay (one week during holidays) and a maximum of three guests plus a $250 security deposit and $85 cleaning fee.

> **Island Insights**
>
> Groups like the Surfrider Foundation Kaua'i and Sierra Club help locals and visitors alike with beach cleanups every month. For a calendar of these 'ecovents,' go to the county-sponsored www.kauaiexplorer.com/guides/cool_happenings.php.

LIWAI'S MAKAI HALE — Cottage $$$$

☎ **822-4500; 4343 'Anini Rd; 2br with loft per week $1950;**

Location, location, location. A good deal for four people, this secluded gem is just 120ft away from the most reclusive part of 'Anini Beach and perfect for those with *keiki*. It's ideal for a family or any group yearning for a beach vacation where leaving the property is nearly unnecessary. It comes complete with a full kitchen, TV, washer/dryer and mini stereo system. Second to its location, the large deck overlooking the water is the cherry on top. Free long-distance calls to mainland US and wi-fi are available. The cost for each additional person (six-person max) is $150. The security deposit is $500 and cleaning fee $175. Between December 15 and January 5, the cost is $2800 per week with a two-week minimum stay.

LIWAI'S MAUKA HALE — Guesthouse $$$$

☎ **822-4500; 4343A 'Anini Rd; 2br house per week $1600**

First, the perks: 400sq ft deck overlooking the ocean, a mere 160ft away. This polished home has a queen bed in its master bedroom with half bath, a second bedroom with two twin beds and another full bath.

Rental includes full kitchen, TV, mini stereo system, washer/dryer, a full bathroom on the ground floor, and outdoor shower. For more than 2 people, $125 each additional person (4-person max). Security deposit $500, cleaning fee $150. Wi-fi access reaches this unit from the larger house (**Liwai's Makai Hale**) if you've got a laptop. Between December 15 and January 5 the cost is $2400 per week with a two-week minimum stay.

PLUMERIA COTTAGE Cottage $$$$

☎ 828-0811; www.surfsideprop.com; 3585 'Anini Rd; 2br with den per week $1525;

Romantic South Seas décor meets well-loved, undeniably chic adornments that have a sort of US Southern charm begging for afternoon naps, early-morning walks to the beach and late-night family card games in the screened-in lanai. Shares part of the property with the **Orchid Cottage** (opposite). Pet ducks swimming along a stream make for a farm-like feel for *keiki*. Sleeps up to five. Guests are invited to pick fruit on the property. Owner Mary Ellen Turk put a unique tropical hot/cold outdoor shower made of fun allusions to the sea. Make reservations at least three months in advance as regulars favor this spot. The cleaning fee is $150. For larger groups, you can combo both this and the guesthouse for $2300 per week, $500 security deposit.

PRINCEVILLE

pop 1698

Princeville is exclusive, elitist and undeniably gorgeous. Its over-the-top gateway fountain puts a new spin on 'gated' community as its luxurious approach to life in paradise comes to fruition, reaching its culmination at the St Regis Princeville, formerly the Princeville Resort.

The neighborhood sprouted as a result of the resort, built in 1985. Before then, the outcrop between the also glorious 'Anini and understated Hanalei were merely unadulterated fields and ranch lands.

Today the 11,000-acre community is a resort town that resembles a suburb, albeit suburbia for folks with money. The single

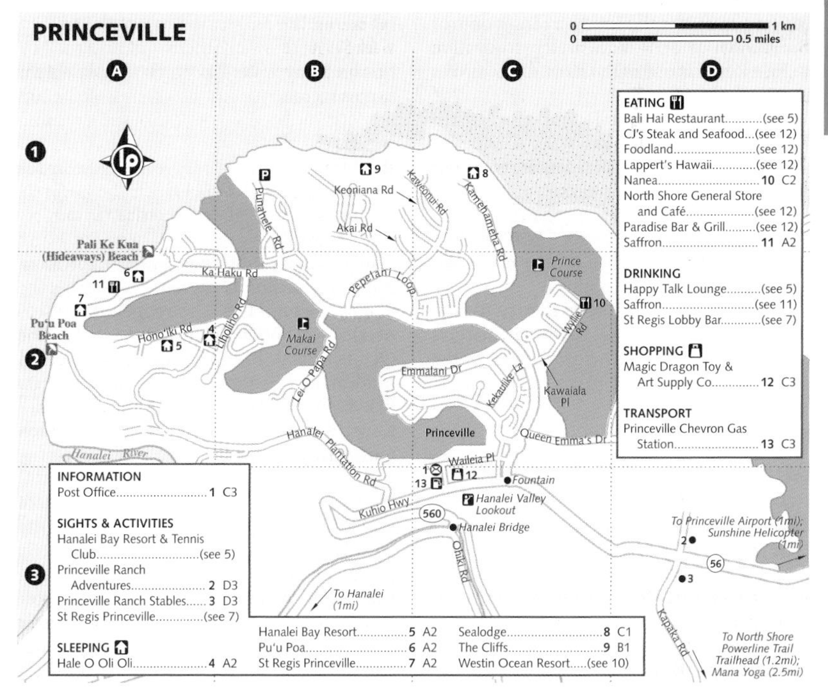

thoroughfare is flanked by two celebrated golf greens and well-marked side streets made up of throngs of condos, terminating at the mother lode of luxury: St Regis Princevillle.

Like much of the island, a car is necessary to get around here, as shopping and dining options aren't within comfortable walking distance.

History

Princeville traces its roots to Robert Wyllie, a Scottish doctor who became foreign minister to Kamehameha IV. In the mid-19th century Wyllie established a sugar plantation in Hanalei (p133). When Queen Emma and Kamehameha IV came to visit in 1860, Wyllie named his plantation and the surrounding lands Princeville to honor their two-year-old son, Prince Albert, who died only two years later. The plantation later became a cattle ranch.

Orientation & Information

Kuhio Hwy changes from Hwy 56 to Hwy 560 at the 28-mile marker in front of Princeville. The 10-mile stretch from here to Ke'e Beach is one of the most scenic drives in the whole state.

In Princeville you'll find the North Shore's only airport, gas station and fire station, plus a shopping center with the basics, such as a supermarket, restaurants and real-estate agencies. The **post office** (☎ 800-275-8777; Princeville Center, 5-4280 Kuhio Hwy; 🕑 10:30am-3:30pm Mon-Fri, to 12:30pm Sat) is located in the shopping center.

Remember, the **Princeville Chevron gas station** (Kuhio Hwy; 🕑 6am-10pm Mon-Sat, to 9pm Sun) is the last stop to buy gas before the end of the road at Ke'e Beach.

Beaches

PALI KE KUA (HIDEAWAYS) & PU'U POA BEACHES

The one complaint about Princeville is the lack of an easily accessible beach. Pali Ke Kua Beach, also called Hideaways Beach, is a magnificent little lozenge of sand, but you must work to reach it. To get here, park in the public lot just after the gatehouse at the St Regis Princeville and take the path between the fences. After several minutes, the trail becomes unbelievably steep, with stairs and ropes to aid your descent. The reward? When the water is calm (and only then), swimming and especially snorkeling are excellent, and the shady, sandy beach is perfect for sunset year-round.

Nearby is another option, Pu'u Poa Beach, between the St Regis Princeville and the mouth of the Hanalei River. To get here, take the path to the left of the gatehouse. Less scenic than Pali Ke Kua, but you can walk from here all the way to the river mouth.

QUEEN'S BATH

This is beautiful but deadly – formed by a lava-rock shelf, natural pools provide a swimming and snorkeling hole that at times gets hit by powerful waves and has been notorious for pulling visitors out to sea. Though the surf at times splashes in softly, any description without stating that it is the most deadly swimming hole on the island would be remiss. If you decide to go, please be smart about it. In 2008 four tourists died there, two of whom were walking along the ledge used to access it when a large wave swept them out to sea. For tips on being water-savvy, go to www.kauaiexplorer.com.

Sights

ST REGIS PRINCEVILLE

☎ 826-9644; www.princevillehotelhawaii.com; 5520 Ka Haku Rd

This is one of those must-sees if you're in the neighborhood, regardless of whether you're staying here. The reopening of this overhauled and renovated spot, slated for October 2009, has been highly anticipated by locals and visitors alike. 'Spectacular' feels like an understatement when speaking of a resort where it's hard to nail down which part offers the most idyllic view. Sunset is without a doubt among the most beautiful the island has to offer at this locale, where it's best to take it in with a highball from the **lobby bar** (p130) or from the deck that feels like you're on a large ship with the crashing waters below.

The presence of the former Princeville Resort caused quite the stir among locals when it was first built in the mid-'80s. It

A study in blue at Pu'u Poa Beach ANN CECIL

has since remained to epitomize exclusivity. One of the two famous golf courses remained operating throughout the renovation, the Prince course, though the stunning, superior Makai course overlooking cliffs with unforgettable, incomparable views remained in sync with the opening dates of the hotel. The St Regis has four hotels that carried over from the previous Princeville Resort but were 'reconcepted' and renamed.

HANALEI VALLEY LOOKOUT

Just north of the Princeville Center on the *mauka* (inland) side of the road is this scenic overlook of the 6-mile Hanalei Valley. Look for the area with parked cars and a gaggle of tourists as this is a popular lookout spot. Though there will be more places between here and Hanalei where you might feel inclined to pull over and take a photo, this is the only 'official' and safe place to do so. A quilt of green marks the nutrient-dense taro, grown more here than anywhere else in the state. Be wary of walking pedestrians and speeding cars when parking here.

Activities

GOLF

There is really no way to describe the **St Regis Princeville Golf Club's** (☎ Prince 826-5000, Makai 826-3580; www.princeville.com; 5-3900 Kuhio Hwy; green fees nonguest/guest Prince $175/150, Makai $125/110) Prince Golf Course, other than to say it is among the most breathtaking in the world. This 18-hole par-72 course, set against sea cliffs, has been featured on several 'best' lists. The 27-hole par-72 Makai Course, c 1971, is also beautiful and challenging for the avid golfer.

HORSEBACK RIDING

Tours with **Princeville Ranch Stables** (☎ 826-6777; www.princevilleranch.com; Kuhio Hwy; tours $65-170; Mon-Sat) offer a beautiful ride, even for beginners, and is also ideal for those who really care about how tour animals are treated. Newbies should wear jeans and plan for a sore bottom. Find the ranch between the 26- and 27-mile markers. The four-hour trip to Kalihiwai Falls is pleasant, and includes picnicking and a swim.

'Opaeka'a Falls KARL LEHMANN

MOUNTAIN BIKING

If technical and definitively challenging rides are your cup of tea, then hitting up the **Powerline Trail** from the North Shore side is scenic, rewarding and worthy of some bragging rights. Though you can bike in and back out, it's best to arrange for pickup at the Kapa'a trailhead or at **'Opaeka'a Falls** lookout. Though it's 11.2 miles, plan for it to feel much longer. The entire ride can be done in about 4 hours with a steady pace. To get there, take the road to the Princeville Ranch Stable and follow to the end to find the trailhead.

YOGA

Located on the *mauka* side of Princeville, Michaelle Edwards's **Mana Yoga** (☎ 826-9230, www.manayoga.com; 3812 Ahonui Pl; per class $20; private sessions per hr $80; 🕑 8:30am Mon & Wed) studio is rustic chic and combines massage, yoga and spinal alignment into her own style that's proven to help heal via natural poses rather than contortionistic ones. Her studio also doubles as a yoga retreat for those wanting a getaway and a rejuvenated return. Single/double studios are $85/$95.

ZIPLINING

PRINCEVILLE RANCH ADVENTURES

☎ 826-7669, 888-955-7669; www.adventureskauai.com; tours $79-125

It's a pleasant morning trek that starts off with a short hike, a long, lazy kayak tour and another hike through a series of ziplines – then a picnic waterfall lunch with a hammock for napping in. Minimum age and weight are 12 years and 80lb. Bring repellent, swim gear and water shoes.

Tours

Leaving out of both Lihu'e and Princeville Airport, **Heli USA Airways** (☎ 826-6591, 866-936-1234; www.heliusahawaii.com; 55min tours $267) offers convenience if you're on the North Shore; however, it was one of two companies on the island to have a fatal crash in 2007, so its safety record is less than perfect. Also operating out of both airports is **Sunshine Helicopters** (☎ 270-3999; www.sunshinehelicopters.com/kauai/tours/princeville_adventure.html; 40-50min tours $345, online booking $285). To view any helicopter company's crash history, visit the National Transportation & Safety Board Website at www.ntsb.gov or Federal Aviation Authority at www.faa.gov.

Eating

LAPPERT'S HAWAII Ice Cream/Cafe $

☎ 826-7393; Princeville Center, 5-4280 Kuhio Hwy; 🕑 10am-9pm

You can smell the waffle cones almost immediately in the parking lot, though whether you catch the sugary scent or become hungry first has yet to be determined. With delicious ice cream and coffee to boot, Lappert's is one of Kaua'i's homegrown treats, and if you're not a diabetic, take this advice: order the Kauai Pie Kona coffee ice cream, toasted coconut, macadamia nuts, fudge and vanilla cake.

NORTH SHORE GENERAL STORE & CAFÉ American $

☎ 826-1122; North Shore General Store & Cafe, Princeville Center, 5-4280 Kuhio Hwy; breakfast $2.75-5, lunch & dinner $7.99-22; 🕑 6am-8pm Mon-Sat

It looks like it's a closed-up shop inside the gas station, but finally, a breakfast, lunch and dinner spot in Princeville that won't break the bank. Get your caffeine hit with a 'red eye' ($2.75) and try a ham or Spam croissant with egg and cheese ($4.99) or Loco Moco or Eggs and Da Kine ($6.99) for a filling breakfast. The hoisin glazed shrimp salad with wontons and udon noodles ($9.99) or fresh falafel burger with tahini yogurt dressing ($7.99) prove healthier for lunch, while any one of their 'hefty burgers' are made with Princeville beef. The scrumptious *paniolo* cowboy pizza ($22.99), topped with chicken, BBQ sauce, pineapple, mozzarella, onions and bacon, is a guilty pleasure.

PARADISE BAR & GRILL
Pub Food $$

☎ 826-1775; Princeville Center, 5-4280 Kuhio Hwy; mains $11-25; 11am-11pm

Burgers, beer and blackened fish are among the decent fare at this little spot, though the service can be frustrating. Consider it only if you've got time to spare and are OK with some attitude.

CJ'S STEAK AND SEAFOOD
Steakhouse/Seafood $$$$

☎ 826-6211; Princeville Center, 5-4280 Kuhio Hwy; dinner mains $22-38; 6-9:30pm

Fans of this spot usually go on and on about its salad bar like it's still the '80s and salad bars are still indicators of to what degree a restaurant is considered posh. In contrast, some might argue today that even the presence of a salad bar knocks its rating down a notch. Yes, CJ's has a great salad bar. But without dating ourselves, let's just say it should be noted for its other claims to fame as well: standard, well-prepared, fine cuts of meats and fresh fish. A cut-and-dry menu without much embellishment, the choices are simple and effective: prime rib, lamb, shrimp, lobster, *'ahi*. You get the picture. Don't expect olive oil, a balsamic cruet or whole-grain bread. Again, without dating ourselves, this is like your favorite upscale steakhouse was uprooted from the late '70s and dropped into today's Princeville – with a baked potato and butter patty on the side and scoop of vanilla for dessert.

SAFFRON
Mediterranean $$$$

☎ 826-6225; 5300 Ka Haku Rd; www.saffron-hawaii.com; mains $17-39; 6-9pm Mon-Thu, to 10pm Fri & Sat

Portions are small and the food is pricey, but the staff is pampering and the menu inventive. Sink into a lounge-like couch while enjoying the Hawaiian tradition of *pupu* (appetizers), met here with a fierce contender in the tradition of tapas. Born and raised in Mexico but also a Spaniard, chef/owner Joaquin Menendez brings a homestyle paella to the table à la Barcelona, with a fusion of other, tasty influences added into the mix. Phyllo-wrapped brie with blueberry relish and green apples, seared *'ahi* with sweet toasted almonds or flan with *liliko'i* glaze are among the more distinctive dishes. If you don't want to splurge too much, order a pizzeta instead of tapas. There's live music here two days a week; see p130.

NANEA
Hawaii Regional $$$$

our pick ☎ 827-8700; Westin Princeville Ocean Resort Villas Clubhouse; breakfast $8-22, dinner mains $31-38; 6:30-10:30am & 5:30-9:30pm

A recent addition to the local dining scene, Nanea has a pleasant plantation-style ambience overlooking a koi pond. The menu has a host of regionalized fusion dishes to choose from, the most notable of which includes scallops *pupu* style, a $20 breakfast buffet spread and an overall 'local,' understated approach to gourmet food. Executive chef and Maui native Kahau Manzu exalts Kaua'i-grown produce, honey and goats' cheese from seven local farms in his menu. The former executive sous chef at Waikiki's renowned Moana Surfrider and sous chef at the Four Seasons Maui has no doubt mastered the art of modest elegance in regional cuisine.

BALI HAI RESTAURANT
Hawaii Regional $$$$

☎ 826-6522; Hanalei Bay Resort

At the time of research, this restaurant was under renovation, with no concrete opening date available, so call ahead to find out if it's opened yet. Upon opening it promises to offer Pacific Rim cuisine, specifically fresh-catch fish with an inventive approach to presentation.

The biggest supermarket on the North Shore, **Foodland** (☎ 826-9880; Princeville Center, 5-4280 Kuhio Hwy; 6am-11pm) has an abundance of fresh produce, prepared sushi, wine, beer, liquor and a better selection overall than Hanalei's **Big Save** (p142).

Drinking

HAPPY TALK LOUNGE

☎ 826-6522; Hanalei Bay Resort

A couple of degrees less stuffy than the resort's Bali Hai Restaurant (p129), at Happy Talk you can take in a draft Bali Hai beer or some tropical drinks like the Coco Banana or Kauai Mudslide with *pupu* like the Namolokama Platter, a combo of watermelon BBQ pork ribs, chicken skewers and tiger prawn katsu, or the Bali Hai crabcakes with curry butter and mango sunrise papaya relish. Live music offerings include jazz and Hawaiian music. This place was closed for renovations at the time of research, so call ahead to ensure it's open.

SAFFRON

☎ 826-6225; 5300 Ka Haku Rd; www.saffron-hawaii.com; 6-9pm Mon-Thu, to 10 Fri & Sat

Exotic martinis, homemade sangria and a high-end wine list certainly don't hurt the already sultry ambience of this truly off-the-beaten-track night spot. Tapas abound to nibble on, as do the pricey but scrumptious cocktails like the pomegranate martini, coco colada or mango *mojito*. Wednesdays and Saturdays have live music, ranging from contemporary Hawaiian to classical guitar.

ST REGIS LOBBY BAR

☎ 826-9644, 800-325-3589; www.princevillehotelhawaii.com; 5520 Ka Haku Rd; 3-11pm

The much anticipated reopening of the St Regis Princeville's 'reconcepted' cocktail-hour staple offers undeniably unforgettable views – we dare say, the best of Hanalei Bay – making this the ultimate for sunset cocktails. At the time of research the lobby bar was under renovation and had yet to be named but was slated to open in October 2009; call ahead to ensure it's open.

Top Picks

NORTH SHORE ENTERTAINMENT

- **Mango Brothers band – Sundays at Hanalei Gourmet** (p141)
- **Karaoke Night – Mondays at Tahiti Nui** (p142)
- **Keli'i Kaneali'i – Tuesdays at Saffron** (above)

Shopping

MAGIC DRAGON TOY & ART SUPPLY CO

ourpick ☎ 826-9144, Princeville Center, 5-4280 Kuhio Hwy; 9am-6pm

A wonderland of whirling, colorful and inspired toys packed into a tiny storefront makes this shop even more magical the longer you're inside. Layers of childhood distractions reveal themselves in turning fans, shiny-packaged objects and old-school Cray-Pas. Kites, sand toys, watercolors, stuffed toys including replicas of Frida Kahlo and Salvador Dali make this intriguing shop among the most original in the Princeville Center. Whether or not you've got children in tow or not, this shop is fun for anyone wanting a moment to honour their creativity or inner child.

Sleeping

Staying in Princeville probably means staying in a condo. If you know exactly which condo you want, simply do a Google search to find all available units. For more privacy, find a vacation home, which typically start around $250 per day. Expect cleaning fees, minimum stays (typically five to seven nights) and other restrictions.

An online agent with an abundance of Princeville rentals is Ahh! Aloha (☎ 866-922-5642; www.kauai-vacations-ahh.com), or check Vacation Rentals By Owner (VRBO; www.vrbo.com) for owner-listed rentals. For other listings sites, see the boxed text, opposite.

HALE O OLI OLI — Cottage $$

ourpick ☎ 714-803-8073; 4126 Kekuanaoa Rd; 3br per week $950, additional days $135

Not your typical Princeville rental, this mellow clean home is chock-full of beach toys like surfboards and snorkel gear, as well as bikes. Reasonably priced, it's a spacious 1600 sq ft that, though not beachside, is a few blocks from the Hanalei Bay Resort. Two of the three bedrooms have queen beds; the third has two twins. Bonuses include the fact that for Princeville, which is rife with side-by-side dwellings,

NORTH SHORE CONDO LISTINGS

If you just can't seem to find a deal with other options, one of your best bets are the many vacation rentals listed with different real estate agencies:

- **'Anini Aloha Properties** (Map p119; ☎ 828-0067, 800-246-5382; www.aninialoha.com; Suite I-1, 4270 Kilauea Rd, Kilauea) Extensive selection of North Shore rentals, including Princeville condos and dream houses from Anahola to Ha'ena.
- **Coldwell Banker Bali Hai Realty** (☎ 866-400-7368; www.balihai.com; 5-5088 Kuhio Hwy) Lots of listings for the North Shore, particularly in Hanalei, 'Anini and Kilauea. On-staff Japanese translator available.
- **Hanalei North Shore Properties** (☎ 826-9622, 800-488-3336; www.hanaleinorthshoreproperties.com) Specializes in unique North Shore vacation rentals, both condos and getaway houses from Anahola to Ha'ena.
- **Vacation Rentals By Owner** (VRBO; www.vrbo.com) The least Kaua'i-specific of these sites, but features vacation rentals worldwide. Use the search function to narrow down your search to see listings for the North Shore of Kaua'i.

this is private and free-standing and sits on a 10,000 sq ft lot with fruit trees bearing avocado, banana and tangerines. Security deposit $200, cleaning fee $150.

ST REGIS PRINCEVILLE Resort $$$$

☎ 826-9644, 800-325-3589; www.princevillehotelhawaii.com; 5520 Ka Haku Rd; r $750-6500;

Thanks to its unforgettable view of Hanalei Bay, the St Regis Princeville is the North Shore's luxe flagship, offering more than your run-of-the-mill upscale resort. Its infinity pool seems to fade into the waters of Hanalei Bay. The resort has four restaurants, including the first Jean-Georges Vongerichten restaurant in Hawaii, and its locally revered lobby bar (opposite). Like any over-the-top resort, 'bigger' is status quo. A 5000-sq-ft infinity pool overlooks Pu'u Poa Beach (p126) and Hanalei Bay. Of course for the price, you're right to expect that even the 'cheapest' rooms are opulent. Decorated with a contemporary Hawaiian design, each has custom-made, regally inspired furniture, one-way viewing glass and marble bathooms. The higher range options include your own round-the-clock butler service, which even offers a personal unpacker. The resort also is home to the Halele'a Spa, an 11,000-sq-ft palatial escape within for massages, replete with couples and VIP treatment rooms. The spa also houses a nail and hair salon and 24-hour fitness center.

At research time, the Starwood property was undergoing renovation to get upgraded from 'the Luxury Collection' to 'St Regis', and slated to open in October 2009.

WESTIN OCEAN RESORT Resort $$$$

☎ 827-8700; www.starwoodhotels.com/westin/property/overview/index.html; 3838 Wyllie Rd; villas $225-780;

Plantation-style architecture that builds on the balminess of island air designed with a bright palate contrasted by rich wood detail. Villas offer a chance to enjoy your fancy digs, with full kitchens that boast marble back-splashes and plenty of prepping space. There's also an upscale but small dining table, flat-screen TV and lanai. Décor is a charming mix of contemporary and pan-Asian, with dark-tone embellishments in furniture harking back to traditional Chinese and Balinese design. Eternity pools, gym, restaurants and washer/dryer access on site.

HANALEI BAY RESORT Resort $$$$

☎ 826-6522; www.hanaleibayresort.com; 5380 Hono'iki Rd; r $205, 1br units from $370;

Location is the name of the game and, though steeply priced, there's good reason: this resort is one of the mainstays of 'luxury' most associate with the area. If you're staying in Princeville, though, you're gonna spend serious cash. Renting an owned unit can save some money, such as with Aloha Condos (☎ 930-1830; www.alohacondos.com). Amenities include 8 tennis courts, several pools and beach access shared with the high-brow St Regis Princeville Resort.

PU'U POA

Condo $$$$

☎ 826-9394, 800-535-0085; www.marcresorts.com; Ka Haku Rd; 2br units $275-500;

Overlooking Hanalei Bay, the décor in Pu'u Poa is almost Floridian, with pastels, outdated details and attempted tropical flair. Again, here, it's location, as it's a stone's throw from the St Regis Princeville. Views are the silver lining. Managed primarily by Marc Resorts, there also is a cheaper Pali Ke Kua condo should you be so inclined. Across the street, Hale Moi cottages has no pool and no view, is noisy and is not recommended.

HANALEI VALLEY

The drive from Princeville toward Hanalei will unveil even more inspired landscapes, soaring birds and ocean views. Misted fields, the silhouettes of palm trees against the sky and afternoon rainbows collaborate to lure you in and push you north.

Sights

HANALEI BRIDGE

The Hanalei Bridge is the first of seven bridges along the drive from the Hanalei River to the end of the road. The county has left the bridge as a historical landmark and, because of this, big trucks will never tear down any road in Hanalei or beyond – and development has been kept a tad at bay.

HANALEI NATIONAL WILDLIFE REFUGE

Anywhere north of Kilauea will set you on a path to the more pristine, the further you go. Following Kalihiwai, you'll catch your first glimpses of the even more vast Edenic landscapes that typify the North Shore. Rolling hills abound as you pass through Princeville, where you'll spot the Hanalei National Wildlife Refuge. The **Hanalei Valley Lookout** (p127), across from the Princeville Center, is a good vantage point for the refuge, rife with fertile taro fields fed by the Hanalei River.

One of the largest rivers in the state, the Hanalei River has nurtured its crops since the first *kanaka maoli* (Native Hawaiians) began cultivating taro in its fertile valley fields. Other crops have come and gone, including rice and oranges. In the mid-1800s, rice paddies were planted here to feed the Chinese sugar-plantation laborers. By the 1930s four rice mills were operating in Hanalei area. Today, taro again dominates, with only 5% of its original acreage. The Haraguchi Mill remains today as a popular site for visitors and school tours (see p140).

The refuge, established in 1972, is closed to the public. However, from the vantage point you might be able to spot the 49 types of bird using the habitat, including the valley's endangered native species: *ae'o* (Hawaiian stilt slender with black back, white chest

A checkerboard of taro fields lines the Hanalei Valley

JOHN ELK III

RULES OF THE ROAD

There is no way to get to the 'end of the road' at Ke'e Beach without being inspired. Undulating, winding strips of road canopied by mammoth trees with glimpses here and there of ocean, valley or river abound. But make like a culturally savvy visitor and avoid 'pulling over' on any shoulder for a photo op, though you're almost guaranteed to see someone else doing this. The first of seven charming one-lane bridges will let you know you're almost in Hanalei (below). Waiting to cross one-lane bridges like the historical one over the Hanalei River slows the pace. Follow this rule of thumb:

- If the bridge is empty and you reach it first, go.
- If a car is crossing ahead of you, follow.
- If you see cars approaching from the opposite direction, yield to the approaching queue cars for at least five vehicles, if not all. That means if you're the sixth or seventh car crossing the bridge, stop and let the opposite side go. And remember to give the *shaka* ('hang loose') sign when someone has let you in.

and long pink legs), *alae ke'oke'o* (Hawaiian coot slate-gray with white forehead), *'alae 'ula* (Hawaiian moorhen dark-gray with black head and distinctive red-and-yellow bill) and *koloa maoli* (Hawaiian duck mottled brown with orange legs and feet).

To get here, turn left onto Ohiki Rd immediately after the Hanalei Bridge. You can enter the refuge only on the Ho'opulapula Haraguchi Rice Mill Tour (p140).

Activities

HIKING

OKOLEHAO TRAIL

You'll want some tread on your shoes, a walking stick (found along the way), mosquito repellent and water for this gorgeous little trek. It's about a 2.5-mile, 1250ft climb and it's sure to get your heart pumping. The Okolehau Trail can be done in about 2 hours and offers one of the most generous payoffs when you get to the top: panoramic views of turquoise and patches of green valley plots, the entire Hanalei Bay and the start of the Na Pali Coast. On a clear day during the winter months, you could even see whales breaching in the distance.

The majority of the first mile is an unrelenting climb up a deceptively steep dirt road. Two plateaus offer scenic overlooks. The first offers views of Hanalei Bay, the Kilauea Lighthouse and taro fields. Following a flat bit of stretch it gets steep again, until you reach the second plateau, with splendid views. Keep your eyes peeled along the way for views of the Hanalei River, gushing waterfalls and blossoming wild orchids. To get to the trailhead, take your first left after Hanalei's first one-way bridge heading north, along Rice Mill Rd. Go down the road about half a mile to a parking lot across from the start of the trail.

Island Insights

In the early 2000s the University of Hawaii conducted genetic modification research on *kalo* (taro plant), which spurred outcry from Hawaiians. In May 2005, it agreed to stop and consult Hawaiians first in future. In March 2008, Kaua'i County Council passed a resolution to support the state legislature by placing a 10-year moratorium on growing or developing genetically modified taro.

The Hawaiian House Agriculture Committee later voted 9-3 to send a bill to the full house that instead instituted a 5-year moratorium, which passed. However, it applies only to Hawaiian varieties of the plant.

HANALEI

pop 478

The surfer chic town of Hanalei has more than its fair share of adults with Peter Pan syndrome and kids with seemingly Olympic athletic prowess. All in all, it's got a hippie-with-money MO coupled with an ingratiating attitude toward otherwise judgmental outsiders. Stroll down its beachfront Weke Rd and you'll see age in defiance, as men in

their sixties wax and preen their surfboards and young 'uns carry their 'guns' (big wave surfboards) toward the beach. Without a doubt beach life is *the* life, and it's been brought here into action.

Orientation & Information

Hanalei town centers on Kuhio Hwy, which is about two blocks up from Hanalei Bay, home of four beaches. Kuhio Hwy is flanked on either side by two small groups of businesses: **Ching Young Village** and **Hanalei Center**. The two centers form the 'downtown' of Hanalei, pulsing with the most of its hustle and bustle with plenty of dining, shopping and water-sport rental options

Hanalei has no bank, but you can find an ATM in the Ching Young Village's Big Save supermarket.

Bali Hai Photo (☎ 826-9181; Ching Young Village; per hr $9; 🕐 8am-8pm Mon-Fri, 9am-5pm Sat, 10am-5pm Sun) Internet access.

Java Kai (☎ 826-6717; www.javakai.com; Hanalei Center, 5-5161 Kuhio Hwy; wi-fi per 2hr $12; 🕐 6:30am-6pm) Lively, open-air hangout spot.

Post office (☎ 800-275-8777; 5-5226 Kuhio Hwy) In the village center.

Beaches

Possibly the best example of what visitors hope for when they envision an active beach life on Kaua'i, **Hanalei Bay** has

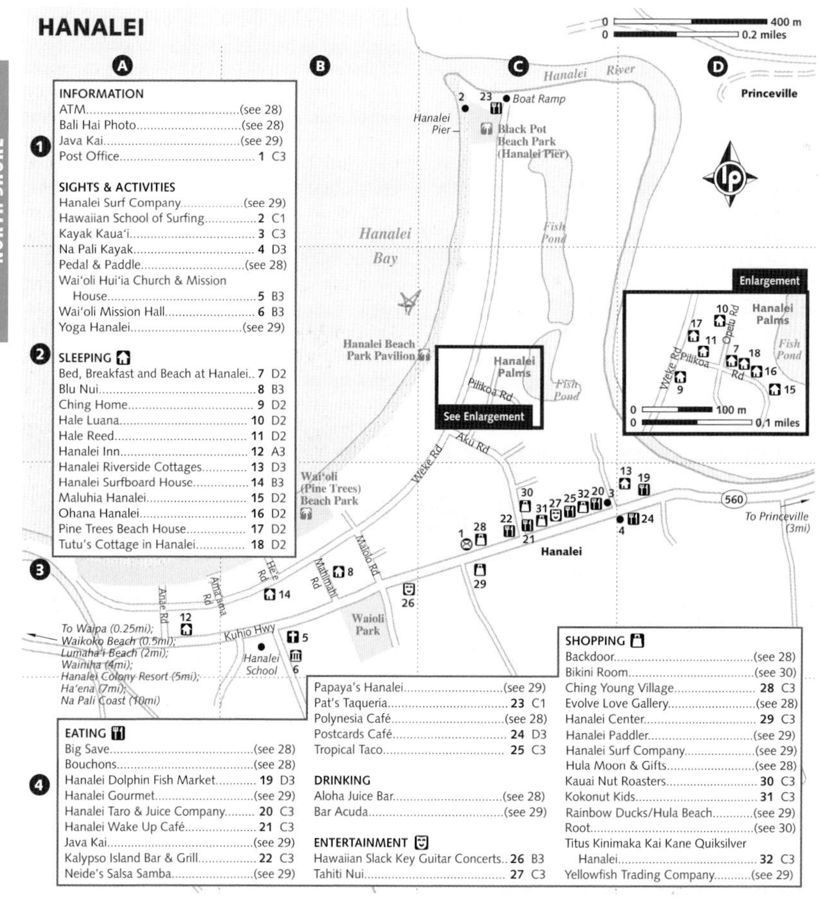

Top Picks

BEST OF HANALEI

- **Waterman voyeurism at Black Pot Beach Park (Hanalei Pier)** (below)
- **Stand up paddle surfing on the Hanalei River** (p139)
- **Sunset swim at Hanalei Pier** (below)
- **Down and dirty at Tahiti Nui** (p142)
- **Underwater bling at Evolve Love Gallery** (p143)

arguably the most beautiful set of beaches on-island, with facilities and easy access. Though it's not always ideal for swimming – during winter months waves can pound relentlessly – it's always fun to sunbathe, read a book or watch surfers rip.

Black Pot Beach Park (Hanalei Pier) and **Wai'oli (Pine Trees) Beach Park** both have rest rooms, showers, drinking water, picnic tables and grills. Family-wise, **Hanalei Beach Park Pavilion** comes in first place, as it has lifeguards as well as facilities. Conditions are best for surfing and bodyboarding; swimming is less than ideal due to the shorebreak.

The beaches are listed here going from the northeastern tip (at the Hanalei River) down the coast to the southwest.

BLACK POT BEACH PARK (HANALEI PIER)

Not lifeguarded, this small section of Hanalei Bay is near the Hanalei River mouth, and usually offers the calmest surf of the oft-wild North Shore swells. Also known as **Hanalei Pier** due to its unmistakable landmark, this stretch of sand shaded by ironwood trees at Hanalei Beach Park is popular mainly with surfers and surf instructors. The sandy-bottom beach slopes gently, making it very safe for beginners. Lessons are typically taught here, just west of the pier, where you find surf schools galore; see p139. In summer, swimming and snorkeling are decent, as are camping and kayaking. As always, use extreme caution during periods of high surf as dangerous shorebreaks and rip currents are common.

At the eastern end of the park the mouth of the Hanalei River opens onto the beach, and you'll find a small boat ramp where kayakers launch for trips up the river. This spot is called **Black Pot**, after a big black wok owned by Henry Tai Hook, who used to cook community meals here in the late 1800s or early 1900s.

HANALEI BEACH PARK PAVILION

Lifeguarded and boasting sweeping views, this is a great place for a picnic, sunset or lazy day at the beach. It's ideally located, though parking can be a challenge; park along Weke Rd if you have to, as it can get crowded.

WAI'OLI (PINE TREES) BEACH PARK

Toward the middle of Hanalei Bay, this park offers respite from the sun. This spot is replete with restrooms and a picnic area. Winter months are when the North Shore is at its highest surf-wise. In April, don't miss the surfing contest Pine Trees Longboard Classic, full of fearless, young, local talent. Pro surfers Andy and Bruce Irons cut their teeth here, and each February they sponsor the Pine Trees Classic, an event for kids to compete, meet their idols and win prizes.

Swimming is dangerous here except during the calmest summer surf. A section, known locally as **Toilet Bowls**, at the end of Ama'ama Rd, has rest rooms and showers.

Hanalei Pier, Black Pot Beach Park PHOTO CREDIT

MIDDLES

At mile marker 4 on the *makai* (ocean) side of the road is a small, woodsy parking area known as Middles parking lot. From here you can walk along the beach or look out to the ocean to see three surf breaks; from left to right they are Waikokos, Middles and Chicken Wings. If you're an experienced surfer, the only way you might be able to tell the difference between Middles and Chicken Wings is at the actual break, which sends waves breaking in two different patterns.

This beach is informally known as Middles because of the break, though the bridge just past the parking lot crosses over Waikoko Stream, and so the shoreline from the bridge onward is formally known as **Waikoko Beach** (below).

WAIKOKO BEACH

Protected by a reef on the western bend of Hanalei Bay, this sandy-bottomed beach with no facilities offers shallower and calmer waters than the middle of the bay.

ISLAND VOICES

NAME: TREVOR CABELL
OCCUPATION: HAWAIIAN CANOE SAILOR; OWNER, ISLAND SAILS (p140)
RESIDENCE: HANALEI

When did you gain your passion about sailing? Living on this island in the middle of the ocean, I think my passion for sailing didn't one day come to me, it was always in me. Sailing is in my blood. My father is a sailor. From my earliest experiences, I can remember fooling around on his boat while [he worked] on it.

What have you and Kuupaaloa your sailing canoe been through? *Kuupaaloa* used to be a paddling canoe. I bought her for $5000. After taking her in the bay and 'swamping' her, she worked. I put in bulkheads, false floors with scuppers and decks to keep her watertight. I built new *amas* [outrigger floats] and glassed all my wood work. The design worked. We sailed her through all the Hawaiian Islands and have worked 12 years at the [St Regis] Princeville Resort doing tours. The canoe has kept us all safe, and I thank her for that.

What do you love most about taking guests on the Kuupaaloa? Neither the canoe nor ocean are judgmental. They don't care where you're from, what nationality you are, how old you are, if you're a boy or girl, or how much money you make. It's common ground for all to enjoy. There's no destination. On the canoe, we're already there. That said, once on the canoe, I enjoy how people are able to come together, relax and step into a world they didn't even know existed.

How has Hanalei changed over the years? Change happens. We must embrace change or get left off to the side.

What would the ideal future Hanalei look like for generations to come? Opportunities. There have to be outlets for young generations to express themselves in every aspect of life: spiritually, culturally, economically, the whole shebang.

Describe the sense of community in Hanalei. There *is* a sense of community in Hanalei like most parts of Hawaii. A whole side of the island is your neighbor, so with it comes responsibility.

It's located a bit north of Waipa. Local surfers call this break 'Waikokos' (literally, 'blood water'); look for them in the water and you'll see where the break is.

Sights

HO'OPULAPULA HARAGUCHI RICE MILL

☎ 651-3399; www.haraguchiricemill.org; Kuhio Hwy

Get an authentic peek at the rich tradition of cultivating taro on Kaua'i on a fully functional, six-generation family-run farm and rice mill with its own wildlife refuge of Koloa duck, cattle egret, black-crowned night heron, *ae'o* (Hawaiian black-necked stilt), Hawaiian coot, and nene (native Hawaiian goose). The Haraguchi family also own the **Hanalei Taro & Juice Company** (p141), and offer a **mill tour** (p140), which includes access to the (otherwise inaccessible) **Hanalei National Wildlife Refuge** (p132).

WAI'OLI HUI'IA CHURCH & MISSION HOUSE

A popular site for quaint church weddings, Wai'oli Hui'ia Church was built by Hanalei's first missionaries, Reverend and Mrs William Alexander, who arrived in 1834 in a double-hulled canoe. Their church, mission hall and mission house remain in the middle of town, set on a huge manicured lawn with a beautiful mountain backdrop.

The pretty green wooden **church** retains an airy Pacific feel, with large, outward-opening windows and high ceilings. The doors remain open during the day, and visitors are welcome. A Bible printed in Hawaiian and dating from 1868 is displayed on top of the old organ. The Wai'oli Church Choir, the island's best, sings hymns in Hawaiian at the 10am Sunday service.

Adjacent are **Wai'oli Mission Hall**, c 1836, and **Wai'oli Mission House** (☎ 245-3202; admission by donation; 9am-3pm Tue, Thu & Sat), a New England house that the Alexanders built in 1837 to replace their grass shack. The Mission Hall, which originally served as the church, was built of coral lime and plaster with a steeply pitched roof to handle Hanalei's heavy rains.

This spot is also the perfect viewing point to watch for flowing water from Mt Namolokama. Though distant, you can spot it from the basketball courts fronting the church. To get to the inconspicuous parking lot, turn *makai* immediately east of Hanalei School. Turn left on the dirt driveway opposite the water hydrant.

Activities

DIVING

A satellite location of the Fathom Five outfit in Koloa, **Ocean Quest Watersports** (☎ 742-6991, 800-972-3078; www.fathomfive.com; 7am, 7:30am & 1pm Mon-Fri) is geared for North Shore dives at Tunnels (March to October). Both PADI-certified divers and newbies can get their introductory dives with a one-hour academic lesson and one- or two-tank dives for around $100/140. They'll bring the gear to you.

If you're certified, **North Shore Divers** (☎ 828-1223; www.northshoredivers.com; dives 8am Mon-Fri Mar-Oct) offers one-/two-tank dives for $79/119 per person (first-time divers can opt for one/two-tank dives for $109/169). For an unforgettable experience, try night diving in summer only for $99. An open water certification course is $450. Meet at the beach.

KAYAKING

While the Wailua River scenery holds more of a royal, sacred background, kayaking is just as peaceful and solitary along the Hanalei River. The approximately 6-mile round-trip journey through the Hanalei National Wildlife Refuge passes beside grassy banks, occasionally canopied by overhanging trees. Your paddling distance can reach 7.5 miles, depending on the water level in the river.

The Hanalei River is perfect for novice kayakers or stand up paddle surfers to practice solo. You can launch your kayak right at the boat ramp. For kayak rentals, try **Pedal & Paddle** (☎ 826-9069; www.pedalnpaddle.com; Ching Young Village; s kayaks per day/week $15/60, d kayaks $35/140; 9am-6pm). It offers the gamut of sports and camping equipment.

NA PALI KAYAK TREK

For the rigorously fit this 'Pepsi challenge' of sorts to compare with other athletic gauntlets that have been thrown down is worth trying. This 17-mile Na Pali Coast trek is not for everyone. Repeat with addendum: not for everyone – in fact only for the athletic elite. This strenuous paddle is possible only from May to September, due to rough seas and shortened daylight. From June to August you can begin this trek at Ke'e Beach (p151) and finish on the West Side, in Polihale (p206). Endurance, aptitude for seasickness and testing your strength will be rewarded with beauty, however, as you navigate around waterfalls, sea caves, spinner dolphins and resplendent sea. If you opt to do this *au naturel* (sans guide, but never without a buddy), be sure to arrange a pickup at the other end of the island or make sure someone knows when to expect you and your counterpart in case of unforeseen emergencies. Though it's possible you'll see other campers boasting walkie-talkies, remember: there is no guarantee if you get into trouble that you'll be rescued. It's a veritable at-your-own-risk endeavor. Always check several days of weather forecasting and ocean conditions before going by calling the National Weather Service hotlines (☎ weather 245-6001, marine forecast 245-3564) for Kaua'i.

Hanakapi'ai is about a mile out from Ke'e Beach. About six more miles you can set up camp at Kalalau. If you started very early, aim for setting up camp at Miloli'i (with a permit), which is at the 11-mile point, 2 miles past Nu'alolo Kai. From there you have the oft-surfless, hot, flat stretch of Polihale, which feels like much longer than the 3 miles it is; it can be less hellish if you opt to do it in its own day.

GUIDED TREKS

Kayak Kaua'i (☎ 826-9844, 800-437-3507; www.kayakkauai.com; Kuhio Hwy; s kayaks per day/week $28/112, d kayaks $52/208; 8am-5pm, to 8pm in summer) Tours include a Na Pali Coast thriller ($185) from May to September, Blue Lagoon kayak and snorkel ($60), or open-ocean paddle on the South Shore winter ($115).

our pick **Na Pali Kayak** (☎ 826-6900, 866-977-6900; www.napalikayak.com; Kuhio Hwy; tours $175) The Na Pali Coast trip is the only tour these folks lead, and their guides have over a decade of experience paddling these waters.

Outfitters Kaua'i (☎ 742-9667, 888-742-9887; www.outfitterskauai.com; Po'ipu Plaza, 2827-A Po'ipu Rd; Na Pali Coast tour $185; reservations 8am-9pm) Located in Po'ipu, but offers tours island-wide.

KITESURFING

You've seen 'em skimming the water, jumping waves and skating across the ocean while attached to a kite that looks as large as an airplane. To take a stab at this undeniably dangerous, intriguing sport (also called kiteboarding), try Keith's Kiteboarding (☎ 635-4341; 3hr lesson $270; by appointment only) for a hands-on course with a teacher who's

Snorkelers are drawn to the lush reefs off the North Shore ANN CECIL

been at it for eight years, or **Aloha Surf and Kiteboarding School** (☎ 635-9293; http://surf.kauaistyle.com; 3 1hr lessons $195; by appointment only).

SNORKELING

While most snorkeling cruises depart from Port Allen (see p189) on the West Side, those starting from the North Shore allow more time at the lushest parts of Na Pali.

Na Pali Catamaran (☎ 826-6853, 866-255-6853; www.napalicatamaran.com) offers four-hour tours (adult/child $135/110), both morning and afternoon, in summer months, generally from May to September. Depending on the waves and the time of year, you might get to venture into some sea caves. Remember: it pounds, and there's no respite from the elements.

For longer, six-hour tours, try **Captain Sundown** (☎ 826-5585; www.captainsundown.com; adult/child 10-12 $162/148). Most of the year he operates out of Lihu'e, so take advantage of using this outlet if you're here during the summer. A character, captain Bob has more than 38 years' experience and takes a lot of pride in what he does.

STAND UP PADDLE SURFING

This increasingly popular sport is a must-do. On the Hanalei River, try **Kayak Kauai** (☎ 826-9844; www.kayakkauai.com; per 24hr $45; 8am-5:30pm, to 8pm in summer) offers an array of athletic equipment and gear, including rentals; it's across the street from Postcards Café. For lessons, hitch up with surfer extraordinaire our pick **Andrea Smith** (☎ 635-0269; 1½hr private lesson $80; 8am-12pm Mon-Fri) for a pleasant introduction to this core-flexing sport. Longtime Kaua'i surfer **Mitchell Alapa** (☎ 482-0749; private lessons per hr $65; 8am-2pm) also offers private lessons.

OUTRIGGER CANOEING

There aren't many activities more Hawaiian than outrigger canoeing, and if you've got the time and are physically fit, this can be a great workout and hands-on way to see the Hanalei River and the bay, as well as its fish, dolphins and *honu* turtles. We recommend **Hawaiian Surfing Adventures** (☎ 482-0749; www.hawaiiansurfingadventures.com; 2hr tours per 4/3/2/1 persons $45/75/100/200; 8am-2pm).

SURFING

Especially if you've never done it, where else will you get a bathwater-warm turquoise sea to skate across under a brilliant sun? Surf lessons are an excellent way to pass the time, and Hanalei, rife with retired surf pros and young up-and-comers alike, is the place to learn.

For lessons, you'll want to be sure to call at least a few days in advance so that if the weather's not appropriate, you can try another day.

Hanalei Surf Company (☎ 826-9000; www.hanaleisurf.com; Hanalei Center, 5-5161 Kuhio Hwy; 2½hr lesson $65-150, surfboards per day/week $20/95, bodyboards per day/week $5/20; 8am-9pm) Surf instructors Russell Lewis and Ian Vernon have an excellent reputation and are especially suited for advanced surfers. Low-key but still pro, chances are good they'll get you standing on your first day.

Hawaiian School of Surfing (☎ 652-1116; Hanalei Pier; 1½hr lesson $65; lessons 8am, 10am & noon) Lessons by legendary pro big-wave surfer Titus Kinimaka or staff. Look for the line-up of boards and red rashguards at the pier. No more than three students per instructor.

Hawaiian Surfing Adventures (☎ 482-0749; www.hawaiiansurfingadventures.com; 2hr group/private lesson $55/75, surfboards per day/week $30/100; 8am-2pm) Longtime Kaua'i surfer Mitchell Alapa and his team give lessons to groups of up to four with a half-hour on land, one hour in the water and another hour of solo practice. Look for the yellow rashguards on the beaches of Hanalei Bay.

Kayak Kaua'i (☎ 826-9844; www.kayakkauai.com; Kuhio Hwy; 1hr lesson $50, surfboards per day $20, bodyboards per day $6; lessons 10am & 2pm) If you rent gear for four days, you get three more days free.

If you're here for a while and considering purchasing a surfboard, 'sponger' or any other watersport equipment, try your luck at the **Watersports Swapmeet** (Hanalei Center, 5-5161 Kuhio Hwy; 9am-12pm first Sat of the month) for some used, some not used, gear; it's in front of the Old Hanalei Schoolhouse.

YOGA

If you're into Ashtanga yoga, your best bet on Kaua'i is classes at **Yoga Hanalei** (☎ 826-9642; www.yogahanalei.com; 2nd fl, Hanalei Center, 5-5161 Kuhio Hwy; per class $15), directed by Bhavani Maki. See the website for class times.

Tours

The Haraguchi family, who also own the Hanalei Taro & Juice Company (opposite), offer the **our pick** **Ho'opulapula Haraguchi Rice Mill Tour** (☎ 651-3399; www.haraguchiricemill.org; Kuhio Hwy; 3hr tour incl lunch per person $65; 10am Wed) tour of their historic rice mill and wetland taro farm by appointment only. You can also see the otherwise inaccessible **Hanalei National Wildlife Refuge** (p132) and learn about Hawaii's immigrant history. Tour numbers are limited to 14. When making your reservation, specify your choice of smoothie and lunch: papaya, banana and guava; coconut, banana and pineapple; or guava, strawberry and banana. Opt for local-style plate lunch like pork with *laulau* (steamed taro leaves) and poi or the taro–hummus veggie.

HAWAIIAN SAILING CANOE

Snorkeling in the morning, cruising in the afternoon or taking sunset on the water, **our pick** **Island Sails** (☎ 212-6053; www.islandsailskauai.com; adult/child $85/65; trips 9am, 10:30am, 3:30pm & 5:30pm) offer a chance to get a taste of the traditional Polynesian sailing canoe. *Honu* (sea turtles), *mano* (sharks), barracuda, dolphins, flying fish and rainbows are among the Edenic elements surrounding the 45ft *Kuupaaloa* built by hand by co-owner Trevor Cabell. The sunset sail is perfect for couples, while those with children can enjoy an early morning ride replete with the pacifying rocking the canoe offers. The afternoon sail is a little rougher, so prepared to get wet. If it's fish you're after, Cabell can help you out with that, too. Bring a wet bag so you can snap a few shots, as well as sunscreen, towel and water bottle. Cabell has a spot for snacks on the canoe as well.

Festivals & Events

Hanalei is revered for its taro heritage, and also is the reason Kaua'i is the largest taro producer in the state. But few can conceptualize how inexorably linked the Hawaiians are to this plant without witnessing some interaction firsthand. In October of

HOMAGE TO TARO

According to Hawaiian cosmology, Papa earth-mother and Wakea sky-father, who also gave birth to the Hawaiian Islands, gave birth to Haloa, a stillborn and brother to man. Haloa was planted in the earth, and from his body came taro (*kalo*), a plant that sustained the Hawaiian people and has long been a staple for Oceanic cultures. By that relationship, man and *kalo* are brothers: each cares for the other.

Kalo is still considered a sacred food rife with tradition and spirituality for Hawaiians. The North Shore's Hanalei (p133) is home to the largest taro-producing farm in the state, where the purple, starchy potato-like plant is grown in pondfields known as *lo'i*. After crossing the first of several one-way bridges in Hanalei, to the left you'll notice the *kalo* growing.

Kalo regained spotlight in the '70s with the 'Hawaiian Renaissance,' a time during which some aspects of the Hawaiian culture enjoyed a modest, long-overdue resurgence. Though dismissed by foreigners as not much more than a glorified, garnet-colored potato, *kalo* is nutrient dense. It is often boiled and pounded into *poi*, an earthy, starchy and somewhat sweet and sticky pudding-like food.

Within the appreciation of *kalo* are the different ways in which families enjoy *poi* – defined as the 'staff of life' in the Hawaiian dictionary. Some families prefer it fresh, while others prefer 'sour *poi*,' or *poi 'awa 'awa*, possibly from the method in which *poi* used to be served – often it sat in a bowl on the table for quite some time.

All traditional Hawaiian households show respect for taro. When the *poi* bowl sits on the table, one is expected to refrain from arguing or speaking in anger. That's because any bad energy is *'ino* (evil) – and can spoil the *poi*.

Tip: because of the spiritual relevance and cultural history of *kalo*, it's disrespectful when visitors dismiss it as bland. So if you happen upon one of many luau on the island to include *kalo*-based *poi* in their smorgasbord, don't jump on the bandwagon to call it 'wallpaper paste.' It's an insult.

even-numbered years, the island enjoys the **Hanalei Taro Festival**, where it's all things taro. Witness the process of turning taro into poi (truly something to behold), or learn about this extraordinary, starchy staple and the laborious ways in which it's cultivated. For more information, contact the **Ho'opulapula Haraguchi Rice Mill** (☎ 651-3399; www.haraguchiricemill.org).

Eating & Drinking

HANALEI TARO & JUICE COMPANY — Sandwiches/Wraps $

our pick ☎ 826-1059; 5-5070-B Kuhio Hwy; smoothies $3-4.50, sandwiches $6.50; 10:30am-5pm Mon-Sat

Their specialty is anything taro-based or homemade. Owned and run by the same family who owns the Haraguchi Rice Mill (see opposite), do yourself a favor and try their buttery, coconut taro *mochi* (rice cake). Co-owner Brad Nakayama likes to liven up things with the purple staple (taro), including spicy taro hummus or taro smoothies made of banana, guava and pineapple.

TROPICAL TACO — Mexican $

☎ 827-8226; 5-5088-A Kuhio Hwy; mains $7-9; 11am-5pm Mon-Sat

Vegetarians on a budget can opt for the straight-up simple duo of beans and cheese on a homemade tortilla found in the Baby Burrito ($4); meat eaters need to dig deeper into their wallet. If arterial health isn't a priority over decadence, try the Fat Jack ($10), a 10-inch burrito stuffed with cheese, beef and beans and deep-fried and topped with sour cream, salsa and lettuce. Though the fish options are hailed as locally caught, you'll need to request that they don't get beer-battered and fried to really taste it.

JAVA KAI — Cafe $

☎ 826-6717; Hanalei Center, 5-5161 Kuhio Hwy; 6:30am-6pm

Truly inspired muffins, black and oily espresso and rich, tropical smoothies for the rise-and-shine internet cafe-hound. Replete with a small wraparound deck for tea- and coffee-sipping and loitering enthusiasts alike, overlooking Hanalei's thriving center. For a real treat, try the Lava Lust smoothie (coconut milk, mango, pineapple juice and raspberry sorbet) or the Vanilla Anu, a cold creamy mix of vanilla, espresso and cream.

HANALEI WAKE UP CAFÉ — Cafe $

☎ 826-5551; cnr Kuhio Hwy & Aku Rd; breakfast $5-7; 6-11:30am

One of the cheapest eats for early grinds; ease and convenience meet a mom-style hot meal at this no-frills breakfast spot. The majority of menu items aren't low in fat but instead decadently caloric. Specialties include the macadamia and cinnamon nut rolls and the breakfast quesadilla with sour cream, cheese and eggs.

PAT'S TAQUERIA — Tacos $

☎ 346-4710; Hanalei Pier parking lot; tacos $4-8; 12-3pm

Where other than Hawaii could a taco truck parked in a beach lot offer gourmet fusion Mexican delicacies as a reprieve from surfing-derived ravenous hunger? Pat Grenz, whose claim to fame includes cheffing at Bar Acuda, serves up fish tacos ($5) and *carne asada* ($4) to be reckoned with. The jalepeño quesadilla ($4) is also a deal. Cash only.

POLYNESIA CAFÉ — Hawaii Regional $$

☎ 826-1999; Ching Young Village; mains $11-17; 8am-9pm

Its slogan proclaims it's 'gourmet food on paper plates.' And the food does take the plate lunch to another level. Favorites include the mac-nut or pecan-pesto *'ahi* plates. Vegetarians can opt for flavorful tofu plates. In the dessert showcase, massive pieces of cake and brownies are irresistible.

HANALEI GOURMET — Pub Food $$

☎ 826-2524; www.hanaleigourmet.com; Hanalei Center, 5-5161 Kuhio Hwy; sandwiches $7-10, dinner mains $14-26; 8am-9:30pm, to 10:30pm summer, live music 8pm Wed & 6pm Sun

The best bets at this lively café/bar/deli are huge sandwiches on house-baked bread. The sit-down meals – from a sampler of lox-style local smoked fish to crunchy macadamia-nut fried chicken – are tasty and unpretentious, if more mainstream American than local. Though not consistent every night, Wednesdays and Sundays offer a good chance for good local music like the Mango Brothers, who play some mean ukulele.

NEIDE'S SALSA SAMBA
Brazilian/Mexican $$

☎ 826-1851; Hanalei Center, 5-5161 Kuhio Hwy; dishes $9-17; 11am-2:30pm & 5-9pm

Unique flavors and a quiet veranda are the main attractions at this little owner-run restaurant serving Mexican and Brazilian fare – from familiar *huevos rancheros* and burritos to traditional Brazilian offerings, such as *panqueca*, a veggie or chicken crepe stuffed with pumpkin.

BOUCHONS
Eclectic/Sushi $$$

☎ 826-9701; www.bouchonshanalei.com; Ching Young Village; lunch 11:30am-4pm, dinner 5:30-10pm

Formerly called Sushi&Blues, this hipster joint on the North Shore still has the same owners, but its service quality has dwindled and its menu for foods other than sushi isn't as exciting. Sit at the sushi bar (open noon to 9pm) or by the open-air seating overlooking the street. They do still offer an abundance of sake, martinis and specials, though Happy Hour (3:30pm to 5:30pm) is the way to go, as they're generally overpriced. There's a large-screen TV for sports, plus some live entertainment on weekends.

POSTCARDS CAFÉ
Hawaii Regional $$$

☎ 826-1191; www.postcardscafe.com; 5-5075 Kuhio Hwy; mains $18-27; 6-9pm

From the outside, the Postcards Café looks like a plain old wooden building. Inside, though, the rustic dining room simultaneously feels special and homey. The creative, healthful, pesci-vegetarian cuisine is well worth the price. Signature items include polenta-crusted taro fritters and the seafood rockets (shrimp, fish and coconut, rolled and fried.)

KALYPSO ISLAND BAR & GRILL
Pub Food $$$

☎ 826-9700; www.kalypsokauai.com; Ching Young Village; mains $12-$30; 11 am-9pm

The gleaming floors and high-def TVs make this spot feel somewhat uppity compared with most of the surrounding restaurants, but the open, airy ambience gives this high-rent show horse the edge over its older, less-sexy neighbors. The menu fuses local grinds such as *ono* – which means 'delicious' in Hawaiian – with mainland-style, by beer-battering it and serving it alongside waffle fries. The *huli-huli* chicken with mango teriyaki falls right off the bone and needs only be chewed for savoring purposes, after having been marinated for 24 hours, stuffed with fruit and slowly roasted, *lah dat* (the local pidgin term for 'just like that'). Macadamia-crusted and locally caught fish is heavenly, with a cream sauce made from *liliko'i.*

BAR ACUDA
Eclectic $$$$

☎ 826-7081; Hanalei Center, 5-5161 Kuhio Hwy; 11:30am-2:30pm & 6-9:30pm Tue-Sat

Most fans of this urban-chic tapas-and-wine bar are mainland tourists or transplants, but there's no denying the culinary mastery. Chef/owner Jim Moffat is from San Francisco, and his seasonal menu features unimpeachable Mediterranean cuisine. Dishes include house-smoked trout with roasted beets and lobster risotto with local sweet corn.

On the run? Try:

Aloha Juice Bar (☎ 826-6990; Ching Young Village; smoothies from $5; 9am-4pm) A more budget-savvy way to get creamy, blended organic and local fruit. Simple pleasure snack: apple banana. Cash only.

Big Save (☎ 826-6652; Ching Young Village; 7am-9pm) Bland and basic, this is the only supermarket west of Princeville.

Hanalei Dolphin Fish Market ☎ 826-6113; 5-5016 Kuhio Hwy; sushi rolls $10-14, lunch $12-14; 10am-7pm) Ceviche, *'ahi poke* and clam chowder make yummy picnic fixings.

Papaya's Hanalei (☎ 826-0089; Hanalei Center, 5-5161 Kuhio Hwy; 9am-8pm) Find tasty deli meals and the usual array of healthy cereals, meat substitutes and soy yogurts. Organic produce is dismayingly expensive.

Entertainment

TAHITI NUI

☎ 826-6277; Tahiti Nui Bldg, Kuhio Hwy; 2pm-2am

This longstanding South Seas–style restaurant and bar was once *the* gathering place on the North Shore – as well as the home of a popular luau. Today the well-worn hangout remains a lively, loud, local favorite. Although dinner is available, go for the bar action at happy hour (4pm to 6pm Monday to Saturday, all day Sunday) and for nightly live music.

TAHITI NUI'S GLORY DAYS

It's changed hands and menus, and has seen its fair share of dated hairdos, bar flies and corresponding beer bellies. But there's a thread of 'Da Nui' that seems to remain the same: it's the liveliest spot in little Hanalei, and, though a dive, it remains *the* North Shore joint extraordinaire for regulars and visitors alike.

In 1964 a Tahitian woman, Louise Hauata, and her husband, Bruce Marston, founded the still-iconic Tahiti Nui (opposite). Its popularity grew and so did its draw – luring such names as Jacqueline Kennedy, who legendarily arrived unexpectedly, preceded by Secret Service agents. Yet despite the fact that it's seen its share of A-listers here you'd never guess it at first glance.

Bruce died in 1975, but Louise continued the spot's luau tradition by augmenting it with renditions of Tahitian songs in English, French or Tahitian. But she was perhaps best known for giving much aloha to her community in times of need.

Louise died in 2003, and Tahiti Nui is now run by her son, Christian Marston; her nephew, William Marston; and John Austin, who's married to celebrated singer Amy Hanaiali'i Gilliom.

Though this crowded, shack-like bar is dive-y, the staff makes up some of the most down-to-Earth money takers on the island. To be sure, this gnarly, well-loved and well-worn hot spot is much like a cherished, old running shoe that, with its stubborn longevity and aptitude for bacteria, lives on.

HAWAIIAN SLACK KEY GUITAR CONCERTS

☎ 826-1469; www.hawaiianslackkeyguitar.com; Hanalei Community Center; adult/child & senior $10/8; 4pm Fri & 3pm Sun

Slack key guitar and ukulele concerts by longtime musicians Doug and Sandy McMaster, year-round, in a refreshingly informal atmosphere.

Shopping

HANALEI PADDLER

our pick ☎ 826-8797; Hanalei Center, 5-5161 Kuhio Hwy; 9am-8pm

Don't miss out on the surfer-chic workout threads by **Andrea Smith** (www.brasilbazar.com) that paddlers and surfer girls alike show up for in droves. These unique cuts that flatter the female form are a godsend for anyone who wants to jump in the water but doesn't feel like showing it all in a butt-cleavage bikini. The shop also carries cute boutique-y dresses and other surf-shop goodies.

KOKONUT KIDS

☎ 826-0353; 5-5290 Kuhio Hwy; 10am-6:30pm Mon-Sat, 10:30am-5pm Sun

Make your kiddies feel cool. After noting all the other mini surfer dudes and dudettes running around this town (with better athletic prowess than some adults), finally you see where they shop.

RAINBOW DUCKS/HULA BEACH

☎ 826-4741; Hanalei Center, 5-5161 Kuhio Hwy; 10am-8pm

Again, you can deck out your entire family in ultra-hip, down-to-earth, beach-inspired clothing. Fun for just a look-see.

HANALEI SURF COMPANY

☎ 826-9000; www.hanaleisurf.com; Hanalei Center, 5-5161 Kuhio Hwy; 8am-9pm

Surf, surf, surf is their MO. Surfer-girl earrings, bikinis, rashies and guy surf shorts, slippers and any other surf gear you might need: wax, shades, the board itself.

BACKDOOR

☎ 826-1900; Ching Young Village; 5-5190 Kuhio Hwy; 9am-9pm

The same owner as Hanalei Surf Company extends to the Los Angeles–inspired name brands and skating lifestyle, hearkening back to the days of Tony Hawk, Velcro and checker-pattern Vans.

EVOLVE LOVE GALLERY

our pick ☎ 826-6441; Ching Young Village; 10am-6pm

Vibrant, inspired paintings, batiks and some serious sea-bling. Sunrise, Ni'ihau

City life on Kaua'i: the commercial area of Hanalei

ANN CECIL

shell and pearl are among the few jewels adorning their work.

YELLOWFISH TRADING COMPANY

☎ 826-1227; Hanalei Center, 5-5161 Kuhio Hwy; 🕑 10am-8pm Mon-Sat, to 7pm Sun

Vintage nostalgic Hawaiiana with everything from old-school wall hangings to kitchenware and unique souvenirs.

KAUAI NUT ROASTERS

☎ 284-2741; 4489 Aku Rd; snacks $6-7; 🕑 11am-7pm Mon-Sat, noon-5pm Sun

Christine Bayley-Wortley has been wholesaling these amazing little treats for years, but finally a retail outlet exists. Concoctions include best-selling coconut almonds, or Kona coffee pecans. Try unique flavors like coconut wasabi, lavender, sesame, butterscotch or praline. Great for take-home gifts or just a high-calorie, sugar binge.

BIKINI ROOM

☎ 826-9711; www.thebikiniroom.com; 4489 Aku Rd; 🕑 10am-5pm, 10am-2pm Sun

Itsy bitsy and teeny weenie, but cheetah and a variety of wild, vibrant prints instead of polka dot. Great for those blessed with a body that just won't quit.

ROOT

☎ 826-2575; 4489 Aku Rd; 🕑 9am-7pm Mon-Sat, 11am-5pm Sun

Good neighbors, this North Shore spot opted out of carrying swimwear like its Kapa'a store so it wouldn't compete with the **Bikini Room** (left). Offers unique lingerie, sleepwear, beachwear, shoes, surfer clothes, yoga wear and a handful of gracious employees, making this a fun spot for window shopping or more.

TITUS KINIMAKA KAI KANE QUIKSILVER HANALEI

☎ 826-5594; 5-5088 Kuhio Hwy; 🕑 9am-9pm Mon-Sat, 10am-5pm Sun

Formerly Kai Kane, this men and women's surf shop recently went corporate as Quiksilver, with Kaua'i's own renowned surfer and household name Titus Kinimaka adding cachet to the mix. Also sells surfboards and paddles.

HULA MOON & GIFTS

☎ 826-9965; Ching Young Village; 10am-6pm
Woodwork, great gift ideas and jewelry make this a fun spot to peruse on a rainy day.

Sleeping

Though it requires a permit, camping at Black Pot Beach Park (Hanalei Pier) is fun, safe, and one of the only methods of keeping your stay on this pricey North Shore stop affordable, if that's a priority. Camp Friday, Saturday and holidays only, with a county permit (see p259).

OHANA HANALEI — Guesthouse $$

☎ 826-4116; www.hanalei-kauai.com; Pilikoa Rd; r per day/week $95/615
Just half a block from the beach, this large studio is one of Hanalei's sweetest deals. The downstairs room is clean and comfy and nicely remodeled, with kitchenette, private entrance, phone, cable TV and convenient parking. The hosts are easygoing, longtime residents who give their guests *lots* of privacy.

HALE LUANA — Cottage $$

☎ 826-6931; Opelu Rd; ste $150
Utterly charming, this enormous loft suite might be your trip highlight. A private entrance leads to the one-bedroom suite, painted in classic white, with a soaring cathedral ceiling. The romantic, open-air spiral staircase overlooks a spacious kitchen and dining room. In the loft bedroom you can laze in bed, gazing at the ocean through a window. Washer/dryer available. There's a one-time cleaning fee of $85.

CHING HOME — Inn $$

☎ 826-9622, 800-488-3336; 5119 Weke Rd; studios per week $600, r/ste per week $850/$950
Clean, hip and perfect for surfers looking for an ideal and less-than-private locale, across from Hanalei Beach Park Pavilion. Upstairs is the airy one-bedroom suite.

BED, BREAKFAST AND BEACH AT HANALEI — B&B $$

☎ 826-6111; www.bestvacationinparadise.com; 5095 Pilikoa Rd; r $105-$120
Location is what makes this a steal, though the owner, perhaps rightfully so, is wary of disturbing the neighbors, so only singles or couples are allowed per reservation (no groups). Across the street from Hanalei Bay (though you can't see the ocean from the rooms), options include a one-bedroom, queen bed and bathroom in the hall for $105 per night or the same with bathroom attached for $120. Rooms are small and there is not much privacy, but the location and price quash such trivial issues. An assortment of boogie boards, beach chairs and beach balls are available for use, and a pleasant deck within earshot of crashing waves makes for a great afternoon. Adding to the bargain is the breakfast served on the lanai; think lemon-coconut coffee cake or banana pancakes with syrup.

HANALEI RIVERSIDE COTTAGES — Cottage $$

our pick ☎ 826-1675; www.hanaleidolphin.com/kauaivacationrental.html; Hanalei Dolphin Center; 2br unit per week $1000;
Launch a canoe, kayak or stand up paddle board right from your backyard on the Hanalei River. Airy, scenic and a stone's toss from the little shops of Ching Young Village, Cottage No 3 has its own wi-fi while the others poach that signal. Sleeps up to four comfortably with two bedrooms and two queen beds. Includes washer/dryer, barbecue and full kitchen.

HALE REED APARTMENT — Apartment $$

☎ 415-459-1858; www.hanalei-vacation.com; 4441 Pilikoa Rd; 2br apt per week from $1000-1500;
Airy and in an ideal location, this spacious little apartment is surprisingly affordable given its location, a short walk to the beach. The ground floor apartment boasts a full kitchen, queen bed and patio perfect for cooking. Can sleep four people, as there are two twin beds as well. There's a partly refundable $300 to $500 security deposit.

HANALEI INN — Inn $$

☎ 826-9333; www.hanaleiinn.com; 5-5468 Kuhio Hwy; r $119;
It's so hard to find good help these days, except here. On-site manager Bill Gaus is a kind soul ready to help point you in the direction of anything you might need (though

it's probably in this book!). Four studios to choose from, each with kitchens and a killer locale, make this a steal. Stay for a week, pay no taxes.

PINE TREES BEACH HOUSE Inn $$$

☎ 826-9333; www.hanaleibayinn.com; 5404 Weke Rd; 1br with loft/1br/r $259/199/139;

The on-site manager for the **Hanalei Inn** (p145) hosts this outfit, but we think this is a better choice – plus it's on the beach frontage road. Four can fit comfortably in the upstairs rental, replete with two queen beds and one futon, while the downstairs studio apartment sleeps two comfortably with one queen bed and a pull-out couch. Both rentals have wi-fi. Stay for a week, pay no taxes.

TUTU'S COTTAGE IN HANALEI Cottage $$$

☎ 826-6111; www.bestvacationinparadise.com; 5095 Pilikoa Rd; 2 br cottage per week $1375

What it lacks in ocean views it makes up for in location. This cozy two-bedroom, one-bathroom standalone cottage is a mere 500ft from the beach, has a covered lanai and mountain views and sleeps three people, max. It's not a particularly good option if you're traveling with children, though.

HANALEI SURFBOARD HOUSE Cottage $$$

our pick ☎ 826-9825; www.hanaleisurfboardhouse.com; 5459 Weke Rd; r $175-225;

This is one of those spots that if you passed it on your way to your boring old rental, you'd be annoyed you hadn't stayed here instead. In true Hanalei style, host Simon Potts takes the white picket fence to another realm with his...surfboard fence, featuring real, used boards. Though pricey, its unforgettable attributes are imaginative interior design and charming Potts himself. The three immaculate studios include kitchenette, wi-fi, TV and unique decor, from vintage Hawaiiana to a shower floor handcrafted with Kaua'i sand. The more expensive detached unit features air-con and surround-sound stereo.

MALUHIA HANALEI Cottage $$

☎ 415-382-8918, 415-310-1919; www.hanaleivacationrental.com; Pilikoa Rd; 2br ste per day/week $150/1050, 3br ste $235/1600

At the end of a quiet cul-de-sac, find an island-style house ideal for large groups. The downstairs two-bedroom unit is a bargain, with compact kitchen, classy tile floor and modern tropical furnishings. There's a partly refundable security deposit of $500.

BLU NUI Cottage $$$

☎ 826-9622, 800-488-3336; 4435 Mahimahi Rd; 2-br unit $1500/wk

Within walking distance of the beach, you're on a side street near Hanalei Bay. Pricey since it lacks a view, but you don't share walls, and the airiness, full kitchen and spaciousness (including garage) makes it feel like it's all your own.

Getting There & Around

Though it's cute walking downtown, you'll need a car to get to Hanalei (buses don't

HONOPU BEACHES

Though hailed as a thrilling side adventure, camping at or even stopping at Honopu Beach is considered by some Hawaiians as disrespectful as it is full of *'iwi* or bones of Hawaiian ancestors. Only very skilled swimmers should venture to **Honopu Beach**, just beyond the Kalalau campsite. You're not allowed to land a boat or surfboard or use any other craft on the beach, so if you opt to go, you have to swim in. The northern part of this beach has an immense waterfall that is beautifully scenic but can push the life force out of you. Currents and rips abound and, of course, an infinite number of other risks are involved when you're frolicking in water below 1900ft cliffs. If you're not deterred from the idea yet, aim to arrive on the southern side but again, be respectful of the fact that it is the burial ground for many. Not a place for yelling, partying or anything you wouldn't do at a cemetery. Once there, you'll see the well-known **Honopu Arch**, featured in such films as *Honeymoon in Vegas, Six Days Seven Nights* and the 1976 remake of *King Kong* featuring Jessica Lange. You can also see the beaches from the water without going to the beach for a more respectful approach to seeing this historic site, either by kayaking past or on a Zodiac or catamaran tour.

cross Hanalei Bridge). Drivers, take note: your last chance to fill the tank was back in Princeville.

For bicycle rentals, try **Pedal & Paddle** (☎ 826-9069; www.pedalnpaddle.com; Ching Young Village; 9am-6pm) for cruisers per day/week $10/30 and mountain-bikes $20/80. **Kayak Kaua'i** (☎ 826-9844; www.kayakkauai.com; Kuhio Hwy; 8am-5pm) also with cruisers $15/60.

AROUND HANALEI

Lumaha'i Beach

Though it's a tidbit of useless knowledge, it's obligatory to mention that this beach is where the famous scene in which Mitzi Gaynor declared her intent to 'wash that man' out of her hair was shot for the 1958 movie *South Pacific*.

The beach, though beautiful, is known on-island as one of the most dangerous for visitors (save Queen's Bath). Way too many visitors have drowned trying to swim at this beguiling spot, dubbed 'Luma-die' as it's infamous for its rough rip currents and powerful waves. The inlet lacks reefs and breaks, so swimming here is flirting with death.

Less morbid is the beach's other nickname, 'Nurse's Beach,' which pays tribute again to Gaynor as a navy nurse in the aforementioned movie. Plan for a nice stroll, however, as it is scenic.

There are two ways onto Lumaha'i Beach. The first and more scenic is a three-minute walk that begins at the parking area 0.75 miles past the 4-mile marker on the Kuhio Hwy. The trail slopes to the left at the end of the retaining wall. On the beach, the lava-rock ledges are popular for sunbathing and photo ops, but beware: bystanders have been washed away by high surf and rogue waves.

The other way to access Lumaha'i is along the road at sea level at the western end of the beach, just before crossing the Lumaha'i River Bridge. The beach at this end is lined with ironwood trees.

Wainiha

Between Ha'ena and Hanalei rests this little spot marked by the 'last chance' Wainiha General Store next to Red Hot Mamas burrito joint. Steeped in ancient history, the narrow, green recesses of Wainiha Valley were the last hideout of the *menehune*, the legendary little people. As late as the 1850s, 65 people in the valley were officially listed as *menehune* on the government census.

> **Island Insights**
>
> Historic structures like Kapa'a's Coco Palms ran into a snag after Hurricane 'Iniki, as all new structures needed to be on stilts to guard against flooding, but altering its structure would preclude it from maintaining its historic status. Along the North Shore, especially in coastal Wainiha and Ha'ena, many houses sit way above the ground for this reason – up to 16ft high – as FEMA flood precautions dictate. Though they may appear to lack stability, the idea is that in the event of a flood, most of the force will pass under the house.

EATING & SHOPPING

There's not much, but some on-the-go groceries can be grabbed at **Wainiha General Store** (☎ 826-6251; 5-6600 Kuhio Hwy; 10am-dusk). For red-hot, filling burritos, sandwiches and somewhat random snacks, head to **Red Hot Mama's** (☎ 826-7266; 5-6607 Kuhio Hwy; meals $8.50; 11am-5pm Mon-Sat).

SLEEPING

COCO CABANA Cottage $$

☎ 826-5141; www.kauaivacation.com/coco_cabana.htm; 4766 Ananalu Rd; 1br $125;

A hot tub, chirping birds, airy ambience and, nearby, swimmable Wainiha River make for a lovely secluded stay. This cute little cottage is perfect for a couple wanting privacy and coziness. It has a queen-size bed, wi-fi and phone.

HALE HO'OMAHA B&B B&B $$

☎ 826-7083, 800-851-0291; www.aloha.net/~hoomaha; 7083 Alamihi Rd; ste $150-175;

It's not that private but if you're down with the whole sharing common space thing, the common spaces are pretty sweet. Plantation style meets the '60s, including a 'great room,' with bar and above-ground hot tub.

Bedrooms are warmly decorated, and bathrooms have dual shower heads for those honeymooners out there.

GUEST HOUSE AT RIVER ESTATE

Guesthouse $$$

☎ **826-5118, 800-390-8444; www.riverestate.com; house $275;**

Airy, huge and open, it's pricey, yes, but one look and you'll see why. Featured in *National Geographic Adventure Traveler* magazine and *LA Times* travel sections, it almost feels like you're on the set of *The Real World: Kaua'i* (because of the lush digs, not because there's a bunch of drunk kids, of course). There's a master bedroom with a king bed, second room with queen, a decked-out kitchen, wraparound lanai, washer/dryer, TV, air-con and anything else you could possibly need.

HA'ENA

Tucked away at the end of the road, landscape, ocean and views don't get more dramatic than at Ha'ena anywhere else on the island. A rural community, Ha'ena is a remote example of where legend meets geography. Two tsunamis struck Ha'ena in the 20th century: the first in 1946 and the second in 1957. Both devastated homes along the beach. Hence any new house built today must be elevated (see Houses on Stilts, p147).

To learn more about Ha'ena's history, visit: www.pacificworlds.com/haena.

Beaches

MAKUA (TUNNELS) BEACH

Thriving with surfers and snorkelers galore, Makua's horseshoe-shaped fringing reef invites beachcombers, too. During summer months you can start snorkeling near the east point and let the current carry you westward. It's safer and less crowded than Ke'e Beach. Expert windsurfers and kiteboarders can be seen on strong winds when waves are choppy (in the 2-to-4ft range). It might be hard to spot them right off the bat, as they're usually way outside the reef, at least 200 yards out in the open ocean.

In winter, high surf conditions mean a tubular break – hence the name Tunnels – ideal for expert surfers and perilous risk for the rest of us. Dangerous rip currents prevail from October to May. It was here on October 21, 2003 that competitive surfer Bethany Hamilton, then 13, lost her left arm in a shark attack. Undaunted, Bethany resumed her surfing career, wrote a book, made a media splash and continues to dominate at national competitions. See www.bethanyhamilton.com for her remarkable story.

To get here, drive past the 8-mile marker and park at either of two spots around the halfway mark between the 8- and 9-mile markers. If you cannot find parking, you might try parking at Ha'ena Beach Park (below) and walking to the right (facing the water) and down along the beach.

HA'ENA BEACH PARK

This is a primo spot for snorkeling, conditions permitting – so go ask the lifeguard first. Ha'ena Beach is yet another beautiful curve of white sand, but beware of astoundingly strong rip currents and shorebreaks from October to May. To the right, you can see the horseshoe shape of Tunnels outlined by breaking waves. To the far left is **Cannons**, a particularly good wall dive, with crevices and lava tubes sheltering all sorts of marine life. There's a snack truck here.

Sights

LIMAHULI GARDEN

☎ **826-1053; www.ntbg.org; self-guided/guided tour $15/20; 9:30am-4pm Tue-Sat**

One of the National Tropical Botanical Gardens (NTBG), it's as impressive in beauty as it is an educational crash course on Kaua'i's flora among native, Polynesian-introduced and modern-introduced alien species. Think mango, guava and plumeria are typical Hawaiian species? Think again. The mammoth Makana Mountain is the backdrop to vibrant plants flourishing from the copious rainfall. Beyond Limahuli Garden's 17-acre visitor-accessible area is the vast 985-acre Limahuli Preserve, where forest is still regaining footing from 1992's Hurricane 'Iniki. Juliet Rice Wichman acquired Limahuli in the '60s with a goal of preserving the valley as a 'living classroom' on ancient Hawaii. In 1976 she gifted the garden to NTBG, and in 1994 her grandson Chipper Wichman gifted the adjoining 985 acres.

Tours are available to the public, but with a self-guided version you can roam at your own pace on a short-but-sweet 0.75-mile loop trail. Perfect for bringing a journal or camera; benches allow for meditative stops.

To get here, turn inland just before the stream that marks the boundary of Ha'ena State Park.

MANINIHOLO DRY CAVE

Directly across Ha'ena Beach Park, Maniniholo Dry Cave is deep and broad and high enough to explore. Drippy and creepy, a constant seep of water from the cave walls keeps the interior damp and humid. The cave is named after the head fisherman of the *menehune* who, according to legend, built ponds and other structures at night.

Activities

YOGA & MASSAGE

If you're going to splurge, do it right at the **Hanalei Day Spa** (☎ 826-6621; www.hanaleidayspa.com; Hanalei Colony Resort; massage per 60/90min $115/195; 🕑 11am-7pm Mon-Sat). Try the detoxifying algae wrap, Ayurvedic herbal mineral mud treatment or Utvartana herbal body rub, or a body polish with Hawaiian sea salt and calming scents like lavender, mandarin or ylang ylang. If you really want to do it, try the couples' deluxe massage ($200), which includes a fruit smoothie or herbal tea.

Eating

MEDITERRANEAN GOURMET

Mediterranean $$$

☎ 826-9875; www.mediterraneangourmet.biz; Hanalei Colony Resort; dinner mains $15-25; 🕑 11am-9pm

Homemade baklava, hand-rolled *fatayer* (spinach pie), babaganush and Turkish coffee are just a few reasons to hit this place up if you're hungry. More reasons? Banana leaf–baked *'ahi* or free-range rosemary rack of lamb. On Wednesday nights the wines are half-price.

Sleeping

For backpackers, **Ha'ena Beach Park** (opposite) has campsites, rest rooms and showers. If you plan to hike the entire **Kalalau Trail**

Tourists exploring Maniniholo Dry Cave (...cave...cave...)

LINDA CHING

(p152), you might want to park and set up a base camp here because your unattended car will probably be safer than parking at Ke'e Beach. See p259 for county camping permit information.

Upscale travelers will find Ha'ena a hotspot for beach-house rentals. A Google search is most effective, but you can also check with the agencies listed in the boxed text, p131.

HANALEI COLONY RESORT

☎ 826-6235, 800-628-3004; www.hcr.com; Kuhio Hwy 560; 2br units from $210;

The only resort west of Princeville, this longstanding condo is near Tunnels Beach. The units are comfortable, with full kitchen and lanai, but quality is mixed: you might find bent screen doors, peeling paint or worn furnishings. Despite its flaws, the remote location is peaceful and the staff is friendly, with a reputation for service.

MERMAID HOUSE

Cottage $$$

☎ 826-8968, 866-369-8968; www.kauai-beach-rental.com; 7341 Ale Lea Rd; 3br $225-250

Close to Makua (Tunnels) Beach, this is the perfect surfer hideaway. A lanai barbecue, two king-size beds, one queen-size bed and two sleepable sofas, along with a full kitchen, make these rustic digs fun for a small group. Cleaning fee $150.

A RIVER HOUSE AND BIRD'S NEST

Guesthouse $$$$

☎ 826-9675; www.wainihariverhouse.com; 5121 Powerhouse Rd; house per week from $1610

It's got a jungle paradise feel, is just a mile from glorious Makua (Tunnels) Beach and close to the Kalalau trailhead. Avocados, lychee, bananas, papayas and mountain apple (a delicacy even to locals) abound. The house boasts a queen bed, full bath, refrigerator and hot plate; minimum stay is one week. It also has a screened-in sleeping area called the Bird's Nest with full bed and half bath.

HA'ENA STATE PARK

Climactic, the 'end of the road,' 230-acre Ha'ena State Park is so pristine compared

NORTH SHORE

PASSIONATE GODDESSES

Legend says that the volcano goddess Pele was napping one day under a hala (screwpine) tree on the Big Island when her spirit was awakened by the sound of distant drums. Her spirit rode the wind toward the sound, searching each island until she finally arrived at **Ke'e Beach** (opposite). Here, above the heiau (ancient Hawaiian religious site), she found Lohi'au, a 16th-century chief, beating a hula drum, surrounded by graceful hula dancers.

Pele took the form of an enchanting woman and captured Lohi'au's heart. They became lovers and moved into his house. In time Pele had to go home to the Big Island, leaving lovesick Lohi'au behind. Later, she sent her sister Hi'iaka to fetch him within 40 days – all the other sisters refused the task, fearing Pele's monumental jealousy, which forbade Hi'iaka even to hug Lohi'au. In return, Pele vowed to watch over Hi'iaka's friend Hopoe, a human woman who lived in a grove of *'ohia-lehua* (a type of scrub or tree).

After Pele left, Lohi'au, heartbroken and distraught, had become deathly ill. When Hi'iaka arrived he was dead and she had to undergo a perilous journey to find his wandering spirit, then perform a series of rituals to revive him. When 40 days passed, Pele, in a fit of rage, brought lava and destruction to the Big Island, killing Hopoe. On her return with Lohi'au, Hi'iaka saw the ruins and knew Pele had not kept her promise so she embraced Lohi'au and placed a lei around his neck.

Pele then circled Lohi'au in a ring of lava fire, which incited Hi'iaka to attack Kilauea Volcano and prepare to let loose the seas. Pele realized her faithlessness in the face of her sister's faithfulness and she relented, telling Hi'iaka where to find Lohi'au's spirit. Lohi'au revived yet again and Hi'iaka then returned to Kaua'i, where they lived until Lohi'au died a mortal death.

You can see Lohi'au's House Site near Ke'e Beach, just a minute's walk above the parking lot – but you must ramp up your imagination into overdrive. At the Kalalau Trail sign, go left along the barely discernible dirt path to a vine-covered rock wall. This overgrown level terrace, which runs back 54ft to the bluff, is the historical home of Lohi'au.

with the modernized rest of the world that it ironically appears Photoshopped. The alluring drive to Ke'e Beach is more than just 'pretty.' You'll likely recognize the distinctive 1280ft cliff commonly known as Bali Hai, its name in the movie *South Pacific*. Hawaiians prefer to use its Hawaiian name, Makana, which aptly means 'gift.'

Sights

WET CAVES

Two wet caves are within the boundaries of Ha'ena State Park. The first, **Waikapala'e Wet Cave**, is just a short walk from the road, opposite the visitor parking overflow area. The second, **Waikanaloa Wet Cave**, is on the south side of the main road.

KE'E BEACH

This beach is a favorite for sunsets and summer snorkeling (in winter months it's out of the question). Divers (expert only – it has a notorious rip current and during winter months is even worse) will enjoy its reef, teeming with fish. There's a famous heiau and gorgeous views, and it's also the start of the Na Pali coast and the adjacent Kalalau trailhead. Expect throngs of visitors. Understandably popular, however, note that Ke'e Beach has always drawn in admirers. The regal beauty of the area has not only drawn in tourists but also beckoned the Hawaiian people, as the first Hawaiians to practice the spiritual dance of hula chose this very spot. Movies like *Thorn Birds* and *Castaway Cowboys* were shot here. As the left side of the ocean draws in an open, powerful current, consider yourself hit over the head with this warning: Ke'e Beach is notorious for sucking swimmers out through a keyhole in the reef when the waters appeared calm, never to return. A safer bet: from the beach you can behold the Na Pali Coast by walking 0.75 miles up through a steep ascent on the Kalalau Trail.

Because parking is limited, the county asks that residents and visitors ride-share or carpool when they can. Parking can be challenging, especially during summer months and weekends. Cars that are obviously rentals (eg Mustangs, Sebrings and PT Cruisers) are also targets for break-ins. You'll find showers, drinking water, rest rooms and a pay phone in the woods behind the parking lot.

KAULU PAOA HEIAU

Ke'e Beach is home to one of the most cherished heiau, said to have the strongest vibrations in the world, second only to Egypt. To this day, those practicing the religious hula come here to receive blessings to pass on through the spiritual dance. You might see lei offerings on the ground, as many leave behind the fragrant flowers out of respect for the dead. If you see a tí leaf encircling a lava rock, that's an offering for Pele, the volcanic goddess. Leave any offerings in place. Enter the heiau through its entryway. Do not cross over its walls, as it is disrespectful and said to invoke bad luck.

NA PALI COAST STATE PARK

The rugged and sheer beauty of the Na Pali (meaning 'the cliffs'), which stretches 22 miles from Ke'e Beach to Polihale on the island's West Side, is difficult to do justice by description. Visiting is an absolute must.

Your tough decision is how you want to see it: by helicopter, hike, or at ocean level, as there are no roads that cover this extreme terrain.

History

Kalalau, Honopu, Awa'awapuhi, Nu'alolo and Miloli'i (see Map p187) are the five major valleys on the Na Pali Coast. Since the first waves of Tahitian settlers, these deep river valleys contained sizable settlements. When winter seas prevented canoes from landing on the northern shore, trails down precipitous ridges and rope ladders provided access.

In the mid-19th century missionaries established a school in Kalalau, the largest valley, and registered the valley population at about 200. Influenced by Western ways, people gradually began moving to towns, and by century's end the valleys were largely abandoned.

Sights & Activities

For views of the Na Pali Coast, hiking the 11-mile Kalalau coastal trail into Hanakapi'ai, Hanakoa and Kalalau Valleys

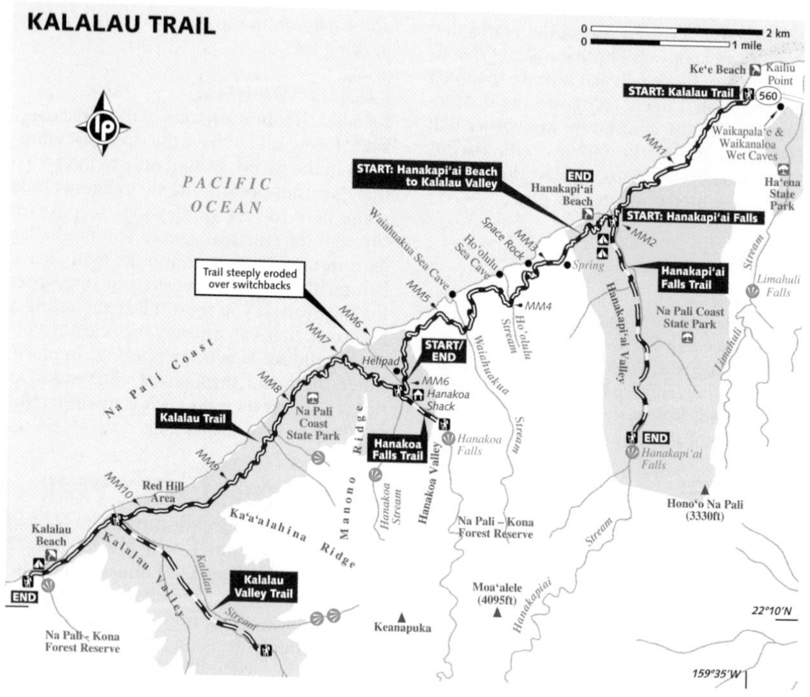

is an adventure that's sure not to disappoint. Unfit for roads, the Na Pali Coast leads to the opposite side of the island, in Koke'e State Park. You won't want to miss hiking the West Side of the island for those views, close in distance but furthest by car. If you're one of those 'ultimate' fitness fanatics, perhaps the Na Pali Coast by sea on a 17-mile kayak adventure is up your alley (p137).

KALALAU TRAIL

Notorious for its difficulty and its dangerous eroded areas, the Kalalau Trail is also revered for the sublime beauty of its dynamic aqua-blue ocean setting and the crystal mountain springs that constantly recarve the 1000-ft-plus Na Pali. You came to Kaua'i seeking a real-life Eden – and hiking this coast is the most intimate way to experience it.

There are three hike options: Ke'e Beach to **Hanakapi'ai Beach**, Hanakapi'ai Beach to **Hanakapi'ai Falls** and Hanakapi'ai Beach to **Kalalau Valley**. There are hunters who can do the entire trail in and out in one day, but most people will either want to opt for the Hanakapi'ai Beach or Hanakapi'ai Falls hike or bring camping gear to make it to **Kalalau Beach**. In winter the trails can become rivers, streams can become impassable and the beaches will just plain disappear from the high surf. Give this trail a second thought before heading out on a rainy day. Always

Island Insights

The **Kalalau Trail** means rugged wilderness, and hikers should be well prepared. The longer the trek, the challenge compounds. Water abounds on the hike but all drinking water must be boiled or treated. Campers should bring only what is necessary. Pack out what you pack in. Garbage and jettisoned weight from departing campers is a serious problem at Kalalau, and it cannot be overstated: take your detritus with you.

Lastly, mosquitoes are voracious. Wear repellent.

NORTH SHORE

be careful of swimming at the beaches along Na Pali as a makeshift sign will tell you of the 30-plus people who have drowned at Hanakapi'ai.

Note that although 11 miles may not sound like much, this is not an 11-mile *walk*. Also remember that means 11 miles *in*, after which point you have to come back out. It is treacherous, steep, and challenging to be sure – but it offers one of the sweetest series of views of ocean, cliff and waterfall you'll ever see. The last section into Kalalau Valley should be done only by the extremely fit. Those who are of average mobility wanting an experience and a half should opt for the Hanakapi'ai River and Beach hike, while those of modest physical prowess should feel justly accomplished with the 4-mile hike to **Hanakapi'ai Falls** (p154). While the falls hike offers a large waterfall pool to frolic in, the county's official stance on Hanakapi'ai Beach is that swimming is not allowed due to the many fatalities in its rough waters. So if you think you'll want some *après*-hike refreshment, perhaps the falls is the way to go.

The state parks office in Lihu'e can provide a Kalalau Trail brochure with a map. Another good source sponsored by the county is www.kauaiexplorer.com. Keep in mind that even if you're not planning to camp, a permit is officially required to continue on the Kalalau Trail beyond Hanakapi'ai. Free day-use hiking permits are available from the **Hawaii State Parks Office** (Map p62; ☎ 274-3444; www.hawaiistateparks.org; Department of Land & Natural Resources, Division of State Parks, Room 306, 3060 Eiwa St, Lihue; 8am-3:30pm Mon-Fri), which also issues the required camping permits for the Hanakapi'ai (one night maximum) and Kalalau (five nights maximum) Valleys. For more information on permits see (p259). You'll need ample time – possibly as much as six to 12 months – in advance to get permits.

KE'E BEACH TO HANAKAPI'AI BEACH

This is the most popular and most crowded hike. You will have to stand to the side of the trail about every 50yd for someone oncoming or passing. It's easy to see why it's so popular, though, as it is a perfect mini–Na Pali experience (4 miles round trip), passing through the small hanging valleys and streams that run through them, offering the panoramic views along the entire coast with Lehua Rock in the distance. You'll end this hike at a white sand beach at the base of Hanakapi'ai Valley: **Hanakapi'ai Beach**. At a mere 2 miles in, plan for about two to three hours for this sojourn, and don't plan on a swim – it's too dangerous. If you want a refreshing treat, continue to the falls.

The Kalalau Trail is the only way to access the rugged, remote Na Pali Coast JOHN ELK III

HANAKAPI'AI BEACH TO HANAKAPI'AI FALLS

our pick For a longer day hike, cross the Hanakapi'ai stream and follow the trail 2 miles up the valley. Hanakapi'ai Falls is spectacular, falling 100ft into a wide pool gentle enough for swimming. Directly under the falls, the cascading water forces you back from the rock face – a warning from nature, as falling rocks are common. The setting is idyllic, though not very sunny near the falls because of the incredible steepness. You'll pass bamboo forests and see some of the most rugged, jagged and inspiring views the island has to offer.

The 4-mile roundtrip hike is relatively flat and pleasant going through the densely forested valley and crossing the stream at several swimming holes. Save the temptation to jump in for the falls, as there's not much that compares with floating in its icy (for Kaua'i) cold waters and looking up at the 200ft foot waterfall. Before you get there, listen for the water. It's sweet, sweet justice as you arrive and jump into this refreshing, clean and clear pool as tropic birds soar above.

The trail itself is periodically washed out by floodwaters, and sections occasionally get redrawn, but path direction basically ascends the side of Hanakapi'ai Stream gradually. The first of three major stream crossings is about one mile or 25 minutes' walk up, at a sign that warns: 'Hazardous. Keep away from stream during heavy rainfall. Stream floods suddenly.' Be particularly careful of your footing on the rocky upper part of the trail. Some of the rocks are covered with a barely visible film of slick algae – worse than walking on ice. During heavy rain, flash floods are likely in the narrow valley, so do this hike only in fair weather.

HANAKAPI'AI BEACH TO KALALAU VALLEY

Going past Hanakapi'ai means you've committed to the whole 22-mile roundtrip hike. The trail takes its longest climb out of Kalalau and proceeds in and out of the valleys along Na Pali. Hanakoa Valley usually marks the halfway point and a rest stop or campground for hikers, depending on how you break up the trail. Past Hanakoa the trail gets noticeably drier and more exposed, and the blue Pacific waters at the base of the cliff taunt you that much more. The last hill to top is the saddle before dropping into Kalalau Valley. It's difficult to say from which vantage point the cliffs look more majestic, from the top at the lookout in Koke'e or here at the bottom. Either way, consider yourself lucky to get to ponder the question. The trail continues across to the western end of the valley where you'll find **Kalalau Beach**.

Lumaha'i Beach (p147)

JOHN ELK III

SOUTH SHORE

Sun. Surf. Sand. The quintessential elements of a beach vacation are guaranteed in Po'ipu, where the weather and waves are welcoming almost year-round. Since the 1970s, huge condos and hotels have mushroomed along the shore, spawning a mass of tourists and a lively (if low-key) resort vibe. While the North Shore's raw beauty is incomparable, the South Shore boasts two world-renowned botanical gardens, plus the undeveloped Maha'ulepu Coast, where lithified sand-dune cliffs and pounding surf make for an unforgettable walk. The quaint, historic Koloa, a former plantation town, is the South Shore's answer to a lively little commercial center.

SOUTH SHORE ITINERARIES

IN TWO DAYS *This leg: 9 miles*

❶ **NATIONAL TROPICAL BOTANICAL GARDEN** (p167) On your first day, catch the morning tour of **Allerton Garden**, a lushly landscaped collection of tropical flora with an interesting history dating back to Queen Emma, the wife of Kamehameha IV.

❷ **KOLOA FISH MARKET** (p161) After the tour, browse the shops and galleries of Koloa, then put together a picnic lunch from this outstanding hole-in-the-wall. Standouts include freshly made *poke* (marinated raw fish), Hawaiian plate lunches and satisfying hunks of *haupia* (coconut dessert).

❸ **PO'IPU BEACH PARK** (p164) Laze away an idle afternoon at this convivial family spot, where you can snorkel, bodyboard or toss a frisbee – or just lie back and wait for a perfect sunset.

❹ **CASA DI AMICI** (p172) This island-inspired Italian bistro is a hidden gem. Locals praise the affordable menu's consistency.

❺ **DIVING TOUR** (p170) On day two, check out Po'ipu's underwater scene, among the island's best. Shore-dive from Koloa Landing or go further and deeper on a boat dive.

❻ **SUNSET WATCHING** (p165) Some of life's finest moments are free. Sit on the stone wall near Brennecke's Beach and watch the sun disappear over silhouetted bodyboarders and into the endless horizon beyond.

❼ **BEACH HOUSE RESTAURANT** (p173) Big spenders, take the 'free sunset' idea a step further by splurging on an oceanfront dinner at this iconic coastal restaurant. Book at least a week ahead.

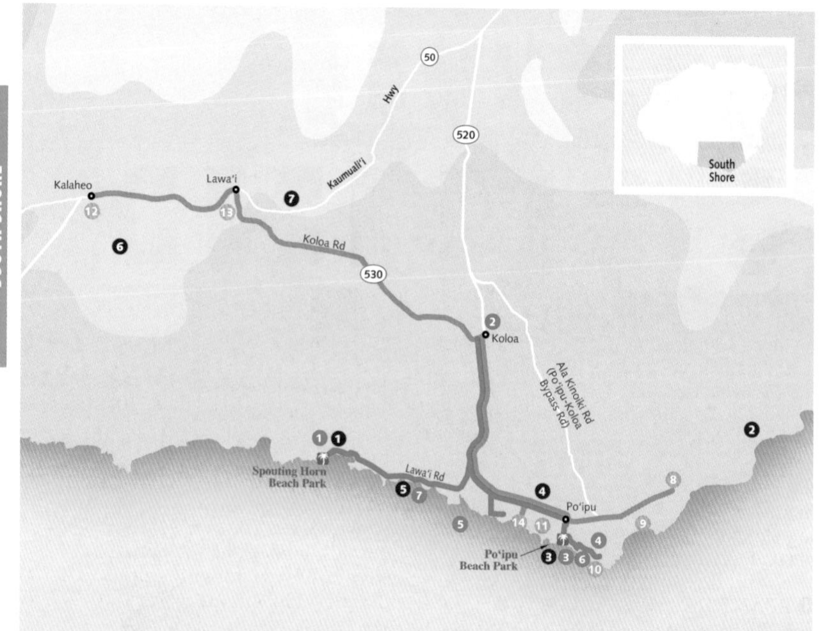

IN FOUR DAYS *This leg: 15 miles*

8 PO'IPU BAY GOLF COURSE (p171) On day three, indulge your PGA fantasies and tread on this famous Po'ipu course, which hosted the PGA Grand Slam from 1994 to 2006.

9 ANARA SPA (p171) If golf isn't your thing, try a massage or facial at the Grand Hyatt's mega spa, which goes all out with a tropical-garden fantasia and lots of alfresco treatment settings.

10 BRENNECKE'S BEACH (p165) If you're into bodyboarding, join the floating throng, awaiting that perfect wave, at this cozy hot spot. If you want to kick back and snorkel, just walk to adjacent **Po'ipu Beach Park (p164)**.

11 PLANTATION GARDENS RESTAURANT & BAR (p172) Set in a historic plantation manor, this longtime restaurant gleams with low-key, classy charm. Before dinner, stroll through **Moir Gardens (p168)**, showcasing cacti, succulents and orchids.

12 KALAHEO CAFÉ & COFFEE CO (p180) Start day four with a leisurely breakfast at this airy hangout in nearby Kalaheo, a mostly residential neighborhood with astoundingly pretty backroads overlooking the coast.

13 LAWAI INTERNATIONAL CENTER (p161) Don't miss the twice-monthly Sunday tours of this quietly powerful site, where 88 miniature Buddhist shrines sit along a rustic, hillside path.

14 SURF TO SUNSET LUAU (p174) If you've never experienced a luau, you might enjoy the Sheraton Kaua'i Resort's beachside dinner and show. Sure, it's commercial and maybe hokey, but the hula, Tahitian and Samoan dancing never fails to impress.

FOR SHOESTRING BUDGETS

1 NATIONAL TROPICAL BOTANICAL GARDEN (p167) The self-guided **McBryde Garden** tour (half the price of the Allerton tour) lets you stroll at your own pace amid palms, orchids and rare native species.

2 MAHA'ULEPU HERITAGE TRAIL (p168) Walk the island's last accessible undeveloped coastline and bear witness to striking limestone cliffs unlike anything else across the Hawaiian Islands.

3 SHORE SNORKELING (p170) Snorkel cruises are exciting but expensive. Take an unstructured approach by renting equipment from **Snorkel Bob's (p160)** and exploring Po'ipu's eye-catching marine life just beyond the shore.

4 PUKA DOG (p172) Sure, it's just a hot dog. But a specialized *puka* (hole) in the toasted bun, plus tropical-fruit relishes, made it a dog to remember.

5 BEACH HOUSE RESTAURANT LAWN (p173) If you can't afford dinner at this fine-dining icon, park yourself on the adjacent grassy knoll and enjoy the free show: lithe local surfers, unobstructed horizon and blazing sunsets.

6 KUKUIOLONO GOLF COURSE (p180) This neighborhood nine-hole course is welcoming, unpretentious and only $8.

7 MARK'S PLACE (p180) Your Hawaiian trip will be sadly incomplete if you leave without having an authentic plate lunch. The trick is choosing the right place. This eatery off the highway is a local fave for classics from teriyaki chicken to grilled mahimahi.

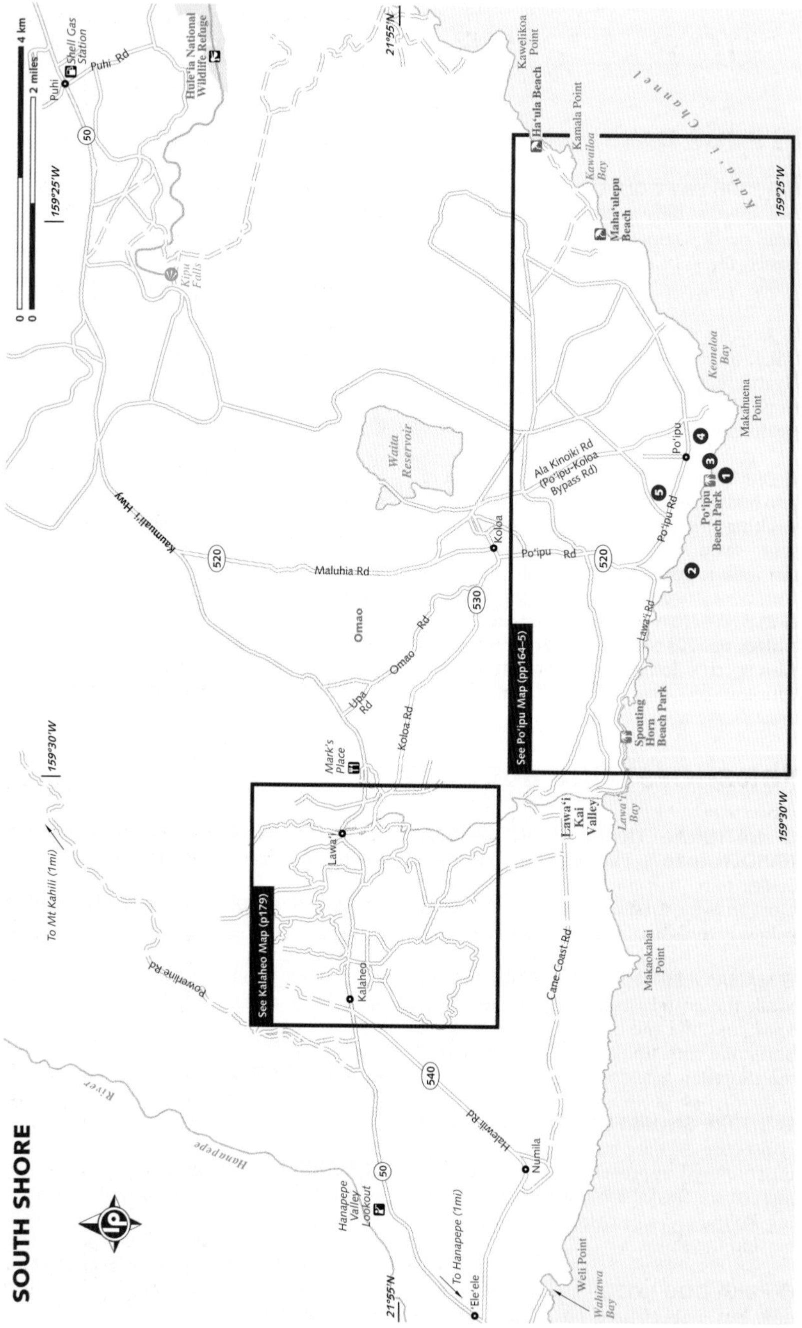

SOUTH SHORE

0 2 miles
0 4 km

159°25'W
159°30'W
21°55'N

Puhi
Shell Gas Station
Puhi Rd
Hule'ia National Wildlife Refuge
Kipu Falls
Waita Reservoir
Kaumuali'i Hwy
Maluhia Rd
Koloa
Omao
Omao Rd
Upa Rd
Koloa Rd
Mark's Place
To Mt Kahili (1mi)
Powerline Rd
See Kalaheo Map (p179)
Lawa'i
Kalaheo
Halewili Rd
Numila
'Ele'ele
To Hanapepe (1mi)
Hanapepe Valley Lookout
Hanapepe River
Cane Coast Rd
Lawa'i Kai Valley
Lawa'i Bay
Makaokahai Point
Weli Point
Wahiawa Bay
See Po'ipu Map (pp164-5)
Ala Kinoiki Rd (Po'ipu-Koloa Bypass Rd)
Po'ipu Rd
Lawa'i Rd
Po'ipu
Po'ipu Beach Park
Spouting Horn Beach Park
Makahuena Point
Keoneloa Bay
Maha'ulepu Beach
Kawailoa Bay
Kamala Point
Ha'ula Beach
Kawelikoa Point
Kaua'i Channel

HIGHLIGHTS

❶ **Best Beach:** Po'ipu Beach Park (p164)
❷ **Best View:** Underwater on a diving trip (p170)
❸ **Best Activity:** Bodyboarding at Brennecke's Beach (p165)
❹ **Best Eco-Conscious Lodging:** Aikane Kaua'i Beach Houses (p176)
❺ **Best Use of Locally Grown Fruit:** Papalani Gelato (p172)

Highlights are numbered on the map on p158.

KOLOA

On the South Shore, all roads lead to Koloa, which was a thriving plantation town until it withered in the years after WWII, when sugar gave way to tourism. Today Koloa's quaint 'Old West' neighborhood contains a pleasant set of affordable shops and restaurants – a welcome complement to the budget-breaking selection in Po'ipu. The adjacent residential towns of Lawa'i and Omao are low-key, neighborly and blooming with foliage.

History

When William Hooper, an enterprising 24-year-old Bostonian, arrived on Kaua'i in 1835, he took advantage of two historical circumstances: Polynesians' introduction of sugarcane to the islands and Chinese immigrants' knowledge of refinery. With financial backing from Honolulu businesspeople, he leased land in Koloa from the king and paid island *ali'i* a stipend to release commoners from their traditional work obligations. He then hired the Hawaiians as wage laborers and Koloa became Hawaii's first plantation town.

Orientation & Information

From the west, Koloa Rd (Hwy 530), which runs between Lawa'i and Koloa, is the best way in and out. From Lihu'e, take the scenic Maluhia Rd (Hwy 520), through the enchanting Tree Tunnel.

Services are minimal:

First Hawaiian Bank (☎ 742-1642; 3506 Waikomo Rd) At the east end of town.

Post office (☎ 800-275-8777; 5485 Koloa Rd) Serves both Koloa and Po'ipu.

Sights

TREE TUNNEL

Driving from Lihu'e to Po'ipu, take Maluhia Rd (Hwy 520) not only for a shortcut but also to pass through the romantic Tree Tunnel, a mile-long canopy of towering swamp mahogany trees (a type of eucalyptus). Pineapple baron Walter McBryde planted the trees as a community project in 1911, when he had leftover trees after landscaping his estate at Kukuiolono (p179).

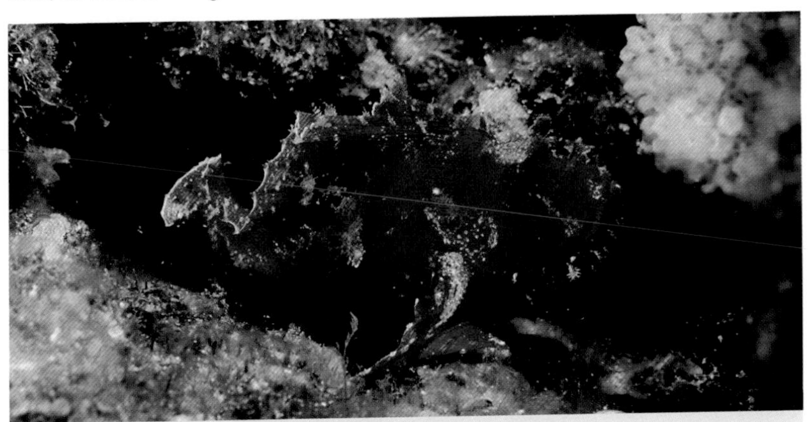

The leaf scorpionfish can be seen while diving off the South Shore

CASEY MAHANEY

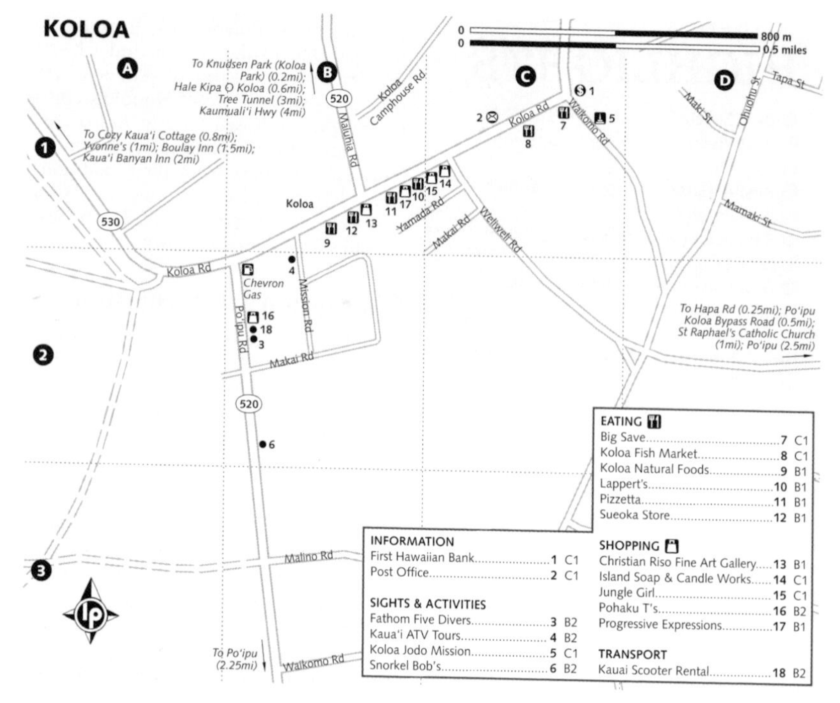

KOLOA HISTORIC BUILDINGS

On the east side of town you'll find the **Koloa Jodo Mission** (☎ 742-6735; 2480 Waikomo Rd; services 6pm Mon-Fri, 9:30am Sun), which follows Pure Land Buddhism, a non-meditating form popular in Japan since the 12th century. The Buddhist temple on the left is the original, which dates back to 1910, while the larger temple on the right is currently used for services.

Kaua'i's oldest Catholic church, **St Raphael's Catholic Church** (☎ 742-1955; 3011 Hapa Rd), is the burial site of some of Hawaii's first Portuguese immigrants. The original church, built in 1854, was made of lava rock and coral mortar with walls 3ft thick – a type of construction visible in the ruins of the adjacent rectory. When the church was enlarged in 1936 it was plastered over, which created a more typical whitewashed appearance.

Activities

Obviously Koloa is landlocked, but it's home to two excellent ocean-sports outfits.

DIVING

The island's best dive outfit, **our pick** **Fathom Five Divers** (☎ 742-6991, 800-972-3078; www.fathomfive.com; 3450 Po'ipu Rd; shore dives $70-140, boat dives $120-330), is run by a husband-and-wife team, Jeannette and George Thompson. They offer the whole range, from Ni'ihau boat dives ($345) to certification courses to night dives (when you might see the Dr Seuss–worthy Spanish Dancer nudibranch, as well as fish that change colors or emit protective substances after dark). Newbies can expect reassuring hand-holding during their introductory shore dives. Groups max out at six and they avoid mixing skill levels. Call well in advance.

SNORKELING

The king of snorkel gear is **Snorkel Bob's** (☎ 742-2206; www.snorkelbob.com; 3236 Po'ipu Rd; rental mask, snorkel & fins per week $9-35; 8am-5pm), which rents and sells enough styles and sizes to assure a good fit. If, after renting, you want to buy an item, your payment deflects part of the cost.

ATV

ATVs typically can't claim to be green, but Kaua'i ATV (☎ 742-2734, 877-707-7088; www.kauaiatv.com; 5330 Koloa Rd; tours $125-175) offers two-seater and four-seater biodiesel vehicles for a reasonable upgrade of $10 per person. (The money is donated to programs that benefit local children.) Most of the fleet (included all of the individual vehicles) are gas-powered, which we cannot recommend. Guides take groups of six to 12 vehicles across upcountry pastureland where you're guaranteed to get dirty, whether merely dusty or soaked in mud. Use their loaner clothing.

Festivals & Events

In late July, **our pick** Koloa Plantation Days Celebration (☎ 652-3217; www.koloaplantationdays.com), the South Shore's biggest annual celebration, spans nine days of family fun with the gamut of attractions (many free), including a parade, block party, rodeo, craft fair, canoe race, golf tournament and guided walks.

Eating

LAPPERT'S
Ice Cream $

☎ 742-1272; Koloa Rd; single scoop $3.65; 6am-10pm

In the 1980s, late founder Walter Lappert introduced the local palate to super-premium ice cream. The signature flavors are bold, tropical-themed, chunky and kid-pleasingly sweet.

Don't Miss

- **Passing under the storybook Tree Tunnel** (p159)
- **Finding that perfect souvenir tee at Pohaku T's** (p162)
- **Playing a round at the twilight rate at Po'ipu Bay Golf Course** (p171)
- **Watching local dancers show off at the Kaua'i Mokihana Festival Hula Competition** (p171)
- **Viewing (or buying) untouristy fine art at Gallery 103 and Gallery +** (p169)
- **Driving Kalaheo's surprisingly scenic backroads** (p181)
- **Sipping a cucumber mojito or lavender piña colada at the Plantation Gardens Restaurant & Bar** (p172)

KOLOA FISH MARKET
Fish Market $

our pick ☎ 742-6199; 5482 Koloa Rd; lunch $4-7; 10am-6pm Mon-Fri, to 5pm Sat

Line up with locals at this hole-in-the-wall serving outstanding *poke* (cubed, marinated raw fish), Japanese-style *bentō* (boxed lunches), sushi rolls and Hawaiian plate lunches. Don't miss the thick-sliced, perfectly seared *'ahi* and rich slabs of homemade *haupia* (coconut dessert).

PIZZETTA
Italian $$

☎ 742-8881; 5408 Koloa Rd; pizzas $17-25, pastas $11-18; 11am-9pm

If this family trattoria had any competition, we'd be more critical. But affordable eateries

LAWAI INTERNATIONAL CENTER

Magical. Enchanting. Stirring. Such words are often used to describe this quiet **our pick spiritual site** (Map p179; ☎ 639-4300; www.lawaicenter.org; 3381 Wawae Rd; call for schedule) in the Lawa'i Valley, northwest of Koloa and Po'ipu. Having originally been the site of a Hawaiian heiau, the site's strong mana (spiritual essence) attracted future generations of worshippers, including Japanese plantation families since the late 1800s.

In 1904, these immigrants placed 88 miniature Shingon Buddhist shrines (about 2ft tall) along a steep hillside path to symbolize 88 pilgrimage shrines in Shikoku, Japan. For years, island pilgrims would journey here from as far as Hanalei and Kekaha. But the site was abandoned by the 1960s, and half of the shrines are scattered in shards.

In the late 1980s, a group of volunteers formed a nonprofit, acquired a 32-acre property and embarked on a backbreaking project to repair or rebuild the shrines. Today all 88 shrines are beautifully restored, and leisurely tours include a detailed history and trail walk. Regardless of the Buddhist shrines being here, the center is a non-denominational sanctuary for all cultures. Visits are allowed only during twice-monthly Sunday tours; call for details.

are scarce around here. Choose from decent gourmet pizzas such as the El Greco (sun-dried tomatoes, artichoke hearts and feta) and filling pastas that won't ravage your wallet. Expect a predominantly touristy clientele.

If your accommodations include a kitchen, you might eat best if you eat in. Local chain supermarket **Big Save** (cnr Waikomo Rd & Koloa Rd; 6am-11pm) has among its best branches here. Don't miss the value-priced *'ahi poke*. Nearby, **Sueoka Store** (☎ 742-1611; 5392 Koloa Rd; 7am-9pm) holds its own with the basics, plus packaged Japanese take-out snacks. Like all health-nut venues, **Koloa Natural Foods** (☎ 742-8910; 5356 Koloa Rd; 10am-8pm Tue-Sat, to 4pm Sun & Mon) ain't cheap, but it carries major natural brands, bulk and packaged items and supplements.

Shopping

CHRISTAN RISO FINE ART GALLERY

☎ 742-2555; www.christianrisofineart.com; 5400 Koloa Rd; 10am-9pm

Browsers are welcome at this informal gallery of paintings and drawings by island artists (including the owner), fine jewelry (including Ni'ihau shell necklaces) and fun collectibles like hand-painted walking sticks (carved from Kaua'i woods by a local artisan and painted by Riso himself). The shop also specializes in custom framing using Hawaiian hardwoods such as koa (see p55) and *kamani*.

ISLAND SOAP & CANDLE WORKS

☎ 742-1945, 888-528-7627; www.kauaisoap.com; 5428 Koloa Rd; 9am-10pm

For a delicious treat with zero calories, breathe deeply inside this flowery, fruity sensation of a shop. Then find your favorite fragrance, such as plumeria, pikake, lavender and vanilla, in a variety of body products. Established in 1984 to recreate the art of soap- and candle-making, the company has grown but still makes everything by hand.

JUNGLE GIRL

☎ 742-9649; 5424 Koloa Rd; 9am-9pm

While not high-end, this little boutique appeals to young and youthful females seeking trendy fashions that won't break the bank. Think beater tanks, hip-slung cargo pants, strappy sundresses and ethnic costume jewelry.

POHAKU T'S

☎ 742-7500; www.pohaku.com; 3430 Po'ipu Rd; 10am-8pm Mon-Sat, to 6pm Sun

This well-stocked shop specializes in Kaua'i-made clothing, crafts and island-themed tees and tanks. Signature shirt designs feature classic island themes including petroglyphs, *honu* (sea turtle) and navigational maps on stonewashed or overdyed colors. Sizes span the whole range and fit Beefy-T loose. Cotton aloha shirts (with traditional coconut buttons), plus kids' shirts and dresses, are locally handsewn and yet affordable.

The rustic shopfronts of Koloa

JOHN ELK III

PROGRESSIVE EXPRESSIONS

☎ 742-6041; www.progressiveexpressions.com; 5420 Koloa Rd; 9am-9pm

Established in 1972, this was the South Shore's first surf shop. Original owners Marty and Joe Kuala sold the shop to the Hanalei Surf Company in 2005 but Joe still designs and crafts boards that are sold here.

Sleeping

Listed below are accommodations in the Koloa, Omao and Lawa'i residential neighborhoods.

BOULAY INN
Inn $

our pick ☎ 742-1120, 635-5539; www.boulayinn.com; Omao Rd; 1br units $85 (cleaning fee $50);

Your money goes far with this airy one-bedroom apartment in quiet residential Omao. The 500-sq-ft unit is comfy more than fancy, sitting atop a garage (no shared walls with the main house). Features include wraparound lanai, full kitchen, private phone line, high ceilings and free use of washer/dryer. The owners are longtime residents who respect guests' privacy. With a sofabed in the living room, it's also ideal for kids or an extra adult.

COZY KAUAI COTTAGE
Cottage $$

☎ 742-1778, 877-742-1778; www.kauaivacationproperties.com/cottage.htm; Omao Rd; cottage s/d $75/100 (cleaning fee $40);

Dreaming of a pastoral retreat? Can't give up modern amenities? You're in luck. This cottage is simple and compact (best for a slim single or couple) but efficiently arranged to include a full kitchen, separate bedroom and comfy living area. The hardwood floor, granite counters and dimmer lights add style, while lots of windows let in cool breezes. The friendly Kaua'i-born owner lives in the main house within sight (but far enough away to ensure privacy).

YVONNE'S
B&B $$

☎ 742-2418; vonne.vonsun@hawaiiantel.net; 3857 Omao Rd; r incl breakfast $95;

A traditional B&B run by a non-traditional woman, Yvonne's two rooms would delight sociable travelers. Each room is comfortingly homey, with Hawaiiana artifacts, charmingly retro furnishings and original modern art. The owner, who lives upstairs, enjoys a good chat and we wouldn't be surprised if guests consider her a friend. While the bathroom is shared, Yvonne typically rents only one room at a time. Three-night minimum.

HALE KIPA O KOLOA
Cottage $$

☎ 742-1802; www.koloakauaicottage.com; 5481 Waiau Rd, Koloa; 2br cottages $125;

A fantastic deal, this airy plantation-style house is close to town and affords much privacy. With two bedrooms, two bathrooms, a full kitchen and washer/dryer, a family or group can settle in without crowding one another. The inland location can be hot, but this cottage features high, insulated ceilings, cool tile floors and clean, white walls. Additional guests cost $15 each.

KAUA'I BANYAN INN
Inn $$

☎ 888-786-3855; www.kauaibanyan.com; 3528-B Mana Hema Pl; r $130-150 (cleaning fee $45);

Although a tad pricey for the neighborhood, the five units are chic enough for the most discerning guests. Each impeccable unit features polished hardwood floors, kitchenette, vaulted ceilings, private lanai and furnishings you'd buy for your own home. Pay more for better views. No kids under 10.

MARJORIE'S KAUA'I INN
Inn $$

Map p179; ☎ 332-8838, 800-717-8838; www.marjorieskauaiinn.com; Hailima St, Lawa'i; r $130-175;

The magnificent vista of Lawa'i Valley from this classy inn will change your life. Well, maybe that's a stretch, but it'll be a trip highlight, for sure. The rooms themselves show off stylish furnishings, and each includes large private lanai and kitchenettes. You're nowhere near the beach, but the elegant 50ft lap pool and poolside BBQ grill compensate nicely.

Getting There & Away

Almost all car, motorcycle and moped rental agencies are in Lihu'e, but **Kaua'i Scooter Rental** (☎ 245-7177; www.kauaimopedrentals.com; 3414 Po'ipu Rd; 8am-5pm) has a branch location in Koloa, just south of the Chevron station.

PO'IPU

pop 1075

Tourists absolutely adore Po'ipu (which ironically can mean 'completely overcast' in Hawaiian) for its dependable sun and easy-access beaches. When it does rain here, you can bet it's pouring on the North Shore. The coast is already blanketed with condos, time-shares, hotels and vacation-rental homes, but such existing developments are minor compared to what's in store (see the boxed text, p170). Alas, no Po'ipu 'town' exists. Therefore dining out is limited and traveling by foot is challenging except along the beaches.

Orientation & Information

There are two entry roads from Kaumuali'i Hwy. Coming from Lihu'e, take Maluhia Rd to the Ala Kino'iki bypass road, which will lead you to the eastern side of Po'ipu. Coming from the West Side, take Koloa Rd to Po'ipu Rd (Hwy 520), which leads to a roundabout. If you veer west, you'll be on Lawa'i Rd (toward National Tropical Botanical Garden); if you veer east, you will remain on Po'ipu Rd, where most beaches and accommodations are located.

For cash, **Bank of Hawaii** (☎ 742-6800; Po'ipu Shopping Village, 2360 Kiahuna Plantation Dr; 8:30am-4pm Mon-Thu, to 6pm Fri) is available but they don't cash checks or traveler's checks at this branch.

Check the website of the **Po'ipu Beach Resort Association** (www.poipubeach.org) for general information on Po'ipu and the whole South Shore.

Beaches

From the Po'ipu Rd thoroughfare, all you see are condos and parking lots. To reach the beaches, you must turn *makai* (seaward) on side streets, such as Ho'owili Rd to reach Po'ipu Beach Park and Kapili Rd for the Sheraton beach.

PO'IPU BEACH PARK

our pick There are no monster waves or idyllic solitude here. But if you're seeking

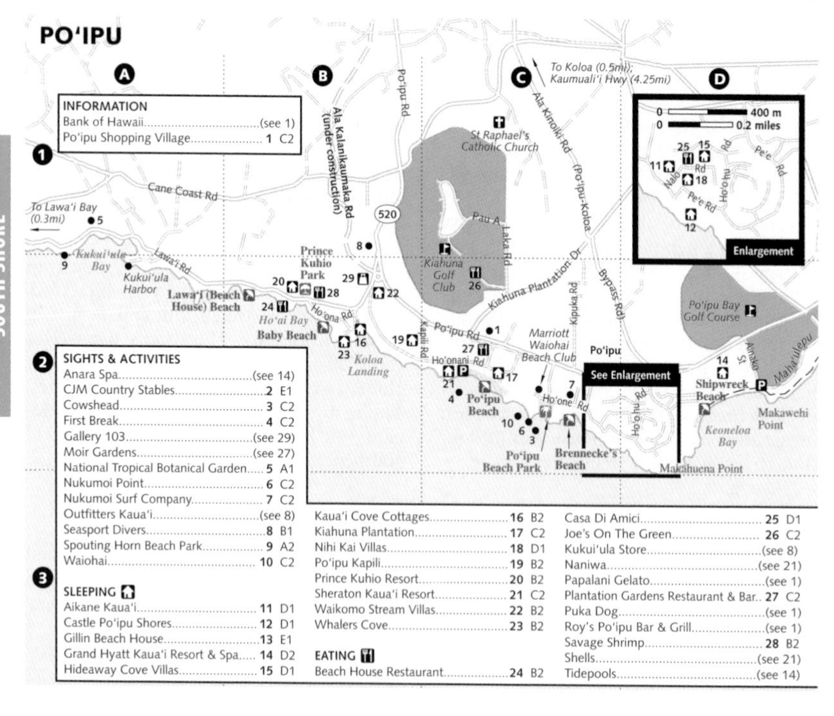

A day at the beach, Po'ipu

MICAH WRIGHT

a safe, lively, family-friendly **beach**, this is it. Located at the end of Ho'owili Rd, it features a lifeguard station and shallow, gentle waters for swimming, snorkeling and beginner diving. The sandy beach is compact (you can see one end from the other) and is jammed on weekends; but you'll have ample elbow room on weekdays. The vibe is convivial; kids without siblings can quickly find playmates, and parents end up recognizing familiar faces among their ilk. Around the beach are grassy lawns, a children's playground, picnic pavilions and tables, rest rooms and showers. What's lacking are eating options.

On the park's western side, **Nukumoi Point** extends a finger of land into the ocean. At low tide, you can walk onto the point and explore tide pools that shelter small fish. Keep your eyes peeled for *honu* (green sea turtles). The best snorkeling is west of the point, where you'll find swarms of curious fish.

To get here, go to the end of Ho'owili Rd. This is an easy-access, drive-up beach, with parking right across the street.

BRENNECKE'S BEACH

Any time, any day, this little beach attracts a big cadre of bodyboarders, bobbing in the water, waiting for the next set. Tourists often sit on the roadside stone wall to enjoy the action (plus the blazing sunsets). No

Top Picks

PO'IPU'S NATURAL WONDERS

- Humpback whales near Spouting Horn Beach Park throughout winter (p168)
- Monk seals resting along the South Shore (p166)
- Lithified sand dunes along the Maha'ulepu Coast (p168)
- Native plants at National Tropical Botanical Garden (p167)
- Perfect sunset views
- Extensive coral-algae reefs and colorful marine life, seen by snorkeling (p170) and diving (p170)

DRINKING
Point (see 21)
Seaview Terrace (see 14)
Stevenson's Library (see 14)

ENTERTAINMENT
Havaiki Nui Luau (see 14)
Surf to Sunset Luau (see 21)

SHOPPING
Kukui'ula Village 29 B2
Po'ipu Plaza (see 8)

RETURN OF THE NATIVE

If you're lucky, you'll chance upon a **monk seal** (Hawaii's official state mammal) hauled out on a beach. Monk seals are endemic (native and exclusive) to Hawaii, but it's a point of conjecture that the first Polynesians killed or drove off the seal population, which had never encountered human predators beforehand. No Hawaiian myths or artifacts even hint at the existence of seals.

They did survive in the **Northwestern Hawaiian Islands** (see the boxed text, p52) but were further decimated by European and Japanese seal traders. The current estimated population of 1200 seals in the Northwestern Hawaiian Islands is declining by 4% annually. In the late 1980s the seals started to return to their original habitat, the main Hawaiian Islands. Surprisingly, they've thrived here. About 100 live in the state, with about 30 making Kaua'i their home. Experts estimate that the seal populations at the Northwestern Hawaiian Islands and the main Hawaiian Islands will average 400 seals in each area within 20 years.

If you see a monk seal, remember that you are intruding in its natural habitat. Keep a distance of 100ft to 150ft and do not provoke it. For more information, see the website of the **Kaua'i Monk Seal Watch Program** (www.kauaimonkseal.com).

surfboards are allowed near shore, so bodyboarders rule. If you want to join in, note that waves break dangerously close to shore. Surf is highest in summer, but the winter action is respectable, too. The beach is flanks the eastern edge of Po'ipu Beach Park.

PO'IPU BEACH

Despite its nicknames Sheraton Beach and Kiahuna Beach, this long swath of sand is not private. It merely fronts the hotel and condo, both of which scored big-time with their location along Po'ipu Beach, which lies west of Po'ipu Beach Park. The waters here are too rough for kids, although an offshore reef tames the waves enough for strong swimmers and snorkelers.

Experienced surfers and bodyboarders can attempt the breaks near the Sheraton, but the waters are famous for sneaker sets (rogue waves that appear from nowhere) and the rocky coast makes it difficult to get offshore and back. South Shore spots tend to be fickle and highly susceptible to winds, tides and swells. Cowshead, the rocky outcropping at the west end of the beach, is an extremely challenging break unless you know how to approach the channel. Expert surfers can attempt offshore spots such as First Break in front of the Sheraton, but beginners should always remain inshore. Waiohai, at the east end of the beach in front of the Marriott Waiohai Beach Club timeshare, also sees major swells.

To get here, drive to the end of Ho'onani Rd.

SHIPWRECK BEACH

Unless you're an expert surfer, bodyboarder or bodysurfer, keep your feet dry at 'Shipwrecks.' But come for an invigorating walk along the half-mile crescent of light-gold sand. You'll have company, as the Grand Hyatt Kaua'i Resort & Spa overlooks much of the beach along Keoneloa Bay. Row after row of waves crash close to shore, giving this beach a rugged, untamed vibe. Toward the left of the bay, to the east, looms Makawehi Point, a gigantic lithified sand dune, which you can ascend in 10 minutes. West of Shipwreck Beach is Makahuena Point, the southernmost tip of Kaua'i; this rocky cliff overlooking crashing waves is today covered with oceanfront condos.

The name comes from, yes, a shipwrecked wooden boat that was washed ashore in the mid-1970s (in 1982, Hurricane 'Iwa swept the boat back to sea). To get here, head toward the Grand Hyatt, turn *makai* on Ainako St and park in the small lot at the end.

Island Insights

In the movie *Six Days Seven Nights* (1998), stunt doubles for Harrison Ford and Anne Heche leap off Makawehi Point. In real life, a few daredevils similarly dive off the rocky cliff, as shown in thrilling YouTube clips. But no one mentions the severe casualties (cracked skulls, spinal damage, bent tailbones) and deaths. In a word: don't.

BABY BEACH

Introduce tots to the ocean at this baby beach (there's another in Kapa'a; p100), where the water is barely thigh high. The sandy shore runs behind a row of beach homes (which are primo vacation rentals) on Ho'ona Rd west of Koloa Landing, so access is easy but parking is tricky (make sure not to block anyone's driveway). Look for the beach access sign, which marks the path to the beach.

LAWA'I (BEACH HOUSE) BEACH

For such a tiny beach, this snorkeling and surfing spot gets some major action. Located almost adjacent to Lawa'i Rd (beside the iconic Beach House restaurant, hence the name), it's in plain view of passersby and not especially scenic or sandy. But during calm surf, the waters are rich snorkel turf, especially for novices, who'll probably meet tangs, parrot fish, needle fish, eels and perhaps turtles, all within a depth of 3 to 15ft. Expect a crowd of vacationers from the nearby timeshares and condos.

The grassy bank by the restaurant makes a fine viewing spot for surfers and sunsets. There are rest rooms, a shower and public parking across the street. Overall, however, choose this beach only if you're staying nearby.

Sights

NATIONAL TROPICAL BOTANICAL GARDEN

our pick NTBG; ☎ 742-2623; www.ntbg.org; 4425 Lawa'i Rd; admission $20-85; 8:30am-5pm

If you're interested in plants and their preservation, a visit to the NTBG's Kaua'i gardens is a must. The gardens are not just stunningly beautiful; they're also a sanctuary for native plants and living laboratories for the staff scientists and other international plant experts. The nonprofit institution strives to propagate tropical and endangered species and manages five gardens (three on Kaua'i, one on Maui and one in Florida).

Of the two gardens located in Po'ipu, the 80-acre Allerton Garden is the showy star, but it requires a pricey guided tour (adult/child 10-12 $45/20; minimum age is 10). Tour guides are generally knowledgeable and enthusiastic, leisurely guiding groups (up to 20) through meticulously landscaped grounds. Highlights include otherworldly Moreton Bay fig trees (seen in *Jurassic Park*), golden bamboo groves, a pristine lagoon and valley walls blanketed with purple bougainvillea during summer. The statuary and water elements somehow blend into the landscape.

The otherworldly Moreton Bay fig trees at Allerton Garden — LUCI YAMAMOTO

A COAST LIKE NO OTHER

The windswept Maha'ulepu Coast resembles no other on Kaua'i: lithified sand-dune cliffs, pounding surf and three pristine beaches still free from mass tourism. Known as Kaua'i's last undeveloped accessible coast, it lies just east of Shipwreck Beach.

This coast comprises a string of beaches: **Maha'ulepu Beach** (Gillin's Beach), **Kawailoa Bay** and **Ha'ula Beach** (running from west to east). Waters are choppy and better suited to experienced swimmers than once-a-year tourists, but hiking is enticing all year round – take the **Maha'ulepu Heritage Trail** (www.hikemahaulepu.org) for a pleasant hike that runs for almost 4 miles from Shipwreck Beach to Ha'ula Beach (you can turn back at any point for a shorter, but still stunning, walk). To reach the trailhead, park in the Grand Hyatt lot at the end of Ainako St. From the beach, head east through the ironwood trees. Along the coast, you will pass spectacular cliffs of lithified sand dunes, tide pools in rocky coves and even the ruins of a heiau.

Near Maha'ulepu Beach you'll see the sole house on the entire coast, the **Gillin Beach House** (☎ 742-7561; www.gillinbeachhouse.com; maximum 6 adults; per week from $3090), originally built in 1946 by Elbert Gillin, a civil engineer with the Koloa Sugar Plantation.

Kawailoa Bay is surrounded by sand dunes to the west and protected by jutting sea cliffs to the east. Windsurfers and kitesurfers skim across the surf here. Ironwood trees backing the beach make a pleasant spot for picnicking. Continue on until you reach Ha'ula Beach, a stunning curved bay with pounding, white-crested waves. The coastline is exposed, so come prepared for sun and wind.

If you must drive, go past the Grand Hyatt, proceed for 1.5 miles on the unpaved road and turn right where it dead-ends at a **gate** (🕑 7:30am-6pm, to 7pm summer). Continue past the gatehouse until you reach the beach parking area. Access hours are strictly enforced.

Besides the Maha'ulepu Heritage Trail website, another excellent resource is *Kaua'i's Geologic History: A Simplified Guide* by Chuck Blay and Robert Siemers. Also see **Malama Maha'ulepu** (www.malama-mahaulepu.org), a nonprofit working to preserve the area, which is owned by Steve Case, the cofounder of America Online.

The adjacent McBryde Garden is less sculpted and fancy than Allerton Garden, showcasing palms, flowering and spice trees, orchids and rare native species, plus a pretty stream and waterfall. The self-guided tour (adult/child 6-12 $20/10; under 5 free) allows you to see the vast grounds without breaking your budget.

MOIR GARDENS

☎ 742-6411; Kiahuna Plantation, 2253 Po'ipu Rd; admission free; 🕑 sunrise-sunset

If cacti are your fancy, this modest display on the grounds of the Kiahuna Plantation condo is worth a look-see. It's a low-key, approachable collection of mature cacti and succulents, interspersed with winding paths, a lily pond and colorful shocks of orchids.

The gardens, established in the 1930s, were originally the estate of Hector Moir, manager of Koloa Sugar Plantation, and Alexandra 'Sandie' Knudsen Moir. The Moirs were avid gardeners who switched from flowering plants to drought-tolerant ones that could naturally thrive in dry Po'ipu.

A sideshow rather than a showstopper, it's worth a stroll if you're staying nearby or dining at the restaurant.

SPOUTING HORN BEACH PARK

Lawa'i Rd (0.2 miles past NTBG)

It resembles a geyser, but Spouting Horn is really a hole situated at the top of a lava cave. When ocean waves pound the shore, they flood the cave and exit through the hole: erupting skyward as a fountain. But waves are unpredictable, so you might need to wait for some action. Fountains are typically under 30ft and last only seconds, but they can reach twice that high during high surf.

Since the 1960s, a bunch of local vendors have sold cheap souvenirs here. But the county will phase them out by 2013 to restore the site to 'peace, rest and beauty.' While the merchandise was mostly foreign-made rubbish, the peddlers do add live-

Island Insights

In 1870 Queen Emma, the wife of Kamehameha IV, traveled from O'ahu to Kaua'i to see the 4200-acre Lawa'i Valley estate, which her Aunt Hikoni had deeded to her. During her visit, she made a celebrated journey to the Alaka'i Swamp – marked today by the **Eo e Emalani i Alaka'i hula festival** (p217) – and big-name missionaries arranged to build a 2-mile-long irrigation ditch to supply the estate with upland water. Once completed, the queen personally helped to cultivate various plants, from native ohia and Polynesian-introduced taro to her signature purple bougainvillea. Her summer cottage still stands on the grounds of **Allerton Garden** (p167), the namesake of Chicago industrialist Robert Allerton, who in 1938 bought and sumptuously landscaped the coastal part of the valley.

liness, local flavor and a chance to avoid corporate retailers.

In any case, the main reason to come here is humpback whale watching in winter, if you want to glimpse them from land.

PRINCE KUHIO PARK

Lawa'i Rd (at Ho'ona Rd)

The simple green space honoring Kaua'i's Prince Jonah Kuhio Kalaniana'ole, born around here in 1871, is looking forlorn nowadays. The lawn is often brown and dry, and visitors rarely enter the grounds, which contain the ruins of an ancient Hawaiian heiau and fishpond. That said, no local would discount the prince's considerable contributions to Hawaii and the Hawaiian people. He was the Territory of Hawaii's first delegate to the US Congress and he spearheaded the Hawaiian Homes Commission Act, which set aside 200,000 acres of land for indigenous Hawaiians, many of whom are still waiting for it.

KOLOA LANDING

Koloa Landing, at the mouth of Waikomo Stream, was once Kaua'i's largest port. In the 1850s farmers used it to ship Kaua'i-grown sugar, oranges and sweet potatoes, and it was the third busiest whaling port among the Hawaiian Islands, surpassed only by Honolulu and Lahaina, Maui. The landing waned after the road system was built, and it was abandoned in the 1920s. Today only a small boat ramp remains.

Underwater, it's another story: Koloa Landing is popular for snorkeling and the best shore diving on the South Shore. Its protected waters reach depths of almost 45ft quickly, so you can almost immediately see underwater tunnels, a variety of coral and fish, sea turtles and, if you're lucky, monk seals. The best sights are located toward the west.

GALLERY 103

www.art103.com; Kukui'ula Village, Ala Kalanikaumaka Rd, Suite 102/103; noon-8pm Mon-Thu, 11am-9pm Fri & Sat, noon-6pm Sun or by appt

For local art that goes beyond no-brainer, easy-sell tropical motifs, visit this classy

Hikers on the Maha'ulepu Coast

LUCI YAMAMOTO

PARADISE AT WHAT PRICE?

Everyone wants a piece of tropical paradise. In Po'ipu, resort development suddenly took off in the mid-2000s when the real-estate market exploded. The island's biggest-ever project is **Kukui'ula** (www.kukuiula.com), a luxury development marked by signs and construction near the Po'ipu Rd roundabout.

The magnitude of the project is staggering: the 1000-acre residential portion will contain 1500 detached custom homes sized from 2000 to 4600 sq ft. Amenities will include a golf course and clubhouse, spa, massive plantation house, a 20-acre park and **Kukui'ula Village**, a 90,000 sq-ft high-end shopping center. Who'll be living here? Buyers are mainly from the US West Coast, such as California and Arizona, and they've got no qualms about the going rate of $1.4 to $3.6 million. About 20 villas and 10 cottages are planned for guests, in case you're short on the down payment.

While the project has spurred worthy endeavors such as the new Gallery 103 and its adjoining annex, Gallery + (see p169), it's mind-boggling to imagine over 1000 new households in this once-lazy beach town.

new gallery. Owner and art photographer Bruna Stude (www.brunastude.com) has assembled an impressive collection by both up-and-comers and established names. The gallery also presents book readings and short films by notable resident artists such as filmmaker Wayne Zebzda and writer-artist collaborators Todd and Linda Shimoda. The adjoining annex, Gallery +, is modeled on museum shops, and offers more affordable drawings, ceramics, fiber art and other collectibles. Everything is original (no commercial giclée prints).

Activities

DIVING

Dive boats and catamaran cruises usually depart from Kukui'ula Harbor, 0.5 miles east of Spouting Horn Beach Park.

The outfit Seasport Divers (☎ 742-9303, 800-685-5889; www.seasportdivers.com; Po'ipu Plaza, 2827 Po'ipu Rd; 2-tank dive $125-155; check-in 7:30am & 12:45pm) leads a range of dives from shore or boat, including a three-tank dive to Ni'ihau ($265), offered only in summer. All dives are guided by instructor-level divemasters; any group with noncertified divers includes an additional instructor. Groups are limited to 18 but the count is typically eight to 12.

Consider nearby Fathom Five Divers (p160), our top pick for diving tours.

SNORKELING

Most snorkeling-tour boats depart from Port Allen, Hanapepe (p189) or Kikialoha Small Boat Harbor (p199) to the Na Pali Coast, but Aloha Kaua'i Tours (☎ 800-452-8113; www.alohakauaitours.com; adult/child 5-12 $80/62.50) leads personalized, half-day shore-snorkeling tours, starting at Lawa'i (Beach House) Beach. Tours include lunch and top-quality equipment, including a wetsuit and optical masks if needed. Led by helpful guides, this is an outstanding introduction for novices.

KAYAKING

For sea kayaking, Outfitters Kaua'i (☎ 742-9667, 888-742-9887; www.outfitterskauai.com; Po'ipu Plaza, 2827-A Po'ipu Rd; reservations taken 8am-9pm) offers a tour (per adult/child 12 to 14 $148/118); the eight-hour paddle makes a good training prelude to the grueling Na Pali voyage (see p217).

SURFING

Po'ipu is a popular spot for lessons because it's got some killer breaks and year-round sun. Beware of large classes, though; four is maximum density.

For lessons, try the following.

Garden Island Surf School (☎ 652-4841; www.kauai-surfinglessons.com; 2hr lesson group/couple/private $75/120/150; lessons 8am, 10am, noon & 2pm) The lesson includes one hour with an instructor and one hour free surfing. Four students per group; minimum age is eight for groups and five for privates.

our pick Kaua'i Surf School (☎ 651-6032; www.kauaisurfschool.com; 2hr lesson group/private $75/175). With 90 minutes of teaching and 30 minutes of free practice, you get your money's worth. A good outfit for kids,

with a special 1hr private lesson for kids aged from four to 12. Also offers multi-day surf clinics and private surf guides.
Surf Lessons by Margo Oberg (☎ 332-6100, 639-0708; www.surfonkauai.com; 2hr lesson group/semi-private/private $68/90/125) One of the longest-running surf schools on Kaua'i, this operation has a fine rep but classes can reach six.

Rentals are found at the following shops.
Nukumoi Surf Company (☎ 742-8019; www.nukumoi.com; 2100 Ho'one Rd; soft-top boards rental per hr/day/week $5/20/60, hard boards $7.50/30/80, bodyboards per day/week $5/15; 7:45am-6:30pm Mon-Sat, 10:45am-6pm Sun) Conveniently located right across from Po'ipu Beach Park.
Progressive Expressions (Map p160; ☎ 742-6041; 5420 Koloa Rd, Koloa; board rental per day/week $20/100; 9am-9pm) Koloa surf shop rents all types of boards, same price.
Seasport Divers (☎ 742-9303, 800-685-5889; www.seasportdivers.com; Po'ipu Plaza, 2827 Po'ipu Rd; surfboard rental per hr/day/week $7/20/100, bodyboards per day/week from $4/15)

HORSEBACK RIDING

If you want a break from hoofin' it yourself, you can hop on a horse at CJM Country Stables (☎ 742-6096; www.cjmstables.com; 2hr tours $98-125; tours 9:30am and 2pm Mon-Sat). The rides are the slow, nose-to-tail, follow-the-leader variety, so they're safe but would bore experienced riders, who could arrange a private ride.

GOLF

The economical Kiahuna Golf Club (☎ 742-9595; www.kiahunagolf.com; 2545 Kiahuna Plantation Dr; green fees incl cart before/after 3pm $95/65, club rental $40) is a relatively forgiving 18-hole, par-70 course designed by Robert Trent Jones Jr. Established in 1983, this compact, inland course uses smaller targets and awkward stances to pose challenges.

The South Shore's jewel is the Po'ipu Bay Golf Course (☎ 742-8711, 800-858-6300; www.poipubaygolf.com; 2250 Ainako St; green fees incl cart non-guest/guest $220/150, club rental $50). This 18-hole, par-72 course adjacent to the Grand Hyatt covers 210 seaside acres. Rates drop at noon ($135) and again at 2:30pm ($80).

SPAS

When Anara Spa (☎ 742-1234; www.anaraspa.com; Grand Hyatt Kaua'i Resort & Spa, 1571 Po'ipu Rd; massage per hr $155-235, facials $165-225) was renovated in 2007, it was an Extreme Makeover, with the spa emerging as a 20,000-sq-ft tropical fantasyland embellished with gardens and waterfalls to sooth the eyes while the face and body indulges in a splurge-worthy menu of delicious services. Access to the lap pool and fitness center is free with a 50-minute spa treatment.

CYCLING

Perhaps due to the lack of bike lanes, cyclists are surprisingly scarce, but Outfitters Kaua'i (☎ 742-9667, 888-742-9887; www.outfitterskauai.com; Po'ipu Plaza, 2827-A Po'ipu Rd; reservations 8am-9pm) rents cruiser (per day $25), road (per day $30) and full-suspension (per day $45) bikes; rates include helmet and lock. Kids' bikes (per day $20) and baby seats (per day $5) are also available.

Tours

Unless you're as water-phobic as a cat, we recommend a snorkeling tour (see p189 and p199) to maximize your cruise experience. But if you're seeking a sunset tour, Capt Andy's Sailing Adventures (☎ 335-6833, 800-535-0830; www.napali.com; Port Allen Marina Center, Waialo Rd; adult/child 2-12/under 2yr $69/50/free) departs from Kukui'ula Harbor between 4pm and 5pm for a scenic two-hour cruise.

Festivals & Events

Prince Kuhio Celebration of the Arts (☎ 240-6369; http://princekuhio.wetpaint.com; admission free) Day-long celebration, in late March, to honor Prince Johah Kuhio Kalaniana'ole, who was born in 1872 on the site of Prince Kuhio Park (p169). Events include live hula and slack key guitar music, plus cultural presentations on Hawaiian *kapa* (bark cloth), *lomilomi* massage, salt making, wood carving and more.
Garden Isle Artisan Fair (☎ 245-9021) When on Kaua'i, buy Kaua'i-made. At this triannual fair in mid-March, mid-August and mid-October, you'll find handcrafted items, Hawaiian music and local *grinds* (eats). Usually located opposite Po'ipu Beach Park.
our pick Kaua'i Mokihana Festival Hula Competition (☎ 822-2166; www.mokihana.kauai.net; Grand Hyatt Po'ipu Resort & Spa; admission $5-10) Three days of serious hula performances in late September, both *kahiko* (ancient) and *'auana* (modern).
Hawaiiana Festival (☎ 240-6369; www.alohafestivals.com; Grand Hyatt Kaua'i Resort & Spa; admission free

excl luau; 8am-noon) Part of the Aloha Festival, this mid-October three-day event features Hawaiian crafts, demonstrations, hula and a luau.

New Year's Eve Fireworks (☎ 742-7444; www.poipubeach.org) Free fireworks on the beach at Po'ipu Beach Park on December 31.

Eating

PAPALANI GELATO Gelato $

our pick ☎ 742-2663; www.papalanigelato.com; Po'ipu Shopping Village, 2360 Kiahuna Plantation Dr; single scoop $3.75; 11:30am-9:30pm

Velvety smooth and subtly sweet, gelato is ice cream for adults. Among the mouth-watering flavors (all homemade on-site), you can't go wrong with classic vanilla bean or pistachio gelato. But, for local color, try the creamy sorbetto, made with fresh, island-grown starfruit, lychee, mango, guava or avocado.

PUKA DOG Fast Food $

☎ 742-6044; www.pukadog.com; Po'ipu Shopping Village, 2360 Kiahuna Plantation Dr; hot dogs $6.50; 11am-6pm

There is only one house specialty. And it's a hot dog, for cryin' out loud. But even Anthony Bourdain couldn't resist a sample: toasty bun, choice of Polish sausage or veggie dog, 'secret' sauce and tropical fruit relish (such as mango and pineapple). Purists might find the toppings overwhelming, however.

SAVAGE SHRIMP Lunch Wagon $

☎ 635-0267; Lawa'i Rd near Prince Kuhio Park; meals $10; 11am-2pm

Follow your nose to the roadside white van for heaping plates of Brazilian-style shrimp cooked with garlic, coconut milk, cilantro and tomatoes. Be prepared for blazing sun and greasy fingers (the shrimp is unpeeled).

JOE'S ON THE GREEN American/Local $

☎ 742-9696; Kiahuna Golf Club, 2545 Kiahuna Plantation Dr; breakfast $5-8, lunch $7-10; 7am-2:30pm

For hot breakfasts under $10, skip the resorts and fill up at this golf clubhouse. Food quality is more greasy-spoon than gourmet, but you can count on the French toast and basic egg dishes. Service is either very good or very bad. If you're in a hurry, go elsewhere.

Top Picks

SOUTH SHORE FOR KIDS

- **Snorkeling at Po'ipu Beach Park** (p164)
- **Shallow lagoon at Baby Beach** (p167)
- **Private lessons on how to surf** (p170)
- **'River pools' at Grand Hyatt Kaua'i** (p178)
- **Fresh-fruit gelato at Papalani Gelato** (left)

PLANTATION GARDENS RESTAURANT & BAR Hawaii Regional Cuisine $$$

☎ 742-2121; www.pgrestaurant.com; Kiahuna Plantation, 2253 Po'ipu Rd; appetizers $9-14, mains $19-27; 5:30-9pm

Set in a historic plantation house, this restaurant is lovely without trying too hard. The menu is mercifully concise and features locally grown ingredients, kiawe (mesquite) grilling for a rich, smoky flavor, and lots of fresh seafood. Kids can choose from fresh fish, chicken fingers, baby back ribs and stir-friend vegetables ($9 to $13). Illuminated by tiki torches at night, the setting is ideal for large gatherings.

CASA DI AMICI Italian $$$

our pick ☎ 742-1555; 2301 Nalo Rd; dinner mains $23-29; from 6pm

Often overlooked due to an obscure location, this ristorante is an unpretentious gem. The chef focuses on using the highest-quality ingredients, such as locally grown greens, black truffles from Italy and homemade sausage. The menu's traditional Italian pastas and meats are joined by multicultural standouts, such as the grilled miso-ginger *'ahi* and paella risotto. The restaurant is on a residential street above Nihi Kai Villas (p176).

NANIWA Japanese $$$$

☎ 742-1661; Sheraton Kaua'i Resort, 2440 Ho'onani Rd; sushi $11-16; dinner mains $28-33; 5:30-9pm Tue-Sat

Despite the island's sizable Japanese population, Japanese restaurants are woefully scarce. The only major sushi bar on the South Shore, Naniwa serves flawlessly fresh, impeccably presented sushi. Your wallet will take a hit, with *nigiri* going for $11 per pair. Big eaters, your best-value option is the Saturday all-you-can-eat dinner buffet, featuring sushi, *poke* (Hawaiian-style marinated, cubed raw fish), *unagi* (broiled eel), tempura and more (adult/child 6-12 $39/19.50).

BEACH HOUSE RESTAURANT
Hawaii Regional Cuisine $$$$

☎ 742-1424; www.the-beach-house.com; 5022 Lawa'i Rd; dinner mains $26-40; ⏲ winter 5:30-9:30pm, summer 6-10pm

There are many oceanfront restaurants in Po'ipu, but only one Beach House. Overrated, perhaps, but it is the iconic spot for sunset dining and worth a splurge. Current chef Todd Barrett's specialties include macadamia-crusted mahimahi and watermelon salad with gorgonzola cheese and just-picked Omao greens. For front-row sunset seating, book a table for 5:30pm, one to two weeks in advance.

SHELLS
Hawaii Regional Cuisine $$$$

☎ 742-1661; Sheraton Kaua'i Resort, 2440 Ho'onani Rd; dinner mains $32-36; ⏲ 6:30-10:30am, 5:30-9pm

While nothing will astonish you about the menu, the preparations are refreshingly elegant, without the cloying 'tropical' sauces that lesser chefs fall back on. Instead, the focus is on local ingredients. Try starting with a hearty salad of Moloa'a tomatoes and Kilauea goat cheese ($13) and proceed to island-caught steamed snapper, pan-seared *shutome* (swordfish) or grilled *'ahi*.

TIDEPOOLS
Hawaii Regional Cuisine $$$$

☎ 742-6260; Grand Hyatt Kaua'i Resort & Spa, 1571 Po'ipu Rd; mains $28-40; ⏲ 5:30-10pm

Surrounded by waterfalls and lagoons filled with *koi* (Japanese carp), the Grand Hyatt's signature restaurant is more romantic oasis than lively nightspot. The surprisingly brief menu presents decent but derivative examples of island fusion, from a grilled peppered *'ahi* with coconut jasmine rice to grilled chicken breast with Okinawan sweet-potato purée. A serene 'special occasion' spot.

ROY'S PO'IPU BAR & GRILL
Hawaii Regional Cuisine $$$$

☎ 742-5000; www.roysrestaurant.com; Po'ipu Shopping Village, 2360 Kiahuna Plantation Dr; appetizers $9-16, mains $37-47; ⏲ 5:30-9:30pm

Still iconic, still wildly popular, Roy's continues to please the foodies. Signature dishes include the melt-in-your-mouth *misoyaki* (miso-marinated) butterfish appetizer and the pesto-steamed *ono* (wahoo) sizzled in cilantro–ginger–peanut oil. Regarding 'atmosphere,' expect a shopping mall setting and notoriously high-decibel dining room. Kids are welcome and can enjoy a $13 four-course meal: quesadilla appetizer, salad, entree (eg grilled *'ahi* or teriyaki chicken) and dessert.

For groceries, indie supermarket **Kukui'ula Store** (☎ 742-1601; Po'ipu Plaza, 2827 Po'ipu Rd; ⏲ 8:30am-8:30pm Mon-Fri, to 6:30pm Sat & Sun) resembles a bodega from the outside, but stocks a good selection of organic produce and dairy, natural whole-grain products, fresh fish and packaged dishes from wholesome meat-free lasagna to *edamame* (boiled soybeans). For a greater selection, go to Koloa's grocers and fish market.

Drinking

Ordering umbrella drinks (think piña coladas and mai tais) will mark you as a tourist, but hey, you're on Kaua'i – go for it. For more creative cocktails, try the **Plantation Gardens Restaurant & Bar** (p217), where the atmospheric bar features rich red walls within the plantation-house dining room.

POINT

our pick ☎ 742-1661; Sheraton Kaua'i Resort; ⏲ 11am-midnight (closed for lunch Mon & Tue)

Being an informal hangout for sunset viewing and people-watching, this bar mixes a great mojito ($9.50 to $11.50) or pours from the tap. For lunch and dinner, reduce costs by eating here from the excellent menu of appetizers and sandwiches.

STEVENSON'S LIBRARY

☎ 742-1234, 800-554-9288; Grand Hyatt Kaua'i Resort & Spa; 1571 Po'ipu Rd; ⏲ 6-midnight

Resembling a too-cool-for-you gentlemen's club, this handsome lounge is rather incongruous with the island scene but serves good (if pricey) sushi, desserts and drinks. Kids are permitted until 9pm, so a romper-room vibe occasionally prevails till then. Highlights include the gleaming 27ft koa-wood bar and live jazz from 8pm to 10pm.

Keoneloa Bay as seen from the Grand Hyatt Kaua'i Resort & Spa (p178) LINDA CHING

SEAVIEW TERRACE

☎ 742-1234, 800-554-9288; Grand Hyatt Kaua'i Resort & Spa; 1571 Po'ipu Rd; 4:30-8:30pm

For free resort 'entertainment,' arrive before sunset on Tuesday, Friday or Saturday for a torch-lighting ceremony and either Hawaiian music or *keiki* (child) hula shows. Call for start time, which varies by season.

Entertainment

Between the two luaus we've listed here, the Sheraton's show gives you more for your money. Also consider driving to Lihu'e for Kilohana Plantation's new and different Luau Kalamaku (p72).

SURF TO SUNSET LUAU

our pick ☎ 742-8205; www.sheraton-kauai.com; Sheraton Kaua'i Resort, 2440 Ho'onani Rd; adult/child 6-12/under 6yr $75/37.50/free; check-in 6pm Fri

We rate the Sheraton's 'Surf to Sunset' luau A (excellent) for oceanfront setting and B (good) for the food and show, which is the standard Polynesian revue. For a commercial luau, the audience size is small at 200 to 300. Beware: humorous emcee expects lots of audience participation.

HAVAIKI NUI LUAU

☎ 240-6456; www.grandhyattkauailuau.com; Grand Hyatt Kaua'i Resort & Spa, 1571 Po'ipu Rd; adult/junior 13-20/child 5-12/under 5yr $94/84/57/free; check-in 5:15pm Sun & Thu

The Havaiki Nui Luau is a well-oiled production befitting the Grand Hyatt setting. But the price is steep, especially if rain forces the show indoors.

Shopping

For years, the only game in town was **Po'ipu Shopping Village** (☎ 742-2831; 2360 Kiahuna Plantation Dr; 9am-9pm Mon-Sat, 10am-7pm Sun), a well-scrubbed if predictable mall with touristy shops (think aloha wear, jewelry, T-shirts and swimwear) and a few notable eateries. By the time of publication, Kukui'ula Village (see the boxed text, p170) should be open.

For the best selection of books (especially nature, botanical and Hawaii titles) and quality gifts, our favorite standby is the **National Tropical Botanical Garden gift shop** (☎ 742-2433; www.ntbg.org/gifts/shop.php; 8:30am-5pm).

Sleeping

The majority of accommodations in Po'ipu are condos, which are available for all budget levels. Rates can vary depending on the owner or agency renting each unit, so we list typical or average rates. Vacation-rental homes can offer more privacy and drive-up access to your door. The two major hotels are high-end Grand Hyatt and the business-class Sheraton Kaua'i. A luxury new hotel, called the **Koa Kea** (www.koakea.com; r from $445), opened in April 2009. With 121 rooms and a beachfront location (near Kiahuna Plantation), this boutique hotel is gorgeously appointed and strives for a personal, family-oriented atmosphere.

Check out the website of the Po'ipu Beach Resort Association (www.poipubeach.org) for additional listings; note that the condo links often go merely to agencies, however. If you decide on a specific condo, always check Vacation Rentals By Owner (www.vrbo.com) for additional rentals; owners might offer better deals than agencies. Also, you can check FlipKey (www.flipkey.com) for specific condo unit reviews. The site is new and lacks a critical mass of reviews, but the existing comments can be helpful.

That said, you don't incur extra fees if you book with agencies, and they can steer you to appropriate properties, especially if you're seeking a vacation-rental home. We recommend the following:

Aikane Po'ipu Beach Houses (☎ 742-1778, 877-742-1778; www. kauaivacationproperties.com/poipu.htm) Choose from a choice crop of dreamy beach houses near Brennecke's Beach.

Kaua'i Vacation Rentals (Map p62; ☎ 245-8841, 800-367-5025; www.kauaivacationrentals.com; 3-3311 Kuhio Hwy, Lihu'e, HI 96766) Longtime all-island agency with excellent variety and quantity of listings. But condo rates can be higher than the average, so compare prices before booking.

our pick The Parrish Collection Kaua'i (☎ 742-2000, 800-742-1412; www.parrishkauai.com; 3176 Po'ipu Rd, Ste 1, Koloa, HI 96756) Well-established agency for condos and vacation homes. Friendly, accommodating staff. Main, on-site agency for Waikomo Stream Villas (below) and Nihi Kai Villas (p176).

Po'ipu Beach Vacation Rentals (☎ 742-2850, 800-684-5133; www.pbvacationrentals.com; PO Box 1258, Koloa, HI 96756) Good prices; although a limited selection, it includes condos and vacation homes.

Po'ipu Connection Realty (☎ 800-742-2260; www.poipuconnection.com; PO Box 1022, Koloa, HI 96756) Condo listings only; good prices and personalized service.

PRINCE KUHIO RESORT — Condo $$

5061 Lawa'i Rd; studios $85-140, 1br units $110-175;

This 90-unit condo is a budget property, so don't expect spiffy furnishings and floors. But it's a great value for the location across the road from Lawa'i (Beach House) Beach (p167). All units have full kitchens and breezy windows, while pleasantly landscaped grounds surround a decent-size pool. Units vary markedly in quality. Find low rates at Po'ipu Connection Realty, Po'ipu Beach Vacation Rentals and www.vrbo.com.

WAIKOMO STREAM VILLAS — Condo $$

☎ 742-2000, 800-742-1412; www.parrishkauai.com; 2721 Po'ipu Rd; 1br units $105-159, 2br units $149-259;

Because it's neither beachfront nor oceanfront, this condo is a real steal. The 60 units are modern, clean and huge (averaging

LONGING LOVERS

Across Kaua'i, the native *naupaka* plant thrives both near the sea and in the mountains. More wide than tall, it has thick, pulpy, bright-green leaves and small white flowers with light-purple streaks. Eight types exist and, intriguingly, feature 'half' flowers: the beach *naupaka* has petals only on the lower half, while the mountain *naupaka* is just the opposite, with petals only on the upper half.

A variety of myths explain this mystery. Some say that the passionate volcano goddess Pele noticed two young Hawaiians very much in love. She desired the young man and approached him as a beautiful stranger, but no matter how she enticed him, he remained faithful to his beloved. Angered, Pele chased him into the mountains, throwing molten lava at him. Her sisters rescued the man from a sure death by transforming him into the mountain *naupaka*. Then when Pele pursued the young woman toward the sea, Pele's sisters changed her into the beach *naupaka*.

Other tales tell of a Princess Naupaka who is forced to abandon her true love, a fisherman, because he is a commoner. Upon their final parting, she gives him half of a flower from her lei. She returns to the mountains and he returns to the sea.

In any case, the unique half-flower of the *naupaka* always emphasizes the universal mourning of lost love.

1100 to 1500 sq ft), with lanai, full kitchen, washer/dryer and high-speed Internet access. The split-level two-bedrooms have soaring vaulted ceilings and an upstairs sleeping loft. With Waikomo Stream running through the gorgeous garden grounds, it's very pleasant – despite proximity to the Po'ipu Rd roundabout.

KAUA'I COVE COTTAGES Apartment $$

☎ 742-2562, 800-624-9945; www.kauaicove.com; 2672 Pu'uholo Rd; studio units $129-165 (cleaning fee $75);

In a low-key neighborhood near Koloa Landing, this trio of 'cottages' (triplex is more apt) deftly blends modern amenities into cozy tropical bungalows. Although studio size is limited, the efficient layout allows bamboo canopy beds, vaulted ceilings, fully loaded kitchenette and lots of windows. Add tastefully exotic decor, lustrous hardwood floors, and parking right outside your doorstep. The only thing missing is wi-fi.

HIDEAWAY COVE VILLAS Apartment $$$

our pick ☎ 635-8785, 866-849-2426; www.hideawaycove.com; 2307 & 2315 Nalo Rd; studios $140-205, 1br units $170-220, 2br units $195-310 (cleaning fees $90-130);

Near Po'ipu Beach Park, these impeccable, modern and professionally managed units are a cut above their peers. All feature private lanai, fine hardwood flooring, genuine art and antiques, name-brand appliances like Cuisinart coffee makers. No detail is forgotten: the full complement of kitchen utensils all match. Casa Di Amici restaurant (p172) is next door, but seems never to be an issue. Computer available in on-site office (8:30am to 1:30pm).

NIHI KAI VILLAS Condo $$$

☎ 742-2000, 800-742-1412; www.parrishkauai.com; 1870 Ho'one Rd; 2br units $159-380;

For moderate spenders who want walkable beach access, here's the ticket. Po'ipu Beach Park is just down the block, although proximity depends on unit location (ie price). Of 70 units, half are well managed by the on-site Parrish agency (p175). At 1000 to 2000 sq ft, they're comfortable, with full kitchens, two or more private lanai, washer/dryer, cable internet access (and even with wi-fi if you're lucky).

KIAHUNA PLANTATION Condo $$$

☎ 742-6411, 800-542-4862; www.outrigger.com; 2253 Po'ipu Rd; 1br units $160- 360, 2br units $240-460;

This aging beauty is still a hot property because it's among the rare accommodations flanking a swimmable beach. Of course, only a few units actually sit on the beach (money talks). Units are comfy, with fully equipped kitchen, living room and large lanai, but furnishings seem worn. Rates are across the board so shop around. On-site agencies include Outrigger and **Castle Resorts** (☎ 742-2200; www.castleresorts.com; 1br units $140-510, 2br units $390-560), but **Kiahuna Beachside** (☎ 937-6642; www.kiahuna.com; 1br units $365-490, 2br units $565) manages the best beachfront properties.

CASTLE PO'IPU SHORES Condo $$$

☎ 742-7700; www.castleresorts.com; 1775 Pe'e Rd; 1br/2br units from $199/299;

Location, location, location. This seemingly ordinary 39-unit condo sidles up to the coast, overlooking lava rock and pounding surf (although no sandy beach). Inside, you'll find consistent features, such as private lanai, full kitchen, washer/dryer and cable TV. The townhouse two-bedroom units in Building C are especially pleasant and spacious. All units have cable Internet access while wi-fi access is sketchy.

AIKANE KAUA'I House $$$

our pick ☎ 742-1778, 877-742-1778; www.kauaivacationproperties.com; 2271 Nalo Rd; 3br house from $250 (cleaning fee $150-195);

A stroll away from Brennecke's Beach, this beach house lets you spread out, with high ceilings, ocean-facing balcony, full kitchen and three bedrooms, each with its own bathroom. It's a green house, insulated and running exclusively on solar energy. Rates vary depending on the number of guests. The friendly owner manages other excellent (and earth-friendly) vacation-rental homes in Po'ipu.

PO'IPU KAPILI Condo $$$

our pick ☎ 742-6449, 800-443-7714; www.poipukapili.com; 2221 Kapili Rd; 1br/2br units from $230/345;

An all-around winner, this 60-unit top-end gem features gorgeously landscaped ground and spacious units (measuring

ISLAND VOICES

NAME: GEORGIA KAKUDA
OCCUPATION: OFFICE MANAGER, CASTLE PO'IPU SHORES (p176)
PLACE OF RESIDENCE: WAIMEA

Where did you grow up? I was born and raised in Waimea, and then I went to school in Missouri to become a teacher. It was a culture shock. It was the 1960s and Midwesterners were so segregated. They knew nothing about Hawaii and would ask if we still lived in grass huts and whether we had any electricity.

How has island life changed since your childhood? I moved back to Kaua'i from Honolulu because I wanted to raise my son in the country. Waimea hadn't changed. We still never locked any doors. We left the car key in the ignition whenever we parked, even at Big Save. Just jump in and go. If we removed the key, we could never find it!

Today, we lock our doors. Nothing's ever happened, but we don't want to invite trouble.

How long have you worked in tourism? I worked at Kiahuna Plantation for 10 years and here at Po'ipu Shores for 20 years. I have repeat guests who return year after year. They're happy to come back and see a familiar face.

Do you enjoy dealing with tourists? When I first started, I was dealing with more tourists than ever in my life. Either you enjoy it or not. You can't be too affected by the rude ones or the complainers.

Believe it or not, some guests complain that the ocean is too loud. They might catch themselves and laugh, or they might not. I tell them, 'I can't turn down the volume.' If people are unhappy at home, they'll also be unhappy on vacation.

Any advice to tourists? Many come unprepared. They ask, 'What should I do today?' If I were traveling somewhere new, I would figure out the highlights and learn about the place. People should do their homework and have an idea why they want to be here.

Do you know the whole island well? Locals tend to stay in their own groove. Once, I didn't go to the North Shore for over 20 years! Another time, I didn't go past Kapa'a for five years. I do go to Lihu'e regularly and I take my grandkids to Koke'e when they visit. When I was growing up, my uncle had a cabin and we'd go every week.

On Kaua'i there are sandy beaches all around. I live near Kekaha. Why drive all the way to Hanalei? Better to enjoy your own backyard than to step on the gas.

1120 to 1820 sq ft) that are consistent in quality, with lots of hardwood, big plush beds, extra bathroom, quality electronics and wired internet access. Ho'onani Rd cuts between the condo and the ocean, but views are nevertheless spectacular (with no obstructing buildings). The closest sandy beach, which fronts the Sheraton, is within walking distance.

SHERATON KAUA'I RESORT Hotel $$$$

☎ 742-1661, 800-782-9488; www.sheraton-kauai.com; 2440 Ho'onani Rd; r with garden view from $240, with ocean view from $460;

The business-class Sheraton has one enviable advantage: a prime stretch of sandy, swimmable, sunset-perfect beach. Rooms are decent, if unmemorable; first-floor ocean

The view from the Hanapepe Valley lookout LINDA CHING

'luxury' rooms are larger due to the tiered architecture. The hotel's open-air design highlights the ocean setting, but the low-end Garden View or Partial Ocean View wings are across the street, nowhere near the beach. Eco-friendly efforts made here include recycling bins and free breakfast coupons for guests who forgo maid service that day.

GRAND HYATT KAUA'I RESORT & SPA Hotel $$$$

☎ 742-1234, 800-554-9288; www.kauai.hyatt.com; 1571 Po'ipu Rd; r garden view $280-430, deluxe ocean view $470-720;

Po'ipu's glamour gal is 602-rooms strong and she loves to show off, with a soaring lobby, tropical gardens, massive spa, world-renowned golf course, oceanfront restaurants and meandering 'river pools.' Inside, the room decor is typically tropical, but obviously a class above. What's missing is a swimmable *real* beach, not just the artificial one. Prices wildly vary, depending on occupancy.

WHALERS COVE Condo $$$$

☎ 742-7571, 800-225-2683; www.whalers-cove.com; 2640 Pu'uholo Rd; 1br/2br units from $349/479;

Po'ipu's most luxurious condo would suit discriminating travelers, who want luxury without a smidgen of tourist fuss. Units are palatial (1300 sq ft on average), elegant and utterly immaculate, and often have gleaming marble floors, granite counters and mansion-worthy furniture. Truly gawk-worthy is the amount of prized koa wood used for the doors and furnishings. Twenty units (out of 38) are available for rental. Daily maid service.

Getting There & Around

To get here from Lihu'e, the quickest way is to exit on Maluhia Rd. Once in Po'ipu, you'll see that it's a sprawled-out town, necessitating a car to go anywhere besides the beach. Navigating is easy, with just two main roads: Po'ipu Rd (along eastern Po'ipu) and Lawa'i Rd (along western Po'ipu). Most attractions, including Po'ipu Beach Park, have free parking lots.

The Kaua'i Bus (p275) runs through Koloa and into Po'ipu, stopping along Po'ipu Rd at Ho'owili Rd (the turnoff to Po'ipu Beach Park). It's an option to get here from other towns but a limited in-town mode.

Because Po'ipu lacks a town center, destinations are scattered. Walking is viable along the main roads and along the beaches, but the vibe is more suburbia than surf town.

KALAHEO

As seen from the highway, Kalaheo is a one-stoplight cluster of eateries and little else. But along the backroads, this neighborly town offers peaceful accommodations away from the tourist crowd. If you plan to hike at Waimea Canyon and Koke'e State Parks but also want easy access to Po'ipu beaches, Kalaheo's central location is ideal.

The town's post office and handful of restaurants are centered around the intersection of Kaumuali'i Hwy and Papalina Rd.

Sights

KUKUIOLONO PARK

Unless you stay in Kalaheo, you'd miss this little park (Papalina Rd; 6:30am-6:30pm), which offers a nine-hole golf course, modest Japanese garden, sweeping views and grassy grounds for strolling or jogging.

Kukuiolono means 'light of Lono,' referring to the torches that Hawaiians once placed on this hill to help guide canoes safely to the shore. In 1860 King Kamehameha III leased the land to Duncan McBryde, whose son, Walter, the pineapple baron, eventually purchased the 178-acre estate. He built the public golf course in 1929 and deeded the entire site for use as a public park upon his death. Walter McBryde is buried near the 8th hole of the golf course.

To get here, turn left onto Papalina Rd from Kaumuali'i Hwy (heading west).

HANAPEPE VALLEY LOOKOUT

This scenic lookout pops up shortly after you pass the 14-mile marker and it offers a

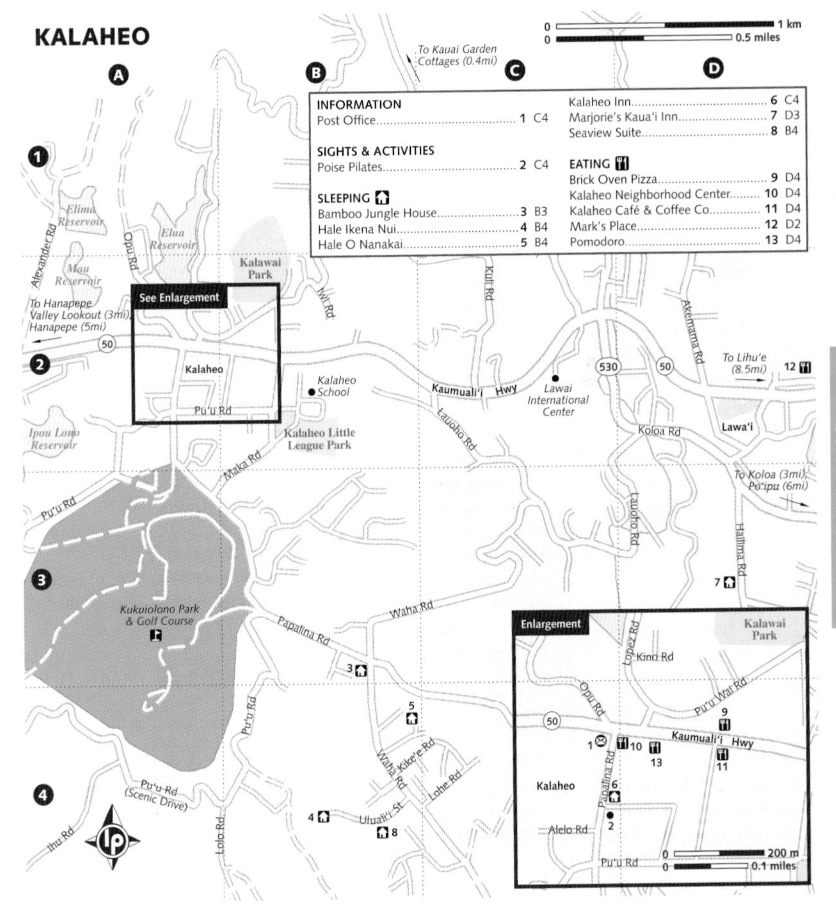

view deep into Hanapepe Valley. The red-clay walls of the cliffs are topped by a layer of green cane, like frosting on a cake. This sight is but a teaser for the dramatic vistas that can be seen at Waimea Canyon.

While old King Sugar might still dominate Hanapepe Valley, look across the highway toward the ocean to see Kaua'i's current major commercial crop – coffee beans – at the **Kauai Coffee Company** (p186).

Top Picks

GOOD-VALUE EATS

- **Kalaheo Café & Coffee Co** (below)
- **Koloa Fish Market** (p161)
- **Casa Di Amici** (p172)
- **Plantation Gardens Restaurant & Bar** (p172)
- **Mark's Place** (below)
- **Pomodoro** (opposite)

Activities

Golf practically for free at **Kukuiolono Golf Course** (☎ 332-9151; Kukuiolono Park, Papalina Rd; green fees adult/child $9/3, pull carts $6; 6:30am-6:30pm), an unassuming, nine-hole, par-36 golf course with spectacular ocean and valley views and zero attitude. Grab a bucket of balls for $2 and hit the driving range, first come, first served.

Stop in for a cup o' joe (p186) JOHN ELK III

For an indoor workout, practice with owner Theresa Ouano (the epitome of fitness) at **Poise Pilates** (☎ 651-5287; www.poisepilates.org; 4432 Papalina Rd; 55min private session $70, mat class $20), a cheerful, well-equipped studio. Prices drop if you buy in multiples.

Eating

MARK'S PLACE

Diner $

our pick ☎ **332-0050; 2-3687 Kaumuali'i Hwy; plates $6-7; 10am-8pm Mon-Fri**

If you're curious about the legendary Hawaiian plate lunch, skip breakfast and come here at noon when you're famished. Classic plate lunches feature generous portions of meaty mains from teriyaki beef to Korean chicken, plus rice and salad. Pickier palates can sample gourmet specials, such as salmon atop greens with soy-*wasabi* vinaigrette. It's located off the highway, east of Kalaheo.

KALAHEO CAFÉ & COFFEE CO

Cafe $$

our pick ☎ **332-5858; www.kalaheo.com; 2-2560 Kaumuali'i Hwy; breakfast & lunch $6-10, dinner $16-26; 6:30am-2:30pm Mon-Sat, to 2pm Sun, 5:30-8:30pm Wed-Sat**

We give a big thumbs up to this roadside café, which boasts a spacious dining room, easy-access parking and a satisfying menu of healthy California-style cooking. Breakfast favorites include a well-stuffed veg wrap and build-your-own omelets, while the lunch hour brings fresh Kalaheo greens and Dagwood-sized sandwiches. Your last temptation: homemade fruit crisp.

BRICK OVEN PIZZA
Pizza $$

☎ 332-8561; Kaumuali'i Hwy; 10-/12-/15-inch pizzas from $11.50/16/24; 11am-10pm Tue-Sun, 4-10pm Mon

Why did Brick Oven become Kaua'i's tourist mecca for pizza? Their pies are fine, but real pizza aficionados might be underwhelmed. That said, vegetarians will welcome the truly meatless combo that's piled with premium veggies and stock-free sauce. And hot pizza does hit the spot after hiking Waimea Canyon.

POMODORO
Italian $$$

☎ 332-5945; Rainbow Plaza, Kaumuali'i Hwy; mains $16-27; 5:30-9:30pm Mon-Sat

Unless you know it's there, you'd never expect such a romantic ristorante in an unmemorable business mall. But locals always cite Pomodoro for traditional dishes such as veal parmigiana ($27) and linguini with white or red clam sauce ($22). Enhanced with candlelit tables and white tablecloths, the setting is intimate yet neighborhood-casual.

Sleeping

SEAVIEW SUITE
Inn $

☎ 332-9744; www.seakauai.com; 3913 Uluali'i St; studios/1br units $75/95;

Choose from two comfy ground-floor units with lovely sunset and ocean views. The one-bedroom suite includes full kitchen, separate living and dining areas and bedding for four. The compact studio, with fully equipped kitchenette, is a steal. Discounted rates if you rent both.

HALE IKENA NUI
B&B/Inn $

☎ 332-9005, 800-550-0778; www.kauaivacationhome.com; 3957 Uluali'i St; r incl breakfast $75, 1br unit $95;

Located at the end of a cul de sac, this spacious in-law apartment (1000 sq ft) includes a living area with sofabed, full kitchen and washer/dryer. Singles can rent the B&B room, which is less private but it includes private bathroom and use of the main house. Bonus: irresistible dog named Bear on site.

KALAHEO INN
Motel $$

☎ 332-6023, 888-332-6023; www.kalaheoinn.com; 4444 Papalina Rd; studio/1br/2br units $83/103/133;

Like most plain Janes, this one is dependable, low-key and quiet. It resembles a typical motel and would best suit budget travelers looking for kitchenette studios. For couples and families, the larger one- and two-bedroom units are decent, but you could do better. All units have basic furnishings, kitchen/kitchenette (with tableware and appliances) and TV-VCR. Wired Internet access is $10 per day; wi-fi access is available only in the office.

KAUAI GARDEN COTTAGES
Inn $$

☎ 332-0877; www.kauaigardencottages.com; 5350 Pu'ulima Rd; studio units $100;

Perched high in the Kalaheo upcountry, this meticulously designed pair of studios gleams with rich Indonesian hardwood floors under soaring cathedral ceilings with cheerful stained-glass accents. The rooms adjoin a vast lanai overlooking a stunningly green valley that gives new meaning to 'valley view.' Two-for-one deal: rent both rooms for only $150 nightly.

DETOUR →

PU'U ROAD SCENIC DRIVE

While the epic journeys along the North Shore and up to Waimea Canyon rank as Kaua'i's top two scenic drives, the South Shore upcountry might surprise you. **Pu'u Rd** in Kalaheo makes a loop past bucolic ranches, generations-old trees and grassy pastureland highlighted by the great Pacific as a fitting backdrop. The lush countryside is a surprise after the dry, red-dirt terrain along the highway.

Pu'u Rd intersects Papalina Dr in two places (either road can be your starting point). We suggest that you drive past Kukuiolono Park (p179) and turn right onto Pu'u Rd to start. It's just over 3 miles back to Kaumuali'i Hwy. It's a winding, one-lane country road with blind curves, so go slow and honk the horn when going around the hairpins.

HALE O NANAKAI

B&B $$

our pick ☎ 652-8071; www.nanakai.com; 3726 Nanakai Pl; r incl breakfast $75-150, 1br units $150-175 (cleaning fee $45);

Guests take first priority at this lovingly designed B&B with accommodations for every budget. Traditional B&B rooms all feature plush carpeting, Sleep Number beds, flat-screen HDTV and a generous continental breakfast. Guests share a huge deck and common area with an awesome coastal view. For more privacy, choose the downstairs apartment, which has a separate entrance and full kitchen.

BAMBOO JUNGLE HOUSE

B&B $$

☎ 332-5515, 888-332-5115; www.kauai-bedandbreakfast.com; 3829 Waha Rd; r incl breakfast $130-170;

In a lovely plantation-style house, the classic B&B experience awaits: friendly hosts, home-cooked breakfasts and 8am gatherings round the morning table. The three rooms are immaculate, featuring snow-white walls, fluffy canopy beds and sparkling French doors. Outside, enjoy a 38ft lap pool amid jungly foliage and lava-rock waterfall. A distinctive property, it's geared toward couples, and no kids are allowed.

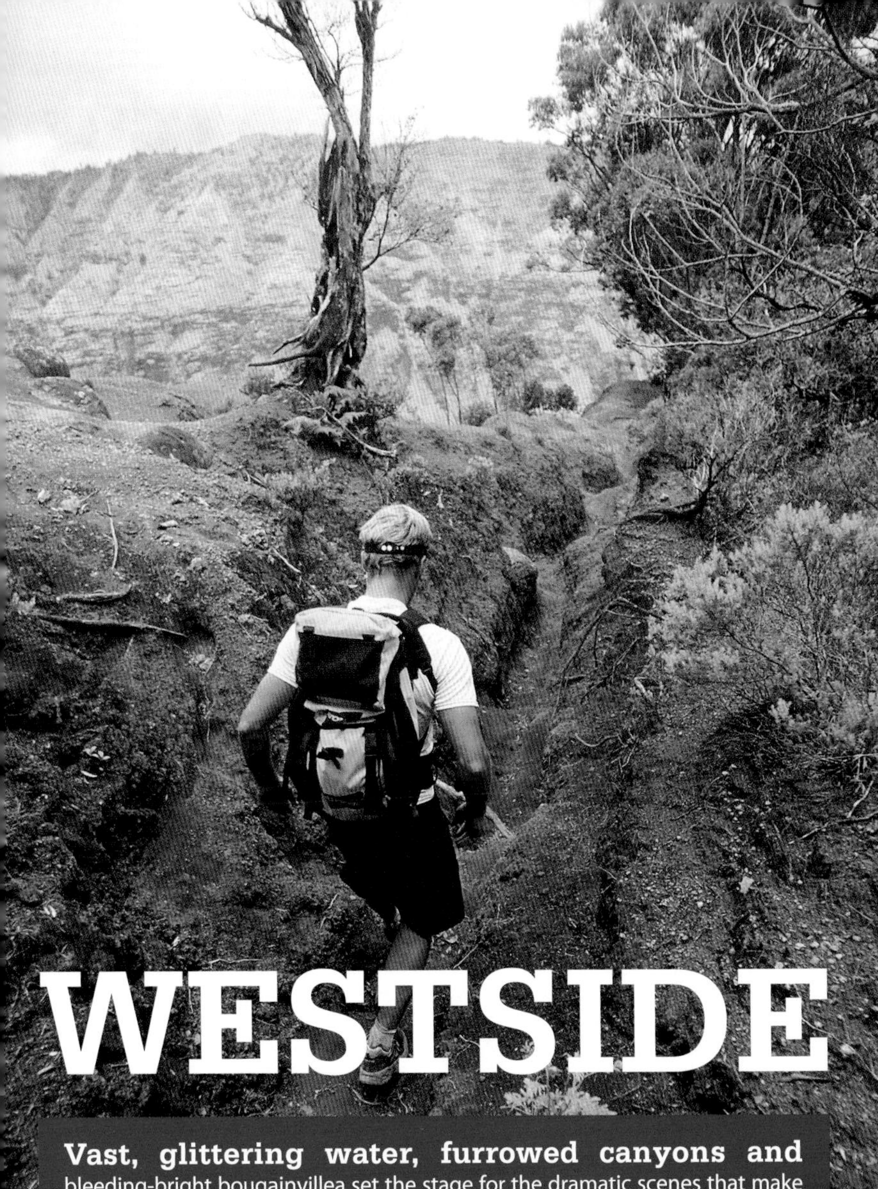

WESTSIDE

Vast, glittering water, furrowed canyons and bleeding-bright bougainvillea set the stage for the dramatic scenes that make up the Westside. Dense with fodder for the hiker-poet, the microclimates of Koke'e conjure images ranging from Gabriel Garcia Marquez's tropical forests to the wilds of AB Guthrie Jr's *Way West*. A dash of *paniolo* (cowboy) peppers the culture here, as does a lifestyle of hunting, surfing and local-style family pride. Churches are unembellished and historical landmarks are sea-battered; revered traditions like salt panning remain intact. The Westside is the least touristy and the most tried-and-true when it comes to sampling a taste of Kaua'i.

WESTSIDE

ITINERARIES

IN TWO DAYS *This leg: 10 miles*

❶ **GET YOUR GRIND ON (p186)** What better way to start your first day in paradise than with espresso and a smattering of pastries? Feast at **Grinds Café**, an aptly named restaurant.

❷ **HISTORIC HANAPEPE WALKING TOUR (p194)** Go at your own pace on this self-guided tour through Hanapepe for souvenirs, Hawaiiana objets d'art and a hearkening back to the 'Old West.'

❸ **SEAWARD (p204)** Take in the pleasant drive to **Kekaha Beach Park**, the last stop before the 'other' end of the road. Lounge all day for the cherry on top: a Westside sunset.

❹ **PACIFIC PIZZA & DELI (p202)** Prepare for a good night of rest with some fresh calzones while taking in the quaint ambience of these mom-and-pop digs.

❺ **NA PALI COAST CRUISE (p189)** Start day two off by experiencing the crown jewel that is the Na Pali Coast from ocean level. No need worry about breakfast; they'll feed you on board.

❻ **SWEETEN THE DEAL (p190)** Give that sea-spent body some sugary reprieve. Near the Port Allen dock, **Kauai Chocolate Company** serves homemade ice cream or tropical truffles like guava, sugarcane cream and macadamia-nut chocolate.

❼ **WRANGLER'S STEAKHOUSE (p202)** Hit up this true *paniolo*-style spot and brace yourself for a rare filet mignon if you're hungry from all that sea-battering madness.

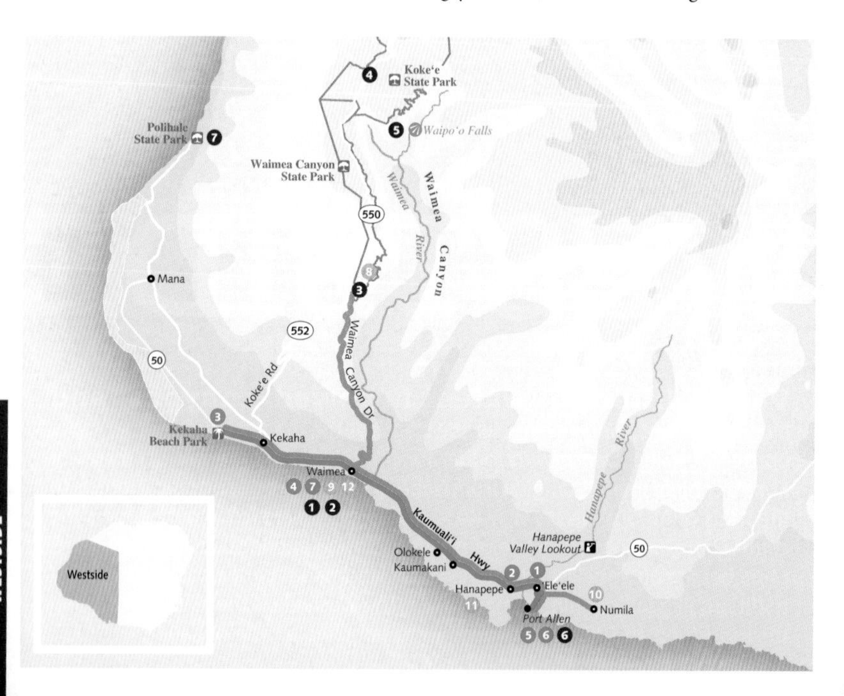

IN FOUR DAYS *This leg: 20 miles*

❽ **WAIMEA CANYON (p206)** Get going as early as you can to enjoy vast dramatic views from car, foot or valley lookout. Whether you'd like a scenic drive, a 30-minute trek or an 8-hour hike, you'll want this entire day to be spent uncovering these wild lands.

❾ **WAIMEA BREWING COMPANY (p202)** Grab some pub food and a locally brewed pint at this perfect-for-winding-down dining spot – you deserve it. If you're a little muddy? *No mattah.*

❿ **KAUAI COFFEE COMPANY (p186)** On your last day, head to where waking up is a specialty. Get some mild exercise by doing the self-guided tour while sipping some savory caffeine or chomp on doughy malasadas at Hawaii's largest coffee growing estate.

⓫ **SALT POND BEACH PARK (p191)** Get today's beach fix and make the mellow scene at this family-style location replete with lifeguard, facilities and local (salt-panning) history.

⓬ **WEST KAUA'I CRAFT FAIR (p203)** Before heading out, get one last taste of exotic goods and multi-syllabic fruits and delicacies, and pick up some travel-approved treats (such as local honey) for your trip home.

FOR ANYONE & EVERYONE

❶ **WEST KAUA'I TECHNOLOGY & VISITOR'S CENTER (p198)** Now an essential part of the new vernacular for the island's Westside, 'high-tech' is the name of the game, coming to fruition in a building that stands out like an aesthetically pleasing sore thumb.

❷ **WEST KAUA'I CRAFT FAIR (p203)** Peruse the work of local artisans working in the tradition of koa wood, Swarovski crystal and batik silk in search of masterful souvenirs.

❸ **WAIMEA CANYON DRIVE (p206)** Discover a sense of the island's age driving up the idyllically immense Waimea Canyon, with inviting views and sobering cliffs that demonstrate its four-million-year past (including the eruption of the volcano that formed Kaua'i (the oldest in the Hawaiian archipelago).

❹ **KOKE'E NATURAL HISTORY MUSEUM (p211)** Get an overview on the flora, fauna, wildlife and native and invasive species that abound and have changed the look of the canyon.

❺ **CANYON TRAIL (p213)** Now that you've gotten acclimated, take this dramatic, relatively short hike to view **Waipo'o Falls (p214)**, which rivals some of the most awe-inspiring views in the world.

❻ **HELICOPTER TOUR (p200)** If hiking isn't enough, rise and shine and take in views that took millions of years to create – by flying over Waimea Canyon (even stopping midway on one of the state park's precipices).

❼ **POLIHALE SUNSET (p206)** Come back to earth's simple, ancient beauty at one of the most, if not *the* most, spiritual places on the entire island: Polihale.

HIGHLIGHTS

1. **BEST BEACH**: Kekaha Beach Park (p204)
2. **BEST VIEW**: Kalalau Lookout (p213)
3. **BEST ACTIVITY**: Snorkeling or whale watching off the Na Pali Coast (p189)
4. **BEST HAWAIIAN COMFORT FOOD**: Ishihara Market gourmet plate lunch (p201)
5. **BEST APRÈS-DINNER SUNSET STROLL**: Kekaha Beach Park (p204)

'ELE'ELE & NUMILA

pop 2040

The small town of **Numila** (meaning 'new mill' in Hawaiian) and its industrial, rural neighbor, **'Ele'ele**, are 'passing through' spots for picking up groceries or doing some aprés-camping laundry.

Information

The **post office** (8am-4pm Mon-Fri, 9-11am Sat) is located in the 'Ele'ele shopping center, found at the 16-mile marker.

Sights

KAUAI COFFEE COMPANY

335-0813, 800-545-8605; www.kauaicoffee.com; Halewili Rd; 9am-5pm

Try a short but sweet self-guided tour of the largest coffee plantation in the state, which operates on 100% renewable energy. If you're with someone special, take a stab at the touristy, but still fun, activity of carving your initials in the leaves of the 'signature tree' fronting the main entrance. Inside, sample coffee flavors such as macadamia-nut brittle, or try the robust Kaua'i Estates coffee. Though it's different from the well-marketed Kona coffee, Kaua'i-grown beans are contenders, no doubt. The pleasant drive on Halewili Rd (Hwy 540) passes hundreds of acres of meticulously plotted coffee trees and intersects Kaumuali'i Hwy near Kalaheo and 'Ele'ele.

Eating

GRINDS CAFÉ Brunch/Cafe $

Map p187; 335-6027; www.grindscafé.net; 'Ele'ele Shopping Center, 4469 Waialo Rd; breakfast $5-10, lunch $5-12; 5:30am-6pm

Lattes, egg scrambles and the sound of loud clinking plates and sports-focused TVs make this greasy spoon a must-stop for lazy morning enthusiasts. Though the menu's got some 'healthier' items than the local diner-standard *loco moco* (hamburger with gravy and fried egg on rice) – arguably not a tough standard to move upwards from in the healthy eats category – expect it to be crowded and awash in a mix of tourists and locals. Though we'd give it a less-than-perfect score when it comes to expedition and efficiency, it earned high marks when it came to friendliness and a willingness to fill patient tummies with the high-calorie makings of a slothful afternoon. Live music at 6pm on Sundays.

Sunset surfing at Kekaha Beach Park (p204)

HOLGER LEUE

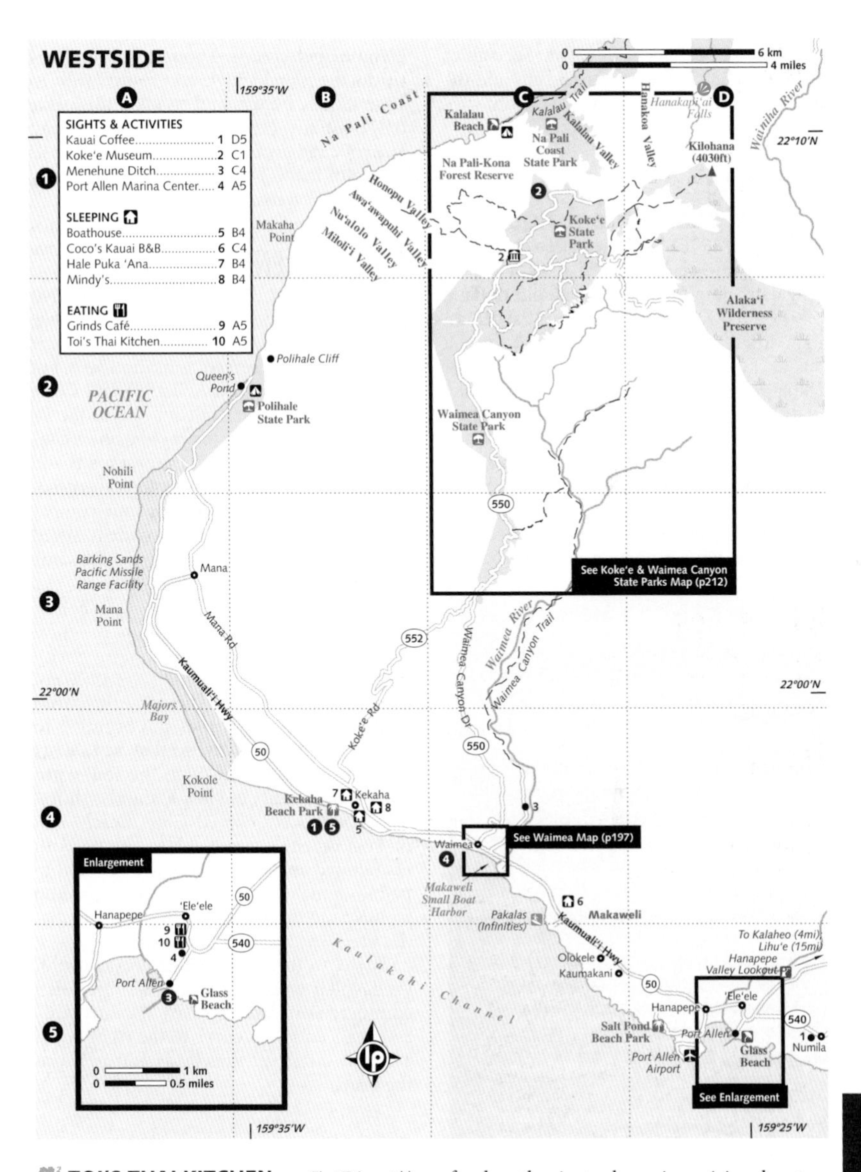

TOI'S THAI KITCHEN Thai/Takeout $$

our pick Map p187; ☎ 335-3111; 'Ele'ele Shopping Center, 4469 Waialo Rd; mains $13-20; lunch 10:30am-1:40pm, dinner 5:30-9pm Tue-Sat

Unassumingly situated in the 'Ele'Ele Shopping Center between the Big Save and post office, this treasure of a find for visitors is a long-time local favorite. Ideal for Thai food enthusiasts, bargain cuisine hunters and vegetarians alike, fragrant, exotic and relatively cheap eats abound here. Owners pluck much of their ingredients from a private garden to create creamy coconut dishes, curries and ginger-seasoned stir-fries. Most meals are spicy and light but hearty, and are coupled with aromatic rice, noodles or fresh papaya salad. Specialties include delicate, savory spring rolls and the Toi Temptation (meat, seafood or tofu with lemongrass and coconut milk).

Shopping

MALIE ORGANICS BOUTIQUE

our pick ☎ 866-767-5727; www.malie.com; 4353 Wai'alo Rd; 9am-4pm Mon-Fri

Singapore plumeria, taro, pineapple, organic pikake and Kaua'i coffee, Amy gardenias, mangoes and Samoan coconuts are just a few of the 'essences' captured by Shaun and Dana Roberts, who started this organic, body- and home-products company in their garage a few years ago. The couple has since partnered with small businesses and sustainable farmers on-island, as well as beginning a brand specifically designed for Koke'e – one that uses the maile vine to help evoke Koke'e State Park, with a portion of the proceeds going to preserve it. Though the company stocks the island's high-end resorts with its sprays, body butters and candles, this is the only boutique. Try the hydrosols, which emit an exotic radiance. The company also boasts products made with sustainable packaging from recycled materials.

Don't Miss

- **Watching surfers rip at the 'for locals only' break, Pakalas** (p200)
- **Mouth texture overload with the *halo halo* (mixed-fruit) shave ice at Jo-Jo's Anuenue Shave Ice and Treats in Waimea** (p200)
- **The refreshing, chocolatey and robust drink-as-meal Pakala's Porter at Waimea Brewing Company** (p202)
- **Post-camping calzones at Pacific Pizza and Deli** (p202)
- **Local-style lunch – stuffed butterfish with noodles, tempura shrimp *bentō* (Japanese box lunch) or smoked salmon *poke* (cubed raw fish) – at Ishihara Market** (p201)
- **A rainy-day movie at the Waimea Theatre** (p200)
- **Poring through odd, dusty, random books at Talk Story Bookstore** (p196)
- **A taste test comparing *liliko'i* (passion fruit) chiffon pies from ol'-school Omoide Bakery and Wong's Chinese Deli** (p195) **to new-school Aunty Lilikoi Passionfruit Products** (p203)
- **Sugarcane, coconut, mango and macadamia-nut truffles at Kauai Chocolate Company** (p190)

PORT ALLEN

More industrial than scenic, the town that serves as a dock for the Pacific Missile Range Facility has evolved with the times: no longer the major port it served as in the 1800s, but the departure point for most Na Pali Coast tours. Alexander & Baldwin, one of the island's largest 19th-century agribusiness concerns that later expanded into railroads and real estate, built a small shopping center that mostly serves as an office for tour companies, but a residential development slated to break ground soon stands to add some liveliness once again to this port town.

Beaches

GLASS BEACH

Trash as art. No, it's not a new take on Marcel Duchamp's famous urinal, but beauty is in the eye of the beholder, so they say. Many a visitor has pored through the well-worn colorful remnants of glass along the shoreline of the aptly named Glass Beach, east of Port Allen. Glass 'pebbles', along with abandoned metals (some with new-found patina, some not so much), have washed up from an old dumpsite nearby, showing that decades of weather, too, can make art.

To get to the little cove, take Aka'ula St, the last left before entering the Port Allen commercial harbor, go past the fuel storage tanks and then curve to the right down a rutted dirt road that leads 100 yards to the beach.

Activities

The Port Allen Marina Center (Map p187), just up from the harbor, has most of the tour offices.

DIVING

Mana Divers (☎ 335-0881; www.manadivers.com; Bay 3, Port Allen Boat Harbor, 4310 Waialo Rd) offers boat dives, night dives and dive charters to Ni'ihau, Lehua Rock and Mana Crack during the months of May through September. They also offer open-water certification courses.

SNORKELING, WHALE-WATCHING & SUNSET CRUISES

Some of the island's best snorkeling can be done while on a sea tour of the Na Pali Coast, the majority of which leave from Port Allen. Waves along the Na Pali Coast are largest September through May, making many of the North Shore and Westside beaches dangerous for snorkeling during that time. With that in mind, on a tour you've got a better chance of seeing marine life even if Mother Nature is refusing to dish out safe snorkeling conditions. Spinner dolphins, *honu* (sea turtles) and whales abound, and catamaran and motorized raft tours offer the rare chance during winter months of seeing the Na Pali first hand, at sea-level (with the exception of a helicopter tour).

When deciding how to view the Na Pali, remember raft tours offer little reprieve

ISLAND VOICES

NAME: KEITH ROBINSON
OCCUPATION: FOUNDER, KAUA'I WILDLIFE RESERVE; CO-OWNER OF NI'IHAU (p219)
RESIDENCE: WESTSIDE

You've spent a great deal of time, energy and your own money to work to preserve rare Hawaiian species on about 100 acres. What do you hope will be your legacy? My hope is my legacy is my endangered species work. The one thing I hope to leave behind is the knowledge that one man working alone was able to, on his own, accomplish endangered species work that multi-gazillion-dollar government agencies or environmental groups were either unwilling or unable to do.

You've led a self-proclaimed 'wildly improbable life.' Tell me about the last two hurricanes. I was out fishing when 'Iwa hit (November 23, 1982). I went up about midnight – I knew the *akule* wouldn't bite until night – and got caught at sea, alone in 30ft waves from the hurricane. Don't ever do that, it's not a good idea – it will very likely ruin your day.

I fell overboard twice that night. The swells were 10ft to 15ft and, trying to come in and tie up, I got caught between the 10-ton boat and the docks. I just barely missed the jump to the dock and fell into the ocean and found myself festooned, the boat lunging around. I was so tired, when I tried to go over the ropes again, I tripped over my own feet and fell back head first into the water a second time. Both times the boat would lunge in against the dock and jerk away, and as it would jerk away the mooring rope between the dock and bow in a split second would go off like a bow-string and when it twanged tight I was yanked out of the water like an arrow leaving a bow. It put a terrible strain on both my arm sockets. On the third try I got onto the dock, tied up the boat with a new rope, but fell in again. I eventually got back on the boat and spent the night there.

My boat and another one that was dry-docked were all that survived – mine and Fujimi Shinagawa's – owned by the only two who never did commercial fishing on Sundays.

Hurricane 'Iniki was a lot easier – I just had to go down to a storage house and deal with some herbicide to prevent a toxic spill. I wandered around in 110- to 120-mile winds, but that experience was mild compared to *'Iwa*. I was on good, solid land and had come out of the shelter about 250 yards away. You did have to brace yourself to not literally be blown away.

from the elements, if any. Catamaran tours usually are packaged with unlimited food and beverage, have a covered area and have restrooms onboard. One item of note: take sensationalistic details about Hawaiian culture – especially pertaining to human sacrifice – with a grain of salt, as some tour companies have embellished the lore greatly over the years.

our pick **Holoholo Charters** (☎ 335-0815, 800-848-6130; www.holoholocharters.com; Port Allen Marina Center, Waialo Rd; 6am-8pm) Watch out for getting used to this kind of life. Crashing turquoise waves, thrilling cliffs, sea caves, waterfalls and food and drink to boot (alcohol included), aboard one of two catamarans: a 50ft sailing 'cat' or a 65ft power vessel. Snorkel tours include a 7-hour Ni'ihau and Na Pali snorkel tour (adult/child aged six to 12 $175/125) and a 5-hour morning tour (adult/child aged five to 12 $135/95). The 2-hour sunset cruise offers the best deal at $79. Save 10% booking online.

Catamaran Kahanu (☎ 645-6176, 888-213-7711; www.catamarankahanu.com; Port Allen Marina Center, Waialo Rd) This Hawaiian-owned catamaran tour is unique in that it offers some informative demos in basket weaving from hau and coconut, as well as a 'touristy' take-home token: coconut leaf roses. Demos also include weaving *ti* leaves and coconut fibers into fishing lines. A 5-hour tour for adult/child aged 4 to 11 years costs $122/80; a 3½-hour tour costs $80/60.

Capt Andy's Sailing Adventures (☎ 335-6833, 800-535-0830; www.napali.com; Port Allen Marina Center, Waialo Rd) Na Pali for 5 to 6 hours of snorkeling (adult/child aged two to 12 $145/104). Plan for getting a little wet, a little cold, and for some sun along the way. The crew will be on the lookout for marine life for you, like flying fish, sea turtles, dolphins and whales, depending on the tour date. Weather permitting, the tour also includes stop at Nu'alolo Kai, an ancient fishing village, with a brief hike.

Blue Dolphin Charters (☎ 335-5553, 877-511-1311; www.kauaiboats.com; Port Allen Marina Center, Waialo Rd) The mother lode of trips is their 'deluxe' Na Pali 7-hour tour with a tryst in Ni'ihau waters (internet/regular price $175/196), while the standard 5-hour Na Pali deal (internet/regular $126/147) still allows for some snorkeling. For an additional $35, they'll take you on a one-tank dive – even if it's your first time.

Kaua'i Sea Tours (☎ 826-7254, 800-733-7997; www.kauaiseatours.com; Aka'ula St, Port Allen) Offers summer Na Pali tours by catamaran (5hr tour adult/child from $139/99), 3-hour tours by raft (internet/regular from $99/109, child $69/73), 3- to 4-hour sightseeing tours of Na Pali or 5-hour dinner/snorkel tour (internet/regular from $139/148, teens $129/137, child $99/109). Raft tours offer the chance to go into sea caves and under waterfalls. Depending on the weather, the tours also offer secluded beach landings to the Nu'alolo Kai archaeological site, an ancient fishing village. The beach visit includes a short, scenic hike. Only a handful of tours have rights to land here so, if you can, take advantage of the unique opportunity.

If less luxe and more rugged is your thing, then a Zodiac raft tour might be for you. Here's one example (see also the Tours section under Waimea; p199): **Captain Zodiac Raft Adventures** (☎ 335-6833, 800-535-0830; www.napali.com; Port Allen Marina Center, Waialo Rd), Capt Andy's sister outfit, which offers a 5½-hour tour (adult/child $129/89) year-round.

Shopping

KAUAI CHOCOLATE COMPANY

our pick ☎ 335-0448; www.kauaichocolate.us; 4341 Waialo Rd; 11am-5pm Mon-Sat, noon-5pm Sun

It's hard to make it back to your car rental with any of these sublime treats left, let alone all the way back to home base. Don't worry, you'll justify it by realizing good chocolate melts quickly and therefore must be eaten.

Fudge, edible body paint (you read that correctly) and truffles with creamy ganaches, mousses and delicate creams of papaya, *liliko'i*, coconut, guava, Kaua'i coffee and sugarcane make it as ridiculous to avoid stopping here as it is gobbling up your goodies quickly with nothing to show for it.

HANAPEPE

pop 2153

Flat facades, a wide street and plenty of old timers and artists make for the eclectic Old West cocktail that is Hanapepe town. Peppered with galleries, its unassuming former main street is a contrast to the old-school plantation locals who still thrive throughout the Westside. 'Old Hanapepe' town used to be home to the island's most bustling flurry of activity, but that torch has since been passed to Lihu'e. When the new 'road' bypassed the old main strip, several businesses were threatened with going belly up. It wasn't until a passionate bevy of real-estate-savvy artists bought up some property that some new life was breathed into Hanapepe, making it the rustic, charming enclave it is today. The old main street now enjoys a Friday Night Art Walk (see the boxed text, p193), when the strip, though small, beats with a joie de vivre, clamoring with lively Westside musicians, charming restaurateurs and grateful gallery owners only too happy to laud visits from 'just looking' patrons.

The small town also boasts the home base of an ongoing Hawaiian tradition unfazed by time: salt panning. The laborious task of collecting the reddish, large crystals of Hawaiian salt is considered a spiritual one, meaning the seasoning – which cannot be bought – is harvested with much local pride.

History

Hanapepe has developed from a thriving, taro-farming, Native Hawaiian community to a commercial center, a military hangout spot and, at present, an artist- and locals-dense enclave. Though Hurricane 'Iniki destroyed many of Hanapepe's historical sites in 1992, 69 remain, of which 43 have met the criteria to be listed on state and national registers.

More than a century ago immigrant entrepreneurs set up shop here. Some were descendants of the Chinese rice growers of the 1860s, others Japanese plantation workers of the early 1900s. By the late 1… Lihu'e became the island's shipping, bu… ness and political seat. When the island's 'road' bypassed the town center, business for many mom-and-pop shops waned. You can catch a glimpse of the past by touring the galleries on the 'old' main street, as many of the buildings have snippets hearkening to their past – it's where businesses such as rice-brokers, cleaners and restaurateurs kept shop.

Hanapepe also has its own cinematic history: it doubled as the Australian outback in the TV miniseries *The Thorn Birds* (1983), the Filipino Olongapo City in the movie *Flight of the Intruder* (1991) and the Hawaiian town in Disney's animated movie *Lilo and Stitch* (2002).

Orientation & Information

Veer *mauka* (inland) onto Hanapepe Rd at the 'Kaua'i's Biggest Little Town' sign.

American Savings Bank (☎ 335-3118; 4548 Kona Rd)

Bank of Hawaii (☎ 335-5021; 3764 Hanapepe Rd) On the western end of Hanapepe Rd.

Beaches

SALT POND BEACH PARK

A beach that feels local but is visitor- and *keiki* (child)-friendly is the simple but lovely Salt Pond Beach Park. Small compared with most Westside beaches, it has

Salt Pond Beach Park

KEVIN LEVESQUE

WESTSIDE

full facilities, including ...ers and campsites. The ...p swimming, and both ...re shallow and OK for ... parental supervision. The beach is known for its salt ponds, where Hawaiians have traditionally made reddish, pink rock salt by panning seawater.

To get here, turn left onto Lele Rd, just after passing the 17-mile marker, then right onto Lokokai Rd. An ideal place for family snorkeling, its rocky, outer fringe means lots of fish and relatively calm waters on the inside of the reef; the added bonus is it's among the few lifeguarded snorkeling spots on the island.

Sights

KAUAI COOKIE COMPANY

☎ 335-5003; 1-3529 Kaumuali'i Hwy, Ste A

Not pretty by any means, this warehouse-/factory-style building, across from Omoide Bakery & Wong's Chinese Deli, houses some of the most appreciated boxed treats on the island. Though some argue the Kauai Cookie is more novelty than delicious, it has an island cult following rivaling the diehard Girl Scouts cookie. Old reliables here like Kona Coffee and Chocolate Chip rarely disappoint.

> **Top Picks**
>
> **WESTSIDE FOR KIDS**
>
> - **Beach day at Salt Pond Beach Park** (p191)
> - **Watching for marine life on a Na Pali snorkel cruise** (p189)
> - **The park, walk and view from Waimea Canyon lookout** (p208)
> - **Tropical Rainbow shave ice at Jo-Jo's Anuenue Shave Ice and Treats** (p200)
> - **Souvenir Ts with native plants at Puahina Moku o Kaua'i Warrior Design** (p195)
> - **Sugar Cane Snax from Kaua'i Granola** (p202)
> - **Trekking the Alaka'i Swamp boardwalk** (p216)
> - **Weather-in-action photographs at Koke'e Natural History Museum** (p211)

SPARKY'S PEACE GARDEN, STORYBOOK THEATRE OF HAWAII

☎ 335-0712; www.storybook.org; 3814 Hanapepe Rd

Great for *keiki,* the Storybook Theatre is a multimedia center, replete with an outdoor classroom ideology, designed for families and artists. It is intended to act as a meeting ground, with several workshops and event-based activities. Though it doesn't keep regular daily hours, it's worth a peek during the weekly Friday Night Hanapepe Art Walk (opposite) as sometimes it offers coinciding children's activities. The **garden** is named after the late Senator Spark M Matsunaga, a peace advocate. The center's studio has also been home to the Russell the Rooster Show – featuring a puppet always happy to 'talk story' (chat) with local residents – for more than 20 years.

GALLERIES

For some permanent art, **Farsyde Tattoo** (☎ 335-2465; www.farsydetattoo.com; 3567 Hanapepe Rd) can make your trip to Kaua'i's Westside even more unforgettable.

DAWN TRAINA GALLERY

our pick ☎ 335-3993; 3840B Hanapepe Rd; 🕒 6-9pm Fri or by appointment

Beautifully raw, realistic and compelling works, as well as affordable prints, can be found in Traina's gallery depicting images that hearken back to the days of precontact Kaua'i. If you see only one gallery, it should be this one. Traina's talent is compounded by her diligent research of, and appreciation for, Hawaiian culture. The gallery also houses the work of Michelle Dick, another talented artist who got her crash course in art when overcoming a nearly fatal illness. Her seductive black and white two-dimensional carvings have attracted a lot of on-island attention in her few years' work.

ARIUS HOPMAN GALLERY

☎ 335-0227; www.hopmanart.com; 3840C Hanapepe Rd; 🕒 10:30am-3:30pm Mon-Thu, to 9pm Fri

Here's a chance to see an artist whose mother was commissioned to sculpt Mahatma Gandi. This Indian watercolorist and photographer offers vibrant works, made with a sumi brush, that capture Kaua'i. The

HANAPEPE ART WALK

Friday evening in Old Hanapepe town offers a candid peek into its milieu of artists, as galleries keep later-than-usual hours, offering the chance to stroll, peruse and dine. The pace picks up around 5pm, when the former main drag is transformed by its augmented, already-heady mix of musicians, art installations and visitors, albeit only till a mere 9pm. Meander through the galleries housing everything from the works of Sunday artists, island-inspired originals, 'Hawaiiana' vintage, photography, paintings spanning post-impressionism to cubism, expressionism and a sampling of Asian. Though art aficionados may snub some of the collections as less-than-cutting edge, remember: Hanapepe is small town – and proud of it.

Many will find the 'art walk' from gallery to gallery is well matched with the gentle ambience of Old Hanapepe's modest Christmas-lit strip, along with its low-key street theatre bands like the Westside cult classic the Happy Enchilata (www.myspace.com/thehappyenchalata) or guitarist Westside Smitty, usually fronting the Talk Story Bookstore. The walk also pairs well with low-rent street vendors like Heather's Monster Tacos, a makeshift tent usually across from the Swinging Bridge. This surly, one-woman show (who has ingratiated herself with local regulars loyal to her homemade tortillas) offers an artform all her own: 'authentic' Tex-Mex out of context. If you'd rather sit or have a more 'island' post-art walk meal, this is the only night of the week when the justifiably popular Hawaiian-American fusion Hanapepe Café (p195) is open for dinner. Best to stop in, make reservations, then do some window-shopping or art critiquing while your name's on the list.

building has kept true to form in that in 1922 it also housed a photographer.

ART OF MARBLING/ROBERT BADER WOOD SCULPTURE

☎ 482-1472; 3890 Hanapepe Rd; 🕑 10am-5pm Sat-Thu, to 9pm Fri

Becky J Wold's work on silk and her husband's in wood make for unique collecting, whether a small paper work by Wold or Cook Island pine work by Bader, pieces are worth a look.

BANANA PATCH STUDIO

☎ 335-5944, 800-914-5944; www.bananapatchstudio.com; 3865 Hanapepe Rd; 🕑 10am-4:30pm Sat-Thu, to 9pm Fri

Koi watercolors, vibrant island art, souvenir ceramic tiles. If any of the B&Bs you've seen bear signage like 'Mahalo for taking off your slippahs,' there's a decent chance it was purchased here. It's functional craft rather than art – though there's plenty to behold in this crowded little space, usually rife with visitors. Certified Ni'ihau shell necklaces (see p220) are on sale here, though there's more traditional work available at the **Ni'ihau Helicopters** (p220) office in Makaweli.

KAUAI FINE ARTS

☎ 335-3778; www.brunias.com; 3751 Hanapepe Rd; 🕑 9:30am-4:30pm Mon-Thu & Sat, to 9pm Fri)

If you're sending something 'home' or want to get your hands on a unique map – including navigational charts – this is a great little spot to peruse. It also sells prints, Ni'ihau shell leis (see p220) and other works.

KAMA'AINA CABINETS KOA WOOD GALLERY GIFTS & FURNITURE

☎ 335-5483; 3848 Hanapepe Rd; 🕑 11am-6pm Mon-Thu & Sat, to 9pm Fri

If you've been lucky enough to see a koa tree on one of your Westside hikes, best to

Inside the Banana Patch Studio ANN CECIL

see its likeness in elegant, polished form. Though investing in much of what is on display could break the bank, it's worth a venture to witness the kind of woodwork that, for Hawaii, has stood the test of time.

AMY LAUREN'S GALLERY

☎ 634-8660; www.amylaurensgallery.com; 3890 Hanapepe Rd; 11am-5pm Mon-Fri, until 9pm Fri

Here's a chance to buy originals instead of giclée, though the latter are usually more affordable. This boutique-style gallery is somewhat of a newbie, and worth a perusal for its vibrant colors and on-site artists.

Tours

Find a copy of Hanapepe's **Walking Tour Map** ($2), which describes the town's historic buildings. Look for the **Swinging Bridge** landmark, which crosses the Hanapepe River. Its funky old predecessor fell victim to 'Iniki, but in a community-wide effort this new bridge was erected in 1996.

INTER-ISLAND HELICOPTERS

☎ 335-5009, 800-656-5009; www.interisland helicopters.com; 1-3410 Kaumuali'i Hwy; flights regular/waterfall $260/$355

Offers door-free flights over the Westside that reveal some of the most rugged views found on Kaua'i.

Please note that unique local weather conditions in this part of the world can present a hazard, and there have been fatalities in various helicopter crashes in this region. To check any tour company's flight record, consult the accident database at the **NTSB** (www.ntsb.gov).

BIRDS IN PARADISE

☎ 822-5309; www.birdsinparadise.com; Burns Field, Puolo Rd; 50min/90min lesson $135/335

Extreme-adventure seekers can take a round-the-island lesson on one of these powered hang gliders for $300. Take the road for Salt Pond Beach Park to reach the airport.

Eating

TARO KO CHIPS FACTORY — Snacks $

☎ 335-5586; 3940 Hanapepe Rd; per small bag $2.50; 8am-5pm

Thinly sliced *kalo* (taro) that's been seasoned, slathered with oil and tortured in a deep wok makes for some crispy, somewhat sweet, but mostly salty, crunching. A great take-home item if you can abstain from chomping until you get to the airport – by then, what's a few more hours?

HAWAIIAN HUT DELIGHTS — Snacks $

☎ 335-3781; 3805 Hanapepe Rd; shave ice from $2; noon-5pm Mon-Fri

Get an old-school snack like Li Hing Mui (dried plum, also known as crack seed) or a quickie rainbow shave ice to go while spending only a smidgen of your budget.

LAPPERT'S HAWAII — Ice Cream/Cafe $

☎ 335-6121; www.lappertshawaii.com; 1-3555 Kaumuali'i Hwy; ice cream $4; 10am-6pm

In 1983, Walter Lappert opened the first of this contagiously addictive chain here in Hanapepe. Order up some locally inspired ice-cream flavors with your coffee – cane-sweetened guava, pineapple and coconut choices put a new spin on fruit-as-meal with creamy, oh-so-refreshing spoonfuls. If you're into chocolate, don't miss the Kauai Pie: Kona-coffee ice cream, chocolate fudge, macadamia nuts, coconut flakes and vanilla cake crunch.

TAHINA'S TASTY TREATS — Fast Food $

☎ 335-0260; 4505 Puolo Rd; lunches $7.75; 11am-5pm Mon-Fri

'Ahi, mahimahi or *opah* (moonfish) make for a yummy approach to the Euro tradition of fish and chips, while other options like fried oysters or shrimp make for a more unusual approach. It also has *boba* (milk tea with tapioca pearls)–style drinks, creamy milkshakes and typical shave-ice flavors.

DA IMU HUT CAFÉ — Cafe $

☎ 335-0200; 1-3959 Kaumuali'i Hwy; 10am-2pm, 5-8pm Mon-Fri, 10-1pm Sat

Try specials like the Imu Hut teri-fried chicken, traditional-style *kalua* pig or any of their Hawaiian plates (especially the fried saimin), which change daily. If you don't want to hang around the mostly local vibe, meals are great to order in advance to take out for a picnic – perfect if it's a sunny day, as the ambience here is a tad stuffy and dimly lit.

BOBBIE'S ISLAND RESTAURANT & CATERING
Hawaii Regional $

☎ 335-5152; 3620 Hanapepe Rd; plate lunch $5.95; 10am-2:30pm Mon-Fri & 5-8:30pm Mon, Thu & Fri

Fish and chips, local-style plate lunches and a killer roast pork gravy; this is a predominantly locals spot and boasts such comforting, high-calorie eats as *loco moco* (hamburger with gravy) and pork *katsu* (Japanese deep-fried cutlets; great for a rainy day or post-hike meal).

KAUA'I PUPU FACTORY
Hawaii Regional/Pupu $

☎ 335-0084; 1-3566 Kaumuali'i Hwy; plate lunch $6.25, 'ahi poke per lb $9; 9am-5:30pm Mon-Fri, to 3pm Sat

On the main street of Old Hanapepe Town, this place is perfect for a picnic plate lunch to make your own mini beach luau. Pick up the local staples like *laulau* (a steamed taro and *ti* leaf bundle with chicken, fish or pork) or *kalua* pork with a scoop of rice, or the *lomilomi* salmon (much like salsa with tidbits of fish here and there) or *poke* (sliced raw tuna, traditionally mixed mixed with soy sauce, sesame oil, green onion, chili pepper, *'inamona* relish or spicy mayo). Be sure to grab some chopsticks.

OMOIDE BAKERY & WONG'S CHINESE DELI
Hawaii Regional/Chinese $

our pick ☎ 335-5066, 335-5291; 1-3543 Kaumuali'i Hwy; mains $7.50-9.75; 9:30am-9pm Tue-Sat

A revered diner that serves up some plantation-local cuisine, where hot homemade island *pake* (Chinese) food soothes the regulars. This well-known spot also serves up fresh-baked, nutritiously lacking white-flour-based comfort eats like sesame–black bean *manju* (a sort of doughnut filled with gritty, slightly sweet paste) and Portuguese sweet bread (similar to what US mainlanders think of as Hawaiian or pineapple bread). If you've got a sweet tooth try their *liliko'i* chiffon pie, a self-proclaimed best.

HANAPEPE CAFÉ & BAKERY
Seafood/Vegetarian $$$

our pick ☎ 335-5011; 3830 Hanapepe Rd; lunch $6-10, dinner $18-25; bakery 7am-3pm; cafe 11am-3pm; dinner 6-9pm Fri only

With walls covered in local art and a quaint ambience, this stop is a must. Breakfasts such as frittata with red potatoes ($8) or quiche and croissant pair well with spicy espresso, while build-your-own garden burgers make a great $7 lunch. But the mainly specials-only dinner menu on Friday takes the cake, with items such as hot-spiced apricot soup, Creole-inspired mahimahi (pink-fleshed fish) bouillabaisse and macadamia-nut spinach salad. Owner Helen Lacono also serves up a genuinely customer-driven attitude. Dedicated to keeping her patrons happy, her famous in-house baked focaccia, multigrain breads and aromatic cinnamon rolls make even East Siders and North Shore recluses trek to the sleepy Westside.

Shopping

PUAHINA MOKU O KAUA'I WARRIOR DESIGNS HAWAII

our pick ☎ 335-9771; www.warriordesignshawaii.com; 3741 Hanapepe Rd

Geared toward locals, this boutique (inside Brook's of Kaua'i) is perhaps best known for its *laua'e, lawa'i, palapalai* ferns and *kilohoku* (stargazer) designs in high-quality ink on locally printed, soft T-shirts. Over the years, local owners Loui and Fumi Cabebe have been sure to consult with *kupuna* (elders) to maintain a culturally savvy business, which has since grown to include warrior designs for men, women and *keiki*. The shop also carries Maui-based Hana Lima soaps with fragrances like coconut-lime and Tahitian vanilla.

JACQUELINE ON KAUA'I

☎ 335-9911; 3837 Hanapepe Rd; 9am-6pm

Friendly and a bit eclectic, Jacqueline makes her mark on her collection in this little consignment store/boutique, where she sews the non-consignment products herself, including Japanese-inspired silk robes and Aloha shirts custom-made while you wait ($45 to $52, usually about one to two hours). Place an order at the beginning of the Hanapepe Art Walk and you're good to go.

JJ OHANA

☎ 335-0366; 3805 B Hanapepe Rd; www.jjohana.com; 8am-6pm Mon-Thu, 9pm Fri

It's not many a venue where you can find both a $2 hot dog and a $7000 necklace. This family-run spot is clad with super-affordable hot daily specials (sometimes

Getting ready for Hanapepe Art Night at Talk Story Bookstore LINDA CHING

chili and rice) along with a wide selection of medium- to high-end souvenirs, such as koa-wood bowls and necklaces, red and blue coral jewelry and Ni'ihau shell leis ($600 to $7000).

TALK STORY BOOKSTORE

☎ 335-6469; www.talkstorybookstore.com; 3785 Hanapepe Rd; 🕑 11am-5pm Mon-Thu, 9pm Fri

The dusty, often hot and oddball-ridden 'Western-most bookstore in the United States' carries everything from vintage erotica, pulp fiction and trashy novelas to archaic piano books and high school required reading. Good for passing the time if you're bored, on a tight budget or simply too tired to walk around.

Sleeping

Salt Pond Beach Park offers convenient camping (see County Parks information on p259 for permit information).

HANAPEPE RIVERSIDE Inn $$

our pick ☎ 261-1693; 4466 Puolo Rd; 1br unit $97, 3-night min

If you want to feel like you can get some fresh Kaua'i air while simultaneously lounging around your new temporary digs (while not breaking the bank at some resort), this decent little upstairs unit has a full kitchen, washer/dryer access, a king-size bed and Hanapepe River views. The only problem is booking, as you have to go through a service. Maximum two people, with a three-night minimum.

WESTSIDE DWELLING Apartment $$

☎ 652-9900; apt $80, cleaning fee $80

If you're looking for a budget deal, these digs are bare-minimum functional meets clean and cozy. This two-year-old ground-floor apartment (four steps) is in a quiet Westside 'hood in the Hanapepe River Valley where most of the neighbors are locals. About 2 miles from Salt Pond Beach Park and a 15-minute walk to 'Old Hanapepe' town. An ideal option for anyone on a budget not looking to spend much time dawdling about in a hotel room. Note: the bed is a futon, which could be an issue for those with back problems.

OLOKELE & KAUMAKANI

The cane fields that abound on the *mauka* (inland) side of the highway are the bread and butter of this region for its owners. 'Olokele' refers to the Olokele Sugar Company, the last remaining sugar producer on Kaua'i and one of two remaining in the state, purchased in 1994 by Gay & Robinson, one of the last of Hawaii's giant sugar companies. It was founded by the children of Eliza Sinclair, who bought the entire island of Ni'ihau (see p219) in the mid-1860s. All told, the Robinson family owns 42,000 acres on Kaua'i, including land purchases in Hanapepe, Kalalau and Wainiha as well as several smaller lots throughout the island.

Kaumakani houses the headquarters of Gay & Robinson, which tries to maintain plantation life in this area (called Makaweli). Nearby Pakala village is home to the boat services to the island of Ni'ihau for its residents, while Kaumakani has Kaua'i's oldest Methodist church.

The road to the Gay & Robinson headquarters and the sugar mill, which comes up immediately after the 19-mile marker on Kaumuali'i Hwy, is shaded by lovely tall trees and lined with classic century-old lampposts. Taking this short drive offers a glimpse into plantation life. Everything is covered with a layer of red dust from the surrounding fields. Quite a few indigenous Ni'ihauans live in this area, many of them working for the Robinsons.

WAIMEA

pop 1787

Waimea ('reddish water') is a popular name in Hawaii; it's also the name of an O'ahu valley and a historical town on Hawai'i the Big Island. But on Kaua'i, it's the name of

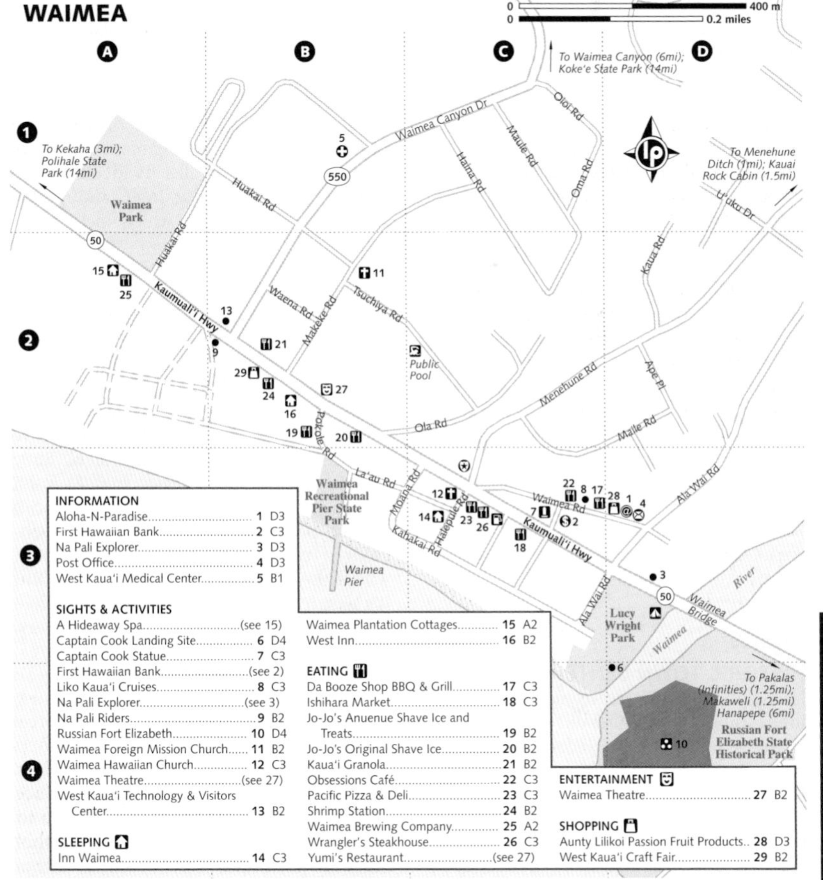

what is arguably the island's richest town – historically speaking.

It was here that Captain Cook of the British navy first landed in 1778 (note the small landing site plaque at Lucy Wright Beach Park). King Kaumuali'i welcomed the first missionaries here in 1820, and by 1852 the first Chinese contract laborers arrived. Rice cultivation began in the Waimea Valley in the 1860s, by Chinese farmers originally contracted to work the sugar plantations. As the commercial sugar industry grew, so did the need for field laborers. In 1884, Waimea Sugar moved in and the settlement evolved into a plantation town.

Today, Waimea thrives as the heart of the Westside, though it's small compared with most life-force cities. One brewpub and a movie theatre are all that speak of Waimea's nightlife, but with playgrounds like Waimea Canyon and Koke'e State Parks just up the hill, who needs a hangover?

Information

Check the website of **West Kaua'i Business and Professional Association** (www.wkbpa.org) to learn more about Waimea.

Aloha-N-Paradise (☎ 338 1522; 9905 Waimea Rd; internet per 30min $4; 7am-5pm Mon-Fri, 8am-12pm Sat;) All-day wi-fi with your own laptop. In the back there's locally roasted coffee drinks and pastries, while the front room has a seating area and art gallery.

First Hawaiian Bank (☎ 338-1611; 4525 Panako Rd) On Waimea's central square.

Na Pali Explorer (☎ 338-9999, 877-335-9909; www.napali-explorer.com; Kaumuali'i Hwy; internet per 30min $3; 7am-5pm) A one-stop shop for internet access, simple souvenirs, light snacks and snorkel-cruise and sportfishing bookings.

Post office (☎ 800-275-8777; 9911 Waimea Rd)

West Kaua'i Medical Center (☎ 338-9431; Waimea Canyon Dr) Emergency services 24 hours.

Sights

HISTORIC TOWN CENTER

Hodgepodge architecture makes for some interesting styles to behold in downtown Waimea, including the Neoclassical **First Hawaiian Bank** (1929) and the art deco **Waimea Theatre** (1938).

Captain Cook's likeness, a replica of the original statue by Sir John Tweed in Whitby, England, stands in the center of town, obscured by trees and the hustle and bustle of Big Save patrons.

Waimea Foreign Mission Church (Makeke Rd) was originally a thatched structure built in 1826 by the Reverend Samuel Whitney. It was changed in 1858 to sandstone blocks and coral mortar by design of another missionary, the Reverend George Rowell.

In 1865 Rowell maligned the congregation and left to create the **Waimea Hawaiian Church** (Kaumuali'i Hwy; services 8:30am Sun), a wooden-frame church that Hurricane 'Iniki destroyed but which has since been rebuilt. It still offers Hawaiian services, a testament to the old-school longevity of the Westside.

WEST KAUA'I TECHNOLOGY & VISITORS CENTER

☎ 338-1332; 9565 Kaumuali'i Hwy; admission free; 9:30am-5pm Mon-Fri

Notice the custom-stained concrete medallions on the corners of the building and their stylized representation of sugarcane honoring the town's sugarcane industry. Well designed to parallel its ideology, this center offers a 2½-hour free walking tour at 9:30am on Monday, which includes an overview of the technology, the building complex and the Waimea theater. At 9:30am on 'Aloha' Fridays, they offer a lei-making class. Call ahead for reservations for larger groups.

LUCY WRIGHT BEACH PARK

While the Captain Cook **landing site** boasts a small plaque on a rock here, the entire park itself was named in honor of Lucy Wright, a revered schoolteacher. As soon as you cross the Waimea Bridge you can see the park, off Ala Wai Rd. Lava rock-colored sand makes for a messy swim, where the Waimea River exits to sea. But it's worth a stroll. The park also has a ball field, picnic tables, rest rooms and showers. Camping is permitted on a flat grassy area, but the roadside site lacks much appeal; see p259 for information about obtaining camping permits.

MENEHUNE DITCH

The first settlers of Kaua'i, called the 'Menehune,' were later conquered by a second wave of Polynesian migrations. At that time, the term became synonymous with a person of low social rank. The translation of *menehune* as 'little people' (ie physically smaller) came from a newspaper article likening them to leprechauns, perhaps for a boost in tourism. Though the *menehune* were small in social status, archaeologists have never found any skeletal remains of less-than-average-size humans anywhere in the Hawaiian islands.

While it's somewhat of a local custom here to blame the *menehune* for the unexplainable, here's a case where they've taken archeologists by surprise. This stone and earthen aqueduct (Map p187) is no doubt an engineering feat, constructed precontact. The legend goes something like this: Ola, a king, ordered Pi, a kahuna (priest), to create a dam and ditch to water his lands west of the Waimea River. Pi contracted the *menehune* living on the canyon rim to build the ditch for payment of one *'opae* (shrimp) per *menehune*. In keeping with typical *menehune* fashion, they finished in one night.

At the end of the 18th century, Captain Vancouver (a former shipmate of Captain Cook who later commanded his own expedition) is said to have noted the walls of the ditch to be around 24ft high. Now, most of the ruins are beneath the road, save one 2ft-high section. However, the ditch is still somewhat functional, diverting water from the Waimea River through the cliff to irrigate the taro patches below.

It's worth a visit; turn at the police station onto Menehune Rd and go almost 1.5 miles along the Waimea River. The ditch is on the left side of the road after a small parking area.

RUSSIAN FORT ELIZABETH

Russia befriended Kaua'i's King Kaumuali'i in the early 1800s; the relationship stood to help Kaumuali'i overcome King Kamehameha and Russia to use Hawaii as an oceangoing stop during its reign as prominent fur traders. The fort was begun in September 1816, but within a year was stopped – perhaps on King Kamehameha's orders or because of general suspicion of the Russians.

Hawaiian troops used the fort until 1864. Now its remains look much like a sea battered lava-rock wall.

Activities

SNORKELING

There are three outfits offering Na Pali Coast tours from Kekaha's Kikiaola Small Boat Harbor, instead of from Port Allen in Hanapepe. Not much of a difference save that you're a bit closer to your destination, so there's a tad more water time.

The art deco–style Waimea Theatre (p202)

AIMEE GOGGINS

WESTSIDE

Liko Kaua'i Cruises (☎ 338-0333, 888-732-5456; www.liko-kauai.com; 9875 Waimea Rd) Run by Kaua'i-born and -raised Native Hawaiian Liko Ho'okano – whose ancestors have hailed from the 'forbidden island' of Ni'ihau – this outfit sails its 49ft power catamaran to the Na Pali Coast for a 4-hour cruise (adult/child aged four to 12 years $120/80). Maximum group size is 34, and tours go as far as Ke'e Beach.

Na Pali Explorer (☎ 338-9999, 877-335-9909; www.napali-explorer.com; Kaumuali'i Hwy; 5hr tour adult/child 5-12 $125/85) Boasts 26ft and 48ft rafts doing snorkel trips on 'rigid-hull' inflatable rafts (hard bottom with inflatable sides), smoother than the all-inflatable Zodiacs. Expect between 16 and 35 passengers. Taken up a notch, the larger raft includes a rest room and canopy for shade.

our pick **Na Pali Riders** (☎ 742-6331; 9600 Kaumuali'i Hwy; www.napaliriders.com; morning adult/child $109/98, afternoon $87) Offers first-hand peeks at the Waiahuakua and Ho'olulu sea caves (weather permitting). Captain Chris Turner is passionate about what he does, and likes to think of this tour as 'National Geographic' in style. Turner offers an intimate setting; small, healthy snack; a CD of photographs and movies taken on the trip; and a feeling you're going out with some of your favorite ragamuffin friends (he likes to travel fast, blare Led Zeppelin and the Rolling Stones, and talk story quite a bit). Remember, it's a no-shade, lots-of-bumps operation, so it's not for the pregnant or injured.

SURFING

Between the 21- and 22-mile markers, you'll notice cars parked on the side of the highway in an area known as Makaweli. This is the access point to a popular surf break called **Pakalas**, dubbed 'Infinities,' said to offer the 'longest lefts' anywhere on-island. There are mixed opinions about what 'keeping it local' means regarding surfing this break. Though those who've been surfing this spot their entire lives aren't going to let you drop in on any waves (so arguably it's not like you're getting in their way), we'd still recommend leaving this break for the locals. Instead, try **Kekaha Beach Park** (p204) or **Polihale State Park** (p206). Of course, Pakalas is a gorgeous *public* beach, and if you'd like to watch some of the best surfers on-island rip, park on the side of the road, take the short dirt path to the beach and keep your eye on the waves.

MASSAGE & YOGA

Traditional Hawaiian massage techniques such as lomilomi are offered at **A Hideaway Spa** (☎ 338-0005; www.ahideawayspa; Unit 40, Waimea Plantation Cottages, 9400 Kaumuali'i Hwy; massage $95-165, spa & skin treatments $55-130; 9am-6pm Mon-Sat), formerly Hart-Felt Massage. The spa also features ayurvedic and spa and skin treatments, as well as oceanfront **yoga classes** ($15; 5pm Tue, 8:30am Sat), ideal for newbies.

Tours

For a unique experience, **Safari Helicopters** (p69), based in Lihu'e, is the only outfit given permission by the Robinson family – owners of Ni'ihau (see p219) and 42,000 acres on Kaua'i – to land in Waimea Canyon. Expect to land atop a cliff overlooking Olokele Valley in Waimea on their 'eco-tour,' which includes a chat with none other than Keith Robinson, the preservationist recluse and treasure-trove extraordinaire who hails from the locally famous family (see the boxed text, p189).

Festivals & Events

Waimea Town Celebration (☎ 338-1332; www.wkbpa.org; admission free) Free fun in mid-February includes rodeo, canoe race, food, crafts, and lei and hula competitions.

Waimea Lighted Christmas Parade (☎ 338-9957) Watch lighted floats through Waimea town. Parade starts at dusk, a week before Christmas.

Eating & Drinking

JO-JO'S ANUENUE SHAVE ICE & TREATS

Shave Ice $

our pick ☎ **338-9963; 4491 Pokole Rd; 11am-5pm**

There are two 'Jo-Jo's', and this one is located roughly between Waimea Theatre and Waimea Landing, next door to Bucky's Liquor & Boiled Peanuts. Does it matter which Jo-Jo's you choose? Absolutely. For our purposes, know this: there are no chemically syrups here – all are homemade without additives and aren't overly sweet. The ice is truly *shaven*, and its syrups don't melt the ice into a ball upon pouring, so you won't break your weak, though determined, plastic spoon.

The delicacy is the dragon-fruit *halo halo*, sandwiched between macadamia-nut ice cream and rich, *haupia* (coconut pudding) topping. Expect your blood sugar level to reach renegade highs and enjoy the coconut resin left behind on your newly smackable lips.

JO-JO'S 'ORIGINAL' SHAVE ICE

Shave Ice $

☎ 635-7615; 9740 Kaumuali'i Hwy; shave ice $2-4; 10am-6pm

Read the boxed text, below, to get a feel for the backstory, and take note: this shave ice is just OK. Don't you want something amazing? Plus, chances are it's hot in here, and it's usually a one-person, slow show.

OBSESSIONS CAFÉ

Cafe $

☎ 338-1110; 9875 Waimea Rd; breakfast & lunch $6-7; 8am-2pm

A great greasy spoon for those yearning for hot, naughty food – which wouldn't be complete on Kaua'i without dishes like the *loco moco*, taken to the next level here in the 'ultimate:' two eggs, hamburger and Portuguese sausage patties, cheddar cheese, onions, mushrooms, rice and gravy ($6.95). Lighter fare includes the Chinese chicken salad ($6), but sedation-inducing sandwiches like the Reuben – with corned beef, sauerkraut and Swiss cheese ($6.75) are the specialty.

ISHIHARA MARKET

Hawaii Regional $

our pick ☎ 338-1751; 9894 Kaumuali'i Hwy; plate lunches $8.75; 6am-8:30pm Mon-Fri, 7am-8:30pm Sat & Sun

The island's most local-style grocer, with cult classics in the deli at back: *'ahi poke* (cubed raw yellowfin tuna mixed with *shōyu*, sesame oil, salt and chili pepper), smoked marlin, stuffed *'ahi* with crab and oxtail soup. Faves like smoked-salmon *poke* run out early, so get here before the lunch rush. They've also got sushi *bentō* (Japanese box lunch), daily specials and marinated ready-to-go meats. Parking is hectic: be patient or park down the street and walk back.

DA BOOZE SHOP BBQ & GRILL

Hawaii Regional $

☎ 338-9953; 9883 Waimea Rd; $7.95 box lunches, keiki menu $2.40; 10:30am-9pm Mon-Sat, to 5pm Sun

While it's got plate lunches like many other local-style outlets, the hickory-smoked BBQ rib specials ($8.50) here combine typical, mainland US meat-eater grinds with Westside flair. Try the sandwich platter ($12) with chicken and pork, rice, macaroni salad (of course) and the homemade BBQ sauce, or the thriftier BBQ burger deluxe ($4.50).

'ORIGINAL' JO-JO'S, SHAVED ICE & THE ART OF MINCING WORDS

Ah, the drama behind the shave ice shops bearing Jo-Jo's name. There are two Jo-Jo's, both claiming 'original' status, for different reasons. To complicate matters further, both are across the street from Waimea High School (the one owned by Aunty Jo-Jo, which we claim is 'better,' is closer to the ocean).

Just like any feud, ask the person on either side and there's a wide gap between the two stories. A middle ground of the tale goes something like this: in the '90s, Aunty Jo-Jo sold her wildly popular, seven-year-old shave-ice shop in Waimea, called 'Jo-Jo's Clubhouse,' to another family. The family had bought the shop largely because of its success borne under the household name Aunty Jo-Jo had created. Over time, locals began to complain that under the new ownership, Jo-Jo's wasn't the same (likely because new owners hadn't been given all the recipes – not the delectable *haupia* topping, let alone the homemade syrups). Its popularity consequently dwindled among locals. Tourists, however, still abound at the 'original' location.

In 2007, Aunty Jo-Jo opened a new shop at a new location (catty-corner from her old digs). The peeved biz owners who bought her namesake just up the street on Kaumuali'i Hwy couldn't produce the contract they claim includes a noncompete clause with Aunty Jo-Jo. That, coupled with the fact that patrons were becoming annoyed with the new owners' less-than-steadfast dedication toward maintaining a 'local' menu (they seem to be perpetually 'out' of their *halo halo* ingredients – a Hawaii shave-ice staple, for example) and that they're a haole (Caucasian)-run business attempting 'local' grinds, hasn't helped their odds with residents so far.

Top Picks

PLANTATION LOCAL EATS

- *Kau kau* **tin (boxed) lunch at Wrangler's Steakhouse** (right)
- *Kau yuk* **(marinated pork) at Omoides Bakery and Wong's Chinese Deli** (p195)
- **Fried saimin at Da Imu Hut Café** (p194)
- *'Inamona 'ahi* **(yellowfin tuna, sea salt, kukui-nut relish and seaweed) at Ishihara Market** (p201)

KAUA'I GRANOLA

Bakery $

☎ 338-0121; www.kauaigranola.com; 9633 Kaumuali'i Hwy; granola $8; 🕑 10am-5pm

The former pie-crust creator for Aunty Lilikoi, baker and owner Cheryl Salazar has found her niche. Salazar is the creator of sugarcane-sweetened Sugar Cane Snax, with tropical trail mixes and dried fruits ideal for when you're heading up to the canyon. Also get a whiff of the macadamia-nut cookies, chocolate-dipped coconut macaroons, and the *liliko'i* or guava crunch granola spread across a buttery cookie sheet. Around Christmas time, don't miss her Aloha shirt- and hula skirt–clad gingerbread men and women – adorable, edible gifts.

SHRIMP STATION

Seafood $

☎ 338-1242; 9652 Kaumuali'i Hwy; dishes $6-15; 🕑 11am-5pm

This is really the spot if you're craving shrimp. Sauteéd scampi-style, beer battered, coconut-flake grilled, in taco form or ground up into a 'shrimp burger' – coupled with papaya-ginger tartar sauce and fries. If you're just along for the ride, Shrimp Station also offers ice cream and random, elementary school–style desserts such as the pushup rainbow pop and the Neapolitan sandwich.

PACIFIC PIZZA & DELI

Italian/Eclectic $$

our pick ☎ 338-1020; 9850 Kaumuali'i Hwy; calzones $6.75, pizza $9.35-25; 🕑 11am-9pm Mon-Sat

While the Hapa-Haole ('half-Caucasian') pizza or calzone is a hands-down favorite with its pesto sauce, sun-dried tomatoes, mushrooms, Canadian bacon, zucchini and pineapple, the Supreme still offers some island influence (includes Portuguese sausage). The Mexican pizza (refried beans, sour cream, cheese) shouldn't disappoint vegetarians with a craving for abundantly filling slices.

WRANGLER'S STEAKHOUSE

Steakhouse $$$

our pick ☎ 338-1218; 9852 Kaumuali'i Hwy; lunch $8-15, dinner mains $17-25; 🕑 11am-9pm Mon-Fri, 4-9pm Sat

While it might seem a bit dusty and dark, this is probably your best bet for getting a Westside *paniolo* experience. The *kau kau* tin lunch hails from the tradition of workers taking lunch in a stackable tin box with three separate containers. Order a hearty *kau kau* tin lunch with shrimp tempura, teriyaki and BBQ meat along with rice and kimchee ($10.95). The restaurant also has a little gift shop where you can buy the *kau kau* tins ($30) – a real gem for local-culture enthusiasts.

WAIMEA BREWING COMPANY

Pub $$$

our pick ☎ 338-9733; www.waimea-plantation.com/dining.php; Waimea Plantation Cottages, 9400 Kaumuali'i Hwy; appetizers $7-13, dishes $9-30; 🕑 11am-10pm Sun-Thu, to 2am Fri & Sat

Tiki torches, live music and inviting plantation-style architecture will beckon you here, as does a long, rotating list of tasty microbrews. (Try a sampler platter for a six-ounce taste of all drafts on hand.) Hearty pub dinners include the honey-mango BBQ ribs ($26.95), teriyaki steak and ale shrimp with wasabi-mashed potatoes ($32.95) and the fish platter ($24.95). If you're on a budget but still hungry, try the Kaho'olawe salad ($13.95), which comes with crunchy candied macadamia nuts, local goats' cheese, pineapple and a guava–balsamic vinaigrette.

Entertainment

WAIMEA THEATRE

☎ 338-0282; 9691 Kaumuali'i Hwy; 🕑 7:30pm Wed-Sun

Perfect for a rainy day or an early-evening reprieve from the sun and sea. Kaua'i is a little behind with new releases, but as this is one of two functioning theatres on-island, it's much appreciated. This art deco theatre is also a venue for the **Hawaii International Film Festival** (www.hiff.org).

Shopping

WEST KAUA'I CRAFT FAIR

Kaumuali'i Hwy (Hwy 50) at Waimea Canyon Dr (Hwy 550); 9am-4pm

Where else could you find fresh malasadas, local fruits and honey and the works of handfuls of artisans? Located just near the entrance of the Old Sugar Mill, this is where local farmers and craftsmen show off their work. Find Swarovski crystal, Limoges-inspired pill boxes, koa-wood bowls and humidors and Ni'ihau shell leis (see p220). Pick up a fresh pineapple for tomorrow's breakfast or munch on longan, starfruit, papaya, banana and lychee while perusing the craft tables.

AUNTY LILIKOI PASSION FRUIT PRODUCTS

866-545-4564; www.auntylilikoi.com; 9875 Waimea Rd; condiments per 10oz $5; 10am-5pm

In 2008 Aunty Lilikoi did it again, taking the gold medal in the Napa Valley International Mustard Competition for her *liliko'i*-wasabi mustard, making it clear that if it's a product with *liliko'i*, Aunty's got it down. Though there's no bakery on-site, her true specialty is arguably her sauces over her famous *liliko'i* chiffon pie – which says a lot. Try the passion-fruit syrup (great for banana pancakes), passion-fruit massage oil (great for honeymooners) and the tasty passion-fruit chap stick (great for after surfing).

Sleeping

KAUAI ROCK CABIN
Cottage $

822-7944, 338-9015; www.a1vacations.com/kauaiwaimearockcabin/1; Menehune Rd; cabin per day/week $50/300, cleaning fee $50

Simple, clean and much like a cabin getaway, this is a studio ideal for one person or a couple. Set in a forest atmosphere, it's got the simple amenities of home, including an umbrella patio set perfect for a lazy afternoon lunch, a king-sized bed, a kitchenette, satellite TV and a phone. About 1.5 miles northeast of town, it's perfect for those wanting to frequent Waimea Canyon during their stay.

COCO'S KAUAI B&B
B&B $$

our pick Map p187; 338-0722; www.cocoskauai.com; r $110, incl breakfast $125;

Stay off the grid at this fabulous little farm, operating on hydroelectric power. The room includes a king-sized bed, its own hot tub, a kitchenette, air conditioning, a BBQ and private garden. In-house treats include samplings of their sugar (perfect for morning coffee) and buttery Malie lotions. Guests can pick local fruits. There is a minimum two-night stay and an additional room ($60) for bigger groups. Owned by one of the Robinsons, owners of Ni'ihau and the Gay & Robinson sugar plantation, bookings for here are recommended two to three months in advance.

INN WAIMEA
Cottage $$

338-0031; www.innwaimea.com; 4469 Halepule Rd; cottages $150/; r from $110;

The cottages and suites here offer a good design mix of plantation roots meets contemporary style. While the two-bedroom cottage (three-night minimum) offers more bang for your buck, the themed rooms (two-night minimum) have standards like coffee makers and a small fridge. The Banana Suite offers unique embellishments, including an iron screen, hot tub and hand-crafted wooden wardrobe, and the Taro Suite has wheelchair access and is ADA-certified.

DETOUR →

YUMI'S RESTAURANT

If you want a dash of charm, ambience and home cooking on the Westside, **Yumi's Restaurant** (338-1731; 9691 Kaumuali'i Hwy; 6am-2:30pm Mon-Fri, 8am-1pm Sat) is located in the art deco Waimea Theatre storefront, to the right of the box office. The spot serves as a relocation of a locally revered Waimea restaurant that, despite being under new ownership, has kept its tasty recipes, including mouth-watering burgers and apple turnovers.

MONOLITHIC DOME B&B B&B $$
651-7009; r $129, $75 cleaning fee $75;
It's all about the novelty, baby. The charming owner made this structure herself, and is understandably proud. It's airy, roomy and randomly intriguing. Upside-down U-shaped – envision a two-story, half-submerged donut. Located near the Menehune Ditch, roughly 2 miles behind Big Save on the *mauka* side of the road, it's got all the modern conveniences you wouldn't associate with a monolithic dome. The bathroom has fresco-painted walls, the queen bed memory foam and high-thread-count sheets, and there's wi-fi throughout. Call for reservations; no drive-bys.

WEST KAUA'I VACATION HOUSE Vacation Rental $$
346-5890; westkauaihouse.com; 2-br apt $135, cleaning fee $50;
Conveniently located on the *mauka* side of the road near the Waimea Big Save, it's a no-frills, clean and homey spot ideal for the thrifty traveler looking for a nice dose of local. Fully furnished and air-conditioned, this getaway does share a wall (it's a duplex). It also has a full kitchen and washer/dryer, as well as a charcoal grill. With two bedrooms and one bathroom, it can sleep up to six people (with a three-night minimum).

WEST INN Inn $$
338-1107, 866-937-8466; www.thewestinn.com; 9686 Kaumuali'i Hwy; r $139;
Likening it to a 'Best Western' is probably the best way to draw a picture of this average, clean, two-story motel-like spot across the street from the Waimea Theatre. Choose either a king or a double bed. Though they boast wi-fi, you must have your own network card. For the price, there are better options elsewhere.

WAIMEA PLANTATION COTTAGES Cottage $$$$
our pick 338-1625, 800-992-7866; www.waimea-plantation.com; 9400 Kaumuali'i Hwy; 1-/2-/3-bedroom cottages from $220/275/325;
These cottages are expensive, no doubt, but charming. The decor offers saliently Westside features, hailing from the tradition of plantation styles while featuring upmarket and modern Hawaiiana-inspired embellishments and several Occidental accoutrements some may not want to live without. The fact that it's a stone's toss from Waimea Brewing Company could be a plus or minus, depending on your lifestyle: it's a convenience for barflies, but for those with young children, it could result in some noise pollution.

KEKAHA

pop 3175

Though there's no town center in Kekaha, the lifeguarded Kekaha Beach Park offers one of the most beautiful sunsets anywhere on-island.

If you're looking for a town with a nearby scenic beach that's located near the base of Waimea Canyon, Kekaha might be the ideal spot to call home during your stay. It is, however, off-the-beaten track and too remote for some. Kekaha houses many military families and is also home to its own eponymous beach park.

Orientation

Kaumuali'i Hwy borders the coastline while Kekaha Rd (Hwy 50), the main drag, lies parallel and a few blocks inland. All you'll find in town are a post office and a couple of stores. On its eastern end, Kekaha Rd and Kaumuali'i Hwy meet near the Kikiaola Small Boat Harbor, a state harbor with a launch ramp.

Beaches

KEKAHA BEACH PARK

The Westside is known for its unrelenting sun and some of the vastest beaches, and Kekaha Beach Park is no exception. Just west of Kekaha town, this long beach is ideal for running, walking or beach combing. Before jumping in, find a lifeguard station and make sure it's OK to go in. Kekaha Beach Park's ocean lacks the reef protection other beaches provide. When the surf is high, currents are extremely dangerous. However, under the right conditions, it can be good for surfing and bodyboarding.

Keep your eyes peeled on the horizon for Ni'ihau island and its offshore islet,

The surf off Kekaha Beach Park, with Ni'ihau visible in the distance ANN CECIL

Lehua. The beach also has one shower just inland from the highway between Alae and Amakihi Rds; rest rooms and picnic tables are nearby.

Sleeping

For more lodging listings, see **Kekaha Oceanside** (www.kekahaoceansidekauai.com).

MINDY'S Vacation Rental $

Map p187; ☎ 337-9275; 8842 Kekaha Rd; s/d $75/85;

Adorable, clean and featuring its own private deck – Mindy's is a steal for the price. A second-story apartment with a full bed, wi-fi and kitchen feels large and open. Though there's no air-conditioning, it's got ceiling fans throughout. Price includes fruit and coffee in the morning.

BOATHOUSE Vacation Rental $

Map p187; ☎ 332-9744; www.seakauai.com; 4518-A Nene St; r $85

Within walking distance of Kekaha Beach, the Boathouse is much like staying in the guesthouse of your favorite (and clean) neighbors. Though a studio, it feels spacious and has its own covered lanai, kitchenette, king-sized bed and TV. Ideal for one person or a couple. Washer/dryer on site.

HALE PUKA 'ANA B&B $$$

Map p187; ☎ 652-6852; www.kekahakauaisunset.com; 8240A Elepaio Rd; suite incl breakfast $139-229;

The long stretch of Kekaha Beach makes for a lovely, reclusive view from this B&B. It's rather pricey, but if you'd rather splurge on the coziness of a B&B than a resort, perhaps this is the one. The high-end Ali'i Suite ($229) has ocean views, a private lanai and cherry wood and bamboo-inspired fixtures; the Hoku Suite ($199) also has ocean views, but is smaller; and the Ku'uipo Suite ($169 to $229) is ground floor. Breakfasts range from healthy (fresh fruit) to guilty pleasure (bacon-and-egg croissant).

BARKING SANDS

Between Kekaha Beach Park and Polihale State Park, the beach stretches for approximately 15 miles. However, ever since the September 11, 2001 terrorist attacks, consistent public access has waned, as it is home to the US Navy base at **Barking Sands Pacific Missile Range Facility** (PMRF; general information

☎ 335-4229, beach access ☎ 335-4111). The missile range facility at Barking Sands provides the aboveground link to a sophisticated sonar network that tracks more than 1000 sq miles of the Pacific. Established during WWII, it's been developed into the world's largest underwater listening device.

POLIHALE STATE PARK

Vast and inspired, Polihale is everything you'd imagine the scenic Pacific to be. The water is crystal-blue, the sand is sugar-white, the beach seems eternal. It is also the *leina* of Kaua'i – the jumping-off point for spirits, where the setting sun leaves a trail for them to follow on the rippling water.

Back on the earthly plane, a rugged access road and inconsistent weather have made this state park somewhat of a headache for the Department of Land and Natural Resources, which closed off the beach for several months in 2008 and prohibited camping after flooding created potential health risks.

There aren't any car-rental vendors who offer insurance for visitors to drive the 5-mile-long dirt road that accesses the park from Mana village, off Kaumuali'i Highway, another snag in the debate over universal access rights to this surfing haven. Locals threatened to protest when a gate was put up to keep visitors out last year, claiming they know the area better than nonresidents and should therefore be allowed access.

Though camping is at times allowed with a permit, whether you decide to drive for a daytrip or more, note that entryway and toilet and shower facilities access is inconsistent – and finding a ride back on this desolate stretch of road should your rental car break down is by no means a sure thing.

WAIMEA CANYON STATE PARK

Gaping, abysmal chasms, dramatic skyscapes and gushing waterfalls make little else compare to Waimea Canyon State Park. Waimea River, Kaua'i's longest, is fed by three eastern tributary canyons – Waip'o, Po'omau and Koa'ie – which bring reddish-brown waters from the mountaintop bog, Alaka'i Swamp. After a good rain, waterfalls gush. Sunny days following rain are ideal for prime views, though hiking can be treacherously muddy.

Waimea Canyon boasts 45 miles of trails that range from delving deep into the rain forest or merely skimming the perimeter, with views that can cause a vertiginous reaction in even the most avid mountain-sport enthusiasts. Trekking around Wai-

Taking in the vistas of Waimea Canyon State Park

JOHN ELK III

THE MARK TWAIN MYTH

It's common knowledge that Mark Twain coined the 'Grand Canyon of the Pacific' moniker, isn't it? Well, while Twain indeed had a way with words, these aren't his.

In their excellent book, *Kaua'i's Geologic History: A Simplified Guide*, Chuck Blay and Robert Siemers debunk this myth. Twain did spend time on the Hawaiian Islands in 1866, writing his oft-quoted letters compiled in *Mark Twain's Letters from Hawaii*. But he apparently never visited the island of Kaua'i nor saw Waimea Canyon, as his writings mention neither.

Further, extensive research by the Bishop Museum in Honolulu discovered that renowned geologist John Wesley Powell began exploring the Colorado River wonder in 1867, ultimately publishing his findings in 1875 – and he never once referred to a 'Grand Canyon.' Only in 1908 did US President Theodore Roosevelt establish the 'Grand Canyon' as a national monument. So, unless Mark Twain also invented the name of the Grand Canyon itself (before it was even on the map), he could not have made the comparison back in 1866. Twain died in 1910.

mea Canyon offers a rare view of the island, housing an abundance of endemic species of wildlife and plants. This includes the largest population of Kaua'i's native fern, the fragrant *laua'e,* alluded to in many of the island's chants and traditions. Also here you might see some of Kaua'i's rare and endangered native forest birds.

Waimea Canyon was formed when Kaua'i's original shield volcano, Wai'ale'ale, slumped along an ancient fault line, creating a sharp, east-facing line of cliffs. Then another shield volcano, Lihu'e, developed the island's east side, producing new lava flows that ponded against the cliffs. Thus the western canyon walls are taller, thinner and more eroded – a contrast that's most theatrically apparent while hiking along the canyon floor. The black and red horizontal striations along the canyon walls represent successive volcanic eruptions; the red color indicates that water seeped through the rocks, creating rust from the iron inside.

Orientation

The southern boundary of Waimea Canyon State Park is about 7 miles up the road from Waimea. You can reach the park by two roads: Waimea Canyon Dr (Hwy 550) starts in Waimea just beyond the 23-mile marker at the Waimea Tech Center, while Koke'e Rd (Hwy 552) starts in Kekaha off Mana Rd. They merge between the 6- and 7-mile markers.

State officials generally prefer visitors to use Waimea Canyon Dr, which is 19 miles long. Either road gets you to Waimea and Kalalau lookouts. Waimea Canyon Dr goes along the canyon. Koke'e Rd is shorter by 3 miles and also offers scenic views, but not of the canyon.

Dangers & Annoyances

Rain creates hazardous conditions in the canyon. Off-road trails can seem a worthwhile risk when dry but become too slick in the rain. The red-dirt trails also quickly become mucky, and river fords rise to impassable levels. Try hiking poles or a sturdy walking stick to ease the steep descent into the canyon.

Note the time of sunset and plan to return well before it's dark. Be aware that daylight will fade inside the canyon long before sunset.

Take enough water for your entire trip, especially the uphill return journey. Any water along the trails would have to be treated.

Cell phones do not work here. If possible, hike with a companion or at least tell someone your expected return time.

Do not forge a new trail or use what appears to be a newly created one. Keep hiking here sustainable and opt for the main trodden path only – even if it seems less challenging.

For more on hiking safely and responsibly, see p42 and the boxed text, p42.

Sights

Along Waimea Canyon Dr, you can see naturally growing examples of native trees, including koa and ohia, as well as invasive

Waipo'o Falls, Waimea Canyon LEE FOSTER

species, such as kiawe. The valuable hardwood koa proliferates at the hunters' check station along the way. Look for the trees with narrow, crescent-shaped leaves.

SCENIC LOOKOUTS

WAIMEA CANYON LOOKOUT

Located at 0.3 miles north of the 10-mile marker, at an elevation of 3400ft. Keep your eyes peeled for the canyon running in an easterly direction off Waimea, which is Koai'e Canyon. That area is accessible to backcountry hikers.

WAIPO'O FALLS

The 800ft waterscape can be seen from a couple of small, unmarked lookouts before the 12-mile marker and then from a lookout opposite the picnic area shortly before the 13-mile marker. The picnic area includes BBQ pits, rest rooms, drinking water, a pay phone and Camp Hale Koa, a Seventh Day Adventist camp.

PU'U HINAHINA LOOKOUT

At 3640ft, there are two lookouts near the parking lot at a marked turnoff between the 13- and 14-mile markers. Although you can't see the lookout from the parking lot, in a few short steps it gives you the illusion of being in the forest overlooking the canyon floor. Overlooking the back of Waimea Canyon, this lookout is also a decent vantage point for the valley floor, with panoramic views to the ocean.

Activities

HIKING

For serious hikers, there are trails that lead deep into Waimea Canyon. During weekends and holidays, pig and deer hunters use these trails.

The Kukui and Koai'e Canyon Trails, two of the steepest on Kaua'i, connect at Wiliwili Camp, 2000ft into the canyon. If the entire trek sounds too strenuous, hike just 1 mile down the Kukui Trail, as you'll reach a bench with an astounding view.

The hiking mileage given for each trail following is for one way only.

ILIAU NATURE LOOP

The 10-minute Iliau Nature Loop makes for a good leg-stretching exercise for those itching to get out of the car but who are ill-equipped to make a big trek. The marked trailhead comes up shortly before the 9-mile marker. Be sure to pass the bench to the left and walk about 3 minutes for a top-notch vista into Waimea Canyon.

The trail is named for the *iliau,* a plant endemic to Kaua'i's Westside; it grows along the trail and produces stalks up to 10ft high. Like the silversword (found only on Maui), *iliau* grows to a ripe old age, then for a grand finale it bursts into blossom and dies.

KUKUI TRAIL

Don't let the fact that it's 2.5 miles in fool you. The climb back out of the valley can be harrowing – definitely for seriously fit and agile hikers only.

The narrow switchback trail covers 2000ft and doesn't offer much in the way of sweeping views, though there's a river at the canyon floor. Keep your eyes peeled for a small sign directing hikers to turn left and hike the steep slope down, with the hill at your back. When you hear the sound of water, you're closing in on the picnic shelter and Wiliwili Camp area, where overnight camping is allowed, but mostly it's hunters who stay.

Expect a steep descent to the bottom of the canyon and intense climb back out afterward. Depending on weather, the sun can be unrelenting but the rain can bring flash flooding (truly seeming immediate) at the river. Don't wander off the trail into the forest area as it could lead you astray. Also remember to pack enough supplies (water, sunscreen, insect repellent).

To get to the trail, find the Iliau Nature Loop trailhead just before the 9-mile marker.

KOAI‘E CANYON TRAIL

Traversing rougly 0.5 miles up the canyon along the Waimea Canyon Trail, you will intersect the Koai‘e Canyon Trail, a moderate trail that takes you down the south side of the canyon to some swimming holes – which should be avoided after rains, because of incredibly quickly rising waters and hazardous flash floods. The trail offers three camps. After the first, Kaluaha‘ulu Camp, stay on the eastern bank of the river – do not cross it. Later you'll come upon the trailhead for the Koai‘e Canyon Trail (marked by a Na Ala Hele sign). Watch for greenery and soil that conceals dropoffs alongside the path. Next up is Hipalau Camp. Following this, the trail is hard to find. Keep heading north. Do not veer toward the river, but continue ascending at approximately the same point midway between the canyon walls and the river.

Growing steeper, the trail then enters Koai‘e Canyon, recognizable by the redrock walls rising to the left. The last camp is

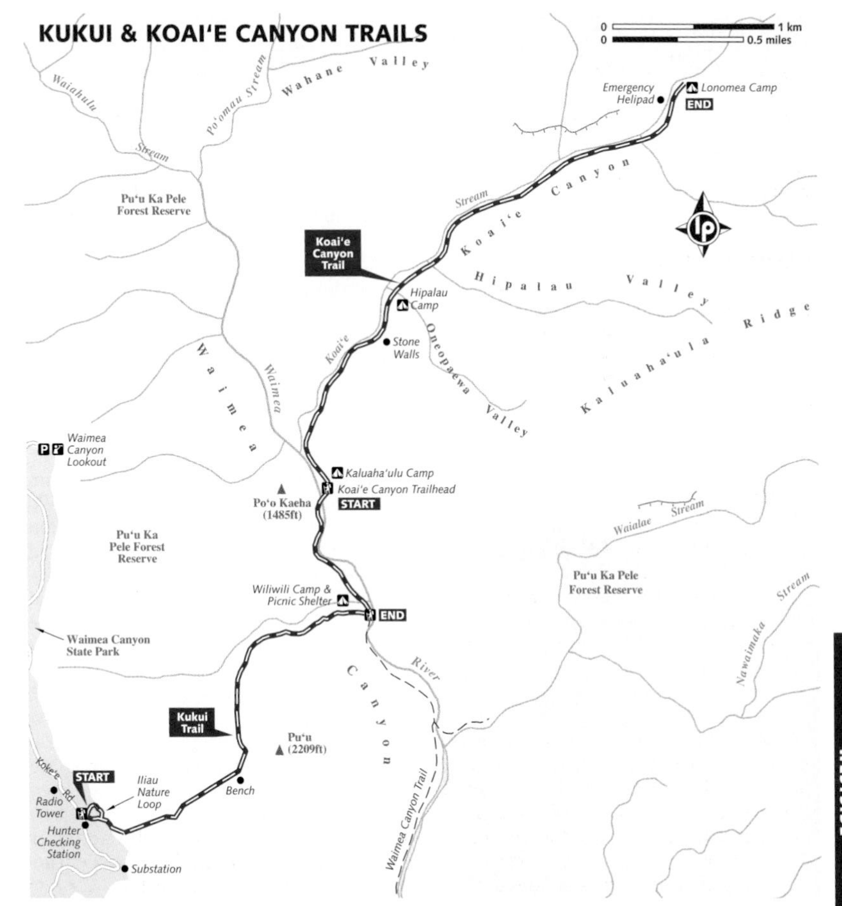

Hikers descending the Waimea Canyon Trail MICAH WRIGHT

Lonomea. Find the best views at the emergency helipad, a grassy area perfect for picnicking. When ready, retrace your steps.

WAIMEA CANYON TRAIL

A difficult, third trail in this area is the 11.5-mile Waimea Canyon Trail, which fords Waimea River. It starts at the bottom of Waimea Canyon at the end of Kukui Trail and leads out to Waimea town. An entry permit is required at the self-service box at the Kukui Trail register.

Top Picks

WESTSIDE WAYFARING

- **Downhill bike ride through Waimea Canyon** (right)
- **Poetically scenic, reasonably short but dramatic Canyon Trail hike to Waipo'o Falls** (p214)
- **Friday Night Art Walk in sleepy Hanapepe town** (p193)
- **Caffeine-enhanced morning stroll at the Kaua'i Coffee Company** (p186)
- **Eleven-mile Nu'alolo rim and 'Awa'awapuhi Trail** (p215) **loop hike at Koke'e State Park**

You might see locals carrying inner tubes for exiting via the river rather than via the return hike.

CYCLING

Coast downhill for 13 miles with **Outfitters Kauai** (☎ 742-9667, 888-742-9887; www.outfitterskauai.com; Po'ipu Plaza, 2827-A Po'ipu Rd, Po'ipu; tour adult/child 12-14 $94/75; check-in 6am & 2:30pm) – there's no technical ability required, as it's on the road, not along some bumpy trail. You'll start at a small dirt pullout past Waimea Canyon Lookout (elevation 3500ft).

The canyon is a mountain biker's dream as mountain bikes are allowed on all 4WD hunting-area roads off of Waimea Canyon Dr. Even when the yellow gates are closed on nonhunting days, it's all fair game – except for Papa'alai Rd, which is managed by the Department of Hawaiian Home Lands and is open for hunting, but not for recreational use.

Sleeping

All four camps on the canyon trails are part of the forest-reserve system. They have open-air picnic shelters and pit toilets, but no other facilities; all freshwater must be treated before drinking. See (p259) for camping permit information.

KOKE'E STATE PARK

The expansive Koke'e (ko-*keh*-eh) State Park is a playground for those who revere the environment. It's home to inspirational views and some of the island's most precious ecosystems. You'll also enjoy some reprieve from the sun, and the microclimates will have you paying attention to the shifts in ambient air.

In ancient times, birdcatchers were the only residents who lived in Koke'e, but the area's resources were important to Hawaiians for forestry, hunting and plant-gathering for leis and medicinal herbs.

An extraordinarily steep trail once ran down the cliffs from Koke'e to Kalalau Valley on the Na Pali Coast – which took the life of at least one Western trekker. Though one of its locally revered charms is its choppy, almost impossible 4WD roads, the state has been working to pave much of Koke'e. Opponents of this have argued it would rob Koke'e of its reclusively rugged character. Another large, potential moneymaker (of equal controversial status) is the state's plans to further modernize Koke'e by adding a helicopter launching pad, which would in turn drive more air-tourism revenues.

Orientation & Information

This park's southern boundary starts beyond the Pu'u Hinahina Lookout. After the 15-mile marker, you'll pass a brief stretch of park cabins, a restaurant, a museum and a campground. Remember, the nearest place for provisions and gas is Waimea, 15 miles away.

The Koke'e Museum provides basic information on trail conditions; you can also call them for real-time **mountain weather reports** (☎ 335-9975).

Dangers & Annoyances

All of the suggestions listed for Waimea Canyon State Park (p207) apply. Further, the higher elevation produces a cooler and wetter climate, so take appropriate attire.

Sights

KOKE'E NATURAL HISTORY MUSEUM

☎ 335-9975; www.kokee.org; entry by donation $1; 🕑 10am-4pm

The Koke'e Natural History Museum showcases detailed topographical maps and local historical photographs. They also have diagrams, botanical sketches of

Kalalau Valley and the Na Pali Coast as seen from Koke'e State Park

ANN CECIL

WESTSIDE

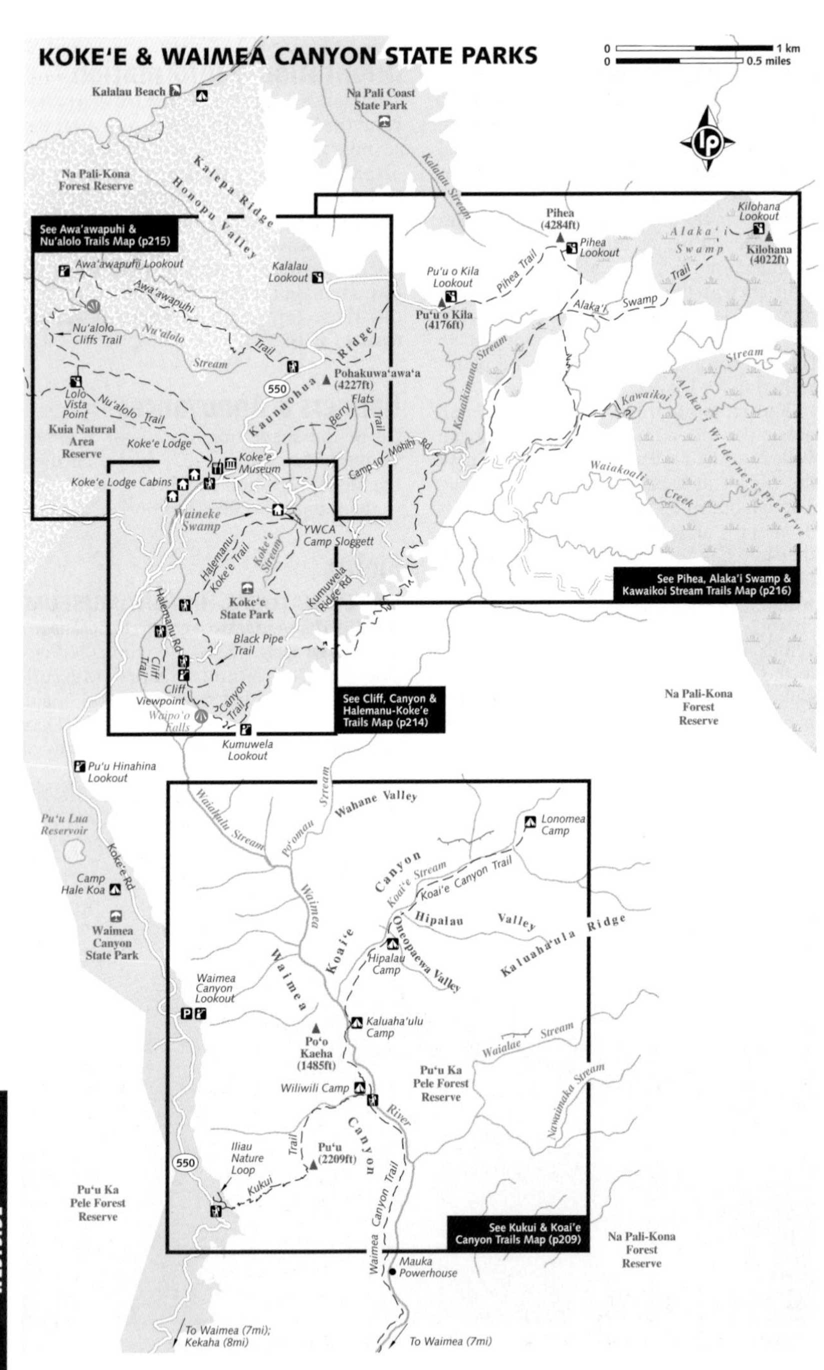
KOKE'E & WAIMEA CANYON STATE PARKS
0 1 km
0 0.5 miles
Kalalau Beach
Na Pali Coast State Park
Na Pali-Kona Forest Reserve
Kalepa Ridge
Honopu Valley
Kalalau Stream
See Awa'awapuhi & Nu'alolo Trails Map (p215)
Awa'awapuhi Lookout
Awa'awapuhi Trail
Nu'alolo Cliffs Trail
Nu'alolo Stream
Lolo Vista Point
Nu'alolo Trail
Kuia Natural Area Reserve
Koke'e Lodge
Koke'e Museum
Koke'e Lodge Cabins
Kalalau Lookout
Kaunuohua Ridge
Pohakuwa'awa'a (4227ft)
550
Berry Flats Trail
Camp 10-Mohihi Rd
Pihea (4284ft)
Pihea Lookout
Pihea Trail
Pu'u o Kila Lookout
Pu'u o Kila (4176ft)
Kilohana Lookout
Kilohana (4022ft)
Alaka'i Swamp Trail
Kauaikinana Stream
Kawaikoi Stream
Alaka'i Wilderness Preserve
Waiakoali Creek
See Pihea, Alaka'i Swamp & Kawaikoi Stream Trails Map (p216)
Waineke Swamp
YWCA Camp Sloggett
Halemanu-Koke'e Trail
Koke'e Stream
Koke'e State Park
Kumuwela Ridge Rd
Halemanu Rd
Black Pipe Trail
Cliff Trail
Cliff Viewpoint
Canyon Trail
Waipo'o Falls
See Cliff, Canyon & Halemanu-Koke'e Trails Map (p214)
Kumuwela Lookout
Na Pali-Kona Forest Reserve
Pu'u Hinahina Lookout
Pu'u Lua Reservoir
Koke'e Rd
Camp Hale Koa
Waimea Canyon State Park
Waimea Canyon Lookout
Waiahulu Stream
Po'omau Stream
Wahane Valley
Waimea
Koai'e Canyon
Koai'e Stream
Koai'e Canyon Trail
Lonomea Camp
Hipalau Valley
Kaluaha'ula Ridge
Oneopaewa Valley
Hipalau Camp
Kaluaha'ulu Camp
Po'o Kaeha (1485ft)
Wiliwili Camp
Waialae Stream
Nawaimaka Stream
Pu'u Ka Pele Forest Reserve
Waimea River
Waimea Canyon
Kukui Trail
Pu'u (2209ft)
Iliau Nature Loop
Waimea Canyon Trail
See Kukui & Koai'e Canyon Trails Map (p209)
Na Pali-Kona Forest Reserve
Mauka Powerhouse
To Waimea (7mi); Kekaha (8mi)
To Waimea (7mi)

native plants and taxidermic representations of some native and invasive wildlife found in Koke'e. There's also a tribute to the late photographer and educator David Boynton, who died in 2007 as he was hiking along a cliff trail to one of his most cherished spots on the Na Pali coastline. Boynton was also a guidebook contributor for Lonely Planet.

The museum has a brochure for the short **nature trail** out back. It offers interpretive information corresponding to the trail's numbered plants and trees, including many native species. During summer weekends, trained volunteers lead **Wonder Walks** (June to September, nominal donation), guided hikes on various trails at Waimea Canyon and Koke'e State Parks. Ask about schedules and reservations.

You'll probably notice in front an array of chickens who have polluted the pristine Koke'e mornings with noise over the past decade; please don't feed them.

KALALAU LOOKOUT

Look for the 18-mile marker, where the ethereal, 4000ft Kalalau Lookout stands up to the ocean, sun and winds with brave, severe beauty. Hope for a clear day for ideal views of Kalalau Valley, but know that even a rainy day can make for some settling clouds that could later disappear – followed by powerful waterfalls and, of course, rainbows.

Though it might be hard to imagine as the terrain is so extreme, as late as the 1920s Kalalau Valley was home to many residents, who farmed rice there. The only way into the valley nowadays is along the coastal Kalalau Trail (see p152) or by kayak (p137).

The paved road continues another mile to **Pu'u o Kila Lookout**, where it dead-ends at a parking lot. This road faces periodic closings. The views of the valley are similar to those of Kalalau Lookout, but it does also serve as the trailhead for the **Pihea Trail** (p215).

Activities

HIKING

Generally speaking, Koke'e is unspoiled. Its sheer size might make it a bit challenging to nail down where you want to start. Know that if you want to avoid hunters (and their dogs) it's best to opt for trails such as **Alaka'i Swamp** or the **Cliff Trail** to **Waipo'o Falls**. While these trails might have some other hikers on them, they're still relatively remote.

A family enjoys a view of the Kalalau Valley from the Pihea Trail ANN CECIL

View from the Awa'awapuhi Trail KARL LEHMANN

The starting point for several scenic hikes, Halemanu Rd is just north of the 14-mile marker on Koke'e Rd. Whether or not the road is passable in a non-4WD vehicle depends on recent rainfall. Note that many rental-car agreements are null and voil off-roading.

CLIFF & CANYON TRAILS

To get to the trailhead, walk down Halemanu Rd for just over 0.5 miles. Keeping Halemanu Stream to your left, ignore a hunting trail-of-use on the right. Then turn right onto the footpath leading to both the Cliff and Canyon Trails.

At this junction, the **Cliff Trail** (0.1 miles) veers right and wanders for less than 0.25 miles uphill to the **Cliff Viewpoint**. This trail is a perfect intro to the canyon's vast views. Short, it's a relatively easy walk for the rewarding Waimea Canyon views it offers.

our pick **Canyon Trail** (1.8 miles) descends a semisteep forest trail, a grove and a dirt luge-like tunnel, which opens up to a vast, red-dirt promontory with cliffs to one side and charming log-steps to guide you further. Shortly thereafter it takes some steep finagling to get to **Waipo'o Falls.** If it's getting too much, you can always turn back around here. Otherwise, after hopping boulders across the stream, follow the trail to Kumuwela Ridge at the canyon rim. The trail ends at **Kumuwela Lookout**, where you can rest at a picnic table before backtracking to Halemanu Rd. Note: avoid holding onto any foliage for stability.

BLACK PIPE TRAIL

For an alternate return from the Canyon Trail you can make a right at the signed intersection of Black Pipe Trail and the Canyon Trail at the top of the switchback where you leave the canyon rim. The trail ends at the 4WD Halemanu Rd where you walk back to the CanyonTrailhead.

HALEMANU-KOKE'E TRAIL

Another trail off Halemanu Rd, which starts further down the road than the Cliff and Canyon Trails is **Halemanu-Koke'e Trail** (1.25 miles). An easy recreational nature trail, it passes through a native forest of koa and ohia trees, which provide a habitat for native birds. One of the common plants found on this trail is banana *poka,* a member of the passion-fruit family and a serious invasive pest. It has pretty pink flowers, but it drapes the forest with its vines and chokes out less-aggressive native plants. The trail ends near YWCA Camp Sloggett, about 0.5 miles from Koke'e Lodge.

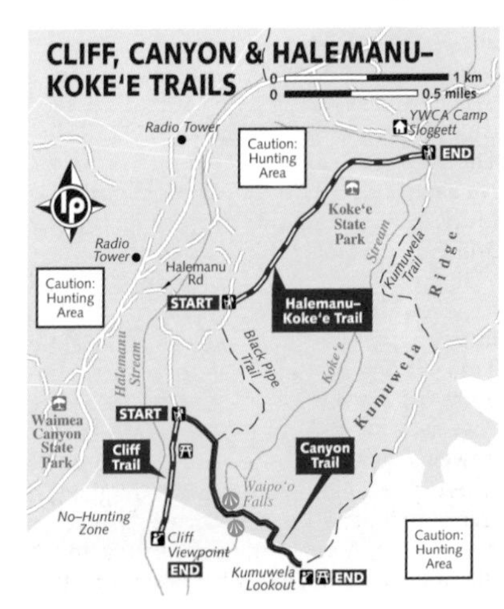

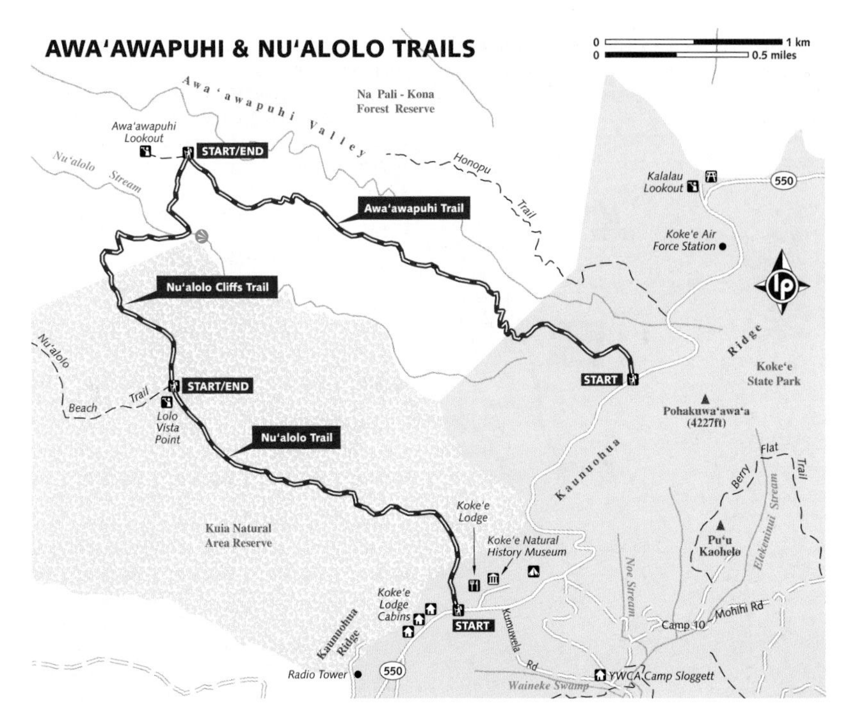

AWA'AWAPUHI & NU'ALOLO TRAILS

our pick Perhaps among the best of the best, the Awa'awapuhi Trail (3.25 miles) and the more challenging Nu'alolo Trail (3.75 miles) offer some of the best of Koke'e. You'll trek along straight 2000ft cliffs. Perhaps nothing is more exhilarating (and vertigo-inducing) than where the trails connect – the **Nu'alolo Cliffs Trail** (2 miles), which has points where it seems you are more of a rock climber or makeshift acrobat than a hiker. The Nu'alolo Cliffs Trail connects to the Nu'alolo Trail near the 3.25-mile mark and to the Awa'awapuhi Trail just short of the 3-mile mark.

If you're undecided as to which trail to take, note that Awa'awapuhi Trail is much less technical and the Nu'alolo Trail is steeper, though arguably each require the same amount of endurance. The Awa'awapui trail does have more traffic, however, and there are some steep steps where you might find yourself hugging a tree. At the end of this trail you'll reach a breathtaking view of the cliffs below, much like the 'Cliffs of Insanity' featured in that Rob Reiner movie that any *Princess Bride* fan would appreciate.

To do this 11-mile hike as a loop, begin with the Nu'alolo Trail (you'll find the trailhead just south of the visitors center). Hike to the bottom of the ridge and look for a sign that says 'Nualolo Cliff Trail.' Follow that to the right, scaling rocks and cutting through tall, eye-level grass (it might feel like you're lost, but you're not), back up through several switchbacks up through a ridge until it intersects with the Awa'awapuhi Trail, which is another signed intersection. Make a right following the Awa'awapuhi Trailhead on Koke'e Rd. Turn right and walk along the side of Koke'e Rd back to Nu'alolo Trailhead for roughly three-quarters of a mile.

PIHEA TRAIL

Some call this easy, but it's all relative. The roughly 3-mile trek begins at **Pu'u o Kila Lookout**. A mere 1 mile in and you'll see the **Pihea Lookout**. Past the vista and a short scramble downhill the boardwalk begins. After another 1.5 miles you will come to

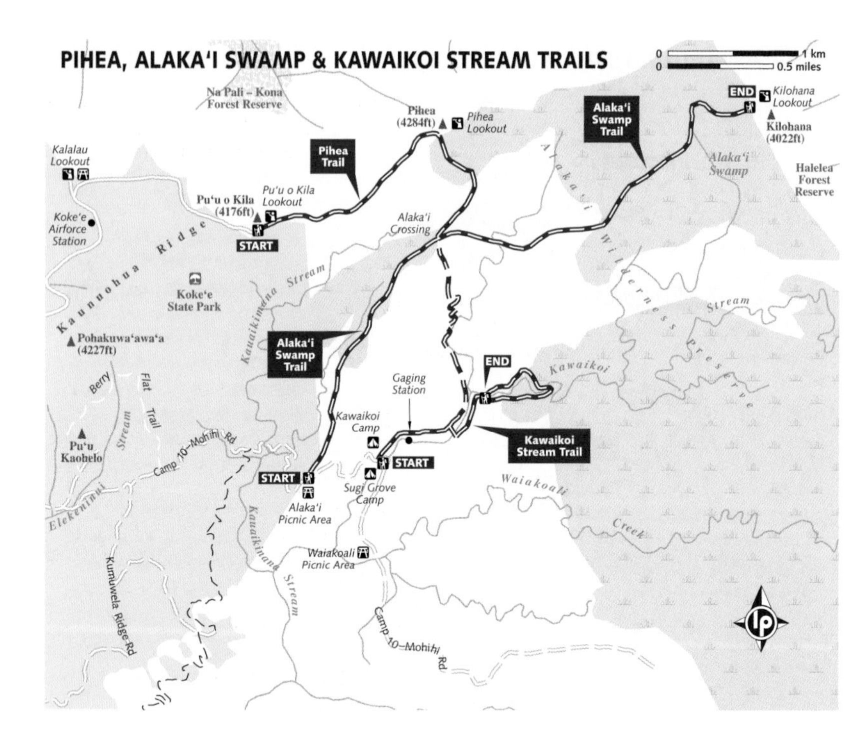

Alaka'i Crossing, intersecting with the **Alaka'i Swamp Trail** (below). A left at this crossing will put you on that trail to the **Kiolohana Lookout**. Continuing straight on the Pihea Trail will take to you the Kawaikoi campground along the Kawaikoi Stream. Most hikers start on the Pihea Trail because the trailhead is accessible by the paved road to Pu'u o Kila Lookout; however, sometimes this road is closed. For another trailhead, begin at the Alaka'i Swamp Trail starting point. The trails are well maintained, with mile markers and signs.

ALAKA'I SWAMP TRAIL

The **Alaka'i Swamp** trailhead begins on a ridge above Sugi Grove Camp on Camp 10-Mohihi Rd. While taking this trailhead covers less steep terrain than you'd find by beginning at the Pihea trailhead, you will need a 4WD to get here, as well as an ability to follow a map along an unmarked dirt road. Park at the clearing at the trailhead. The trail begins as a wide grassy path for roughly 0.5 miles, where the boardwalk begins. It continues through small bogs and intermittent forests until it reaches the **Alaka'i Crossing**, where it intersects the **Pihea Trail** (p215). Continue straight through the crossing and you'll see that the boardwalk becomes a series of steep steps to the **Kawikoi Stream**, and then a steep series of switchbacks up the other side. Beyond here, the boardwalk is relatively flat, continuing through the almost otherworldly terrain of the Hawaiian bogs, with knee-high trees and tiny, endemic carnivorous plants. The boardwalk ends at **Kilohana Lookout**, where, with a little luck, you'll see views of Wainiha Valley and even beyond to Hanalei Bay.

KAWAIKOI STREAM TRAIL

Head to Sugi Grove Camp by going down Camp 10 Rd (4WD only). Cross over the **Kawaikoi Stream** for this nice little nature walk, which follows the stream through the forest. The trail rises up on a bluff at the end of the stream and then loops around back down to a cold, dark swimming hole before returning you back to where you started.

On top of the world: Kalalau Valley JOHN ELK III

KALALAU LOOKOUT TO PU'U O KILA LOOKOUT

This mellow, 2-mile hike offers a pleasant walk along the closed road linking two lookouts. A two-lane strip of asphalt, currently closed to traffic, connects the park's premier viewpoints of the Kalalau Valley, and in early morning and late afternoon, as the fog is wafting overhead, it is a delightful birding walk. You won't see as many species as in the forest itself, but it's worth the amble.

Festivals & Events

Hula *halau* (troops) from all over Hawaii participate in the one-day **Eo e Emalani i Alaka'i** (☎ 335-9975; www.kokee.org/festivals; admission free; 🕒 10am), an outdoor dance festival at Koke'e Natural History Museum in early October, commemorating Queen Emma's 1871 journey to Alaka'i Swamp. The festival includes a royal procession, hula, music and crafts.

Eating & Sleeping

KOKE'E LODGE
Diner $

Map p212 & p215; ☎ 335-6061; snacks $3-7; 🕒 9am-3:30pm

Rustic but without the charm, this restaurant's strong point is mostly convenience.

THE OTHERWORLDLY ALAKA'I SWAMP

Thanks to its unique ecosystem, the Alaka'i Swamp was designated as a Wilderness Preserve in 1964 and is managed by the state. You'll see dwarf trees and mossy undergrowth amid a series of misty bogs. Here and there toppled trees show a massive network of roots, spreading horizontally as the hard-packed soil prevents them from penetrating more than a foot or so deep. The flora is subdued rather than flashy and includes many natives, from *ohia lehua* (a tree with orange-red flowers) to *mokihana* (a vinelike tree with green berries) to maile (a vine with aromatic leaves and bark).

In the swamp there are 10 times more native birds than introduced birds. (Elsewhere in Hawaii, introduced birds outnumber natives many times over.) Many of these species are endangered, some having fewer than 100 birds remaining. The Kaua'i *'o'o*, the last of four species of Hawaiian honeyeaters, was thought to be extinct until a nest with two chicks was discovered in Alaka'i Swamp in 1971. However, the call of the *'o'o* – that of a single male – was last heard in 1987.

You'll notice that the **Alaka'i Swamp Trail** (opposite) is virtually completely spanned with wood planks. It was not created to be 'nice' but rather because the trail was previously so muddy that hikers would often go off-trail to find stable footing. This created multiple trails in place of just one; hence hikers trampled more ground and caused more environmental harm. The Department of Land & Natural Resources, Forestry & Wildlife Division, started laying planks around 1989 to preserve the swamp. It was a time-consuming (and overly ambitious, according to some) process that got delayed when Hurricane 'Iniki hit in 1992. Today the project continues, with a plan to cover more of the Pihea Trail.

CAMPING IN KOKE'E STATE PARK

Even though it's Hawaii, don't be fooled: Koke'e campgrounds are at an elevation of almost 4000ft and the nights are cold. Take a sleeping bag, waterproof jacket, change of warm clothing, extra socks and hiking shoes instead of sneakers. See p259 for details on obtaining permits.

The most accessible camping area is the Koke'e State Park Campground, which is north of the meadow, just a few minutes' walk from **Koke'e Lodge** (p217). The campsites sit in a grassy area beside the woods (perfect for splaying out a blanket and taking a nap), and have picnic tables, drinking water, rest rooms and showers. Further off the main track, Kawaikoi and Sugi Grove campgrounds are about 4 miles east of Koke'e Lodge, off Camp 10-Mohihi Rd (4WD only) in the forest reserve adjacent to the state park. Each campground has pit toilets, picnic shelters and fire pits. There's no water source, so you'll need to bring your own or treat the stream water. These forest-reserve campgrounds have a three-night maximum stay.

The Kawaikoi campground sits on a well-maintained 3.5-acre grassy field, and it's recommended if you are camping in a large group (say, 10 or more). The Sugi Grove site is picturesque, under sugi trees, a fragrant softwood native to Japan that's commonly called a pine but is actually a cedar. This site is shaded, making it ideal during hot summer months. It is close to the Kawaikoi stream.

Still, convenience goes a long way all the way up in Koke'e, where you're a 30-minute drive away from any other dining options. Granola (of course, it's hiking country) and other breakfasts are served, along with soup and sandwiches.

KOKE'E LODGE CABINS — Cabin $

Map p212 & p215; ☎ 335-6061; PO Box 819, Waimea, HI 96796; cabin $50

Minimally maintained, the 12 cabins here are for folks seeking a remote, rustic, rather grimy experience – pretend you're reliving your dorm life (without a phone, TV or loud music). All cabins include a double and four twin beds, kitchen, shower, wood stove (your only heating source), linens and blankets.

YWCA CAMP SLOGGETT — Campground/Cabin $

Map p212 & p215; ☎ 245-5959; www.campingkauai.com; campsites per person $15, dm $25, 1-br cabin $85

Choose either a cabin or bunkhouse, or camp on the grass. The cabin has a king-sized bed, full kitchen, bathroom and woodburning fireplace. The bunker has a kitchenette, two bathrooms and a fire pit. You provide sleeping bags and towels. No reservations are needed to camp.

NI'IHAU

Relatively small in population when Captain Cook anchored off it January 29, 1778, there are fewer than 300 inhabitants on Ni'ihau today.

Ni'ihau, long dubbed by passing tour boats as the 'Forbidden Island,' is privately owned by the Robinson family (and part of the US). Its 'forbidden' mystique – caused by lack of access to the public – also has a fascinating backstory. Only Robinson family members and Native Hawaiian residents and their guests are allowed there, coupled with a few government employees.

The fact that the Robinson family has been able to keep Ni'ihau relatively isolated has helped allow a culture all its own to be preserved: Hawaiian is the primary spoken language, adding to its time-capsule quality, as is a religious temperance introduced by the Robinsons that's been in place now for roughly 146 years.

History

The culture of Ni'ihau and its people are inexorably linked to the Robinsons. Since their purchase of the majority of the island from King Kamehameha V in 1863, a purchase he is said to have approved of in part because of the anti-drinking practices of the Robinson family, the isolated Ni'ihau has remained the only majority Native-Hawaiian–speaking island in existence.

Deciding there was too much drinking in Scotland (and haggis and bagpipes, according to Keith Robinson, great-great-grandson of co-purchaser Eliza Sinclair), the family left between 1830 and 1850, heading to New Zealand, Tahiti and Vancouver in search of a homeland in keeping with their moral ideals. After first negotiating with King Kamehameha IV, they finally bought Ni'ihau from King Kamehameha V in 1864, for $10,000 in gold. The purchase began a new era of ranching on Ni'ihau: Sinclair brought the island's first sheep from New Zealand.

Keith and his brother Bruce Robinson are highly protective of Ni'ihau's isolation and its people. The family owns a significant amount of Kaua'i land and a sugar company (see p196).

Keith and Bruce Robinson are unpretentious outdoorsmen. Both are fluent in Native Hawaiian, just like any Ni'ihau resident. Bruce Robinson is married to a Ni'ihauan woman.

Thanks to its isolation since the purchase and quarantine during a 1950s outbreak of polio, the island has been able to avoid many diseases, including AIDS. To this day, residents' medical care needs are met either by the Robinsons' insurance or the US Department of Social Services.

Population & Lifestyle

Ni'ihau's population is mostly Native Hawaiian. The island's population has dropped from 600 in the 1980s to 160 in 2007 (the latest available data). Most residents live in Pu'uwai ('heart'), a settlement on the dry western coast. It's a simple life; water is collected in catchments, and the toilets are in outhouses. Residents hardly live 'without,' however. Though all residents are 'off the grid,' most have found ingenious ways to harness power, and several utilize hydro or wind sourcing, often backed up by gasoline generators. Cell phone signals reach some of the island, which also relies on a radio communication system.

Ni'ihau has a schoolhouse where teachers host classes from kindergarten to 12th grade. Courses are taught in Hawaiian until fourth grade. Students learn English as a second language.

Ni'ihau business and Sunday church services are conducted in Hawaiian. Throughout the islands, the Hawaiian language spoken by Ni'ihauans is known as the purest remaining, differing at times from the evolving language to come out of University of Hawaii–Hilo's College of Hawaiian Language, which has birthed words to define modern terms. Some have critiqued new UH-Hilo terms as sounding too similar to western languages. An example is the word *kamepiula* for computer; in an attempt to stay truer to non-westernized Hawaiian language, critics opt for using the two older Hawaiian words *lolo uila*, literally 'electrical mind.'

Geography & Environment

A mere 17 miles from Kaua'i, Ni'ihau is the smallest of the inhabited Hawaiian Islands: 18 miles long and 6 miles at the widest point, with a total land area of almost 70 sq miles and

45 miles of coast. Ni'ihau rainfall averages a scant 12in annually because the island is in Kaua'i's rain shadow. Its highest peak, Paniau, is only 1250ft tall and cannot generate trade wind–based precipitation.

Unique to the island are its shells: warm-hued and delicate sea jewels from the island are strung into exquisite and coveted leis costing from $125 to $25,000. In late 2004, Governor Linda Lingle signed a bill mandating that only items made of 100% Ni'ihau shells and crafted entirely in Hawaii can carry the Ni'ihau label. Residents of Ni'ihau make exquisite leis for sale at the **Ni'ihau Helicopters** office (below), which they use for bartering trips to and from Kaua'i.

Almost 50 endangered monk seals live on Ni'ihau, monitored by Bruce Robinson. Unfortunately, the draw of the pristine has threatened Ni'ihau. Its waters have suffered depletion by sport and commercial fishers who sail in to fish and pick *'opihi* (edible limpet) from the island's shorebreaks. The outside world also has threatened Ni'ihau fisherman and residents, who couldn't eat fish between January and March of 2009, after a dead baby humpback whale and thousands of fish were found washed up on a Ni'ihau shore. Though officials conducted necropsies, and despite speculation that the state's poisoning of neighboring Lehua island days earlier (to kill rabbits and rats that were eating endangered plants) was the reason, no cause has been determined.

Economy & Politics

The island economy has long depended on Ni'ihau Ranch, the sheep and cattle business owned by the Robinsons. But it was always a marginal operation on windy Ni'ihau, with droughts devastating herds. In 1999 Ni'ihau Ranch closed.

The family has been able to keep the island relatively undeveloped by allowing some temporary US government projects. Keith Robinson joked of the preference in allowing military projects on-island over development: 'The military comes and goes. After a military project is over, it usually gets rusted down to nothing.'

Allowing some tourist access is one of the prices to pay for owning a private island. Much of the tourist access the Robinsons allow is to help pay for services for Ni'ihauans, such as a recently purchased helicopter used for MEDEVAC services.

While it's difficult to find a comparative relationship to explain the dynamic between the Robinsons and Ni'ihauans, the Robinsons view themselves as protectors. And though that's the kind of paternalism that can rub outside Native Hawaiian groups the wrong way, for the most part Ni'ihauans don't seem to mind.

In fact, the common thread between the Robinsons and Ni'ihauans seems a steadfast allegiance from both sides. That carries over even on Kaua'i, as Ni'ihauans who've emigrated seem to stay in Robinson territory, on Kaua'i's Westside. Many who move to Kaua'i work for the Robinsons and live on their property, often in the Makaweli area. Kaua'i's only church conducted in Hawaiian also is on Kaua'i's Westside in Waimea, attended mostly by Ni'ihauans.

For the Ni'ihauans who don't make it to Kaua'i, samplings of Kaua'i are brought to them via barge roughly twice a month. Soda and poi (fermented taro paste) are among items brought over.

Politically, Ni'ihau falls under the jurisdiction of Kaua'i County. In 2004, George W Bush got 39 of 40 votes cast by Ni'ihauans. In 2008, Ni'ihau's precinct was one of only three of Hawaii's 538 precincts to vote for John McCain over President Barack Obama. McCain received 35 votes and Obama received four votes, despite Hawaii being Obama's strongest state in the nation.

Visiting Ni'ihau

Although outsiders are not allowed to visit Ni'ihau on their own, the Robinsons offer **helicopter tours** (Ni'ihau Helicopters; ☎ 877-441-3500; www.niihau.us; 12550A Kaumuali'i Hwy, Makaweli; half-day per person $365; office 8am-2pm Mon-Fri), which take off from Burns Field in Port Allen (p188). A half-day excursion includes lunch, snorkeling and swimming off the island's shores; bookings must be made well in advance. The Robinsons also offer **hunting safaris** as part of the island's conservation and wildlife management program (see the above website for more information).

KAUA'I FOR FAMILIES

With its phenomenal natural beauty and rural vibe, Kaua'i always appeals to honeymooners and adventurers. But it's also perfect for families, especially active, outdoorsy ones. Instead of visiting museums or shopping malls, kids can snorkel amid tropical fish, zipline in forest canopies or enjoy sandy beaches galore, with bodyboarding hot spots and shallow, toddler-sized lagoons. Add to their deeper appreciation of Kaua'i with a visit to historical attractions, from a replicated ancient Hawaiian village to a splendid plantation manor (complete with vintage train and horse-drawn carriages). And don't think a luau show is too hokey – the fire dancer will leave your kids spellbound!

PRACTICALITIES

The Basics

Not much can go wrong on Kaua'i. It's a tiny tropical island and part of the USA. Here, temperatures never drop below 65°F, driving distances are relatively short, and everyone speaks English! Still, proper planning will ease the burdens of traveling with kids. Depending on your kids' ages and interests, you can either tone down or ramp up your own itinerary. Obviously, you can't hike the steepest trails or go scuba diving if you're traveling with an infant, but you'll find equally enjoyable substitutes. You might even appreciate the change of pace. Lonely Planet's *Travel with Children* has lots of valuable tips and interesting anecdotes.

Set up a home base, or two on either side of the island, choosing accommodations based on your top priorities. Resorts such as the Grand Hyatt Kaua'i Resort & Spa (p178) and Kaua'i Marriott Resort (p77) can offer spectacular swimming pools and other such distractions. But parents might prefer the convenience and cost savings of a full kitchen and washer/dryer, which often come with condos and various vacation-rental cottages, beach houses and in-law apartments. Kids and babies are generally welcome except at some upscale B&Bs.

Note that hotel rates typically allow underage children to stay free with their parents and might even provide roll-away beds or cribs. Vacation-rental rates often apply only to doubles; kids above a certain age might count as extra guests and entail $10 to $25 each per night. Always ask about policies and bedding before booking.

Most car-rental companies (see p276) lease child-safety seats (cost per day $10 to $12, per week $50 to $60), but they're not always on hand; reserve in advance. Driving is easy but traffic can stymie your schedule and cause missed reservations. Leave early and avoid morning, evening and weekend midday rush hours.

Supplies, such as disposable diapers and infant formula, are sold islandwide, but try

Kid-pleaser Kamalani Playground at Lydgate Beach Park (p83) LUCI YAMAMOTO

AM I OLD ENOUGH?

- **To Go Ziplining** Minimum age ranges from seven to 12, depending on the company. But participants must also meet weight minimums that can range from 70lb to 100lb.
- **To Kayak the Wailua River** Most tours have no minimum age restrictions, but ask yourself whether your child is ready for the 30- to 45-minute hike to Uluwehi Falls. Babies sit either on a parent's lap or in a special seat, but you'll need a backpack carrier for the hike. More feasible might be kayaking tours of the Hanalei River.
- **To Hike the Kalalau Trail** While the entire trek would daunt most adults, the first leg to Hanakapi'ai Beach (or even just a mile in) is now a popular family activity. Gauge whether your kid can scramble over rocks and roots before attempting this hike, although you can always turn back when they've had enough.
- **To Take a Snorkel Cruise to Na Pali** Depending on the outfit and type of boat (catamaran, raft), tours might set minimum ages set from five to eight. Larger boats might allow tots as young as two to ride along. Consider whether your child can handle four to six hours at sea.
- **To Operate a Moped** You must have a driver's license to operate a moped, which means, for example, that Hawaiian teens must be 16. Rental companies also require that those under 18 are accompanied by a parent who also rents a moped.
- **To Ride a Helicopter** Most tour companies set minimum ages (eg two to five) and some also set minimum body weights (eg 35lb). Toddlers must be strapped into their own seat and pay the full fare. We recommend waiting till your kid can actually appreciate the flight before taking them along.
- **To Take a Surfing Lesson** Most instructors don't set an age minimum. Kids who are part fish (and can swim comfortably in the ocean) are fine candidates for lessons.

shopping in Lihu'e and on the East Side for the best selection and prices. Facilities for diaper-changing and breastfeeding are scarce; chances are you'll need to improvise in the back seat. Be discreet.

Licensed daycare is offered by two agencies on Kaua'i. Both have good reputations, but leaving your children with strangers is always dicey. **Babysitters of Kaua'i** (☎ 632-2252; www.babysittersofkauai.com; up to 2 siblings $18 per hr, 3hr minimum) offers sitters who are insured, licensed, TB tested, background checked and CPR and first-aid certified. Babysitters come to your location (eg hotel or condo) islandwide. **People Attentive to Children** (PATCH; ☎ 246-0622; www.patchhawaii.org) is a referral service to licensed childcare providers. If you describe to them your needs, they'll send you a list of providers. Parents must take their kids to the provider's location; there's no on-call services. Rates vary according to the provider but on average, it's $10 per hour.

The island's small-town vibe means that no place is formal, whether in attitude or attire. There's no need to pack your kids' designer jeans or collector's kicks. Wear T-shirts, shorts and *rubbah slippahs* to blend in.

Eating with Kids

Hawai'i is a family-oriented and unfussy place, so all restaurants welcome children. High chairs are usually available, but it pays to inquire ahead of time. Even Kaua'i's finest resort restaurants accommodate children (often with kid-specific menus). That said, consider your child's temperament: neighboring tables will not appreciate noisy interruptions during their four-star, wallet-draining meal.

If restaurant dining is inconvenient for your family, no problem! Eating outdoors is among the simplest and best island pleasures. Pack finger foods for a picnic, stop for smoothies at roadside stands, and order plate lunches or fish wraps at patio counters. Accommodations providing full kitchens are convenient for eat-in breakfasts, especially if you stock up on fruit at farmers markets.

The food itself should pose little trouble, as Kaua'i grocers stock mainstream national brands. A kid who eats nothing but Honey Nut Cheerios will not go hungry here. But the local diet, with its abundant variety of cuisines and sweet treats, will probably tempt kids away from mainstream habits.

Discounts

For big-ticket items, such as air travel and lodging, you'll generally end up paying adult costs for kids. Unless they're infants, they'll occupy regular seats and beds. But you can save on pricey activities, including snorkeling cruises to ziplining tours, depending on the outfit and on your kids' ages. In addition to activity discounts, admission fees for museums, gardens and commercial luau are often reduced for kids and teens. Shop around online to find the best deals for your kids. Remember to take along proof of age.

OUTDOOR ACTIVITIES

At Sea

Half of Kaua'i's 111 miles of coastline are lined with sandy beaches, so it almost behooves you to try a bunch of ocean activities. If your child cannot swim or fears the ocean, try one of Kaua'i's gentle 'baby beaches' in Po'ipu (p167) or Kapa'a (p100) for toddlers. Lydgate Beach Park (p83) is an ideal starter beach for grade schoolers or anyone who needs well-protected waters. Although not lifeguard-staffed, 'Anini Beach Park (p123) has consistently calm waters (thanks to a massive offshore reef) and would be ideal for kids. In general, however, pick lifeguard-staffed beaches if you and your kids aren't strong swimmers or are unfamiliar with the Pacific Ocean.

The whole family can learn to snorkel on Kaua'i: shore snorkeling can be done daily if you're staying near an appropriate beach. But also indulge in a thrilling cruise to snorkel the iconic Na Pali waters. If your kid has never sailed before, a smoother catamaran ride might be safer than a zippy raft adventure, but it all depends on the child's personality and comfort at sea.

Surf lessons are another fun family activity. While Kaua'i beaches might seem crowded, they're nowhere near as jammed as Maui and O'ahu beaches, so beginner groups are generally small and personalized. If 'catching a wave' is a mystery to your kid, go bodyboarding before trying to surf. It's much easier to learn and will give the child that all-important seed of confidence.

Island Insights

Especially on the North Shore, the surfing lifestyle is pervasive, attracting many youngsters to the sport from an early age. If hooked, kids tend to become devotees, catching waves every day after school. The talented ones, dubbed 'grommets' ('groms' for short), dream of turning pro the way young urban hoopsters fixate on making the NBA, often neglecting considering other, more realistic alternatives. Those who do succeed in competitions often attract sponsors, such as Hurley and Dakine, and opt for home-schooling.

Top Picks

BEACHES FOR KIDDIES

- **Po'ipu Beach Park** (p164) Gentle waters for snorkeling and swimming, with lots of convivial families on the sand
- **Salt Pond Beach Park** (p191) A locals' swimming beach that's accessible without an exhausting hike
- **Lydgate Beach Park** (p83) Two pools protected by rock walls, plus two jumbo playgrounds
- **'Anini Beach Park** (p123) Pristine waters smooth as glass and relatively uncrowded
- **Baby Beach** (Poipu, p167; Kapa'a, p100) Thigh-high lagoons, perfect for babies and toddlers

For lifeguard-protected beaches, see the boxed text, p37.

On Land

While you can bring your kids along to gardens, parks, activity tours and the majority of attractions, some are especially geared toward children. At Lydgate Beach Park (p83), for example, you'll find two massive (and massively appealing) playgrounds with swings, slides, bridges and mysterious nooks and crannies. Na 'Aina Kai Botanical Garden (p118) includes a special children's area with a wading pond, jungle playground, treehouse and more. Smith's Tropical Paradise (p83) is a family-friendly park where

Local families love Anahola Beach Park (p108)

LUCI YAMAMOTO

there are no time limits to strolling the island-themed 30-acre grounds.

Hiking is big on Kaua'i and if your kids think this activity is boring or pointless, this might be the place to change their minds. But it's important to pick the right hike for your kids' ages and stamina. (Of course, you can always try a long but moderate trail and turn back after a reasonable distance.) At Waimea Canyon State Park (p206) and Koke'e State Park (p211), you'll find trails ranging from simple nature walks to strenuous treks (which would daunt most parents) amid the striking landscape of a gargantuan lava gorge and rugged forestland.

For more adventure, try ziplining, horseback riding, or bicycling along the Eastside coastal path.

Top Picks

FAMILY ACTIVITIES

- **Exploring the palatial playgrounds at Lydgate Beach Park** (p83)
- **Whooshing from tree to tree on a zipline tour** (p67 and p128)
- **Romping in the Children's Garden at Na 'Aina Kai Botanical Gardens** (p118)
- **Sailing to snorkeling waters off the Na Pali Coast** (p189 and p199)
- **Floating in nostalgic inner tubes along irrigation ditches and tunnels** (p68)
- **Hiking at Waimea Canyon or Koke'e State Parks** (p206 and p211)
- **Cooling off with a frozen-fruit 'frostie' at Banana Joe's Fruit Stand** (p119)
- **Enjoying a leisurely beach day at Po'ipu Beach Park** (p164)
- **Bicycling along the east coast on Ke Ala Hele Makalae** (p102)
- **Riding a historic train at Kilohana Plantation** (p64)

CULTURAL ACTIVITIES

Kids are often intrigued by stories of faraway places and people. So why not introduce them to Hawaiian history and culture during your trip?

Traditional grass hut, Kamokila Hawaiian Village (p84) LINDA CHING

Top Picks

SHOPPING FOR KIDS

- **Recycled crayons from Island Soap & Candle Works** (p121 and p162)
- **Children's books (with audio CDs featuring renowned Hawaiian singers) by Dr Carolan and Joanna Carolan** (www.bananapatchpress.com)
- **Locally sewn aloha wear from Kapaia Stitchery** (p74) **and Keiki Kovers** (www.keikikovers.com)
- **Cool clothes for cool kids at Kokonut Kids** (p143)
- **Hand-painted ceramic-tile clocks at Banana Patch Studio** (p193)
- **Magic Dragon Toy & Art Supply Co** (p130)

A good starting place is Kamokila Hawaiian Village (p84), a modest but pleasantly leisurely site where kids can envision an ancient settlement. Some teens might appreciate Kaua'i Museum (p64), but its simple, glass-encased displays will probably seem too much like a school excursion for most. Budding botanists might enjoy Limahuli Garden (p148), where they can learn which plants the ancient Hawaiians knew or simply enjoy strolling the terraced garden path. Kilohana Plantation (p64) offers fun rides, either in carriages drawn by Clydesdale horses or on a historic railroad.

If you're staying at a large resort, your kids could enroll in professionally supervised 'day camps,' which span either half- or full-day sessions. Kids might learn to hula dance, hear Hawaiian stories, go pole fishing or make lei and other handcrafts. Note that programs vary in their emphasis on Hawaiian-related activities.

Such camps are available at the Sheraton Kaua'i Resort (p177), Kiahuna Plantation (p176), Grand Hyatt Kaua'i Resort & Spa (p178), Applicable ages vary, but range from three to 12. Rates also vary in the $45 to $70 range per full-day session. Some programs are open to nonguests.

HISTORY & CULTURE

The Hawaiian Islands existed long before aloha shirts and beach resorts. Many today focus on vacationland Hawaii, the place that arose *after* Captain Cook's fateful arrival, *after* the sugar-plantation era, *after* statehood, *after* the Hiltons and Hyatts set up shop. Before Western contact, the Native Hawaiian *'aina* (land) and people had a culture all their own, and its post-colonial transformations still incite regret and rage, as well as deep pride. Of course, today's Hawaii is a multicultural quilt, bound by traditional Hawaiian culture but touched by the succession of immigrants who followed, from 19th-century plantation workers to modern-day transplants seeking 'the good life.'

HISTORY

THE FIRST SETTLERS

Most archaeologists believe that the first humans migrated to the Hawaiian Islands from the Marquesas Islands around AD 500. This settlement marked the end of a 2000-year period of migration by ancient seafarers originally from Southeast Asia. They traveled eastward into Polynesia (a vast triangle of Pacific islands with New Zealand, Easter Island and Hawai'i at its three points), settling first in Samoa and Tonga and then spreading to the farthest reaches.

Some speculate that they undertook perilous voyages due to famine or overpopulation, while others believe that chiefs wanted new lands to rule without competition from their rivals. Still others believe that the ancient voyagers were like modern-day astronauts: driven by curiosity of the unknown.

Whatever the reason, they managed the journeys in double-hulled canoes 60ft long and 14ft wide, sans any modern navigational tools, whether compasses, radar, radios or satellites. Instead they relied on the 'star compass,' a celestial map based on keen observation (and perfect memory) of star paths.

They had no idea what, if anything, they would find thousands of miles across open ocean. Experts estimate that Hawai'i's discoverers came from the Marquesas Islands and sailed for four months straight with no stops to restock food and water. They brought plants and animals that would be useful for settlement – now that's positive thinking.

Island Insights

The word *kapu* (taboo) originally encompassed all of the various prohibitions on behavior. Today, it generally means 'no trespassing' or 'off-limits.' It appears mostly on makeshift signs posted on private property: 'KAPU. KEEP OUT. THIS MEANS YOU.'

THE ANCIENT WAY OF LIFE

Ancient Hawaiians believed that the ruling aristocracy of hereditary kings and chiefs were direct descendants of the gods. Hence, no one dared question their authority and mana (spiritual essence). In the social order, the highest class were the *ali'i nui* (high chiefs), who ruled one of the four major islands. One's rank as an *ali'i* was determined by the mother's family lineage, making Hawai'i a matriarchal society.

The second class comprised *ali'i 'ai moku* (district chiefs) who ruled island districts and *ali'i 'ai ahupua'a* (lower chiefs) who ruled *ahupua'a*, pie-shaped subdistricts extending from the mountains to the ocean. Also ranked second were kahuna (masters), experts in important skills such as canoe building, religious practices, healing arts and navigation.

The third, and largest, class were the *maka'ainana* (commoners), who were not chattel of the *ali'i* and could live wherever they pleased, but who were obligated to support the *ali'i* through taxes paid in kind with food, goods and labor.

The final *kauwa* (outcast) class was shunned and did not mix with the other classes, except as slaves. No class resented

1778

British captain James Cook becomes the first Westerner to discover the Hawaiian Islands when he lands at Waimea Bay on Kaua'i. In 1779, Captain Cook is killed at Kealakekua Bay on Hawai'i.

1810

Kamehameha the Great unites the major Hawaiian Islands under one kingdom, which is called Hawai'i after his home island. He took 20 years to accomplish this singular feat.

1820

First missionaries arrive at Kailua Bay on the Kona Coast. By then, Kamehameha I was dead and the *kapu* system abolished, so Hawaiians readily convert to Christianity.

their position, for people accepted the 'natural order' and based their identity on the group than on their individuality.

Although the hierarchy might sound feudal in the European sense, Hawaiian society was quite different because *ali'i* did not 'own' land. It was inconceivable to the Hawaiian mind to own land or anything in nature. Rather the *ali'i* were stewards of the land – and they had a sacred duty to care for it on behalf of the gods. Further, the ancients had no monetary system or concept of trade for profit. They instead exchanged goods and services through customary, reciprocal gift giving (as well as through obligations to superiors).

Strict religious laws, known as the *kapu* (taboo) system, governed what people ate, whom they married, when they fished or harvested crops, and practically all human behavior. The *kapu* often discriminated against women, who could not dine with men or eat bananas, coconuts, pork and certain types of fish.

AN ISLAND APART

Kaua'i has always embraced its distinction from the other Hawaiian Islands. Here are a few examples:

- It is the only island not conquered by King Kamehameha the Great.
- It's relatively distant from the other major islands, which lie clustered together.
- It strives to perpetuate a rural, un-Waikiki quality. No building can exceed the height of a coconut tree, meaning that Kaua'i has no skyscrapers.
- It has no mongooses.

FROM HAWAIIAN KINGDOM TO US TERRITORY

Captain Cook & the European Invasion

When esteemed British naval captain James Cook inadvertently sighted the uncharted island of O'ahu on January 18, 1778, the ancient Hawaiians' 500 years of isolation were forever lost. This singular event transformed Hawai'i in ways inconceivable at the time.

Strong winds on that fateful day pushed Cook away from O'ahu and toward the island of Kaua'i, where he made landfall on January 20 at Waimea Bay (p197). Cook promptly named the islands the Sandwich Islands, after his patron, the Earl of Sandwich.

Cook and his men were enthralled with Kaua'i and its inhabitants, considering them to be robust and handsome in physical appearance, and friendly and generous in trade dealings. Meanwhile the Hawaiians, living in a closed society for hundreds of years, found the strange white men to be astounding. Most historians believe that they regarded Cook as the earthly manifestation of the great god Lono.

After two weeks, Cook continued to the Pacific Northwest for another crack at finding the elusive Northwest Passage across North America. Searching in vain for eight months, he returned south to winter in the Hawaiian Islands.

In November 1778, Cook sighted Maui for the first time, but did not land, choosing instead to head further south to explore the nearby island of Hawai'i with its towering volcanic mountains. After landing in picturesque Kealakekua Bay in January 1779,

1835

First successful commercial sugar plantation is established in Koloa on Kaua'i. Early Polynesians brought sugarcane to the islands, but they only chewed its juices and never refined it.

1860

Robert Crichton Wyllie, a Scot who served as the Kingdom of Hawai'i's minister of foreign affairs, names his North Shore sugar estate Princeville, to honor the son of King Kamehameha IV and Queen Emma.

1893

The Hawaiian monarchy, under Queen Lili'uokalani, is overthrown, ending 83 years of the Hawaiian monarchy. In 1895, some Hawaiian royalists attempt a counterrevolution, and the deposed queen is placed under house arrest for nine months.

HISTORY PAGE-TURNERS

- **Kaua'i: The Separate Kingdom** (Edward Joesting) Definitive history of Kaua'i emphasizes its iconoclastic bent.
- **Kaua'i: Ancient Place-Names and Their Stories** (Frederick B Wichman) Traditional stories about island sites give context and meaning to sightseeing.
- **Ancient Hawai'i** (Herb Kawainui Kane) Renowned artist-historian's gorgeously illustrated book stirs the imagination about old Hawai'i.
- **Shoal of Time: A History of the Hawaiian Islands** (Gavan Daws) Classic textbook covering the period from Captain Cook's arrival to statehood.
- **Pau Hana: Plantation Life and Labor in Hawaii, 1835–1920** (Ronald Takaki) Well-researched account of Hawaii's sugar-plantation laborers and subsequent unique multiculturalism.

Cook's luck ran out. He ultimately overstayed his welcome on Hawai'i, diminished his godly status and skirmished with the Hawaiians over a stolen shore boat. A battle ensued, killing Cook, four of his men, and 17 Hawaiians.

The Hawaiian Kingdom

Among the Hawaiian warriors in the battle that felled Captain Cook was a young, exceedingly tall and physically strong man named Paiea. In two decades between 1790 and 1810, this charismatic leader, who became known as Kamehameha the Great, would accomplish what no other chief had ever done before: rise through military conquests to be the *mo'i* (king) of the islands of Hawai'i, Maui, Moloka'i and O'ahu.

To make his domain complete, Kamehameha tried to conquer the island of Kaua'i, but was thwarted by the formidable island chief Kaumuali'i. Kamehameha did, however, manage to negotiate a diplomatic agreement with the chief, which put the island under Kamehameha's new kingdom, but gave Kaumuali'i the right to rule the island somewhat independently.

Kamehameha is credited with unifying all of the islands, bringing an end to the interisland rivalries and wars, and establishing a peaceful and solidified kingdom. He was widely acknowledged as being a benevolent and just ruler, much loved by his people until his death in 1819.

Enter the Missionaries

When Kamehameha died, his 23-year-old son Liholiho (Kamehameha II) became *mo'i* and his wife, Queen Ka'ahumanu, became *kuhina nui* (regent) and co-ruler. Both of them were greatly influenced by Westerners and eager to renounce the *kapu* system. In a shocking snub to tradition, the two broke a strict taboo against men and women eating together and later ordered many heiau (temples) and *ki'i* (idols) destroyed. Without the oppressive but stabilizing ancient traditions, Hawaiian society was in chaos.

Thus the first missionaries to Hawai'i chanced upon a fortuitous time and place to arrive. The American Congregationalists from Boston landed in Kailua Bay on April 19, 1820, just 11 months after King Kamehameha died in almost the exact spot. The Hawaiian people were in great social and

1900

Hawaii becomes a US territory and then takes 59 years to achieve statehood – longer than any other territory in the union.

1925

The first air flight between the mainland and Hawaii is made. Eleven years later, Pan American launches the first commercial mainland–Hawaii flights.

1941

Japanese forces attack Pearl Harbor and the US enters WWII. Most of the Japanese in Hawaii are spared from internment camps because they are necessary laborers in the sugar fields.

political upheaval and many, particularly the *ali'i* (chiefs), found the Protestant faith an appealing replacement.

The Hawaiians had no written language, so the missionaries established a Hawaiian alphabet using Roman letters and zealously taught them how to read and write. This fostered a high literacy rate and publication of 100 Hawaiian-language newspapers. Eventually, however, the missionaries banned the Hawaiian language in schools, to distance Hawaiians from their 'hedonistic' cultural roots.

They prohibited hula dancing because of its 'lewd and suggestive movements,' denounced the traditional Hawaiian chants and songs that honored 'heathen' gods, taught women to sew Western-style clothing and abolished polygamy, which was accepted and necessary in the isolated island group.

Many missionaries became influential advisors to the monarch and received large tracts of land in return, prompting them to leave the church altogether and turn their land into sugar plantations. It is often said that the missionaries came to do good – and did very well.

King Sugar

When foreigners quickly saw that Hawai'i was ideal for growing sugarcane, they established small plantations using Hawaiian labor. But by then the native population had severely declined, thanks to introduced diseases. To fill the shortage, workers were imported from overseas starting in the 1860s, first from China, and soon after from Japan and the Portuguese islands of Madeira and the Azores.

FOREIGN INVASION

When news of Captain Cook's discovery spread, a flood of European and American foreigners came to explore the Hawaiian Islands. The islands were a prime Pacific waystation for traders and whalers, and by the 1820s had a foreign resident population of about 500. British, America, French and Russian traders would travel to the Pacific Northwest for furs and stop in Hawai'i to resupply their ships and to buy *'iliahi* (fragrant sandalwood), a valuable commodity in China. Then they would trade the furs and sandalwood for exotic Chinese silks, spices and furniture. Due to the greed of both traders and Hawaiians, *'iliahi* was virtually decimated and remains rare today.

By the 1840s, Hawai'i was the whaling capital of the Pacific, with over 700 whaling ships stopping at Hawaiian ports annually. Here, they restocked supplies and transferred their catch to ships bound for the US eastern seaboard, allowing for longer and more lucrative hunting trips.

The foreigners brought not only new religious, social, political and dietary habits, but also a slew of lethal infectious diseases (such as STDs, tuberculosis, measles and leprosy). In 1778, Captain Cook found a thriving native population of about 400,000 (estimates range from 100,000 to one million). By 1878, a century later, the count dropped to an estimated 40,000. Today, there are only 5000 to 7000 pure Hawaiians worldwide. The number of part-Hawaiians has steadily increased, however. About 250,000 Hawaii residents (20% of the total population) identify themselves as part–Native Hawaiian.

1946

A tsunami generated by an earthquake in the Aleutian Islands kills 176 people across the islands. The Big Island is hardest hit with 61 deaths, while 14 people die on Kaua'i's North Shore.

1959

On August 21, 1959, Hawaii becomes the 50th US state. Opponents had argued that island labor unions were communist and that the islands were too remote.

1961

Elvis Presley films *Blue Hawaii* at Wailua's Coco Palms Resort. The resort becomes the go-to destination for Hollywood stars and fans, but it has been closed since Hurricane 'Iniki damaged it in 1992.

The influx of imported foreign labor and the rise of the sugar industry had a major impact on the islands' social structure. Caucasian plantation owners and sugar agents rose to become the elite upper economic and political class, while the Hawaiians and foreign laborers became the lower class, without much of a middle class in between.

The sugar industry boomed during the American Civil War (1861–65), when Hawai'i became the northern states' sugar source. After the war, the industry languished until 1875, when the US ended foreign import taxes and sugar production skyrocketed from 21 million pounds in 1874 to 114 million pounds in 1883.

Overthrow of the Monarchy

In 1887 the members of the Hawaiian League, a secret antimonarchy organization run by sugar interests, wrote a new constitution and by threat of violence

HAWAIIAN DIACRITICAL MARKS

If you're stumped by the spelling of Kaua'i (instead of 'Kauai'), relax. That upside-down, backward apostrophe is the *'okina*, a diacritic that signals a glottal stop in the pronunciation of Hawaiian words. We include the *'okina* in all uncommon Hawaiian words (unless it's omitted in business names), but we omit it for Hawaiian words commonly used in English (eg luau and lanai). Note that another Hawaiian diacritical mark, the *kahako* (long vowel), is omitted for Hawaiian words, although a long-vowel mark is included for Japanese words (eg *bentō*).

The *'okina* can dramatically change a word's meaning. For example, lanai (with no *'okina*) means porch or balcony, while Lana'i refers to a Hawaiian island. The vast majority of people pronounce island names incorrectly, but it's simple if you just observe the *'okina* placement. Thus Kaua'i is *kaua-i*, not *ka-wai*.

Since the late 1990s and early 2000s, state and county governments have advocated including the diacritics in all place and street names. Thus you will see them, especially the *'okina*, in newspapers, advertisements, street signs, government websites and so forth. The switch has been patchy but it's very clear which way the islands are headed. (Ironically, some elderly Native Hawaiians actually prefer spelling Hawaiian words without the diacritics because they learned to read and write using the Hawaiian Bible, which was written without the marks.) Non-native speakers sometimes get too eager to use the *'okina*, which inevitably ends up appearing where it does not belong. Before you plop an *'okina* willy-nilly into any Hawaiian word, check the online **Hawaiian dictionary** (www.wehewehe.org).

As for the official spelling of Hawaii, the US government recognizes Hawaii to be the official state name under the Admission Act of 1959. Thus, while state and county governments have embraced the *'okina*, the federal spelling is used for interstate and international dealings.

In this book, Hawai'i (with the *'okina* glottal stop) refers to the island of Hawai'i ('the Big Island') and to the pre-statehood Hawaiian Islands. Hawaii (without the *'okina*) refers to the state. We use this distinction to avoid confusion between the island and the state, though technically speaking the *'okina* should appear in both.

1975

A Micronesian navigator and Hawaiian crew sails the voyaging canoe *Hokule'a* from Hawaii to Tahiti (2400 miles) without any modern means of navigation.

1976

The grassroots organization Protect Kaho'olawe 'Ohana files a lawsuit in the Federal District Court to halt the US Navy's use of Kaho'olawe island as a practice bombing site.

1982

On November 23, Hurricane 'Iwa slams the Hawaiian Islands with estimated gusts reaching 120 mph across Kaua'i and O'ahu. Statewide, the damage totaled $312 million (1982 USD) but only one person, a seaman aboard a Navy vessel, died.

PROMISED LAND

Hawaiians had no concept of land ownership. The gods owned the lands, and people were stewards with a *kuleana* (right) to cultivate it. In practical terms, the king controlled the lands and foreigners had no means to own any.

In the 1840s, Americans sought to secure long-term property rights. In 1848, they got the Hawaiian government to enact the **Great Mahele**, a revolutionary land reform act that redistributed all kingdom lands in three parts: crown lands, chief lands, and government lands (for the benefit of the general public).

Two years later the government went further and allowed foreign residents to buy land. Haole sugar growers and land speculators bought huge parcels for minimal sums from chiefs lured by quick money and from commoners ignorant of deeds, taxes and other legal requirements for fee-simple land ownership.

Native Hawaiians lost much of their land and struggled with ensuing economic problems. In 1920, Kaua'i native son **Prince Kuhio** (congressional delegate for the Territory of Hawai'i) got the US Congress to pass the **Hawaiian Homes Commission Act**, which set aside almost 200,000 acres of government land for Native Hawaiians to lease for $1 per year. It sounds terrific, but much of the set-aside lands are remote and lack basic infrastructure, such as roads and access to water and electricity. Also, regardless of the 'free' land, lessees must build their own homes, which many applicants cannot afford.

Applicants end up waiting for years, even decades. Today there are over 19,000 residential applicants waiting across the state. Only about 8300 leases have been granted since 1920.

forced King David Kalakaua to sign it. This constitution, which became known as the 'Bayonet Constitution,' limited voting rights and stripped the monarch's powers, effectively making King Kalakaua a figurehead.

When Kalakaua, Hawai'i's last king, died in 1891, his sister and heir, Princess Lili'uokalani, ascended the throne. She tried to restore the monarchy, but on January 17, 1893, the leaders of the Hawaiian League, supported by both US Department of State Minister to Hawai'i John L Stevens and a 150-man contingent of US marines and sailors, forcibly arrested Queen Lili'uokalani and took over 'Iolani Palace in Honolulu – a tense but bloodless coup d'état. The Kingdom of Hawai'i was now the Republic of Hawai'i.

Island Insights

Born in Lihu'e on Kaua'i, **Eric Shinseki** is a highly decorated, retired four-star general, currently serving as US Secretary of Veterans Affairs. He became famous during his tenure as Army Chief of Staff when he clashed with Secretary of Defense Donald Rumsfeld during the run-up to the war in Iraq. Shinseki wisely predicted the need for far more troops in postwar Iraq ('in the order of several hundred thousand soldiers') than what Rumsfeld had proposed.

Shinseki, who is Japanese, is the first Asian four-star general in the US military and the only Asian-American to be promoted to the Army's top position.

1983

Kilauea Volcano on Hawai'i starts its latest eruption, which is ongoing. The longest eruption in recorded history, it has engulfed roads and even the entire village of Kalapana.

1986

The luxury Princeville Resort is built, spurring massive development of the North Shore's sprawling planned community.

1992

The eye of Hurricane 'Iniki passes directly over Kaua'i on September 11, killing six and causing more than $1.8 billion (1992 USD) in damage. 'Iniki is the most powerful hurricane to hit the Hawaiian Islands in recorded history.

ANNEXATION, WAR & STATEHOOD

American interests continued to push hard for annexation, while Hawaiians fought to prevent this final, formal acquisition. In 1897, more than 21,000 people (almost half of the population of Hawai'i) signed an anti-annexation petition and sent it to Washington. In 1898, President William McKinley nevertheless approved the annexation, perhaps influenced by the concurrent Spanish-American War, which highlighted Pearl Harbor's strategic military location.

Statehood was a tough sell to the US Congress, but a series of significant historical events paved the way. In 1936, Pan American airlines launched the first commercial flights from the US mainland to Hawai'i, thus launching the trans-Pacific air age and the beginning of mass tourism. Wireless telegraph (and later telephone) service between Hawai'i and the mainland alleviated doubts about long-distance communication. Most important, WWII proved both the strategic military role of Pearl Harbor and the loyalty and heroism of Japanese immigrants.

During WWII, the Japanese were initially banned from joining the armed forces, due to great suspicion about their loyalty. In 1943, the US government yielded to political pressure and formed an all-Japanese combat unit, the 100th Infantry Battalion. While only 3000 men were needed for this unit, more than 10,000 men volunteered.

By the war's end, another all-Japanese unit, the 442nd Regimental Combat Team, composed of 3800 men from Hawaii and the mainland, had received more commendations and medals than any other unit. The 100th Infantry also received special recognition for rescuing the so-called 'Lost Battalion,' stranded behind enemy lines in France.

While still a controversial candidate, especially to Southern conservatives, both Democrat and Republic, the islands were finally admitted as the 50th US state in 1959.

THE HAWAIIAN RENAISSANCE

After WWII, Hawaii became America's tropical fantasyland. The tiki craze, surfer movies, aloha shirts and Waikiki were all Westernized, commercial images, but they made Hawaii iconic to the masses. Simultaneously, Hawaiians were increasingly marginalized by Western social, political and economic influences. The Hawaiian language had nearly died out, land was impossible for most Hawaiians to buy, and most

GOODBYE SUGAR

The demise of the sugar industry caused a sea change in the Hawaiian Islands' economy. After all, it went from being the state's largest (with 26 plantations) in 1960 to a lost cause (with only two plantations) by the 1990s. Hawaii's sugar industry couldn't compete with cheaper foreign markets. In September 2008 Kaua'i's Gay & Robinson (p196) plantation was one of two holdouts statewide (the last remaining plantation is on Maui) when the Robinsons announced that they would cease sugar operations and switch to ethanol production.

Today, the economic drivers are tourism (which drives construction), the military, seedcorn research and, occasionally, the film industry.

1994

The Po'ipu Bay Golf Course hosts the annual PGA Grand Slam of Golf from 1994 to 2006. Tiger Woods takes first place for five consecutive years, from 1998 to 2002, and then two more in 2005 and 2006.

2000

Senator Daniel Akaka first introduces the Native Hawaiian Government Reorganization Act ('Akaka Bill'), which recognizes Hawaiians' indigenous status and allows limited self-governance. The bill has repeatedly stalled in Congress and remains on the floor.

2004

The National Oceanic and Atmospheric Administration's National Weather Service designates Kaua'i County as a 'StormReady' and 'TsunamiReady' community, based on its warning system and other 'readiness' requirements.

EYE OF THE STORM

Almost two decades after Hurricane 'Iniki blasted the island, residents can still give blow-by-blow accounts of their survival on September 11, 1992. 'Iniki blew in with sustained winds of 145mph and gusts of 165mph or more (a weather-station meter in mountainous Koke'e broke off at 227mph). It snapped trees by the thousands and totally demolished 1420 homes (and swept over 60 out to sea). Another 5000 homes were severely damaged while over 7000 sustained minor damage. Most of the island lacked electricity for over a month, and some areas lacked power for up to three months. Thirty-foot waves washed away entire wings of beachfront hotels, particularly those in Po'ipu and Princeville.

During the immediate aftermath, residents were remarkably calm and law-abiding despite the lack of power, radio or TV. Communities held parties to share and consume perishable food. Looting was minor, and when grocers allowed affected residents to take what they needed, they insisted on paying.

Miraculously, only four people died, but the total value of the damage to the island was $1.8 billion. The tourist industry bounced back by the late 1990s and today is thriving. While locals notice the changed landscape, newcomers would never realize the havoc wreaked 15 years ago. Unfortunately a couple of Kaua'i's native bird species have not been spotted since 'Iniki.

Because 'Iniki struck during daylight, many residents recorded the event in real-time with camcorders. The best footage was compiled into an hour-long video ($24.95), which you can order at www.video-hawaii.com/iniki.html.

of the traditional ways of life that had supported an independent people for over 2000 years were lost. Without these, Hawaiians lost much of their own identity and even felt a sense of shame.

The 1970s introduced a cultural awakening, due largely to two events: in 1974 a small group called the **Polynesian Voyaging Society** (www.pvs.hawaii.org) committed themselves to building and sailing a replica of an ancient Hawaiian voyaging canoe, to prove that the first Polynesian settlers were capable of navigating the Pacific without the use of Western technology such as sextants and compasses. When the *Hokule'a* made its maiden 4800-mile roundtrip voyage to Tahiti in 1976, it instantly became a symbol of rebirth for Hawaiians, prompting a cultural revival unparalleled in Hawaiian history.

The same year, a small grassroots group, the Protect Kaho'olawe 'Ohana (PKO), began protesting the treatment of Kaho'olawe, an island the US military had used as a training and bombing site since WWII. The PKO's political actions, including the island's illegal occupation, spurred new interest in reclaiming not only Kaho'olawe (which the Navy relinquished in 2003) and other military-held lands, but also Hawaiian cultural practices, from hula to lomilomi massage.

Public schools started teaching Hawaiian language and culture classes, while Hawaiian immersion charter schools proliferated. Hawaiian music topped the charts, turning island-born musicians into now-legendary superstars. Small but vocal contingents began pushing for Hawaiian sovereignty, from complete secession from the United States to a nation-within-a-nation model.

2006

Torrential rainstorms for over 40 days in February and March cause Kaloko Dam on the North Shore to break, causing a flash flood of 300 million gallons of water into the ocean. Seven people are swept away to their deaths.

2007

Almost 300 Kaua'i residents protest the inaugural arrival of the Superferry at Nawiliwili Harbor. At least 34 swim into the ship's path to block the 350-foot-long Alakai from landing.

2008

After 119 years in business, Kaua'i's last remaining sugar plantation, Gay & Robinson, ends its sugar operations due to rising fuel, fertilizer and other costs. The company, founded in 1889, is planning to move into ethanol production.

THE CULTURE

ISLAND IDENTITY

Ask residents why they like Kaua'i and they'll likely say, 'It's not Waikiki!' Among the major Hawaiian Islands, Kaua'i is the smallest and most rural. With no towns over 10,000 people, no skyscrapers and only one way to navigate the island, there's no mistaking that you're on an island. All the Neighbor Islands are considered 'country,' if not *da boonies* (the boondocks), compared to Honolulu, but Kaua'i remains the most 'countrified' – by choice.

Defining a typical Kaua'i person is almost impossible, now that the population includes a sizable contingent of transplants from the US mainland and abroad. They might be post-college wanderers or surfer dudes, but most are wealthy retirees or middle-aged career switchers seeking idyllic seclusion. Many hail from California and the Pacific Northwest – outdoorsy types who discover a superior outdoors here.

Born-and-raised Kauaians tend to be easygoing and low-key. The Asians, especially, tend to avoid public confrontations and 'making waves.' Multigenerational locals take pride in their roots, such as their high school alma mater, and they enjoy knowing and being known in the community. Kauaians are well aware of their 'underdog' status, and when their local kids beat the statewide competition in sports or debating, the victory is especially sweet.

The influx of mainland haole has diluted traditional communities (eg Hawaiian taro and fishing villages, plantation towns and ethnic communities), especially on the North Shore, which is priced beyond most locals' means. Many of the newcomers bring fresh ideas about environmentalism and sustainability, slow growth and slow food. Locals generally support such trends, which parallel the Hawaiian concept of aloha *'aina* (love of the land). But the newcomers' interests occasionally clash with those of locals who are simply trying to eke a living here. Costco and Wal-Mart might be anathema to a mainlander trying to escape from chain retail, but they were heralded by budget shoppers who had always felt gouged by the existing 'monopoly' by local businesses. And the monster truck remains the status vehicle among local dudes.

Regional Differences

Despite the island's compact size, each geographical location has its own distinct vibe. Lihu'e (p57), the county seat, is a functional town where people go to work, not to play. Hanapepe (p190) is a sleepy plantation town-cum-artists colony, quaintly shabby. Hanalei (p133) is a surf town, dominated by suntanned blonds and affordable only by multimillionaires. Wailua's (p82) upcountry remains a favorite residential area, where backyard gardens guarantee all the starfruit and avocados you can eat.

WHO ARE YOU?

Haole White person (except local Portuguese). Often further defined as 'mainland haole' or 'local haole.'
Hapa Person of mixed ancestry, most commonly referring to *hapa haole* who are part-white and part-Asian.
Hawaiian Person of Native Hawaiian ancestry. It's a faux pas to call any Hawaii resident 'Hawaiian' (as you would a Californian or Texan), thus ignoring the existence of an indigenous people.
Kama'aina Person who is native to a particular place. A Waimea native is a *kama'aina* (literally defined as 'child of the land') of Waimea and not of Lihu'e. It assumes a deep knowledge of and connection to the place. In the retail context, '*kama'aina* discounts' apply to any resident of Hawaii (ie anyone with a Hawaii driver's license).
Local Person who grew up in Hawaii. Locals who move away retain their local 'cred,' at least in part. But longtime transplants (see below) never become local. To call a transplant 'almost local' is a welcome compliment, despite its emphasis on the insider/outsider mentality.
Neighbor Islander Person who lives on any Hawaiian Island other than O'ahu.
Transplant Person who moves to the islands as an adult.

Local pride runs deep in Hawaii

LUCI YAMAMOTO

Visitors who drive around the island multiple times might assume that locals similarly circumnavigate the island, but residents tend to stick to their regions – except for stocking up or buying cheap gas at Costco.

LIFESTYLE

On Kaua'i, urban pursuits are few. Most residents focus on the outdoors. The ocean is the primary playground, and families often own their own fishing boats. Surfing, especially in Hanalei and Po'ipu, is the sport of choice. Local Asians tend to give it up once they're adults, while Hawaiians and haole transplants keep riding until old age.

The workday starts and ends early, and most find a comfortable work/home balance. Childcare is shared with grandparents and relatives, typically eager babysitters. Retirees often congregate in friendly gangs for morning golf or coffee, and virtually all residents develop a green thumb.

Not surprisingly, Kaua'i locals tend to follow traditional lifestyle patterns (which parallel the standard 'American dream'). They tend to marry early and stick to traditional male and female domestic roles (it's still odd for a wife not to take her husband's surname). The easy lifestyle, especially in surf towns like Hanalei, seems to squelch ambitions to travel the world or attend mainland schools.

Locals and transplants tend to diverge in their careers and ambitions. Locals tend toward more conventional, 'American dream' lives, meaning marriage, kids, a modest home, stable work and free nights and weekends. Mainland transplants are here for other reasons: retirement, a dream B&B or organic farm, art, youthful experimentation. Here, they are free to be unconventional.

Urban Influences

City pursuits – shopping, theater, cinema and museums – are minimal. The sole major shopping mall is Kukui Grove Shopping Center (p74) in Lihu'e, but it offers just the basics, sans upscale designer or department stores. Kauaians are generally down-to-earth types, blasé about mainland fashion trends or the latest high-tech gizmo. It takes eagle eyes to spot a Prius or an iPhone – and there is little need to own a suit and tie on this island! With only three

ALL IN THE 'OHANA

In Hawaii, locals define 'family' much more inclusively than do mainstream mainlanders. Here, the *'ohana* (family) can extend beyond bloodlines to friends, teammates, coworkers and classmates. If people demonstrate the *'ohana* spirit,' it means that they are generous and welcoming, like family should be.

Hanai (adopted or foster) children are common in Hawaiian families. To be a *hanai* child or to *hanai* a child is not odd or pejorative in Hawaii. Instead, *hanai* children are fully accepted into the family.

Locals might refer to a 'calabash cousin,' meaning a close friend akin to a cousin but not a blood relation. More commonly, you'll hear locals refer to 'aunty' or 'uncle' even if the person is not related at all. These elders are beloved community members, and calling them aunty or uncle connotes respect and affection.

Island Insights

Throughout this book, the Entertainment listings are sparse. As one former New York musician put it, '9pm is Kaua'i's midnight!' This might reflect the early-bird routines of most islanders, who rise at dawn to catch the waves, beat the heat and get to work on time.

public high schools on the island, education remains a weak point. Parents, especially if they're mainland transplants, try to get their kids into private schools.

But you might be surprised at how much Lihu'e and the Eastside resemble a mini version of mainland suburbia, with strip malls and guaranteed commute traffic. Despite Kaua'i's compact size, the island is entirely auto-dependent. Public bus transit is negligible, sidewalks are rare, and residential neighborhoods are miles from commercial centers. The cost of living, including gas, groceries and electricity, is sky-high here (not to mention the stratospheric real-estate market).

When Kauaians travel, they go mostly to Honolulu to shop (a popular hobby among locals) but prefer the Hilo (Big Island), its kindred sibling, which shares a similar small-town character. Farther destinations include the US mainland (particularly Vegas), Japan and Southeast Asia, often visited in tour groups.

POPULATION

The state's population, approaching 1.3 million, is heavily concentrated on O'ahu, where Honolulu is the state's only true city. According to the US Census estimate for 2007, the population of Kaua'i County was about 63,000, while the de facto population (including visitors) was almost 82,000. The figures for town populations date back to the 2000 Census, which showed the largest town to be Kapa'a with almost 9500 people, followed by Lihu'e with 5675, Wailua Homesteads with 4600 and Kalaheo with almost 4000.

Whites constitute just over 31% of the population, followed by full- or part-Native Hawaiians at 24%, Filipinos at almost 14% and Japanese at 11.5%. The remaining 18% are people with mixed ethnic backgrounds. The seemingly high number of Native Hawaiians is rather misleading because only a tiny percentage has greater than 50% Hawaiian blood. The number of 'pure' Hawaiians has dropped steadily ever since Captain Cook's arrival; experts estimate their number to be under 5000 nationwide.

Different ethnicities congregate in different towns. Lihu'e has the largest concentration of Japanese (almost 30%), while its surrounding communities of Puhi and Hanama'ulu are both 50% Filipino. Kalaheo is known as 'Portuguese town.' The North Shore is predominantly Caucasian, from Kilauea (at 45%) to Hanalei (at 56%) to Princeville (at a whopping 80%). Eastside towns Wailua and Kapa'a show the most even distribution among ethnicities, while Anahola is over 70% Native Hawaiian.

Kaua'i's daytime and nighttime populations highlight why Eastside highway traffic is a nightmare: during the day, county capital Lihu'e's population of almost 5675 practically doubles due to commuting workers.

MULTICULTURALISM

The overwhelming majority of Kaua'i's current immigrants are white, so the island's diversity is based on historic minorities: Native Hawaiians and plantation immigrants (predominantly Filipino and Japanese). This unique ethnic mix differs from mainland majority-minority populations, in which the 'minorities' are Latino or black.

During plantation days, whites were the wealthy plantation owners, and their legendary surnames remain household words (eg Wilcox Memorial Hospital and Rice St). Their ingrained privilege is one reason why some resentment toward haole lingers. Granted, those prominent families were often close allies of the high-ranking Hawaiians – or even related by marriage. As time passes and the plantation era fades away, the traditional stereotypes, hierarchies and alliances have softened. But, for years, the immigrants would capitalize on plantation nostalgia during political elections, emphasizing their insider status as former plantation laborers.

That said, no ethnic group ever kept exclusive; instead they freely adopted and shared cultural customs, from food to festivals to language. Folks of all colors dance hula, craft hardwood bowls, play the ukulele and study the Hawaiian language. Cultural festivals, such as Chinese New Year or Japanese Obon, attract mixed crowds.

Due to intermarriage, one cannot always assume a person's race or ethnicity from their surname. Many Hawaiians have Caucasian or Asian surnames, for example. If you observe Kamehameha Schools students, who must prove any quantum of Hawaiian ancestry, you'll see features that appear Chinese, Japanese or Caucasian, among the Hawaiian faces. It's also common, in multiethnic families, for siblings to vary in skin, eye and hair colors, which locals find amusing.

Generally, locals feel bonded with other locals. While tourists and transplants are welcomed with open arms, they must earn the trust and respect of the locals. It is unacceptable for an outsider to assume an air of superiority and to try to 'fix' local ways. If white, such people will inevitably fall into the category of 'loudmouth haole.'

RELIGION

Ancient Pantheon

Ancient Hawaii was a polytheistic society. The four major gods were Ku, god of war and masculine power; Kane, god of fresh water, sunlight and procreation; Kanaloa, god of the ocean and ocean winds; and Lono, god of peace and agriculture. Dozens of demigods and deities reigned over the natural and supernatural worlds. Among those still worshipped today are Pele, goddess of volcanoes; Laka, goddess of hula; and Hina, goddess of the moon.

Most deities had *kinolau* (earthly counterparts), which could be animate or inanimate objects, such as rocks, animals and trees, or other natural elements, such as wind and rain. Virtually everything in the earthly world were the *kinolau* of a deity; therefore, all things were considered to have mana (spiritual essence).

Ancient Hawaiians believed that when humans die, their spirits live on in the form of *'aumakua* (guardian spirits) that protect living family members. *'Aumakua* adopt earthly forms such as sharks, geckos, birds or fish. A reciprocal relationship existed: *'aumakua* would provide guidance and protection to the living, who in turn were duty-bound to revere and protect their guardian spirits on earth.

Modern Religious Mix

The Hawaiians replaced their ancient religion with Christianity after King Kamehameha's death, and most remain devout Christians today. But they didn't abandon all of their old values and rituals, which still appear. Christian sermons often include both Hawaiian and English words, and public ceremonies, such as groundbreaking, feature a kahuna to bless the land. Hawaiian activism against development is rooted in *aloha 'aina* (love of the sacred land).

Today, most residents do not claim adherence to a particular faith, and the religious milieu is tolerant rather than dogmatic. Still, for such a small island, Kaua'i has dozens of churches and temples, especially on the Westside. The largest religious group is Roman Catholic, due to the significant Filipino population, followed by the Church of Jesus Christ of Latter-Day Saints, which has attracted many South Pacific converts. Mainstream Protestant Christianity is struggling with declining

THROW A SHAKA

The hand sign known across the islands as 'shaka' signifies thanks, solidarity and friendly greetings. Folks develop their own personal shaka style: facing up or down, one hand or two, stock still or lots of shaking. Here's how to do it:

- Extend your thumb and pinky finger.
- Keep your three middle fingers (index, middle and ring) curled.
- Face the back of your hand to your audience.
- Smile and give a shake. Shaka, brah!

BACKYARD GRAVEYARDS

Ancient burial sites lie underneath countless homes and hotels throughout Hawaii. Construction workers often dig up *iwi* (bones) and *moepu* (funeral objects), while locals swear by eerie stories of equipment malfunctioning until bones are properly reinterred and prayers given.

In 1990, Congress enacted the **Native American Graves Protection and Repatriation Act** (www.hawaii.gov/dlnr/hpd/hpburials.htm), which established burial councils on each island to oversee the treatment of remains and preservation of burial sites. To Native Hawaiians, desecration of *iwi* is a major affront (and illegal).

Kaua'i's most recent case involved Ha'ena's **Naue Point**, the site of some 30 confirmed *iwi*. At the time of research, the landowner had already poured concrete despite protests when a state judge ruled that the State Historic Preservation Division (SHPD) must consult the burial council. In November 2008, the burial council recommended that the SHPD reject the landowner's burial-treatment proposal and revoke its building permit.

What happens next? Could a landowner lose the right to build? Probably not. Most likely, the state will approve a burial-treatment proposal to remove the *iwi* and reinter them offsite (an outcome that Hawaiians find woefully inadequate).

Many hotels and condos were built on land with *iwi* now sitting in storage or still underground. And what happens to those restless spirits? Believe it or not, Po'ipu's Grand Hyatt Resort has a director of Hawaiian and community affairs who does blessings somewhere on resort grounds at least once a month to quell some 'spiritual disturbance.'

membership, while evangelical churches are burgeoning. Buddhism is prevalent among the Japanese, and their temples are often important community centers, while the spectacular Kaua'i Hindu Monastery (p84) in Wailua belies the minuscule number of Hindus here.

Across the island, ruins of heiau (ancient Hawaiian religious sites) exist as partial stone structures and walls. Most are modest in scope, and if one is unfamiliar with their significance, they will resemble a mere pile of rocks. Hawaiians located heiau on spiritually powerful sites; to understand a heiau requires an appreciation of stark, untouched nature.

Island Insights

It might be short-lived, but a **lei** makes an uplifting, in-the-moment souvenir. In daily life, locals continue to wear leis for special events, such as weddings and public ceremonies. Ancient leis were subtle in their beauty, made of modest berries, fragrant maile leaves and other greenery. Today's popular tourist leis feature fragrant or showy flowers, such as plumeria or dendrobium orchids. See masterpiece leis at Kaua'i Museum's annual **lei contest** (p69).

ARTS

Defining Hawaii art is a conundrum. Does it include non-traditional genres? Should artists be *kama'aina* (locally born and raised)? Must the subject matter be local? Minds will differ, of course, but here we try to focus on artists who live in Hawaii and focus on local themes. While we try to identify the best *kama'aina* artists, we must recognize the many talented transplants who come here and produce notable works.

Music

Traditional Hawaiian music meant *mele oli* (solo chants), performed a capella at rituals or ceremonies, and *mele hula* (hula chants), accompanied by dance and rhythm instruments. While stirring, *mele* were repetitive and not quite melodic. But once missionaries arrived, Hawaiians sang hymns with gusto and soon were composing songs still sung today. Queen Lili'uokalani's 'Aloha 'Oe' is a prime example.

Once string instruments arrived, Hawaiians displayed their musical gifts by making three instruments their own. The resonant Hawaiian steel guitar *(kika kila)* is fundamental to the signature Hawaiian sound. Most cite Joseph Kekuhu as the inventor of the iconic lap guitar in the 1880s; by the 1900s, he and other Hawaiians burst on the international scene, introducing both the instrument and *hapa-haole* (Hawaiian music with English lyrics) to Americans and Europeans.

The ukulele is popular to the point of Hollywood cliché. While always present in the background to accompany *hula 'auana* (modern-style hula), it's also a solo instrument for bestselling musicians such as Eddie Kamae and Jake Shimabukuro (who became a YouTube hit with his mesmerizing cover of George Harrison's 'While My Guitar Gently Weeps').

Slack key guitar (*ki ho'alu*, which means 'loosen the key') is not an instrument but a fingerstyle method in which the strings are slacked from their standard tuning. Since Gabby Pahinui first recorded his slack key tunes for the public in the 1940s, it's become the most famous and commercially successful Hawaiian genre. In fact, since the Grammy Award for Best Hawaiian Music Album was established in 2005, four of the five winners have been slack key compilations featuring some of the living legends.

Hawaiian vocalists are known for a distinctive falsetto style called *ha'i*, which stresses the breaks between lower and upper registers. Among females, the archetype is the late Genoa Keawe, whose impossibly long-held notes in the song 'Alika' set the standard (and set it high). Other notables include jazz-turned-Hawaiian songbird Amy Hanaiali'i and the 20-something superstar Raiatea Helm, widely considered to be Keawe's successors.

Since the early 1900s, Hawaii music has shifted between Westernized and Hawaiian sounds. Nowadays, the trend is toward Hawaiian lyrics, both modern pop compositions and traditional chanting with little accompaniment. The singer who best captured both worlds is the late Israel Kamakawiwo'ole, whose rendition of the classic 'Over the Rainbow' enchanted audiences worldwide.

To hear a diverse selection of Hawaii music, stream the radio station at www.hawaiianrainbow.com. An excellent online CD retailer is www.mele.com.

Hula

Modern audiences assume that hula is entertainment or creative expression. But ancient Hawaiians regarded hula as much more. They had no written language, so hula and chanting served as essential communication, to record historical events, myths and legends. It was also a religious offering to the gods.

Today's commercial hula shows, which emphasize swaying hips and nonstop smiling, might be compelling but they're not 'real' hula. Serious students join a *hula halau* (school), where they undergo rigorous training and adopt hula as a life practice.

But *hula halau* have embraced the utterly modern concept of competition. In major competitions in Hawaii and California, dancers vie in *kahiko* (ancient) and *'auana* (modern) categories. *Kahiko* performances are raw and primordial, accompanied only by chanting, and they use a bent-knee stance to allow dancers to absorb earth's energy. *Kahiko* dancers' costumes show primary colors and often lots of skin. Accompanied by harmonious singing and string instruments, *'auana* seems more like mainstream hula, with Western-influenced dresses and pants, sinuous arm movements and smiling faces.

One of the best venues to view serious hula is the Kaua'i Mokihana Festival Hula Competition (p171) in Po'ipu.

Native Hawaiian Arts & Crafts

Traditional Hawaiian woodwork is found across the island, ranging from keepsake rocking chairs and masterful calabash bowls to affordable desk accessories and kitchen utensils. See Robert Bader's graceful Norfolk-pine platters at the Art of Marbling (p193) in Hanapepe, Davison Arts (p106) in Kapa'a for furniture and the Koa Store (p74) in Lihu'e for handmade koa souvenirs, from chopsticks to display canoe paddles.

Christian missionaries introduced patchwork quilting to Hawaiians, who designed their own elegant, non-scrap appliqué method. Classic Hawaiian quilts feature a single, stylized flora shape appliquéd on a white background cloth. Painstakingly handstitched throughout, a genuine Hawaiian quilt costs thousands of dollars. See exquisite antique quilts at the Kaua'i Museum's (p64) biennial quilt exhibit in early summer.

Thanks to a small group of master weavers, *lauhala* (pandanus-leaf) weaving is hanging on. But genuine creations are hard to find. A good starting point is the Edith King Wilcox Gift shop (p74) in Lihu'e.

In addition to traditional arts and crafts, look for contemporary Kaua'i-made products, ranging from Malie botanical soaps (p188) made with local flora to Kapaia Stitchery's hand-sewn handbags and quilts (p74). For more ideas, see the list on p50.

The best advice, whether you've got a budget of $10 or $10,000: beware cheap, foreign, mass-produced imitations. Buy locally made.

Literature

Hawaii's first examples of literature were ancient Hawaiian myths and legends, originally transmitted by oral tradition. But in modern times, novels by nonlocal writers, such as James Michener's *Hawaii,* dominated Hawaii literature.

In the 1970s and 1980s, novels and poems by local authors expanded the definition of Hawaii literature. A good intro to the pidgin vernacular and local personalities is *Growing Up Local: An Anthology of Poetry and Prose from Hawai'i,* a compendium published by Bamboo Ridge Press, a pioneer in the genre. See the publisher's website – www.bambooridge.com – to get familiar with notable local writers.

For traditional myths and legends of Kaua'i, you can't go wrong with master storyteller Frederick B Wichman's anthologies, including *Touring the Legends of Koke'e* and *Touring the Legends of the North Shore,* both published by the **Kaua'i Historical Society** (www.kauaihistoricalsociety1914.com).

Cinema & TV

That's no Hollywood set – Kaua'i's spectacular beaches, jungles and cliffs have starred in over 75 movies and TV shows. It all started in 1933 when director Lois Weber brought a film crew to shoot *White Heat.* Later, in *South Pacific* (1957), the North Shore's Lumaha'i Beach, with Makana mountain in the background, became an

HAWAIIAN QUILTING *Lisa Dunford*

With its vibrant colors and graphic patterns, the striking beauty of Hawaiian appliqué quilts is easy to see. But look more closely and discover the story behind the beauty. Each part has meaning, and each design is thought to contain the very spirit of the crafter – early quilts were even buried with their makers so their souls couldn't go wandering.

Missionaries introduced quilting to the islands in the 1800s, but Hawaiian women already sewed *kapa* (pounded-bark cloth) to make bedding, imprinting the top with natural motifs. Most scholars believe appliqué quilting took hold because of its 19th-century popularity in the US and easy adaptation to *kapa*-like designs. (Local lore has it that patchwork quilting was rejected because island women didn't have fabric-scrap bags – who are we to argue?)

Even today, traditional quilts usually have one bright fabric – say, magenta – which is cut into a repeating pattern after being folded in fourths or eighths (remember making paper snowflakes in grade school?). The bright fabric is then appliquéd, usually by hand, onto a white or natural-color foundation cloth, and the design is quilted around in an echoing pattern.

At the center of the quilt is the *piko* (navel); an open center is seen as a gateway linking the spiritual world and the physical one, while a solid core symbolizes the strength of the family. A border symbolizes the continuity of life. Fruits and plants have meaning, too, but you won't see any human figures (it's believed they could come alive at night). Some typical symbols:

- breadfruit – abundance
- pineapple – hospitality
- mango – wishes granted
- taro – strength

If you want to buy one of these treasures, expect to pay thousands. (If prices are low, the quilts were likely made in the Philippines.) Better still, create your own! Ask the friendly staff at Kapaia Stitchery (p74) for tips.

WHAT IS ART?

Most artwork by Kaua'i artists is highly commercial: colorful, representational works that appeal to the tourist eye. Unique pieces (usually less marketable) that go beyond the stereotypes do exist, but they're harder to find, displayed mainly in Honolulu museums and galleries. On Kaua'i, try the following galleries as starting points: Art 103 (p169), Artists of Kaua'i (p106), Ship Store Galleries (p93), the cluster of galleries in Hanapepe (p192) and **Ola's Hanalei** (☎ 826-6937; www.olashanalei.com; Hanalei Dolphin Center, 5-5016 Kuhio Hwy; 10am-9pm).

Notable fine artists (to name only a few) include:

- **Margaret Ezekiel** Pastel drawings of cloudscapes or the human figure
- **Bruna Stude** (www.brunastude.com) Elegant B&W underwater photography
- **Mac James** (www.macjamesonkauai.com) Nature paintings and drawings with contemporary environmental themes
- **Carol Bennett** Meditative paintings of underwater movement
- **Liedeke Bulder** (www.liedekebulderart.com) Classic botanical paintings and skyscape watercolors
- **A Kimberlin Blackburn** (www.akimberlinblackburn.com) Uninhibitedly colorful, stylized sculptures and paintings.

icon. Elvis Presley's *Blue Hawaii* (1961) will forever give Coco Palms Resort (closed indefinitely) that star cachet.

More recently, *Raiders of the Lost Ark* (1981) used the rugged landscapes near Hule'ia Stream outside Lihu'e and the Kalalea Mountain north of Anahola to stand in for South American jungles. In Steven Spielberg's blockbuster 1993 film *Jurassic Park*, Allerton Garden (p167) in the Lawa'i Valley became the valley of the dinosaurs – and reprised the set for two sequels, *The Lost World: Jurassic Park* (1997) and *Jurassic Park III* (2001). In *Six Days Seven Nights* (1998), stunt doubles for Harrison Ford and Anne Heche jump off Makawehi Point at Shipwreck Beach, while in *Dragonfly* (2002), upland Wailua's dense forestland becomes the Venezuelan jungle where Kevin Costner's wife mysteriously disappears.

State and county officials continue to woo Hollywood to shoot in Hawaii, eager for the multimillion-dollar boost to the local economy. In 2006, state lawmakers sweetened tax incentives for production companies, raising the existing 4% credit for production costs to 20% on Neighbor Islands (and to 15% on O'ahu).

In 2007, Ben Stiller filmed the $100-million *Tropic Thunder* on Kaua'i, giving the island a huge economic boom. The *Tropic Thunder* team hired 350 local crew members (in a total crew of 778), plus hundreds of local extras. They rented houses or stayed at the two Wailua hotels for some 13 weeks. They patronized local restaurants, bars and countless businesses. They filmed across the island, from Grove Farm in Lihu'e to Hanalei. Overall, the film is estimated to have contributed a whopping $60 million to the island's economy.

But some islanders allege that the film sets caused environmental damage, such as altered streams, flattened bamboo groves

LOCAL LITERATURE FOR ALL AGES

- **All I Asking For is My Body** (Milton Murayama) First published in 1975, this 1980 American Book Award winner is a realistic account of the Japanese-American experience around WWII.
- **Saturday Night at the Pahala Theatre** (Lois-Ann Yamanaka) The breakthrough collection of poems by this prolific writer won the 1993 Pushcart Prize and proved that pidgin English can be literary.
- **Kauai Tales** (Frederick B Wichman) This beautifully illustrated collection (the first in a series of four) gives imaginative context to real-life places on Kaua'i.
- **Where Are My Slippers? A Book of Colors** (Dr Carolan and Joanna Carolan) With lost slippers, zoo animals, rhymes and colorful illustrations, this is a guaranteed go-to fave. See the Carolans' entire collection of children's books at www.bananapatchpress.com.

LEARN THE LINGO

While English is the standard language used in Hawaii, you'll quickly realize that it's a far cry from mainland English. Here, locals use a combination of pidgin, Hawaiian and English (with a dose of Japanese and Chinese, too).

It sounds more challenging than it is. Local kids grow up with this hodgepodge but they're taught in public schools to use standard English in academic and professional settings.

Most agree with this distinction, but a once-renegade, now-respected group called Da Pidgin Coup (www.hawaii.edu/satocenter/dapidgincoup.html) at the University of Hawai'i advocates recognition of pidgin (which they call Hawai'i Creole English) as a legitimate language.

The best-known champion of pidgin is Lee Tonouchi, a writer, playwright and lecturer at Kapi'olani Community College on O'ahu, who was hired in the English Department with an application written entirely in pidgin. His books include *Da Word* (short stories), *Living Pidgin: Contemplations on Pidgin Culture* (essays) and *Da Kine Dictionary* (pictorial dictionary). In addition to Tonouchi's titles, find Douglas Simonson's classic *Pidgin to Da Max*, a laugh-out-loud cartoon dictionary.

Download a free **Hawaiian Language & Glossary** PDF from www.lonelyplanet.com/hawaiian-language. For now, here are some common words and phrases:

Hawaiian

aloha – love, hello, welcome, goodbye
hale – house
kane – man
kapu – taboo, restricted
mahalo – thank you
makai – a directional, toward the sea
mauka – a directional, toward the mountains (inland)
pau – finished, completed
pono – goodness, justice, responsibility
wahine – woman

Pidgin

brah – shortened form of *braddah* (brother)
chicken skin – goose bumps from cold, fear, thrill
coconut wireless – the 'grapevine'; local gossip channels
da kine – whatchamacallit; used whenever you can't think of the appropriate word
fo' real? – Really? Are you kidding me?
high makamaka – stuck-up, snooty, pretentious; literally high 'eyes,' meaning head in the air
howzit? – Hey, how's it going? As in 'Eh, howzit brah?'
rubbah slippahs – literally 'rubber slippers,' flip-flops
talk story – chitchat or any casual conversation
to da max – used as an adjective or adverb to add emphasis, as in 'Da waves was big to da max!'

and scorched 'war zones' and toxic damage from pyrotechnics. They criticize the lack of oversight by the State Department of Land and Natural Resources (or any other authority).

We could not prove the allegations either way, but conclude that Kaua'i's movie 'industry' will always entail a fine balance. Some embrace the island's long history on the silver screen. Some value the big economic boost. Some view the 'commodification' of the *'aina* (land) as never justifiable. Minds differed over *Tropic Thunder* and will differ again the next time Hollywood comes to town.

For more information about the industry, contact the **Hawaii Film Office** (www.hawaiifilmoffice.com).

FOOD & DRINK

Island-caught fish. Island-grown produce. Island-casual setting. The trendiest tastes and coolest eateries may launch in Honolulu, but Kaua'i likes to keep it simple. Whether you're savoring four-star Hawaii Regional Cuisine or sampling that curious Spam *musubi,* you'll find a fascinating fusion of flavors – from Polynesian staples such as taro, banana and coconut to Japanese teriyaki, Chinese noodles and Hawaiian *kalua* pork. On a small island, the choice of outstanding eateries is scant – so get psyched to hunt down the best fish markets, indie bakeries and splurge-worthy chefs, and shop at daily farmers markets for just-picked bananas, papayas, avocados and much more.

THE ISLAND DIET

Hawaii is a US state, so Americans will find the familiar fast-food chains, supermarkets stocked with national brands, and conventional menus of pancakes and Caesar salads. But if you plunge in and go local, you'll find that the food gives real insight into the people, the history and the land. (What a fantastic excuse to eat up!)

Defining the island diet is no simple matter. It's multiethnic, yet distinct from classic ethnic cooking. It's got a full-fledged highbrow cuisine, yet its iconic dishes are lowbrow local *grinds* (akin to street food). The only way to understand the island diet is to partake of its pleasures. Below, we describe three major categories, all of which have the following in common:

First, the primary starch in Hawaii is sticky, medium-grain white rice. Jasmine rice is tolerated with Thai food, but flaky rice is considered haole (Caucasian) food (and Uncle Ben's is considered inedible).

Second, the top condiment is soy sauce (ubiquitously called by its Japanese name, *shōyu*), which combines well with sharp Asian flavors, such as ginger, green onion and garlic.

Third, meat, chicken or fish is often integral to a dish. For quick, cheap eating, locals devour anything tasty, from Portuguese sausage to hamburger steak to corned beef. But the dinner-table highlight is always seafood, especially succulent, freshly caught *'ahi* (tuna).

Fourth, non-local classics (such as pizza and bagels) are usually disappointing. Also bear in mind the idiosyncratic local definitions: in Hawaii, 'barbecue' typically means teriyaki-marinated.

Finally, while Kaua'i's top restaurants can hold their own among statewide peers, you generally won't find the cutting-edge culi-

Coconut shrimp plate with chili sauce

AIMÉE GOGGINS

GO FISH

Fresh sashimi-grade *'ahi* for $10 per pound? You're not dreaming. Perhaps that's why locals eat twice as much seafood as the per-capita US national average. *'Ahi* is the local favorite for eating raw, but *mahimahi* and *ono* are also popular for cooking.

The **Hawai'i Seafood Buyers' Guide** (www.hawaii-seafood.org) is a fascinating, one-stop resource (whether you're interested in catching, selecting or eating island fish).

The following species are most commonly eaten in Hawaii:

'ahi – yellowfin or bigeye tuna, red flesh, excellent raw or rare
aku – skipjack tuna, red flesh, strong flavor; *katsuo* in Japanese
kajiki – Pacific blue marlin; *a'u* in Hawaiian
mahimahi – dolphin fish or dorado, pink flesh, popular cooked
nairage – striped marlin; *a'u* in Hawaiian
onaga – red snapper, soft and moist
ono – wahoo, white-fleshed and flaky
opah – moonfish, firm and rich
'opakapaka – pink snapper, delicate flavor, premium quality
'opelu – mackerel scad, pan-sized, delicious when fried
shutome – swordfish, succulent and meaty
tako – octopus, chewy texture
tombo – albacore tuna, light flesh, mild flavor, silky texture

nary creativity that you'd find on O'ahu and even on Maui or Hawai'i the Big Island.

A terrific resource on Hawaii cuisine and its budding locavore movement is **Edible Hawaiian Islands** (www.ediblehawaiianislands.com), available free islandwide or by subscription.

Hawaii Regional Cuisine

If pineapple-topped entrées epitomized Hawaii cuisine till the late 1980s, locals are partly to blame. Fine dining in Hawaii meant copycat 'continental' fare that hid the basic appeal of local ingredients: locally caught fish, locally grown produce and locally raised meat.

While there were many decent, mid-range Japanese and Chinese eateries, Hawaii lacked an actual unique local cuisine. Further, the local appetite for cheap, filling food (never mind that they're made with canned goods) did nothing to push the gourmet envelope.

In the late 1980s Hawaii's top chefs finally shone the spotlight on the islands. They partnered with local farmers, ranchers and fishers to gather the freshest ingredients, and they found inspiration in the varied ethnic cuisines. Often, they transformed down-home comfort food into dressed-up masterpieces. The movement was dubbed 'Hawaii Regional Cuisine,' and the pioneering chefs such as Alan Wong, Peter Merriman and Roy Yamaguchi became celebrities.

Today Hawaii Regional Cuisine can be defined broadly to include restaurants that highlight fresh local ingredients, such as the Mediterranean-inspired tapas restaurant Bar Acuda Tapas & Wine (p142) but the classics include celebrity chef Roy Yamaguchi's namesake (p173), Tidepools (p173), the Beach House Restaurant (p173), Postcards Café (p142) and Hanapepe Café (p195).

KAUA'I GOES LOCAVORE

Hawaii Regional Cuisine started as a four-star phenomenon, but it is defined not by fanciness but by simplicity: local, seasonal, organic ingredients, handpicked if possible. Top chefs insist on top quality, and small farmers have stepped up with excellent crops.

The locavore trend, spurred by Hawaii Regional Cuisine, might help struggling island farms survive. Regrettably, 90% of the state's basic food supply is imported, including 80% of fresh milk. (When O'ahu's last dairy closed in early 2008, only two Big Island dairies were left statewide.) Kaua'i's only commercial dairy is Kauai Kunana Dairy (p118).

Fresh local produce is a highlight of Hawaii's food scene

LUCI YAMAMOTO

Kaua'i's major commercial crops are coffee, taro and seed corn, but at farmers markets you can find the gamut of fruits and vegetables. It's simple: shop at farmers markets (see the boxed text, p253). Buy local produce. You'll eat better and also help sustain Kaua'i's budding new farming industry. For more on sustainable agriculture, see p46.

Local Food

Cheap, filling and tasty, local food is the stuff of cravings and comfort. Such food might be dubbed 'street food' but street vendors are uncommon, except at farmers markets. No list is complete without the classic plate lunch, a fixed-plate meal containing 'two scoop rice,' macaroni-potato salad and your choice of a hot protein dish, such as *tonkatsu* (breaded, fried pork cutlets), fried mahimahi or teriyaki chicken. Often eaten with disposable chopsticks on disposable plates, they are tasty and filling. Typically fried, salty, gravy-laden and meaty, plates now include grilled fish, brown rice and green salad.

The local palate prefers hot rice or noodle entrées to cold cuts and sliced bread. Thus another favorite is *saimin*, a soup of chewy Chinese egg noodles and Japanese broth, garnished with colorful topping such as green onion, dried nori, *kamaboko* (steamed fish cake), egg roll or *char siu*.

Top Picks

LOCALLY GROWN

- **Oliver Shagnasty's Kaua'i Natural Raw Honey** (sold locally)
- **Kauai Kunana Dairy goat cheese and bath products** (www.kauaikunanadairy.com; see p118)
- **Sheldonia Farm organic greens grown in Omao on the South Shore** (served at fine restaurants such as the Beach House Restaurant (p173), Shells (p173) and Roy's (p173)
- **Organic coffee from Blair Estate Organic Coffee Farm** (☎ 800-750-5662; www.blairestatecoffee.com; $30 per lb)
- **Organic vanilla beans and palm-blossom honey from Steelgrass Farm** (www.steelgrass.org/giftshop; see p83)
- **Grass-fed beef (gamier 'real' beef) raised in Lawa'i on the South Shore by Medeiros Farm** (☎ 332-8211; 4365 Papalina Rd, Kalaheo; 8am-5pm Mon-Fri, 8:30am-3pm Sat)
- **Organic ginger from Kolo Kai Organic Farm** (www.kolokaiorganicfarm.com)

Look for locally grown products at farmers markets (p253), Papaya's (Waipouli, p97, and Hanalei, p142), Banana Joe's (p119), Java Kai (Kapa'a, p104, and Hanalei, p141) and other venues islandwide.

In a hurry, pick up a *bentō* (prepackaged Japanese-style box lunch containing rice, meat or fish, and Japanese garnishes such as pickles, at deli counters and corner stores. And you can't go home without trying a Big Island invention called *loco moco,* a bowl of rice, two eggs (typically fried over-easy) and hamburger patty, topped with gravy and a dash of *shōyu.*

Consider yourself lucky if you snag an invitation to a *pupu* (appetizer) party at a local home. Go casual and expect an endless spread of grazing foods (forget the cheese and crackers), such as fried shrimp, *edamame* (boiled soybeans in the pod) and *maki* (rolled) sushi. A must-try is *poke* (pronounced 'PO-keh'), Hawaii's soul food, a savory dish of bite-sized raw fish (typically *'ahi*), seasoned typically with *shōyu,* sesame oil, green onion, sea salt, *ogo* (seaweed) and *inamona,* a flavoring made of roasted and ground *kukui* (candlenut).

Nowadays kids veer toward mainstream candy and gum, but the traditional local treat is mouth-watering Chinese crack seed, preserved fruit (typically plum, cherry, mango or lemon) that, like Coca-Cola or curry, is impossible to describe. It can be sweet, sour, salty or licorice-spicy. Sold prepackaged at grocers or by the pound at specialty shops, crack seed is mouthwatering and addictive.

Top Picks

POKE BY THE POUND

- **Pono Market** (p104)
- **Koloa Fish Market** (p161)
- **Ishihara Market** (p201)
- **Fish Express** (p71)
- **Hanalei Dolphin Fish Market** (p142)

On a hot day, nothing can beat shave ice, which consists of a mound of ice, shaved as fine as powdery snow, that's then packed into a cup and drenched with various sweet syrups in eye-popping hues. Purists stick with only ice but, for added decadence, try one with sweet azuki-bean paste or ice cream underneath.

Native Hawaiian

Utterly memorable in rich, earthy flavors and native ingredients, Hawaiian food is like no other. Today, several dishes are staples in the local diet, but they're generally harder to find than other cuisines. The best venues for good, authentic Hawaiian food are plate-lunch shops, diners, fish markets and supermarket delis. Commercial luau buffets include all the notable dishes, but the quality can be mediocre.

Guava-and-lemon shave ice LINDA CHING

THE OTHER PINK MEAT

Simply put, locals love Spam. Yes, *that* Spam. It's a local comfort food, typically eaten sliced and sautéed to a light crispiness in sweetened *shōyu*. Expect to see Hormel's iconic canned ham product served with eggs for breakfast or as a *loco moco* option. It's especially enjoyed as Spam *musubi* (rice ball topped with fried Spam and wrapped with dried seaweed, or *nori*) – folks of all stripes savor this only-in-Hawaii creation that's culturally somewhat akin to an easy, satisfying PB&J sandwich.

The affinity for Spam arose during the plantation era, when canned meat was cheap and easy to prepare for *bentō* (box) lunches. In Hawaii, unlike on the mainland, there's no stigma to eating Spam. If you acquire a taste for it, plan a trip to Honolulu for the annual **Waikiki Spam Jam** (www.spamjamhawaii.com) and go wild in your own kitchen with *Hawai'i Cooks with SPAM: Local Recipes Featuring Our Favorite Canned Meat,* written by prolific cookbook author Muriel Miura.

Perhaps the most famous (or infamous) Hawaiian dish is poi, or steamed and mashed wetland taro, which was sacred to ancient Hawaiians. Locals savor the bland to mildly tart flavor as a starchy palate cleanser, but its slightly sticky and pasty consistency can be off-putting to nonlocals. Taro is highly nutritious, low in calories, easily digestible and versatile to prepare. Also try taro chips (made with dryland/upland 'Chinese' taro), available from local grocers.

Locals typically eat poi as a counterpoint to strongly flavored fish dishes such as *lomilomi* salmon (minced salted salmon tossed with diced tomato and green onion) and *poke* (see p249). In case you're wondering, salmon is actually an imported food, first introduced to Hawaiians by the crews of whaling ships.

No Hawaiian feast is complete without *kalua* pig, which is traditionally roasted, whole, underground in an *imu,* a sealed pit of red-hot stones. Cooked this way, the pork comes out smoky, salty and quite succulent. Nowadays *kalua* pork is typically oven-roasted and seasoned with salt and liquid smoke. At commercial luaus, a pig placed in an *imu* is only for show (and it couldn't feed 300-plus guests anyway).

A popular restaurant dish is *laulau,* a bundle of pork or chicken and salted butterfish, wrapped in taro leaves, and steamed in *ti* leaves. When cooked, the melt-in-your-mouth taro leaves blend perfectly with the savory meats.

Another food hardly seen on menus is raw *'opihi,* which you might see locals picking off shoreline rocks.

DRINKS

On 3000 acres in 'Ele'ele, Kaua'i Coffee Company (p186) produces 60% of the state's coffee, but its beans lack the international cachet of Kona coffee. The company grows mainly the shrubby, wind-resistant Yellow Catuai variety, which they machine-harvest. Aficionados tend to prefer the hand-picked Typica variety, which is grown by the five-acre **Blair Estate Organic Coffee Farm** (www.lbdcoffee.com), a family-run business with deep roots in the island coffee industry.

Café culture has taken root, with baristas brewing espresso at deli counters, indie hangouts and, of course, Starbucks. Local old-timers balk at paying $3-plus for coffee, but today's youth are eager converts to lattes and cappuccinos. Still, Kaua'i's handful of cafés close by dinnertime and exude a hippie, not hipster, vibe.

While fresh fruit is plentiful at farmers markets, fresh fruit juice tends to be pricey and sold mainly at health-food markets and roadside fruit stands, such as the Coconut Cup (p104), which makes tropical smoothies to order. An offshoot of the smoothie is the frosty, an icy dessert with the texture of ice cream, made by puréeing frozen fruit in a food processor. Try it at Banana Joe's Fruitstand (p119). Forgo the supermarket cartons and cans, which tend to be sugary drinks.

Unique to Hawaii are two fruit-juice 'tonics' nowadays marketed mainly to tourists: *'awa* (kava), a mild sedative, and *noni* (Indian mulberry), which some consider to be a cure-all. Both fruits are pungent, if not repulsive, in smell and taste, so they are typically mixed with other juices.

Among alcoholic beverages, beer is the local drink of choice. Kaua'i's two microbreweries are Waimea Brewing Company (p202), with a full restaurant–pub in Waimea; and **Keoki Brewing Company** (☎ 245-8884; www.keokibrewing.com; 2976 Aukele, Lihu'e), which sells two popular ales islandwide, Keoki Gold (golden) and Keoki Sunset (amber).

Wine is gaining in popularity among the upper-income classes, and all top-end restaurants offer a decent selection. For retail bottles, connoisseurs will appreciate the **Wine Garden** (☎ 245-5766; 4495 Puhi Rd, Puhi; 🕑 10am-6:30pm Tue-Sat), located along the highway just south of Lihu'e.

CELEBRATIONS

To celebrate is to feast. Whether a 300-guest wedding or an intimate birthday party, a massive spread is mandatory. If not, why bother? Most gatherings are informal, held at parks, beaches or homes, featuring a potluck buffet of homemade dishes. On major American holidays, mainstream foods appear (eg Easter eggs and Thanksgiving turkey) alongside local fare such as rice (instead of mashed potatoes), sweet-potato tempura (instead of yams) and hibachi-grilled teriyaki beef (instead of roast beef).

Now that agri-tourism and gourmet cuisine are trendy, food festivals are garnering much attention. The Hanalei Taro Festival (p141), a biennial event (even-numbered years), features poi-pounding and taro-cooking contests. More extravagant (from $85 to $100) but still informal stand-up events are the Spring Gourmet Gala (p69), featuring grazing stations of food-and-wine pairings by big-name chefs, and Taste of Hawaii (p91), a line-up-and-sample extravaganza dubbed the 'ultimate Sunday brunch.'

Many public festivals and events offer lots of family-friendly outdoor food booths, serving much more than standard concession grub. The Waimea Town Celebration (p200), Koloa Plantation Days Celebration (p161), Coconut Festival (p103) and Kaua'i County Farm Bureau Fair (p70) showcase not only local culture but also local food, from shave ice to plate lunches.

Island Insights

County law prohibits retail sales of alcohol past 11pm. If you're too late, bars are your only option for midnight drinking.

Luaus

In ancient Hawaii, a luau commemorated auspicious occasions, such as births, war victories or successful harvests. Today, only commercial luaus offer the elaborate

IS CHOCOLATE THE NEW COFFEE?

The world's 'chocolate-growing belt' extends 20 degrees north and south of the equator; the key producers are West Africa, Brazil, Ecuador, Malaysia and Indonesia. Today, the Hawaiian Islands, which fall at the belt's northern edge, are inching their way into the industry. Cacao is among the specialty crops that sustainable-agriculture proponents are touting for Hawaii's next generation of farmers.

The forerunner is the Big Island's Original Hawaiian Chocolate Factory, a mom-and-pop farm that's been producing 100% Kona chocolate since 2000. Making chocolate is no cheap or overnight venture, and it's commendable that they do all of their own processing, packaging and marketing, all while growing cacao on their six-acre farm (and buying the rest from 60 other farmers on the island). Since 2005, a second company, O'ahu's Dole-owned Waialua Estate, started growing cacao, which it now ships to San Francisco's Guittard Chocolate Company for roasting, grinding and final processing. Both companies sell their chocolate online.

There are many fine chocolate makers (using imported chocolate) across the Hawaiian Islands. But if you're curious about *100% Hawaii-grown chocolate*, your choices dwindle to a handful. On Kaua'i, cacao farming remains in the simmering stage (it takes thousands of mature plants to produce enough cacao for steady commercial production), but **Steelgrass Farm** (see the boxed text, p83) offers a fascinating farm tour that traces how cacao beans transform into chocolate bars.

Hawaiian feast and hula dancing that folks expect. A $75 to $100 ticket buys you a highly choreographed Polynesian dance show and an all-you-can-eat buffet of luau standards – usually toned down for the Western palate – such as poi, *kalua* pig, steamed mahimahi, teriyaki chicken and *haupia* (coconut custard).

For the most impressive show, Kilohana Plantation's Luau Kalamaku (p72) offers a compelling theatrical production and professional-caliber dancers. If setting is important to you, the Sheraton Kaua'i Resort features the only luau on a beach (p174), performed for a relatively small audience (200 to 300 people). The long-running luau at Smith's Tropical Paradise (p83) is a family affair and, while touristy, the multicultural performances with dancers of all age has its appeal.

Private luau celebrations, typically for weddings or first birthdays, are often large banquet-hall gatherings. The menu might be more daring – perhaps include raw *'a'ama* (black crab) and *'opihi* (limpet) – and the entertainment more low-key. No fire eaters.

Don't Miss

- **Chocolate-tasting tour at Steelgrass Farms** (p83)
- **Homemade taro chips from Taro Ko Chips Factory** (p194)
- **Steaming noodle soups at Hamura Saimin** (p70)
- **Garlic shrimp at the Savage Shrimp van** (p172)
- **Befriending locals who'll bestow homegrown avocados and starfruit on you**
- **Hawaiian plate lunch and taro-coconut mochi at Hanalei Taro & Juice Co** (p141)
- **'Ono (delicious) plate lunches at Mark's Place** (p180)
- **Spam musubi and homemade manju (Japanese sweet-bean-filled pastry) at Pono Market** (p104)
- **Poke rolls (in rice paper) from Duke's Canoe Club** (p72)
- **Coconut almonds, Kona-coffee pecans and other addictive, crunchy, nutty treats at Kauai Nut Roasters** (p144)

Island Insights

Hawaii is the only US state commercially producing coffee and chocolate.

WHERE TO EAT & DRINK

There's no need to bring a tie or heels to Kaua'i, as even fine dining is island-style casual. Destination eateries tend to cluster in the resort areas and largest towns, meaning Po'ipu, Princeville and Hanalei. The Eastside is best for moderate prices, and scattered here and there are gems such as Hanapepe Café (p195).

There's a local/tourist divide in restaurant choices: tourists are willing to pay a premium for waterfront setting and go-for-broke quality; hence they flock to the Beach House Restaurant (p173), Tidepools (p173), Duke's Canoe Club (p72) and other resort-y restaurants.

Local prefer good value, meaning tasty food and generous portions, never mind the lack of pretty view or decor. They're regulars at diners such as Ono Family Restaurant (p104), Tip Top Café & Sushi Katsu (p70) and Garden Island Barbecue & Chinese Restaurant (p71). For a dinner splurge, locals pack into Kintaro (p92), night after night.

On the road, take-out food will save time and money. Take advantage of Kaua'i's plethora of fish markets for *poke* (see Top Picks box, p249, for recommendations) and gourmet-quality fish plates. Lihu'e's Fish Express (p71) has an especially diverse menu of takeout fish entrées. Omnivores not counting calories should indulge in local-style plate lunches, *loco moco* and saimin at delis and diners. For family dining, see p223.

HABITS & CUSTOMS

In most households, home cooking is integral to daily life, perhaps owing to the slower pace, backyard gardens and obsession with food. Meals are early and on the dot: typically 6am breakfast, noon lunch and 6pm dinner. At home, locals rarely (perhaps never) serve formal sit-down meals with individual courses. Even when entertaining, meals are typically served potluck style with a spread of flavorful dishes that will seem ridiculously clashing to the unfamiliar palate.

If invited to a local home, show up on time and bring dessert. Remove your shoes at the door. And don't be surprised if you're forced to take home a plate or two of leftovers.

Except at top resort restaurants, the island dress code means that T-shirts and flip-flops are ubiquitous. But the older local generation tends toward neat, modest attire. Kaua'i restaurants typically open and close early; late-night dining is virtually nonexistent. In general, locals tip slightly less than mainlanders do, but still up to 20% for good service and at least 15% for the basics.

Top Picks

SWEET TREATS

- **Fresh malasadas (Portuguese sugar-coated doughnuts) at Kaua'i Malasadas** (p70)
- **Organic gelato and sorbetto at Papalani Gelato** (p172)
- **Exquisite coconut macaroons from Icing on the Cake** (p91)
- **Shave ice from Hawaiian Blizzard** (p104) **or Jo-Jo's Anuenue Shave Ice and Treats** (p200)
- **Gooey coconut–vanilla bean tapioca from Sweet Marie's Hawaii** (p97)
- **Liliko'i chiffon pie from Hamura Saimin** (p70) **or Omoide Bakery** (p195)
- **Tropical granola, trail mix and cookies that rival mom's, all from Kaua'i Granola** (p202)
- **Homemade baklava at the Mediterranean Gourmet** (p149)

VEGETARIANS & VEGANS

Though locals love their sashimi and Spam, vegetarians and vegans won't go hungry on Kaua'i. A handful of restaurants cater to vegetarian, vegan, fish-only or health-conscious diets. Alas, Kaua'i's star vegan restaurant, Blossoming Lotus, closed in 2008, but other notable venues include Postcards Café (p142) and Hanapepe Café (p195), which focus on vegetarian and fish dishes. The high-end Hawaii Regional Cuisine menus always have vegetarian options. Asian eateries offer varied tofu and veggie options, but beware of meat- or fish-based broths.

The most economical way to ensure no meat or animal ingredients is to forage at farmers markets and health food stores.

FARM-FRESH PRODUCE

Locally grown produce is woefully scarce at supermarkets, and the steep prices might steer you away. But instead of resorting to mainland-grown options, try shopping at **farmers markets**:

Monday

- Noon at Knudsen Park, Maluhia Rd (Hwy 520), Koloa
- 3pm at Kukui Grove Shopping Center, Kaumuali'i Hwy (Hwy 50), Lihu'e (Map p60)

Tuesday

- our pick 2pm in Waipa, inland side of Kuhio Hwy, slightly west of Hanalei. This is the choice one!
- 3pm at Kalaheo Neighborhood Center, Papalina Rd, Kalaheo
- 3pm at Wailua Homesteads Park, Malu Rd (Map pp84–5)

Wednesday

- 3pm at Kapa'a New Park, Kahau St, Kapa'a (Map p101)

Thursday

- 3:30pm at Hanapepe Town Park, behind the fire station
- our pick 4:30pm at Kilauea Neighborhood Center, Keneke St, Kilauea (Map p119)

Friday

- 3pm at Vidinha Stadium, Ho'olako Rd and Kapule Hwy, Lihu'e (Map p60)

Saturday

- 9am at Kekaha Neighborhood Center, Elepaio Rd, Kekaha
- 9am at Christ Memorial Episcopal Church, Kolo Rd, Kilauea (Map p119)
- 9:30am near Hanalei Community Center, Hanalei, Kuhio Hwy

FOOD GLOSSARY

Hawaii cuisine is multiethnic and so is the lingo. In addition to this glossary, see www.lonelyplanet.com/hawaiian-language for a free downloadable Hawaiian Language & Glossary chapter covering pidgin and Hawaiian pronunciation tips.

adobo – Filipino chicken or pork cooked in vinegar, *shōyu,* garlic and spices
arare – *shōyu*-flavored rice crackers; also called *kaki mochi*
'awa – kava, a native plant used to make an intoxicating drink
bentō – Japanese box lunch
broke da mout – delicious; literally 'broke the mouth'
char siu – Chinese barbecued pork
crack seed – Chinese-style preserved fruit; a salty, sweet or sour or both snack
donburi – meal-sized bowl of rice and main dish
furikake – a catch-all Japanese seasoning or condiment, usually dry and sprinkled atop rice; in Hawaii, often used for *poke*
grind – to eat
grinds – food; *'ono kine grinds* is good food
guava – fruit with green or yellow rind, moist pink flesh and lots of edible seeds
haupia – coconut-cream dessert
hulihuli chicken – rotisserie-cooked chicken
imu – underground earthen oven used to cook *kalua* pig and other luau food
inamona – roasted and ground *kukui* (candlenut), used to flavor *poke*
izakaya – a Japanese pub serving tapas-style dishes
kalo – taro
kalua – Hawaiian method of cooking pork and other luau food in an *imu*
kamaboko – cake of puréed, steamed fish; used to garnish Japanese dishes
katsu – Japanese deep-fried cutlets, usually pork or chicken; see *tonkatsu*
kaukau – food
laulau – bundle of pork or chicken and salted butterfish, wrapped in taro and *ti* leaves and steamed
li hing mui – sweet-salty preserved plum; type of crack seed; also refers to the flavor powder
liliko'i – passion fruit

A *bentō* (Japanese box lunch) is a great takeout option LUCI YAMAMOTO

loco moco – dish of rice, fried egg and hamburger patty topped with gravy or other condiments
lomilomi salmon – minced, salted salmon, diced tomato and green onion
luau – Hawaiian feast
mai tai – 'tiki bar' drink typically containing rum, grenadine, and lemon and pineapple juices
malasada – Portuguese fried doughnut, sugar-coated, no hole
manapua – Chinese steamed or baked bun filled with *char siu*
manju – Japanese steamed or baked cake, often filled with sweet bean paste
mochi – Japanese sticky-rice cake
nishime – Japanese stew of root vegetables and seaweed
noni – type of mulberry with smelly yellow fruit, used medicinally
nori – Japanese seaweed, usually dried
ogo – crunchy seaweed, often added to *poke; limu* in Hawaiian
'ohelo – shrub with edible red berries similar in tartness and size to cranberries
'ono – delicious
'ono kine grinds – good food
pho – Vietnamese soup, typically beef broth, noodles and fresh herbs
poi – staple Hawaiian starch made of steamed, mashed taro
poke – cubed, marinated raw fish
pupu – snacks or appetizers
saimin – local-style noodle soup
shave ice – cup of finely shaved ice sweetened with colorful syrups
shōyu – soy sauce
soba – thin Japanese buckwheat-flour noodles
star fruit – translucent green-yellow fruit with five ribs like the points of a star and sweet, juicy pulp
taro – staple plant with edible roots and stems (used to make poi) and edible leaves (eaten in *laulau); kalo* in Hawaiian
teishoku – Japanese set meal
teppanyaki – Japanese style of cooking with an iron grill
tonkatsu – Japanese breaded and fried pork cutlets, also prepared as chicken *katsu*
tsukemono – Japanese pickled vegetables
ume – Japanese pickled plum
unagi – freshwater eel, usually grilled and served with sweet sauce over sushi rice

PLANNING YOUR TRIP

A tropical vacation on Kaua'i is almost a no-brainer, with world-class beaches coming with comfy US standards of living. Your main pre-trip planning will be booking accommodations and a car. Budget travelers, especially, should book early to snag decent deals.

Most visitors will land in Honolulu first, making a two-island hop (O'ahu and Kaua'i) a convenient option. This combination gives a please-all blend of urban and rural, but if you've got only a week, we highly recommend spending the entire time on Kaua'i.

WHEN TO GO

With mild temperatures year-round, there's no real off-season regarding climate. But it is cooler and rainier in winter (November through March), the season most prone to torrential rainstorms that can cause major flooding. That said, winter does offer the thrill of whale watching.

Surf conditions also vary greatly by season. Hanalei Bay, for example, is a placid lagoon in summer and an experts-only surfing mecca come winter. Such seasonal changes might affect your plans if you want to kayak the Na Pali Coast (or even sail there on a snorkeling cruise), possible only during summer. For more on weather and ocean safety, see the Climate section of the Directory (p264) and the Outdoor Activities & Adventures chapter (p30).

Avoiding the 'tourist season' is growing impossible as it's spread and become a year-round phenomenon. But avoid the winter high season (mid-December through March), when prices soar at many hotels and condos. The best times to go are fall (September through early December) and spring (mid-April through June), when prices are generally lower and holiday vacationers are gone.

During major holidays (see p267), including Thanksgiving, Christmas, and the New Year, occupancy is high, if not booked solid.

You might also consider planning your trip to include some of Kaua'i's colorful indie festivals and events (p262).

COSTS & MONEY

Kaua'i is veering toward the high end in accommodations and dining, but remains affordable for most budgets with proper planning. Accommodations will be your biggest expense, followed by airfare and car rental. While rates run the gamut, most studio or one-bedroom rates fall between $100 and $200; for an ocean view, expect to pay $200. Big-name resorts start at $250 and skyrocket toward the thousands. Decent digs under $100 are rather scarce.

Families and groups can economize by renting houses or condo units with kitchens, and sharing expenses. Solo travelers are hit hardest and need to be savvy about finding studios or special single rates.

In general, the North Shore is the priciest region on the island, especially for solo travelers seeking studio or minimal space.

DON'T LEAVE HOME WITHOUT...

- Necessary specialty items (eg maternity swimsuit)
- Hiking shoes that you don't mind getting red-dirt dirty
- Sport sandals for everyday walking
- UV-protection sunglasses for ocean glare
- Wide-brimmed sunhat
- Travel umbrella or rain poncho for random showers
- Binoculars for whale watching and birding
- Snorkel gear if you're particular about fit and quality
- Identification cards (eg student, automobile association, AARP) for possible discounts

CLIMATE CHANGE & TRAVEL

Climate change is a serious threat to the ecosystems that humans rely upon, and air travel is the fastest-growing contributor to the problem. Lonely Planet regards travel, overall, as a global benefit, but believes we all have a responsibility to limit our personal impact on global warming.

Nearly every form of motorized travel generates CO_2 (the main cause of human-induced climate change), but planes are far and away the worst offenders, not just because of the sheer distances they allow us to travel, but also because they release greenhouse gases high into the atmosphere. The statistics are frightening: two people taking a round-trip flight between Europe and the USA will contribute as much to climate change as an average household's gas and electricity consumption over a whole year.

Climatecare.org and other websites use 'carbon calculators' that allow travelers to offset the level of greenhouse gases they are responsible for with financial contributions to sustainable travel schemes that reduce global warming – including projects in India, Honduras, Kazakhstan and Uganda.

Lonely Planet, together with Rough Guides and other concerned partners in the travel industry, support the carbon offset scheme run by climatecare.org. Lonely Planet offsets all of its staff and author travel. For more information, check out our website, www.lonelyplanet.com.

The swankiest accommodations can be found at top-end resorts and vacation-rental homes, especially those in Po'ipu and along the North Shore.

Airfares vary too greatly for any generalities, except a tip on timing: fares rise during the winter high season, especially around the holidays. For land transportation, there is no question: you must rent a car.

CHOOSING ACCOMMODATIONS

In this book, accommodations are listed in price order, from lowest to highest, in the Sleeping sections of each regional chapter. Ratings range from \$ (under \$90), \$\$ (\$90 to \$170), \$\$\$ (\$170 to \$270) to \$\$\$\$ (over \$270). Room rates are listed for single (s) or double (d) occupancy; if there's no rate difference for one or two people, the general room (r) rate is listed. Unless otherwise noted, breakfast is not included, bathrooms are private and the room is available year-round. Listed rates do not include taxes of 11.41%. Smoking is prohibited indoors. For a key to the icons used in this book, see the Quick Reference on the inside front cover.

At many hotels and condos, rates rise during the winter high season (mid-December through March) and on major holidays, festivals and events. In high-demand times, the best accommodations are booked months (even a year) in advance. See below for specific information about each lodging type.

Regarding bargaining or haggling, don't bother. In Hawaii, it's just not a widespread practice. Hotel or condo staffers have no authority to grant special discounts, while innkeepers and B&B owners might simply refuse the room.

B&Bs, Inns & Vacation Homes

The terminology can be fuzzy, but in this book, B&Bs either serve full or continental breakfasts or provide groceries for guests to prepare on their own. While also located in owner-occupied homes, inns do not include breakfast. Inn units can be spacious suites, including kitchenette, private access and other apartment amenities. Vacation homes refer to freestanding, fully equipped residences, from cottages to mansions. The

HOW MUCH?

- **Shave ice** \$3
- **Ziplining tour** \$120
- **Pound of poke** \$10
- **Plate lunch** \$7
- **Luau show** \$85

For additional price information, see the Quick Reference page on the inside front cover.

TYING THE KNOT ON KAUA'I

Kaua'i was a 'destination wedding' site long before the term was even coined. Today, about 90% of all weddings on the island involve nonresidents. So while it's not a novel idea, getting hitched on Kaua'i is also a well-oiled process, and uncomplicated. In addition to choosing a wedding site, which might require planning ahead, be aware of the state's marriage license requirements, listed at the end of this box.

In choosing a wedding site, think about your budget and style. A Kaua'i wedding can be anything from a gala formal banquet to a barbecue picnic at the beach. Consider the following locations for starters:

- **Ritzy resorts**, including the St Regis Princeville Resort (p131), Grand Hyatt Kaua'i Resort & Spa (p178) in Po'ipu, and Kaua'i Marriott Resort (p77) in Lihu'e
- **Beaches** (of course), but you need a permit for weddings on state land (see http://hawaii.gov/dlnr/land/forms-1/forms)
- **Gardens**, including Na 'Aina Kai Botanical Gardens (p118) and Smith's Tropical Paradise (p83)
- **Vacation-rental properties**, but ask agents about fees and rules
- **Wacky settings**, including underwater in scuba gear, horseback riding to the backcountry, midair in a helicopter – you get the idea

Even simple weddings will entail advance planning, especially regarding licensing and beach permitting. One way to avoid errors (and unneeded stress) is to hire a good wedding planner. We highly recommend Mike and Martina Hough's **Kauai Island Weddings** (www.kauaiislandweddings.com) for their thorough knowledge of island venues, buoyant photography (including 300 digital images) and do-it-all versatility.

Bear in mind the state's marriage requirements before locking in your plans:

- Minimum age is 16. If under 18, parental consent is required.
- Valid photo identification is required (driver's license or passport).
- A completed application form is required prior to the marriage license appointment. You can either download the form at www.hawaii.gov/health or request the form by phone (☎ Honolulu 808-586-4544, 🕑 8am-4pm Monday to Friday) or by mail (State of Hawaii Marriage License Office, PO Box 3378, Honolulu, HI 96801).
- You must meet with a marriage license agent, who must witness your signing of the form.
- You must contact the marriage license agent for an appointment prior to arrival. Some agents do not book appointments over two weeks before the event. Both parties must be present. For a list of agents, call ☎ 241-3498; you can leave messages, which are promptly returned, on this pre-recorded information line.
- The current licensing fee is $60 (cash only), payable to the agent at the appointment. The agent might charge an additional $5 fee.
- The marriage license is issued immediately and remains valid for 30 days only in Hawaii (which means you must conquer any cold feet within a month or else pay $60 again for another license).

number of residential accommodations is burgeoning, with Wailua Homesteads, Hanalei and 'Anini teeming with vacation rentals.

Quality varies wildly, and you can usually predict the quality level by the price. While B&B and inn rooms sometimes drop under $100, most cost between $100 and $175. Many require a minimum stay of two or three days and offer discounts for extended stays. Some refuse child guests to maintain a quiet, immaculate or 'romantic' setting. Vacation homes typically start at about $150; note the extra-guest cost, $15 on average. Most residential accommodations require a minimum stay of two or three nights; weekly discounts often apply. Vacation homes are typically owned by non-resident mainlanders, managed by local agencies.

For an extensive, if overwhelming, selection of vacation-rental listings, see **Vacation Rentals By Owner** (VRBO; www.vrbo.com). With VRBO listings, caveat emptor. There is no quality guarantee, so you're on your own if problems arise.

Agents can steer you to trusted accommodations and offer helpful advice. See listings in Po'ipu, Princeville, Lihu'e and Wailua.

Camping & Cabins

Kaua'i offers camping at all levels of 'roughin' it.' Some campgrounds, such as 'Anini Beach Park (p123), are within view of houses; others, such as the campsite in Kalalau Valley (p152), are miles from civilization. For camping supplies and rentals, the best rental sources are Pedal & Paddle (p137) and Kayak Kaua'i (p138), both in Hanalei. You can also buy gear from Pedal & Paddle or from big-box retailers like Kmart and Wal-Mart in Lihu'e.

STATE PARKS

State park campsites can be found at Na Pali Coast State Park (Hanakapi'ai and Kalalau Valleys; p152), Koke'e State Park (see the boxed text, p218). Permits are required from the **Hawaii State Parks office** (Map p62; ☎ 274-3444; www.hawaiistateparks.org; Department of Land & Natural Resources, Division of State Parks, 3060 Eiwa St, Room 306, Lihu'e, HI 96766; 8am-3:30pm Mon-Fri), obtainable either in person or by mail. Fees range from $5 to $10 per night, and time limits are enforced.

For remote backcountry camping in Waimea Canyon State Park (p210) and Koke'e State Park (see the boxed text, p218), there is no charge. The **Division of Forestry & Wildlife** (Map p62; ☎ 274-3433; www.hawaiitrails.org; Department of Land & Natural Resources, Division of Forestry & Wildlife, 3060 Eiwa St, Room 306, Lihu'e, HI 96766; 8am-4pm Mon-Fri) issues free, backcountry camping permits for four sites in Waimea Canyon, two sites (Sugi Grove and Kawaikoi) in the Koke'e State Park area, and the Waialae site near the Alaka'i Wilderness Preserve.

COUNTY PARKS

The county maintains seven campgrounds on Kaua'i. Moving clockwise around the island, these are: Ha'ena Beach Park (p149), Black Pot Beach Park (Hanalei Pier; p145), 'Anini Beach Park (p124), Anahola Beach Park (p108), Hanama'ulu Beach Park (p64), Salt Pond Beach Park (p191) and Lucy Wright Beach Park (p198). The best are the coastal parks at Ha'ena and 'Anini; the latter is particularly secluded and idyllic. The parks at Anahola and Hanama'ulu tend to attract a rougher, shadier crowd and are not recommended for solo or female campers. Each campground is closed one day a week for cleaning and for preventing permanent squatting.

Camping permits cost $3 per night per adult camper (children under 18 free) and are issued in person or by mail (at least one month in advance) at the **Division of Parks & Recreation** (Map p62; ☎ 241-4463; www.kauai.gov; Lihu'e Civic Center, Division of Parks & Recreation, 4444 Rice St, Suite 150, Lihu'e, HI 96766; 8:15am-4pm).

WHAT TO ASK ABOUT VACATION RENTALS

Booking a condo or house, sight unseen, is always a leap of faith. Even if an agent or owner is not trying to stiff you, there's still a chance of misunderstanding. To avoid big disappointment, ask key questions such as these:

- Is my unit 'oceanfront' or 'beachfront'? Oceanfront might mean rocky cliffs. Ask if beachfront waters are swimmable.
- What are the rental terms (eg minimum stay, deposit, check-in and check-out times), payment method and cancellation policy?
- How and when do you get the key? In Hawaii, agents often leave keys with your rental-car company at the airport or they put them in a lockbox and give you the combination.
- Does wi-fi reach all rooms?
- How noisy are the neighborhood chickens?
- For cottages and houses: how near are nearest neighbors and nearest town?
- For B&Bs: what type of breakfast is served?

Note: asking about air-con is unnecessary because tradewinds and ceiling fans work wonders.

Requirements include a signed waiver, application and payment by cash, cashier's check or money order only.

Permits can also be obtained at four satellite locations on weekdays from 8am to noon, but only cashier's checks or money orders are accepted:

Hanapepe Recreation Center (☎ 335-3731; 4451 Puolo Rd)

Kalaheo Neighborhood Center (☎ 332-9770; 4480 Papalina Rd)

Kapa'a Neighborhood Center (☎ 822-1931; 4491 Kou St)

Kilauea Neighborhood Center (☎ 828-1421; 2460 Keneke St)

Top Picks

BUDGET SLEEPS

- **Aloha Hale Orchids** (p106)
- **Garden Room** (p94)
- **Boulay Inn** (p163)
- **Kauai Rock Cabin** (p203)
- **Bunk House at Rosewood Kaua'i** (p93)
- **Westside Dwelling** (p196)
- **Orchid Tree Inn** (p107)
- **Mindy's** (p205)
- **Cozy Kauai Cottage** (p163)
- **Green Acres Cottage** (p122)

Condominiums

Condominiums can offer much more than comparable hotel rooms: they're generally larger, often with separate bedroom(s) and kitchen. They're also more likely to include free wi-fi and washer/dryer, plus a bunch of homey amenities, such as books, DVDs, towels, appliances and beach equipment. If you're lucky, you'll land a renovated unit with hardwood floor, 400-count sheets and even a computer for guests. But therein lies the frustrating thing about condos: each unit is individually owned and, even within the same complex, inconsistencies abound.

For saving money, condos are best for those staying a week or longer, otherwise the mandatory cleaning fee (which averages $75 to $100 for a studio or one-bedroom unit) negates any savings. Most condos require three- to seven-day minimum stays. Prices drop if you stay longer: the weekly rate is typically six times the daily rate and the monthly is three times the weekly.

Most condos are rented through agencies, which are listed in the Po'ipu (p174) and Princeville (p130) sections because of their overwhelming concentrations there. Also search through Google and VRBO, to bypass agencies and perhaps to snag better deals. That said, rental agencies can be helpful in emergencies such as 2am plumbing disasters.

Hostels

Hosteling is sketchy on Kaua'i. Two are open in Kapa'a, but due to consistently negative reports from travelers we have not included them in this book. Also, with dorm beds costing $25 to $30 per night, couples and groups can do better by sharing a budget room elsewhere.

Hotels & Resorts

Hotels suit those who want a full-time staff, daily housekeeping and amenities such as pools and restaurants. Kaua'i has relatively few hotels, but they come in all levels, including luxury mega-hotels, dubbed 'resorts,' in Princeville, Po'ipu and Lihu'e; midrange options on the East Side and basic motels islandwide. (Note: the term 'resort' also refers to general resort areas, such as Princeville.)

One fundamental rule applies to hotels: never pay rack rates. Major hotels (particularly the largest and priciest) commonly undercut their published 'rack rates' to remain as close to capacity as possible. Rates madly fluctuate on the basis of occupancy, so book a room well in advance through the hotel's

BOOK ACCOMMODATIONS ONLINE

For more accommodation reviews and recommendations by Lonely Planet authors, check out www.lonelyplanet.com/hotels. You'll find the true, insider lowdown on the best places to stay. Reviews are thorough and independent, and best of all, you can book online.

A rental cottage at Rosewood Kaua'i (p93)

LUCI YAMAMOTO

website (for discounted internet rates) or through packagers.

Within a given hotel, rates depend mainly on the view. An ocean view can cost 50% to 100% more than a parking-lot view (euphemistically called a 'garden' or 'mountain' view).

TRAVEL LITERATURE

The Hawaiian Islands have always intrigued visitors, including writers who try to capture their uniqueness and complexity. Surprisingly, there is little contemporary travel writing about Kaua'i, beyond travel guides and histories. Thus the following is a mix of historical accounts is a mix of historical travelogue, memoir and cultural analysis.

For other history recommendations see the boxed text, p230; for fiction, see p242.

A Kaua'i Reader (edited by Chris Cook, 2007) This compelling collection of stories and historical accounts covers the gamut, from menehune legends to first-hand descriptions of Hurricane 'Iniki and big-wave surfing.

Aloha Kaua'i: A Childhood (Waimea Williams, 2004) This well-written memoir vividly describes 1950s Kaua'i, before the tourism boom, when simpler island values reigned.

Ha'ena: Through the Eyes of the Ancestors (Carlos Andrade, 2008) Written by a Ha'ena native and University of Hawai'i professor, this is a personal look at the land's sway on all aspects of native life.

Letters From Hawaii (Mark Twain, written 1866) Observant, irreverent, wise and witty, Twain's 25 letters from four months in the 'Sandwich Islands' in 1866 reveal both his pre-fame literary genius and the exoticism of 19th-century island life.

Travelers' Tales Hawai'i: True Stories (various authors, revised ed 2005) Featuring such writers as John McPhee, Jan Morris, Barbara Kingsolver and Maxine Hong Kingston, this varied collection of fine essays on Hawaii is an entertaining introduction to its culture and quirks.

Check the websites of Hawaii-based publishers **Bess Press** (www.besspress.com), **Mutual Publishing** (www.mutualpublishing.com) and **Island Heritage Publishing** (www.welcometotheislands.com) for a mind-boggling selection of Hawaii-related books.

INTERNET RESOURCES

About.com: Hawaii (http://hawaii.about.com) While geared toward mainstream travelers, this encyclopedic site is thorough, current and readable.

our pick **HawaiiHistory.org** (www.hawaiihistory.org) This comprehensive resource on Hawaii's history offers outstanding timelines, articles and photos.

our pick **Kaua'i Explorer** (www.kauaiexplorer.com) A must-see on Kaua'i's beaches and ocean safety, with a handy Q&A forum.

Kaua'i Visitors Bureau (www.kauaidiscovery.com) Run by Kaua'i's marketing agency, this site is a good, if predictable, starting point.

Kaua'i Wedding Professionals Association (www.kauaiwedpro.com) For listings of wedding planners, photographers, florists, caterers and other usual suspects.

LonelyPlanet.com (lonelyplanet.com) Concise basic information on Hawaii and travel planning, plus hotel reviews.

TryKauai.com (www.trykauai.com) Established by longtime Kaua'i resident Lilly 'Lilikoi' Dowling, this no-fee booking site offers colorful photos, reviews, firsthand info and a homey touch.

FESTIVALS & EVENTS CALENDAR

See regional chapters for more listings.

FEBRUARY

Waimea Town Celebration (Waimea; p200)
mid-February
Waimea town comes alive with food, craft and game booths, a beer garden, canoe race, rodeo and good old-fashioned family fun.

APRIL

Spring Gourmet Gala (Lihu'e; p69)
early April
Hawaii's top chefs present food-and-wine pairings that would impress the snobbiest of gourmands at this fundraiser for Kaua'i Community College's culinary arts program.

MAY

Kaua'i Polynesian Festival (Lihu'e; p69)
late May
A visual feast for cultural dance, this is your chance to see expert Tahitian, Maori, Samoan and Hawaiian dancers perform with gusto.

May Day Lei Contest and Fair (Lihu'e; p69)
May 1
Simple strings of plumeria (frangipani) are mere child's play next to the floral masterpieces entered in the annual Kaua'i Museum lei contest.

JUNE

Taste of Hawaii (Wailua; p91)
first Sunday in June
Known as the 'Ultimate Sunday Brunch,' this casual affair showcases local chefs, gourmet food booths and no-holds-barred sampling.

JULY

Koloa Plantation Days Celebration (Koloa; p161)
late July
The South Shore's biggest event celebrates the island's multicultural history with a parade, block party, craft fair, sports competitions and guided walks.

AUGUST

Kaua'i County Farm Bureau Fair (Lihu'e; p70)
late August
Old-fashioned county fairs still draw crowds on Kaua'i, with carnival rides, a livestock show, hula performances and, of course, local 'grinds' (food).

SEPTEMBER

Kaua'i Composers Contest & Concert (Lihu'e; p70)

mid-September

Blend Hawaiian-style music genres with the gamut of local talent, and you get this lively, feel-good event, which originated in 1984 and grew into today's signature event of the islandwide Kaua'i Mokihana Festival.

OCTOBER

Coconut Festival (Kapa'a; p103)

early October

There's something for everyone at this festival honoring the coconut, including cooking demos and contests, food booths, craft vendors and live music.

Annual Eo e Emalani i Alaka'i Festival (Koke'e State Park; p217)

early October

A moving reenactment of Queen Emma's historic 1871 journey to Alaka'i Swamp, this outdoor hula festival showcases dancing and the island reverence for Hawaiian history.

NOVEMBER

'Kaua'i Style' Hawaiian Slack Key Guitar Festival (Lihu'e; p70)

mid-November

Witness top musicians from across the islands performing what's becoming Hawaii's most famous musical genre. Best of all, admission is free.

DECEMBER

Lights on Rice Parade (Lihu'e; p70)

early December

Who doesn't like a parade? Especially one that's brightly lit and full of Christmas cheer, along Lihu'e's Main Street.

Waimea Lighted Christmas Parade (Waimea; p200)

mid-December

Historic Waimea's lighted parade epitomizes small-town charm with a brilliant display of floats and marching units, amid a town dripping with Christmas lights.

New Year's Eve Fireworks (Po'ipu; p172)

December 31

Throughout Hawaii, New Year's Eve means rousing fireworks, from backyard firecrackers and sparklers to festive displays such as this show at Po'ipu Beach Park.

DIRECTORY & TRANSPORTATION

CONTENTS

PRACTICALITIES

BUSINESS HOURS

In this book, reviews do not include opening hours if they follow the typical time frames listed below. For restaurants, we indicate 'breakfast,' 'lunch,' and 'dinner' if hours are standard. But if businesses' opening hours differ by over 30 minutes in either direction, reviews do specify them.

Banks 8:30am-4pm Mon-Fri, some to 6pm Fri & 9am-noon or 1pm Sat
Bars & Clubs to midnight daily, some to 2am Thu-Sat
Businesses 8:30am-4:30pm Mon-Fri, some post offices 9am-noon Sat
Restaurants breakfast 6-10am, lunch 11:30am-2:30pm, dinner 5-9:30pm
Shops 9am-5pm Mon-Sat, some also noon-5pm Sun

CHILDREN

The island's social scene is very informal and family-oriented, so travelers with kids will fit right in. See our Kaua'i for Families chapter (p221) for advice on traveling with kids.

CLIMATE

Kaua'i might be compact, but its climate varies markedly around the island: the Westside and South Shore tend to be dry and sunny, while the North Shore and Eastside see regular showers. Of course, the biggest factor is elevation, so you'll notice an increase in precipitation as you head *mauka* (inland).

Climate also varies by season. Rain is a given in winter (November to March), particularly on the North Shore. The upside is that showers are usually sporadic, and interspersed with sunshine. That said, winter downpours can be torrential, causing dangerous flash floods.

Since the island is only 33 miles wide and 25 miles from north to south, it's easy to

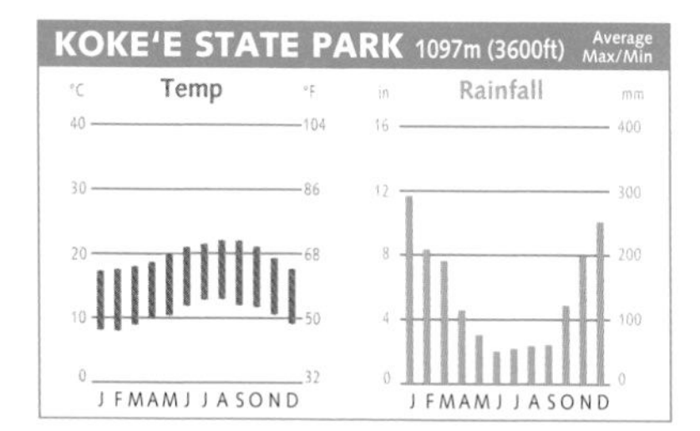

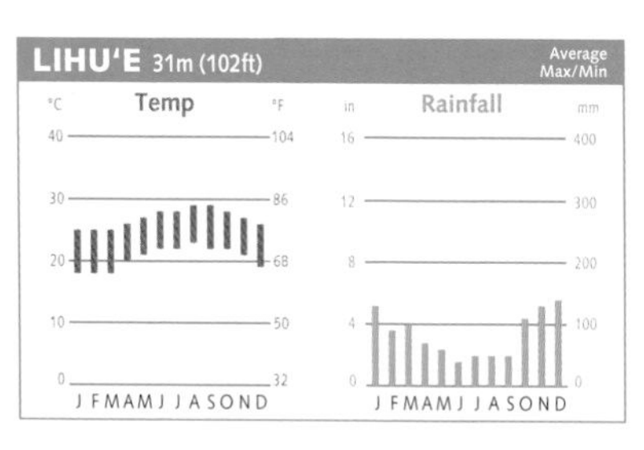

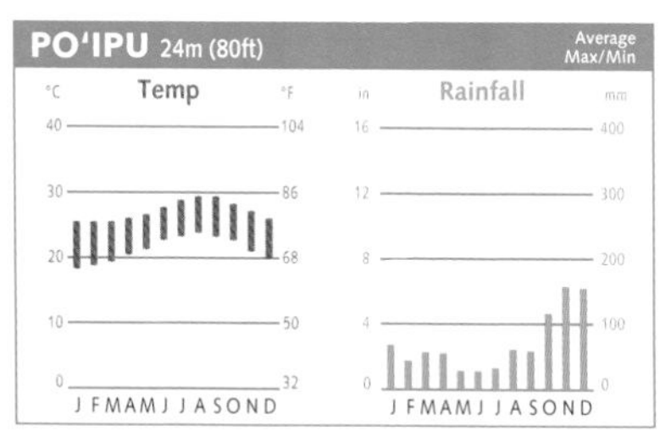

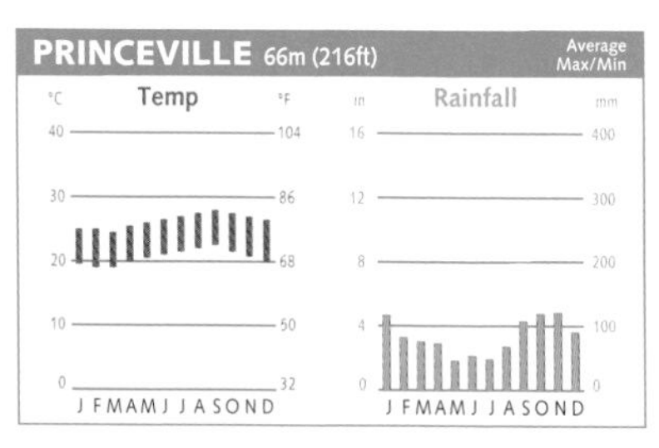

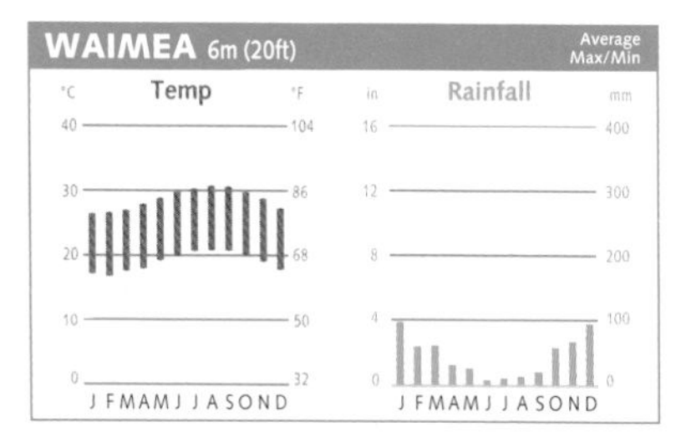

escape to your preferred climate. Temperatures drop at higher elevations (eg at Koke'e State Park) but never to any extremes.

The climate charts, left, give temperature and rainfall averages for popular island destinations. For other information on seasonal differences, see p256.

DANGERS & ANNOYANCES

The majority of visitors leave with pleasant memories, but if you're an unfortunate victim of an accident or crime, contact the **Visitor Aloha Society of Hawaii** (VASH; ☎ 808-926-8274; www.visitoralohasocietyofhawaii.org).

Drug addiction on the island generally involves 'ice' (crystal methamphetamine) or *pakalolo* (marijuana). Visitors can avoid drug trouble by being on guard at deserted beaches and parks (eg Nawiliwili Beach Park, Keahua Arboretum) after dark. On a relatively unpopulated island with virtually no nightlife, you can often find yourself alone, with no one to call for help. Solo travelers, especially, will find it safest to hang out in public places.

The greatest threat to Kaua'i visitors is also a major attraction: the ocean. Drownings are staggeringly frequent among tourists. If you're heading to the beach, please heed the ocean safety tips on p34.

Flooding

During heavy rains, rivers can suddenly rise and threaten people's safety, especially during hiking. Never try to ford an overflowing river. Flooding also affects access to the North Shore, if bridges are closed. If you are stuck on one side, you will have no choice but to wait it out.

Scams

Be wary of tourist information booths that actually lure visitors into buying timeshares. Sellers use freebies, from luaus to cruises, to attract an audience for their 'no obligation' pitches. Don't waste your time.

While relatively innocuous, the fake 'Hawaiian' souvenirs sold at cheap tourist traps are a scam that hurts makers and sellers of genuine Hawaiian products. If the label states 'Made in China' (or any other foreign origin), why bother?

BUZZ OFF

The biggest annoyance on Kaua'i comes in a tiny package: mosquitoes! With the island's wet climate, it's no surprise that the mosquito population thrives. The Hawaiian Islands are home to four types of pest mosquitoes. One species, the Asia tiger mosquito, a daytime biter that arrived in Hawaii 100 years ago, was introduced to the US mainland in 1985 but is not found on the West Coast. Thus people from California and other western states have likely never encountered this aggressive species and, when bitten, developed those unsightly (and irritating) red welts. Island residents often seem unbothered despite bare arms and legs.

Mosquitoes are most prevalent in rainy areas with lots of standing water (which make good breeding sites). When hiking on the Kalalau Trail, any of the Eastside trails or in any forested area, be sure to wear insect repellent. Along windswept coasts (eg Maha'ulepu Beach) and at high elevations (eg Koke'e State Park), you'll find few or no mosquitoes.

DEET is the most widely used and effective repellent for mosquitoes. Use the lowest effective percentage, such as 20% (it's sold up to 35%). If you're allergic to DEET, you could treat your clothing or try a natural repellent, such as Burt's Bees or Avon Skin-So-Soft, but they're not as effective. If you're dining at an outdoor restaurant, ask for a mosquito coil.

Theft & Violence

Violent crimes are relatively infrequent on Kaua'i, especially in populated areas. The main crimes against tourists are car break-ins, especially at roadside parks, campgrounds and parking lots that are slightly deserted – too far from town for police to patrol yet close enough to be a druggie hangout. The very-remote beaches, trails and campgrounds tend to be cleaner and safer because they are less accessible.

Some beaches, surf spots, swimming holes and rural neighborhoods are unofficially considered locals only, so haole (white) tourists might encounter resentment and even violence. Avoid confrontation (you'll be outnumbered) and heed *kapu* (No Trespassing) signs on private property.

Tsunamis

Of all natural disasters, tsunamis have killed more people statewide than all others combined. During the 20th century, Kaua'i was hit by two major tsunamis. Both ravaged the North Shore, causing 14 deaths in 1946 and demolishing 75 homes and washing out six essential bridges in 1957. Today, new homes built in tsunami-prone areas (flood zones) must be built high off the ground.

If you're at the coast when a tsunami occurs, immediately head upland. The front section of local telephone books provides maps of safety evacuation zones and areas susceptible to tsunamis.

DISCOUNT CARDS

While the biggest savings come from '*kama'aina* discounts' given to state residents (or anyone with a valid Hawaii driver's license), nonresidents can cut costs with discounts for children, students, seniors, automobile-club members and the military. Remember to bring your ID cards for proof of membership.

FOOD

In this book, reviews are listed in price order, from lowest to highest, in the Eating section of each regional chapter. Ratings range from $ (under $12), $$ ($12 to $20), $$$ ($20 to $28) to $$$$ (over $28) for the price of one main dish. The price estimates do not include taxes, tips or beverages. Recommended grocers are listed below the restaurants. For more on Hawaii's unique cuisine, see the Food & Drink chapter (p245).

GAY & LESBIAN TRAVELERS

The state of Hawaii is very popular with gay and lesbian travelers. This is not surprising, considering the state's strong legislation to protect minority groups and a constitutional guarantee of privacy that extends to sexual behavior between all consenting adults. That said, overt 'couples' behavior, whether handholding or kissing, is rarely exhibited at all, much less by same-sex couples. Locals tend to keep their private lives to themselves.

Kaua'i's gay community is spread over the island, but concentrated more on the Eastside and North Shore. Donkey Beach (see the Detour box, p110), between Kapa'a and Anahola, is well known as a gay-friendly, clothing-optional, 'alternative' beach (despite the official ban against nudity).

HOLIDAYS

The following state holidays will affect visitors only slightly, except for the three major ones: Thanksgiving, Christmas and New Year's Day. During those holidays, air travel will be pricey and packed. For other significant dates, see the Festivals & Events Calendar (p262).

New Year's Day January 1
Martin Luther King Jr Day third Monday in January
Presidents Day third Monday in February
Kuhio Day March 26
Good Friday Friday before Easter Sunday
Memorial Day last Monday in May
King Kamehameha Day June 11
Independence Day July 4
Statehood Day third Friday in August
Labor Day first Monday in September
Election Day second Tuesday in November
Veterans Day November 11
Thanksgiving fourth Thursday in November
Christmas Day December 25

INTERNATIONAL TRAVELERS

Entering Hawaii

PASSPORTS & VISAS

US entry requirements remain in flux post-9/11, so all foreign visitors should confirm visa rules before traveling. The introductory portal for US visa information is the website for the **US Department of State** (http://travel.state.gov/visa).

Except for visitors from Canada, Mexico, Bermuda and the 35 countries that qualify for the Visa Waiver Program, foreign visitors to the USA need a visa. (Of course, Canadians and other non-US-citizens do need passports.)

The Visa Waiver Program allows citizens of the following 35 countries to enter the USA for stays of 90 days or less without first obtaining a US visa: Andorra, Australia, Austria, Belgium, Brunei, the Czech Republic, Denmark, Estonia, Finland, France, Germany, Hungary, Iceland, Ireland, Italy, Japan, Latvia, Liechtenstein, Lithuania, Luxembourg, Malta, Monaco, the Netherlands, New Zealand, Norway, Portugal, San Marino, Singapore, Slovakia, Slovenia, South Korea, Spain, Sweden, Switzerland and the UK. As of January 2009, citizens of the 35 countries in the US visa waiver program must register online with the government, at least three days before their visit, at https://esta.cbp.dhs.gov. The registration is valid for two years.

Your home country determines the validity period for a US visitor visa, while US officials set the length of your US stay at the port of entry. To remain in the US longer than the date stamped on your passport, you must go to the Honolulu office of the **US Citizenship & Immigration Service** (☎ 532-3721; www.uscis.gov; 595 Ala Moana Blvd, Honolulu, O'ahu) before the stamped date to apply for an extension.

Upon arriving in the US, all foreign visitors must have their two index fingers scanned and a digital photo taken. For more information, see the Travel Security section of the **US Department of Homeland Security** (www.dhs.gov) site.

CUSTOMS

Visitors to the USA (including Hawaii) can bring in 1L of liquor and 200 cigarettes duty-free; age minimums of 21 years for

READ THIS BOOK, NOW FORGET IT!

We love travel guides, we really do. But we also know that there's no replacement for a spirit of discovery. The very best travel experiences, not just in Kaua'i but anywhere, are the ones you create yourself. They are the unexpected people you meet, the wonderful restaurant you find while escaping the rain, the trails you follow that no one mentioned.

Even in small, heavily visited places like Kaua'i, there are tons of 'undiscovered' places. Indeed, we've sprinkled this book with detours to help inspire your own independent explorations. In other words, read this book, then forget it. Put it down. It's your trip.

liquor and 18 years for tobacco apply. Additionally, visitors can bring up to $100 worth of gift merchandise duty-free into the USA.

Hawaii has stringent restrictions against bringing any fresh fruits and plants to the islands, to prevent entry of invasive species. Think twice about traveling with your pet – the rabies-free state enforces strict pet quarantine laws, though you can slice the time to five days if you meet specific requirements. (For information on bringing in assistance animals, see Travelers with Disabilities, p271.) For complete details, contact the **Hawaiian Department of Agriculture** (☎ 808-483-7151; hawaii.gov/hdoa/ai/aqs).

Consulates in Hawaii

In the state of Hawaii, all foreign consulates are located on O'ahu, in Honolulu:

Australia (☎ 524-5050; Penthouse, 1000 Bishop St)
Germany (☎ 946-3819; 252 Paoa Pl)
Italy (☎ 531-2277; Suite 201, 735 Bishop St)
Japan (☎ 543-3111; 1742 Nu'uanu Ave)
Netherlands (☎ 531-6897; Suite 702, 745 Fort St Mall)
New Zealand (☎ 595-2200; 3929 Old Pali Rd)
Philippines (☎ 595-6316; 2433 Pali Hwy)

INTERNET ACCESS

Nowadays many accommodations offer high-speed internet access. At B&Bs, it's usually wireless, but a surprising number of hotels and condos offer only wired, in-room connections. Ask about rates as they can be exorbitant, especially at high-end resorts.

In this book, accommodations and other reviews with the 💻 symbol indicate those that provide computers for guest use, while reviews that have the 📶 symbol indicate that wi-fi is available.

Most towns have a few internet cafes or business centers offering wi-fi and computers (the average rate is about $2.50 per 15 minutes). This book recommends internet access spots for each town, but also check out **Wi-Fi Free Spot** (www.wififreespot.com), a handy (but not exhaustive) wi-fi directory.

LEGAL MATTERS

You are entitled to an attorney from the moment you are arrested. The **Hawaii State Bar Association** (☎ 537-9140, 800-808-4722; www.hsba.org) is one starting point to find an attorney. If you can't afford one, the state must provide one for free.

In Hawaii, anyone driving with a blood alcohol level of 0.08% or higher is guilty of driving 'under the influence.' Possessing marijuana and narcotics is illegal (but smoking a joint rarely leads to arrest unless other crimes are involved). Hitchhiking and public nudity (eg at nude beaches) are crimes rarely enforced.

While the **Department of Commerce & Consumer Affairs** (Big Island ☎ 974-4000; www.hawaii.gov/dcca) deals primarily with residents' issues, visitors who want to lodge a complaint

PLUGGING INTO KAUA'I

- **Electricity** Voltage is 110/120V at 60 cycles, with a standard US plug.
- **Measurement** As on the US mainland, distances are measured in feet, yards and miles; weights in ounces, pounds and tons; liquid volumes in cups, pints, quarts and gallons.
- **Newspapers & Magazines** The island's major daily is the *Garden Island*. For foodie news, pick up a free copy of *Edible Hawaiian Islands*, which is based on Kaua'i. Freebie tourist magazines, such as *101 Things to Do* and *This Week Kaua'i* are handy for general info and cost-cutting coupons.
- **Radio** Kaua'i broadcasts about a dozen FM and two AM radio stations. For 100% locally produced, non-commercial radio, tune in to KKCR 90.9FM.
- **TV** All the major US TV networks and cable channels are represented.
- **Video** Video systems use the NTSC standard, which is incompatible with the PAL system. Encoded DVDs are region 1.
- **Laundry** Most condos, B&Bs, inns and vacation-rental homes include free or inexpensive use of washers and dryers; hotels typically offer coin-operated laundry facilities.
- **Surf Reports** Online reports are available at www.kauaiexplorer.com/ocean_report and www.kauaiworld.com/surfreport.

against a business should contact the Department's Consumer Resource Center.

MAPS

If you plan to stick to towns and highways, the maps in this book will probably suffice. But if you want to explore unpaved roads or find secluded B&Bs, the atlas-style *Ready Mapbook of Kaua'i* (☎ 985-9777; www.hawaiimapsource.com; $10) is indispensable.

For ocean sports, see **Franko's Maps** (www.frankosmaps.com) for outstanding full-color, fold-up, waterproof maps ($6 to $10) that pinpoint snorkeling, diving, surfing and kayaking spots and also identify tropical fishes. The *Nelles Map of Kaua'i* ($7), a fold-up road map, is a minimalist alternative to the *Ready Mapbook*. The *UH Press Map of Kaua'i* by James Bier ($4) is a detailed geographical map.

Only geographers, backcountry explorers and map fiends would need topographic maps, but if you want one, first try **TopoZone** (www.topozone.com). Also, hikers should get the detailed topographical trails map ($5 in person, $6 by mail) from **Na Ala Hele** (☎ 274-3442; www.hawaiitrails.org), the trails unit of the Division of Forestry & Wildlife.

MONEY

Prices quoted in this book are in US dollars ($), the only currency used in Hawaii. The dollar (commonly called a 'buck') is divided into 100 cents. Coins come in denominations of one cent (called a 'penny'), five cents ('nickel'), 10 cents ('dime'), 25 cents ('quarter') and, in limited circulation, the rare 50-cent piece ('half-dollar') and two versions of $1 coins. Notes come in one-, five-, 10-, 20-, 50- and 100-dollar denominations.

See Quick Reference inside the front cover for exchange rates and the Planning Your Trip chapter (p256) for basic info on costs.

ATMs, Cash & Checks

Automated Teller Machines (ATMs) provide quick cash and a convenient substitute for traveler's checks, but withdrawals using other banks' cards do incur surcharges of $1.50 to $2. Hawaii's two largest banks, **Bank of Hawaii** (www.boh.com) and **First Hawaiian Bank** (www.fhb.com), both have extensive ATM networks that will give cash advances on major credit cards and allow cash withdrawals with affiliated ATM cards. Look for ATMs at banks and supermarkets, shopping centers, convenience stores and gas stations.

Foreign currency can be exchanged for US dollars at Honolulu International Airport and at main bank branches on Kaua'i.

Personal checks are usually not accepted, especially if drawn from a non-Hawaii bank.

> **LEGAL AGE**
>
> The legal age in Hawaii varies by activity:
> - Drinking: 21
> - Driving: 16
> - Sex: 16
> - Voting: 18

Credit Cards

Major credit cards are widely accepted on Kaua'i, but not by many small businesses, including eateries and residential accommodations (eg B&Bs and inns).

Tipping

In restaurants, it's standard practice to tip at least 15% for good service and 10% if it's mediocre. Leaving no tip is rare and requires real cause.

Traveler's Checks

Traveler's checks seem archaic but they do offer protection from theft and loss. They're accepted like cash by most vendors, but mom-and-pop shops might not.

Keep a record of all check numbers (and separate from the checks themselves). For refunds on lost or stolen traveler's checks, call **American Express** (☎ 800-992-3404) or **Thomas Cook** (☎ 800-287-7362).

PHOTOGRAPHY

All camera supplies, such as print and slide film, digital memory cards and batteries, are available on Kaua'i. Disposable underwater cameras (which average around $15) are ideal for capturing those snorkeling and kayaking adventures.

To burn a CD or DVD with your images, most internet cafes and business centers will charge you for computer time and for the CD (about $1) or DVD (about $3). Film users: develop each roll as you finish it because the island's high temperature and humidity accelerate the deterioration of exposed film.

Don't pack unprocessed film (including the roll inside your camera) into checked luggage because exposure to high-powered X-ray equipment will cause it to fog. While the scanners used for carry-on baggage are less powerful, to be safe, carry your film separately and submit it to airport security officials for a 'hand check.'

For a quickie course on taking good shots, consult Lonely Planet's *Travel Photography*.

POST

Mail delivery to and from Hawaii via the **US postal service** (USPS; ☎ 800-275-8777; www.usps.gov) is reliable but takes a little longer than similar services across the US mainland (about 10 days for air mail and four to six weeks for parcel post).

First-class mail between Hawaii and the mainland goes by air and usually takes three to four days. For 1st-class mail sent and delivered within the US, postage rates are 42¢ for letters up to 1oz and 27¢ for standard-size postcards.

International airmail rates for letters up to 1oz or postcards are 72¢ to Canada or Mexico and 94¢ to other countries.

You can receive mail c/o General Delivery at Kaua'i post offices, but according to the official rule you must first complete an application in person. Bring two forms of ID and your temporary local address. The accepted application is valid for 30 days; mail is held for a maximum of 15 days. But exceptions are sometimes made, so ask. Hotels and other accommodations might hold mail for incoming guests.

SHOPPING

The best way to remember Kaua'i is to buy Kaua'i-grown or Kaua'i-made items. For locally grown edibles, an easy pick is coffee, but see the varied list on p248 to suit any palate. Other edible souvenirs sold islandwide include Aunty Lilikoi (www.auntylilikoi.com) passionfruit products, Anahola granola (www.anaholagranola.com) and baked goods from local bakeries.

Locally made art and crafts abound in galleries across the island, particularly in Hanapepe (p192). Look for paintings, koa-wood crafts and Ni'ihau shell jewelry. Remember, genuine items are meticulously crafted and never cheap. See p241 for more on traditional Hawaiian art and crafts.

The **Kaua'i Made** (www.kauaimade.net) website promotes vendors selling products made on Kaua'i, by Kaua'i residents, using Kaua'i materials, but its list is limited and misses many outstanding products.

Flowers, such as orchids, can fly with you to the US mainland if they are inspected and approved by the **US Department of Agriculture** (☎ 245-2831), which has an office at Lihu'e airport.

One last point: bargaining is rarely done here, except perhaps at farmers markets (although prices are already so low that it'll seem rather petty).

TELEPHONE

Always dial '1' before toll-free (☎ 800, 888 etc) and domestic long-distance numbers. Also, while the Hawaii state area code ☎ 808 applies to all islands, it must also be dialed for interisland calls (between islands).

Pay phones are readily found in shopping centers, beach parks and other public places. Local calls include all calls within the island and cost 25¢ or 50¢. Interisland calls are long distance and more expensive. Hotels often add a hefty service charge of $1 or more per call made from a room phone.

Private prepaid phone cards are readily available – check convenience stores, supermarkets and pharmacies.

Cell (Mobile) Phones

Verizon has the most extensive cellular network across the islands, but AT&T and Sprint also have decent coverage. While coverage on Kaua'i is good in major towns, it's spotty or nonexistent in rural areas.

Asian and European phones won't work in the US unless they are quad-band phones, supporting all four major GSM bands (850, 900, 1800 and 1900).

Long-Distance & International Calls

To make international calls direct from Hawaii, dial ☎ 011 + country code + area code + number. (An exception is to Canada, for which you dial ☎ 1 + area code + number – but international rates still apply.)

For international operator assistance, dial ☎ 0. The operator can provide specific rate information, including the cheapest time periods for calling.

If you're calling Hawaii from abroad, use the international country code for the US (☎ 1), followed by the area code ☎ 808 and the seven-digit local number. You must also dial the area code also when calling from one island to another.

TIME

Hawaii does not observe daylight saving time, probably because it has 11 hours of daylight in midwinter (December) and 13½ hours in midsummer (June). In midwinter, the sun rises around 7am and sets around 6pm. In midsummer, it rises before 6am and sets after 7pm.

TOURIST INFORMATION

For mainstream information, the **Kaua'i Visitors Bureau** (Map p62; ☎ 245-3971, 800-262-1400; www.kauaidiscovery.com; Suite 101, 4334 Rice St, Lihu'e) website is a good starting point and includes accommodations listings. The statewide **Hawaii Visitors & Convention Bureau** (☎ 800-464-2924; www.gohawaii.com; Suite 801, 2270 Kalakaua Ave, Waikiki, O'ahu) offers only general info but might be handy for island hoppers.

> **Island Insights**
>
> Upon arrival, set your internal clock to 'Hawaiian time.' This means slow down and forget the wristwatch. (When locals are late, they blame it on Hawaiian time.)

Available at the airport and at brochure stands islandwide, the free tourist guides **101 Things to Do** (www.101thingstodo.com) and **This Week** (www.thisweek.com) contain handy, current info and maps, plus discount coupons.

TOURS

Here, 'tours' refer to group sightseeing options. For activity tours (snorkeling cruises, ziplining adventures, etc), see the Outdoor Activities & Adventures chapter (p30), plus the regional chapters for details.

Bus tour companies offer whirlwind regional tours (eg Fern Grotto, Waimea Canyon, North Shore), but these allow only superficial 'stop-and-click' sightseeing. Forgo them unless you're a non-driver with no other option. Typical rates range from \$50 to \$88 for adults and \$36 to \$70 for children, depending on the tour itinerary.

Kaua'i Paradise Tours (☎ 246-3999, 800-404-3900; kauaiaufdeutsch@msn.com; 6/8hr tour \$66/88) Personalized tours narrated in English or German.

Polynesian Adventure Tours (☎ 800-622-3011; www.polyad.com)

Roberts Hawaii (☎ 866-898-2519; www.robertshawaii.com)

See p274 for group package tours, which can be a steal. Such tours merely package air, hotel and car bookings, so you're not stuck with a group during your stay. See p275 for cruises to and between the Hawaiian Islands.

An excellent option for learning is **Elderhostel** (☎ 800-454-5768; www.elderhostel.org), which offers tours (including accommodations, meals and lectures) for those aged 55 and older. Most of the themed trips are multi-island and focus on Hawaiian history, culture and geography.

TRAVELERS WITH DISABILITIES

Kaua'i's major hotels and condos are equipped with elevators, TTD-capable phones and wheelchair-accessible rooms (which must be reserved in advance). But most accommodations are relatively small and might lack such amenities.

For general information, see the Kaua'i County visitor FAQ page at www.kauai-hawaii.com/visitor-faq) and click on Information. The **Disability and Communication**

Access Board (DCAB; ☎ 586-8121; www.hawaii.gov/health/dcab; Room 101, 919 Ala Moana Blvd, Honolulu, O'ahu) also provides a tip sheet specifically for Kaua'i at www.hawaii.gov/health/dcab/docs/TravelKauai.pdf.

Guide dogs and other assistance animals are not subject to the general quarantine rules for pets, if they meet the Department of Agriculture's minimum requirements; see www.hawaii.gov/hdoa/ai/aqs/guidedogs for details. All animals must enter the state at Honolulu International Airport.

Wheelchair-accessible transportation must be planned in advance. On Kauai there are currently no car rental agencies with lift-equipped vehicles. **Gammie HomeCare** (☎ 632-2333; www.gammie.com; #4, 3-3215 Kuhio Hwy, Lihu'e; 8:30am-5pm Mon-Fri) rents portable ramps, wheelchairs, hospital beds, walking aids and other medical equipment. **Wheelchair Getaways of Hawaii** (☎ 800-638-1912; www.wheelchairgetaways.com) rents wheelchair-accessible vans.

For general information, try the **Society for the Advancement of Travel for the Handicapped** (SATH; ☎ 212-447-7284; www.sath.org; Suite 610, 347 Fifth Ave, New York, NY 10016), which has a website and a quarterly magazine.

Kaua'i County provides a Landeez all-terrain wheelchair at lifeguard stations at Po'ipu Beach Park (p164), Lydgate Beach Park (p83) and Salt Pond Beach Park (p191).

VOLUNTEERING

With numerous openings, flexible schedules and on-the-job training, **National Tropical Botanical Garden** (South Shore ☎ 332-7324, ext 228, North Shore ☎ 826-1053; www.ntbg.org/donate/volunteer.php) is an ideal place to volunteer. In addition to long-term positions, such as docents and nursery assistants, there are opportunities for visitors to 'vacation and volunteer.'

The **Koke'e Resource Conservation Program** (☎ 335-9975; www.krcp.org) accepts short-term volunteers and eight-week interns to help with weed-control projects in and around Koke'e, Waimea Canyon and Na Pali Coast State Parks. The work involves strenuous hiking and use of herbicides. In exchange for work, bunk-bed housing is provided at the Civilian Conservation Corps Camp, a remote site suited to folks who would welcome solitude. Volunteers and interns must provide their own health insurance.

Hawaiian Islands Humpback Whale National Marine Sanctuary (☎ 246-2860; www.hawaiihumpbackwhale.noaa.gov), a statewide organization, has formal programs only on Maui, but volunteer opportunities do exist on Kaua'i. Contact Jean Souza, the Kaua'i Programs Coordinator, at jean.souza@noaa.gov.

WOMEN TRAVELERS

Kaua'i presents few problems specific to women travelers, and may be more relaxed and comfortable than many mainland destinations. Of course, women (especially solo travelers) should be wary of isolated beaches, campsites and hiking trails. County parks and secluded picnic sites, eg Keahua Arboretum, are notorious for late-night partying.

Kaua'i's compact size and small-town atmosphere make solo travel easy. Group tours and lessons give singles the option to meet others. That said, accommodations will always cost more for singles, especially because few places differentiate between single and double rates. Hiking and swimming alone is never wise, and solo travelers, particularly females, should try to find a trusted companion or group when venturing to isolated areas.

For help after a sexual assault, call Kaua'i's **Sexual Assault Hotline** (☎ 245-4144).

WORK

US citizens can legally work in Hawaii, but short-term employment will probably mean entry-level jobs in restaurants and hotels. With specific outdoor skills (eg scuba diving) one can explore employment with activity operators. The same goes for those with massage or cosmetology training, who might find work at resort spas. If you're qualified for serious 'professional' jobs, decent opportunities are scarce and comparatively low-paying.

But the entire state tends does to need teachers and nurses. Also, residential construction is booming, and there's a shortage of licensed carpenters, plumbers, painters, electricians and roofers.

Check the listings in newspaper classifieds and the Kaua'i page of **Craigslist** (http://honolulu.craigslist.org/kau).

GETTING THERE & AWAY

AIR

Virtually all travelers to Kaua'i arrive by air, and the vast majority stops first at Honolulu International Airport. If you have a layover in Honolulu, make sure the ticket agent marks your baggage with Lihu'e (LIH) as the final destination.

US domestic and international airfares vary too much for generalizations about the cheapest carriers or months. But you can count on across-the-board fare hikes from mid-December to mid-March.

Airports

All commercial flights land in Lihu'e, mostly via Honolulu, which is 25 minutes away by air. Most commercial helicopter tours depart from Lihu'e, but some use two other, smaller airports on the island: Burns Field (see p194) in Hanapepe and Princeville Airport (see p128).

Lihu'e Airport (LIH; ☎ 246-1448; www.hawaii.gov/dot/airports/kauai/lih; visitor info 6:30am-9pm)
Honolulu International Airport (HNL; ☎ 836-6413; www.honoluluairport.com)

Airlines

The vast majority of incoming flights from overseas and the US mainland arrive on O'ahu at Honolulu International Airport. From there, travelers must catch an interisland flight to Kaua'i.

Here are the four interisland carriers:

go! (airline code YV; ☎ 888-435-9462; www.iflygo.com) Discount carrier.
Hawaiian Airlines (airline code HA; ☎ 800-367-5320; www.hawaiianair.com) Hawaii's largest airline: the most flights, and fares comparable to go!'s.
Island Air (airline code WP; US mainland ☎ 800-323-3345, Neighbor Islands ☎ 800-652-6541; www.islandair.com) Only one or two flights to/from Lihu'e per day.
Mokulele Airlines (airline code MW; ☎ 426-7070; www.mokuleleairlines.com) Partner with Alaska Airlines.

THINGS CHANGE...

The information in this chapter is particularly vulnerable to change. Check directly with the airline or a travel agent to make sure you understand how a fare (and ticket you may buy) works, and be aware of the security requirements for international travel. Shop carefully. The details given in this chapter should be regarded as pointers and are not a substitute for your own careful, up-to-date research.

The following airlines fly directly to Lihu'e Airport from the US mainland:

Alaska Airlines (airline code AS; ☎ 800-252-7522; www.alaskaair.com)
American Airlines (airline code AA; ☎ 800-223-5436; www.aa.com)
United Airlines (airline code UA; ☎ 800-241-6522; www.ual.com)
US Airways (airline code US; ☎ 800-428-4322; www.usairways.com)

Airlines flying into Honolulu include the following:

Air New Zealand (airline code NZ; ☎ 800-262-1234; www.airnz.co.nz)
Air Pacific (airline code FJ; ☎ 800-227-4446; www.airpacific.com)
China Airlines (airline code CI; ☎ 800-227-5118; www.china-airlines.com)
Continental (airline code CO; ☎ 800-523-3273; www.continental.com)
Delta (airline code DL; ☎ 800-221-1212; www.delta.com)
Korean Airlines (airline code KE; ☎ 800-438-5000; www.koreanair.com)
Philippine Airlines (airline code PR; ☎ 800-435-9725; www.philippineair.com)
Qantas Airways (airline code QF; ☎ 800-227-4500; www.qantasusa.com)

Tickets

Ah, the art and science of finding the lowest airfares. The internet is by far your best tool. First try the travel websites that broadly search multiple airline and travel booking sites: **Kayak** (www.kayak.com) and **Farecast** (www.farecast.com) are two good ones.

Otherwise, go to the booking sites directly and compare prices between them:

- www.travelocity.com
- www.expedia.com
- www.orbitz.com
- www.cheaptickets.com

US MAINLAND

Airfares have fluctuated wildly since late 2008, but the lowest round-trip fares from the US mainland to Honolulu are generally $500 to $600 from the East Coast and $350 to $400 from the West Coast. Fares rise markedly during peak travel periods.

Booking a direct flight to Kaua'i might cost more, but you'll save time and reduce the chance of missing baggage. Direct flights depart from West Coast cities such as Los Angeles, San Francisco and Seattle.

Package tours, which can include airfare, hotel and car, can be a bargain for traveling couples who would stay at affiliated hotels anyway. But single travelers will find no savings since they base rates on double occupancy. **Pleasant Hawaiian Holidays** (☎ 800-742-9244; www.pleasantholidays.com) offers departures from numerous US mainland cities. **Sun Trips** (☎ 800-786-8747; www.suntrips.com) offers packages from Oakland, California.

An interesting option for flexible summer travelers is **Airtech** (☎ 212-219-7000; www.airtech.com) and its Space-Available FlightPass, a standby ticket that can be the cheapest way to fly between the West Coast and Kaua'i (as well as to O'ahu, Maui and the Big Island).

WITHIN HAWAII

Airfares fluctuate due to availability and price competition among the carriers, but one-way fares to Kaua'i generally range from $50 to $90. Hawaiian Airlines, the largest interisland carrier, offers the most flights, which is handy if you need to reschedule. It typically matches the fare offered by discounter go! airlines, which has the next best selection of flights. Island Air flies smaller aircraft and has only one or two flights daily. Whichever airline you choose, book early for the lowest prices.

AUSTRALIA

Hawaiian Airlines flies nonstop between Sydney and Honolulu. Both Qantas and its budget subsidiary, **Jetstar** (www.jetstar.com.au), fly to Honolulu from Sydney and Melbourne (via Sydney, but without changing planes).

For bookings, try **Flight Centre** (☎ 1300-133-133; www.flightcentre.com.au) and **STA Travel** (☎ 1300-733-035; www.statravel.com.au).

CANADA

Air Canada and WestJet offer direct flights to Honolulu from Vancouver; flights from Calgary, Edmonton and Toronto connect via Vancouver.

Hawaiian Airlines also has flights from Vancouver, Calgary, Edmonton and Toronto, with stopovers in Phoenix and in Honolulu.

Booking agencies include **Travel Cuts** (☎ 866-246-9762; www.travelcuts.com) and **Travelocity** (☎ 877-282-2925; www.travelocity.ca).

JAPAN

Japan Airlines flies directly between Honolulu and Tokyo, Osaka, Nagoya or Fukuoka. Fares vary according to departure city and season, but they always rise during Golden Week in May, the Obon festival in August and around the New Year.

All Nippon Airways (ANA) flies to Honolulu from Tokyo, Sapporo and Kumamoto. Continental and Northwest have several flights to Honolulu from Tokyo and Osaka; ticket prices are comparable to those offered by Japan Airlines.

For bookings, start with **STA Travel** (☎ 03-5391-2922; www.statravel.co.jp).

NEW ZEALAND, MICRONESIA & SOUTH PACIFIC ISLANDS

Continental has nonstop flights from Guam to Honolulu, and Air New Zealand flies from Auckland.

Hawaiian Airlines flies to Honolulu from Tahiti and American Samoa. Air New Zealand offers roundtrip tickets from Fiji to Honolulu via Auckland. It also flies to Honolulu from Tonga, the Cook Islands and Western Samoa.

Agents serving New Zealand include **Flight Centre** (☎ 0800-24-35-44; www.flightcentre.co.nz) and **STA Travel** (☎ 0800-474-400; www.statravel.co.nz).

UK & CONTINENTAL EUROPE

United, American and all of the national carriers fly between Honolulu and various European cities. The most common route to Hawaii from Europe is west via New York, Chicago or Los Angeles. If you're interested in heading east with stops in Asia, it may be cheaper to get a round-the-world ticket instead of returning the same way.

London is arguably the world's headquarters for 'bucket shops' specializing in discount tickets. Two good, reliable agents for cheap tickets in London are **STA Travel** (☎ 0870-162-7551; www.statravel.co.uk) and **Trailfinders** (☎ 0845-058-5858; www.trailfinders.com).

SEA

Cruises

The colossal cruise ships seen throughout Hawaii are predominantly island-hoppers that originate in Honolulu. But there are occasional ships that originate in California or Vancouver. On either type of cruise, don't expect to spend more than one day on Kaua'i.

The North American cruises range from 10 to 19 days; the average 15-day tour from California costs about $1500 to $1900 per person and include daylong stops on O'ahu, Maui, Kaua'i and the Big Island. Cruise lines include the following:

Holland America Cruise Line (☎ 877-724-5425; www.hollandamerica.com) Departures from San Diego or Vancouver.

Princess Cruises (☎ 800-568-3262; www.princess.com) Rates are generally steeper than Holland's; departures from Los Angeles and Vancouver.

The only company running interisland cruises is **Norwegian Cruise Line** (☎ 800-327-7030; www.ncl.com) and its *Pride of America* liner, distinctly painted with Old Glory. Seven-day trips (starting in Honolulu and stopping in Maui, Hawai'i Island and Kaua'i) range from about $1200 (no view) to $1650 (balcony). The ship docks at Nawiliwili Harbor on Thursdays for one night.

Ferry

In late 2007, the **Hawaii Superferry** (www.hawaiisuperferry.com) launched its first commuter ferry, the *Alakai*, amid heated controversy. While the O'ahu–Maui route was active for just over a year, all service was terminated indefinitely in March 2009 due to legal troubles (see the boxed text, p54).

GETTING AROUND

TO/FROM THE AIRPORT

Almost all visitors rent cars from agencies located at Lihu'e Airport. Those forgoing rental cars can catch cabs; see the Lihu'e chapter (p78) for more information.

BICYCLE

Kaua'i is compact enough for road cycling, but the going can be tough. Winter months are particularly wet, but showers are common year-round. Dedicated bicycle lanes are rare, and roads can be narrow, winding and heavily trafficked. Riding along the North Shore, which has narrow, shoulderless roads that zigzag over steep cliffs, is impossible.

An 18-mile coastal bicycle path is slated to run from Lihu'e all the way to Anahola, and the path is partly completed. Selective bike transportation is feasible, but the path currently seems geared toward recreation rather than commuting.

Bicycle-rental shops are found in Waipouli (p96), Kapa'a (p102), Hanalei (p146) and Po'ipu (p171). In general, bicycles are required to follow the same state laws and rules of the road as cars.

Since 2001, the state has legally required bike helmets for riders under 16 and for passengers in bike seats or trailers. Furthermore, rental shops cannot rent to riders under 16 unless they wear a helmet.

BUS

The county's **Kaua'i Bus** (☎ 241-6410; www.kauai.gov; 3220 Ho'olako St; per trip adult/senior & youth 7-18 $1.50/75¢; 🕒 5:15am-7:15pm Mon-Fri, reduced schedule on Sat, no service on Sun) is fine for traveling along major highway towns and stops, but its routes and runs are limited. Schedules are available online and at island businesses including Big Save, Kukui Grove Center and Safeway. All buses stop in Lihu'e. The number of trips per route varies; for example, for intra-Lihu'e travel, there's an average of eight departures on weekdays, but for longer routes, such as Lihu'e to Po'ipu, you are stuck with one daily departure from each end.

A few caveats about bus travel on Kaua'i: drivers will accept only the exact fare; a monthly pass costs $15; you can transport a bodyboard (but not a surfboard), folding baby stroller or bicycle; stops are marked but might be hard to spot; and the schedule does not include a map.

Buses are air-conditioned and equipped with bicycle racks and wheelchair ramps.

CAR

Automobile Associations

The **American Automobile Association** (AAA; ☎ O'ahu 808-593-2221, Neighbor Islands 800-736-2886; www.aaa-hawaii.com; #A170, 1130 N Nimitz Hwy, Honolulu, O'ahu), which has its only Hawaii office in Honolulu, provides members with maps and other information. Members get discounts on car rental, air tickets and some hotels and sightseeing attractions, as well as emergency road service and towing (☎ 800-222-4357). For information on joining your regional AAA, call ☎ 800-564-6222. AAA has reciprocal agreements with automobile associations in other countries, but bring your membership card from home.

Driver's License

An international driving license, obtained before you leave home, is necessary only if your country of origin is a non-English-speaking one.

DRIVING DISTANCES & TIMES

Average driving distances and times from Lihu'e are listed below. Allow more time during morning and afternoon rush hours and on weekends.

Destination	Miles	Time
Anahola	14	25min
Hanalei	31	1hr
Hanapepe	16	30min
Kapa'a	8	15min
Ke'e Beach	40	1¼hr
Kilauea Lighthouse	25	40min
Po'ipu	10	20min
Port Allen	15	25min
Princeville	28	45min
Waimea	23	40min
Waimea Canyon	42	1½hr

HIGHWAY NICKNAMES

Locals call highways by nickname rather than by number. Here's a cheat sheet:

Hwy 50 Kaumuali'i Hwy
Hwy 51 Kapule Hwy
Hwy 56 Kuhio Hwy
Hwy 58 Nawiliwili Rd
Hwy 520 Maluhia Rd (Tree Tunnel) and Po'ipu Rd
Hwy 530 Koloa Rd
Hwy 540 Halewili Rd
Hwy 550 Waimea Canyon Dr
Hwy 552 Koke'e Rd
Hwy 560 Kuhio Hwy (continuation of Hwy 56)
Hwy 570 Ahukini Rd
Hwy 580 Kuamo'o Rd
Hwy 581 Kamalu Rd and Olohena Rd
Hwy 583 Ma'alo Rd

Fuel & Towing

Fuel is readily available everywhere except in remote areas such as Waimea Canyon and the North Shore beyond Princeville. Gas prices are steep across the state and especially high on Kaua'i, where prices per US gallon run 50¢ to 75¢ more than the mainland average. Prices also vary greatly on the island, with lows found on the Eastside and the reigning high at Princeville. Check current prices at www.kauaiworld.com/gasprices.

If you get stuck on the road, towing is mighty expensive and therefore to be avoided at all costs. Figure the fees at about $65 to start, plus $6.50 per mile you must be towed. How to avoid it? Don't drive past Keahua Arboretum or to other off-road destinations without 4WD, for instance, and never drive any vehicle in deep sand.

Rental

Unfortunately, renting a car often costs more on Kaua'i than on the other major Hawaiian Islands, so it's even more critical to shop around and to doggedly check online rates (which constantly rise and fall to reflect availability). At best, weekly rates drop to $250 for compact cars (and slightly more for full-size), plus taxes and fees

UNDERSTANDING DRIVING DIRECTIONS

If you ask for driving directions, be prepared for the local lingo. Here's a summary of the mainland-versus-local style of giving directions:

Mainland style	Local style
North, south, east and west points	*Mauka* ('toward the mountain'; inland) and *makai* ('toward the ocean'; coastal)
Highway numbers	Highway nicknames (see boxed text, opposite)
Cross-streets or mile markers	Landmarks (eg 'across from the Lihu'e McDonald's')
Mileage	Estimates (eg 'about halfway to Kealia Beach')

that increase the base estimate by about 20%. Rates rise to $350 to $450 weekly for limited-availability bookings. Rental rates generally include unlimited mileage. Rates for 4WD vehicles range average about $70 to $120 per day (before taxes and fees), but all agencies prohibit driving off-road. (Read: you can try it, but if you get stuck and call them for help, they'll charge a penalty fee.)

Consider the *total* price when shopping around. Remember that rates depend on season and availability and are volatile, changing by the day or even by the hour.

Having a major credit card greatly simplifies the rental process. Without one, some companies will not rent to you, while others require prepayment, a deposit of $200 per week, pay stubs, proof of return airfare and possibly more.

The state's minimum age for driving a car is 18 years, but most rental companies enforce a minimum age of 25 (or 21 with an extra fee of $25 per day).

Car-rental companies are located at Lihu'e Airport. The familiar major agencies are generally reliable:

Alamo (☎ 800-327-9633, Lihu'e 246-0645; www.alamo.com)
Avis (☎ 800-331-1212, Lihu'e 245-7995; www.avis.com)
Budget (☎ 800-527-0700, Lihu'e 245-9031; www.budget.com)
Dollar (☎ 800-800-4000, Lihu'e 246-0622; www.dollar.com)
Hertz (☎ 800-654-3011, Lihu'e 245-3356; www.hertz.com)
National (☎ 888-868-6207, Lihu'e 245-5636; www.nationalcar.com)
Thrifty (☎ 800-847-4389, Lihu'e 866-450-5101; www.thrifty.com)

The sole local agency, **Island Cars** (Map p60; ☎ 246-6000, 800-246-6009; www.islandcars.net; 2983 Aukele St, Lihu'e), offers consistently cheap rates, but car quality is less consistent.

Road Conditions & Hazards

Highway congestion is terrible, especially between Lihu'e and Kapa'a, where rush-hour traffic is a given. To combat commuter traffic into Lihu'e on weekdays, a 'contra-flow' lane is created from 5am to 10:30am on Kuhio Hwy (Hwy 56) in the Wailua area; this turns a northbound lane into a southbound lane by reversing the flow of traffic.

During major rainstorms, roads and bridges can flood. Areas particularly prone include the North Shore bridges and anywhere near rivers and streams. Rain or shine, stay alert for one-lane-bridge crossings and heed the advice in the boxed text, p133. Whenever there's no sign on one-lane stretches, downhill traffic must yield to uphill traffic.

Driving off-road often means through rough, muddy and remote 4WD-only wilderness. Conditions are hazardous and you'll probably be miles from help and cell phone access. If you have never driven a 4WD vehicle before, don't do your trial run here.

Island Insights

Street addresses on Kaua'i might seem oddly long and complicated, but there's a pattern. The numerical prefix in street addresses along Kaua'i's highways (eg 3-4567 Kuhio Hwy) refer to one of five districts on Kaua'i: 1 refers to Waimea and vicinity, including Ni'ihau; 2 is Koloa and Po'ipu; 3 is Lihu'e to the Wailua River; 4 is Kapa'a and Anahola; and 5 is the North Shore.

Nighttime driving can be tricky along rural roads, especially on the North Shore. Expect few street lamps and winding, narrow roads.

Road Rules

As in North America, drivers keep to the right-hand side of the road. Turning right at a red light is permitted (after stopping and yielding to oncoming traffic, of course) unless a sign prohibits it. Seat belts are required for drivers and front-seat passengers, as well as back-seat passengers under the age of 18. The crime of driving while intoxicated (DWI) is legally defined as having a blood alcohol level greater than 0.08%.

Note the strict rules for child passengers: kids aged three and under must use infant/toddler safety seats; those aged four to seven must use a booster seat (unless the child is 4ft 9in tall and can properly use a seat belt). Most car-rental companies can rent child-safety seats if reserved in advance.

Speed limits are posted *and* enforced. If stopped for speeding, expect a ticket; the police rarely give mere warnings. Most accidents are caused by excessive speed.

While drivers tend to speed on highways, however, in-town driving is courteous and rather leisurely. Locals don't honk (unless a crash is imminent), they don't tailgate and they let faster cars pass. Do the same, and you'll get an appreciative thank-you wave or *shaka* sign (local hand greeting; see the boxed text, p239) in return.

For tips on negotiating one-lane bridges, see the boxed text, p133.

THREE GOLDEN RULES OF THE ROAD

- Don't honk your horn unless necessary for safety.
- Don't speed in residential neighborhoods.
- Let faster drivers pass whenever it's safe to do so.

HITCHHIKING

Hitchhiking is officially illegal statewide, though this law is not rigidly enforced. But it's not a common practice among locals, either. Along the North Shore, folks are more likely to offer rides. Please keep in mind that hitching is always a risk, especially for solo travelers.

MOPED & MOTORCYCLE

For motorcycle rentals, the go-to place is Harley-Davidson (p78), which has a 26-bike fleet in Puhi, just outside Lihu'e. For mopeds, try Kauai Scooter Rental (p78).

You need a valid motorcycle license to rent one, but a standard driver's license will suffice for mopeds. The minimum age for renting a motorcycle is 21; for a moped, it's 16.

Note that we're using the term 'moped,' but others might use 'scooter.' Regardless of terminology, all motorized bikes with an engine size of 49cc or less are classified the same. State law prohibits more than one rider per moped, and requires that they be driven in single file at a maximum of 30mph. Also, mopeds are not to be driven on sidewalks or freeways, but rather on roads with lower speed limits or on the highway shoulder.

The state requires helmets only for motorcycle or moped/scooter riders under age 18. Rental agencies provide free helmets for all riders and the smart ones use them.

Finally, if you hate riding in the rain, think twice about renting a bike here.

TAXI

Locals rarely use taxicabs so you'll find only a dozen companies. Fares are based on mileage regardless of the number of passengers. Since cabs are often station wagons or minivans, they offer good value for groups. The standard flag-down fee is $3, plus 30¢ per ⅛ additional mile. Cabs line up at the airport during normal business hours, but they don't run all night or cruise for passengers; for any rides outside a trip from the airport, you'll need to call ahead.

Taxi companies include **Akiko's Taxi** (☎ 822-7588), in the Lihu'e–Kapa'a area; **North Shore Cab** (☎ 826-4118; www.northshorecab.com), based in Princeville; and **Southshore Cab** (☎ 742-1525) in Po'ipu.

BEHIND THE SCENES

LUCI YAMAMOTO *Coordinating Author*

A fourth-generation native of Hawai'i, Luci Yamamoto grew up with hula lessons and homegrown bananas, but longed for four seasons and city sidewalks. She got as far as college in Los Angeles and law school in Berkeley, followed by a brief stint practicing law and a career change toward writing. Over the years, especially after working on Lonely Planet's *Hawaii, Big Island* and *Kaua'i* titles, she's come full circle from her youthful offhandedness about her extraordinary home islands. Currently living in Vancouver, she feels privileged when *kama'aina* still consider her a 'local girl.' For this book, Luci wrote the Outdoor Activities & Adventures, Green Kaua'i, Lihu'e, Eastside, South Shore, Kaua'i for Families, History & Culture, Food & Drink, Planning Your Trip and Directory & Transportation chapters.

AMANDA C GREGG

One of Amanda C Gregg's earliest memories was jumping on a Maui hotel bed with her little sister, announcing plans to someday live in Hawaii – and here she is, calling Kaua'i's Eastside home. Growing up in Massachusetts, the ocean was Amanda's first love; travel, second. After studying in Spain, Amanda received English and fine arts degrees and a Master's in Journalism from CU–Boulder. Since, she's worked as a newspaper reporter, editor and travel writer on the mainland and on Kaua'i. Chasing her newest passion, outrigger canoeing, she got the opportunity to paddle in the 32-mile Na Pali Challenge and 18-mile Queen Lili'uokalani races. For this book, Amanda wrote the North Shore and Westside chapters and the Ni'ihau boxed text.

DEDICATION

This 2nd edition of *Kaua'i* is dedicated to David Boynton, whose passion for and knowledge of Kaua'i's native forests have educated and inspired generations.

LONELY PLANET AUTHORS

Why is our travel information the best in the world? It's simple: our authors are passionate, dedicated travelers. They don't take freebies in exchange for positive coverage so you can be sure the advice you're given is impartial. They travel widely to all the popular spots, and off the beaten track. They don't research using just the internet or phone. They discover new places not included in any other guidebook. They personally visit thousands of hotels, restaurants, palaces, trails, galleries, temples and more. They speak with dozens of locals every day to make sure you get the kind of insider knowledge only a local could tell you. They take pride in getting all the details right, and in telling it how it is. Think you can do it? Find out how at **lonelyplanet.com**.

THIS BOOK

This 2nd edition of *Kaua'i* was written by Luci Yamamoto and Amanda C Gregg. Contributions were also made by Jake Howard and Lisa Dunford. The previous edition was written by Luci Yamamoto. This guidebook was commissioned in Lonely Planet's Oakland office and produced by:

Hawaii Product Development Manager & Commissioning Editor Emily K Wolman
Coordinating Editor Ali Lemer
Coordinating Cartographer Andrew Smith
Managing Editor Sasha Baskett
Managing Cartographer Alison Lyall
Assisting Editors Melissa Faulkner, Cathryn Game, Carly Hall, Fionnuala Twomey
Indexer Sarah Stewart
Series Designer Gerilyn Attebery
Layout Designer Jim Hsu
Managing Layout Designers Sally Darmody, Laura Jane, Indra Kilfoyle
Cover Designers & Image Researchers Yukiyoshi Kamimura, Marika Kozak, Nic Lehman, Michael Ruff, Kate Slattery
Project Manager Eoin Dunlevy
Language Content Coordinator Quentin Frayne

Thanks to Michaela Klink Caughlan, Lucy Birchley, Emele Freiberg, Mark Germanchis, Brice Gosnell, Bronwyn Hicks, Lauren Hunt, Abbot L Moffat III, Anthony Phelan, Paul Piaia, Raphael Richards, Julie Sheridan, Christina Tunnah, Vivek Waglé, Juan Winata

Internal photographs p40, p76, p92, p95, p112, p113, p127, p138, p144, p193, p205, p211, p213, Ann Cecil/Lonely Planet Images; p7, p19, p46, p51, p58, p88, p100, p108, p122, p135, p149, p174, p178, p196, p226, p249, p262, Linda Ching/Lonely Planet Images; p66, p75, p132, p153, p154, p155, p162, p180, p206, p217, p263, John Elk III/Lonely Planet Images; p15, p227, p262, Greg Elms/Lonely Planet Images; p208, Lee Foster/Lonely Planet Images; p21 (top & bottom), p22, p37, Amanda C Gregg; p45, p199, p221, p246, Aimée Goggins; p17, Peter Hendrie/Lonely Planet Images; p115, p128, p214, Karl Lehmann/Lonely Planet Images; p49, p186, p262, Holger Leue/Lonely Planet Images; p191, Kevin Levesque/Lonely Planet Images; p18, p159, Casey Mahaney/Lonely Planet Images; p17, Mark Parkes/Lonely Planet Images; p78, Merten Snijders/Lonely Planet Images; p183, Woods Wheatcroft/Lonely Planet Images; p31, p57, p63, p121, p165, p210, Micah Wright/Lonely Planet Images; p8, p9, p10, p12, p13, p14, p16, p20, p71, p79, p86, p105, p167, p169, p222, p225, p237, p245, p248, p254, p261, p263, Luci Yamamoto

THANKS from the Authors

Luci Yamamoto
Mahalo nui loa: to Jon Letman of NTBG, Andrea Brower of Malama Kaua'i and Richard Sugiyama, my Kaua'i insiders; to Rosemary Smith, Chris White and Michaelle Edwards for their generosity; and to my fascinating Island Voices: Sylvia Akana, Luke Hitchcock, Georgia Kakuda, Kenneth Kubota, Anson Lardizabal and Louisa Wooten. I owe much to Nanette Napoleon and to the late David Boynton, whose respective writings on history and wildlife were invaluable to my work. To

SEND US YOUR FEEDBACK

We love to hear from travelers – your comments keep us on our toes and help make our books better. Our well-traveled team reads every word on what you loved or loathed about this book. Although we cannot reply individually to postal submissions, we always guarantee that your feedback goes straight to the appropriate authors, in time for the next edition. Each person who sends us information is thanked in the next edition – and the most useful submissions are rewarded with a free book.

To send us your updates – and find out about Lonely Planet events, newsletters and travel news – visit our award-winning website: lonelyplanet.com/contact.

Note: We may edit, reproduce and incorporate your comments in Lonely Planet products such as guidebooks, websites and digital products, so let us know if you don't want your comments reproduced or your name acknowledged. For a copy of our privacy policy visit lonelyplanet.com/privacy.

THE LONELY PLANET STORY

Fresh from an epic journey across Europe, Asia and Australia in 1972, Tony and Maureen Wheeler sat at their kitchen table stapling together notes. The first Lonely Planet guidebook, *Across Asia on the Cheap*, was born.

Travelers snapped up the guides. Inspired by their success, the Wheelers began publishing books to Southeast Asia, India and beyond. Demand was prodigious, and the Wheelers expanded the business rapidly to keep up. Over the years, Lonely Planet extended its coverage to every country and into the virtual world via lonelyplanet.com and the Thorn Tree message board.

As Lonely Planet became a globally loved brand, Tony and Maureen received several offers for the company. But it wasn't until 2007 that they found a partner whom they trusted to remain true to the company's principles of traveling widely, treading lightly and giving sustainably. In October of that year, BBC Worldwide acquired a 75% share in the company, pledging to uphold Lonely Planet's commitment to independent travel, trustworthy advice and editorial independence.

Today Lonely Planet has offices in Melbourne, London and Oakland, with over 500 staff members and 300 authors. Tony and Maureen are still actively involved with Lonely Planet. They're traveling more often than ever, and they're devoting their spare time to charitable projects. And the company is still driven by the philosophy of *Across Asia on the Cheap*: 'All you've got to do is decide to go and the hardest part is over. So go!'

commissioning editor Emily K Wolman and coauthor Amanda C Gregg: I couldn't have done it without you. Special thanks, as always, to MJP and to my family.

Amanda C Gregg

Mahalo to the poetry that is Kaua'i. To my family: Donald, Bettina, Kimberly and Timothy, for unconditional love and unprecedented generosity. To Imaikalani, *ku'uipo, koa haku mele,* for profound love: here's to you. To author Greg Benchwick, commissioning editor Emily K Wolman and coordinating author Luci Yamamoto, for guidance and influence. To Island Voices Keith Robinson, Andrea Smith and Trevor Cabell for time, candor and grace. To Mohala and Danita Aiu, Gil Chang and Davianna McGregor, PhD, for inspiration and support. To District Health Officer Dileep G Bal, MD, MS, MPH and his wife, Muktha, for treating me like a daughter.

THANKS from Lonely Planet

Many thanks to the travelers who used the last edition and wrote to us with helpful hints, useful advice and interesting anecdotes: Emma Blewett, Ally Boggs, Jeannie Holtz, Bettina Kaltenhaeuser, Karen Kedmey, Heh Shin Kwak, Laurent Luce, Deb Vantriet.

INDEX

000 Map pages

000 Map pages

ACCOMMODATIONS

000 Map pages

ACTIVITIES

BEACHES

GREENDEX

GOING GREEN

It seems like everyone's going 'green' these days, but how can you know which businesses are actually eco-friendly and which are simply jumping on the sustainability bandwagon?

The following listings have all been selected by Lonely Planet authors because they demonstrate an active sustainable-tourism policy. Some are involved in conservation or environmental education, and many are owned and operated by local and indigenous operators, thereby maintaining and preserving Hawaiian identity and culture.

We want to keep developing our sustainable-tourism content. If you think we've omitted someone who should be listed here, or if you disagree with our choices, email us at talk2us@lonelyplanet.com.au. For more information about sustainable tourism and Lonely Planet, see www.lonelyplanet.com/responsibletravel.

MAP LEGEND

ROUTES

- Primary
- Secondary
- Tertiary
- Lane
- Unsealed Road
- One-Way Street
- MM29 Mile Marker
- Walking Tour
- *Walking Trail*
- *Walking Path*
- *Track*

TRANSPORT

- Ferry
- Rail

HYDROGRAPHY

- River, Creek
- Intermittent River
- Swamp
- Reef
- Glacier
- Water

BOUNDARIES

- State, Provincial
- Marine Park
- Regional, Suburb
- Cliff

AREA FEATURES

- Airport
- Beach
- Building
- Forest
- Land
- Market
- Park, Reserve
- Sports

POPULATION

- CAPITAL (NATIONAL)
- Large City
- Small City
- CAPITAL (STATE)
- Medium City
- Town, Village

SYMBOLS

Sights/Activities

- Beach
- Bodysurfing
- Buddhist
- Canoeing, Kayaking
- Christian
- Diving
- Golf
- Monument
- Museum, Gallery
- Point of Interest
- Pool
- Ruin
- Snorkeling
- Surfing, Surf Beach
- Trail Head
- Windsurfing
- Winery, Vineyard
- Zoo, Bird Sanctuary

Eating

- Eating

Drinking

- Drinking
- Café

Entertainment

- Entertainment

Shopping

- Shopping

Sleeping

- Sleeping
- Camping

Transport

- Airport, Airfield
- Bus Station
- Cycling, Bicycle Path
- General Transport
- Parking Area
- Petrol Station
- Taxi Rank

Information

- Bank, ATM
- Hospital, Medical
- Information
- Internet Facilities
- Police Station
- Post Office, GPO

Geographic

- Lighthouse
- Lookout
- Mountain, Volcano
- National Park
- Beach Park
- Picnic Area
- Shelter, Hut
- Spot Height
- Waterfall

Although the authors and Lonely Planet have taken all reasonable care in preparing this book, we make no warranty about the accuracy or completeness of its content and, to the maximum extent permitted, disclaim all liability arising from its use.

LONELY PLANET OFFICES

Australia
Head Office
Locked Bag 1, Footscray, Victoria 3011
☎ 03 8379 8000, fax 03 8379 8111
talk2us@lonelyplanet.com.au

USA
150 Linden St, Oakland, CA 94607
☎ 510 893 8555, toll free 800 275 8555
fax 510 893 8572, info@lonelyplanet.com

UK
2nd Fl, 186 City Rd
London EC1V 2NT
☎ 020 7106 2100, fax 020 7106 2101
go@lonelyplanet.co.uk

Published by Lonely Planet Publications Pty Ltd
ABN 36 005 607 983

Cover photographs Beach on the Na Pali Coast, Frans Lanting/Corbis (front); Sandals floating off the Na Pali Coast, Woods Wheatcroft/Lonely Planet Images (back top); Sunset over Hanalei Pier and Hanalei Bay, Ann Cecil/Lonely Planet Images (back bottom).

Printed by Toppan Security Printing Pte. Ltd.
Printed in Singapore.